just JAVA™

SECOND EDITION

THE SUNSOFT PRESS
JAVA SERIES

▼ ***Core Java,*** *Second Edition*
Gary Cornell & Cay S. Horstmann

▼ ***Graphic Java***
David Geary & Alan L. McClellan

▼ ***Instant Java,*** *Second Edition*
John A. Pew

▼ ***Java by Example,*** *Second Edition*
Jerry R. Jackson & Alan L. McClellan

▼ ***Just Java,*** *Second Edition*
Peter van der Linden

just

JAVA™

SECOND EDITION

PETER van der LINDEN

SunSoft Press
A Prentice Hall Title

The publisher offers discounts on this book when ordered in bulk quantities.
For more information, contact Corporate Sales Department, Prentice Hall PTR ,
One Lake Street, Upper Saddle River, NJ 07458. Phone: 800-382-3419; FAX: 201- 236-7141.
E-mail: corpsales@prenhall.com.

Editorial/production supervision: *Joanne Anzalone*
Cover design director: *Jerry Votta*
Cover designer: *Anthony Gemmellaro*
Cover illustration: *Paul Chesley, Tony Stone Images*
Manufacturing manager: *Alexis R. Heydt*
Marketing manager: *Stephen Solomon*
Acquisitions editor: *Gregory G. Doench*
SunSoft Press publisher: *Rachel Borden*

10 9 8 7 6 5 4 3 2 1

ISBN 0-13-272303-4

SunSoft Press
A Prentice Hall Title

This text is dedicated to the ancient Greek Alcibiades. He was tutored by Socrates, but in my view far out shone his tutor in accomplishments. In 450BC or thereabouts, it is said that Alcibiades invented the hammock. Alcibiades was actually trying to invent the fishing net, but he was somewhat of a klutz, and there was a high wind on the day he did a "dry-run" of the first prototype.

I would also like to mention the fine products of the Mendocino Brewery, Hopland, California. Their fine products, especially Red Tail Ale, help sustain the morale of programmers throughout the region.

Contents

Chapter 5

More Sophisticated Techniques, 155

Introduction

"In a five year period we can get one superb programming language. Only we can't control when the five year period will begin."

      —Alan Perlis, uncle of Algol-60

Why I Wrote This Book

Just imagine that you have been given the opportunity to design the ultimate programming language! What would you put in it?

Well, first of all, objects. And plenty of 'em. Object-oriented programming is moving to general acceptance as a superior implementation technique. Perhaps like me, you would want support for multi-threading. Better reliability and error handling are important, so let's find room for exceptions. Programmers need help with tiresome details, so let the compiler take care of making sure that all source files are up-to-date in a link.

And so on, and so on. I think you can see where this starts to lead. In the 1995 Pebble Beach Concours car show in California, one of the exhibits was a Rolls-Royce which had been similarly pieced together out of bits and pieces of the best. The Rolls featured a body from a 1931 Phantom II, modern racing carburetors, a custom-built chassis, and the engine from a Spitfire aeroplane. The 12 cylinder 28-liter Merlin engine used in the Spitfire was also built by Rolls-Royce. All of these

Bounty paid for corrections!

Every book on a technical subject has errors when it goes to press. That's even more true when the technical subject is as new as Java is. The goal of this author is to ruthlessly search out inaccuracies in this text, and eliminate them in future printings.

The general website for this book, containing reader feedback, sample programs, and the current errata sheet is http://www.best.com/~pvdl

There's a bounty of $1 per error to the first person who brings a programming correction to the attention of the author, so it can be corrected in future printings. The policy is that all errors will be corrected, but the bounty is reserved for programming related things in the English version (because that's the only one I can change directly).

Please send your corrections and feedback by e-mail to pvdl@best.com.

components are the best of their type, but put together the whole is an ill-matched over-complex mess that doesn't seem much fun to drive. Just as a duck is adapted to fly, walk, and swim, but does all three poorly, this aero-engined car can't fly, and is almost impossible to drive with finesse. It has covered an average of just 50 miles per year since it was completed a decade ago. Apart from anything else, you can't stray far from a gas station when you only get 2 m.p.g. A careless stamp on the throttle could twist the chassis. The engine is mounted backwards so the prop. shaft comes out where the propeller used to go.

Too many good things—an airplane-engined car

The vehicle was commissioned by an eccentric and rich used-car dealer, and must be driven gingerly at all times. It develops around 1000 bhp (a Corvette has about 20% of this), but heavy-footedness on the accelerator pedal could set the clutch on fire, or screw the mainshaft right out of the gearbox. The result of this "throw in everything good" design is an impractical and nearly undriveable vehicle. The question then is, "Is Java like this?"

The answer is a resounding "No!" For one thing, Java wasn't commissioned on the whim of an eccentric. Rather it was a considered approach designed by a top engineer, trying to solve practical problems. Aspects of Java have been borrowed from other languages, but they have been carefully integrated into the whole. Practicality is the hallmark throughout. Design decisions have been made with good judgment and thoughtfulness. Java benefited greatly from the C++ experience—seeing what was needed, what worked, and what should be discarded.

Once every generation or so in the computer industry, a new technology arises that is so compelling, and so well-fitted to the issues of the day, that it sweeps everything away before it. This happened in the 1960s with the shift to transistor logic, eventually leading to large scale integrated circuits. It happened again in the early 1980s with the unexpected success of the IBM PC. It was the right product at the right time, given credibility by the right company.

On the software side, a paradigm shift happened in 1982 through 1984 with spreadsheet software. Lotus123, and Visicalc before it, met people's needs so well that Lotus shot to prominence in a wave of profitability that other companies could only dream of.

And it is happening with Java right now. The success of Java represents the convergence of several unstoppable industry trends:

- Popularization of the Internet
- Consumer electronics merging into PC and telephone technologies
- Computer industry drive to interactive multimedia everything
- Rejection of the complexity of C++
- Desire for independence from Microsoft/Intel desktop monopolies

The speed of adoption of Java by programmers everywhere has been truly remarkable. However it is not Java per se that the industry seeks, but a resolution to the challenges raised by the issues above. Java is the only serious contender to address these issues. As a result, it has met with immediate and overwhelming acceptance. Java is not just another language. Because Java addresses these issues it is the beginning of a phenomenon that is changing the nature of computing.

Java is particularly convenient for use in Internet applications, but it is a general purpose language too. Its features will be quickly understood by programmers, if explained in the right way. What programmers need now is a book on Java that combines three elements:

1. An introduction to Java, relating it to more familiar languages,

2. Clear explanations, describing the significance of new features with their common pitfalls, and

3. Short practical examples that can be tried by readers using the compiler supplied.

This is a beginners book on Java, intended for people who are already programmers. You can use this book if you have knowledge of any language: Pascal, or Visual Basic, Fortran, or Ada. Knowledge of C or C++ will give you a head start. Our central theme is to provide some easily accessible answers to the question "what's new and different about Java?"

We assume knowledge of programming, but nothing else. The text starts by setting the context: the explosion in popularity of the Internet. It then provides an introduction to Object-Oriented Programming before launching into a bottom-up appraisal of Java. This material is essential. If you don't understand OOP or the World Wide Web, you'll never understand the language, or how the libraries fit together, how applets work, and why certain events fit with certain methods. The accompanying CD has a Java compiler system for Windows 95, Windows NT, the Macintosh, and Solaris 2 which includes everything you need to try Java.

What You'll Need

As everyone knows, the only real way to learn a programming language is to write some programs in it. For that you need the Java system and a Java-capable browser. This book comes with a CD that contains the Java compiler system. However, you may want to to download a Web browser or later release of Java as explained in Chapter 12 (You should have familiarity with utilities like anonymous FTP used for retrieving files from Internet hosts).

In theory, you could forgo the Web browser and Internet access, and just learn Java application programming on your local system. In practice, however, this would be a mistake. You would be missing a key part—seamless client-server programming on the network—which is responsible for the vast interest in Java.

How To Use This Book

Sometimes we do things in an order that looks funny from the table of contents. Sometimes we mention a topic only to say we're deferring discussion to a later section. This is because learning a subject isn't usually done in a depth-first manner. When you learn a foreign language you don't learn all the adjectives, followed by all the nouns finishing with all the verbs. If you did it that way you wouldn't be able to utter a whole sentence until you had completed all the lessons! It's the same with learning a programming language: it's best to cover enough to get you going, then look at the next thing by building on that, and eventually revisit anything that needs further attention. It gives a funny look to the table of contents though.

I tried to map out this book in three stages: first by covering the roots of Java and the resurgence of Object-Oriented Programming up front; then providing practical examples with clear explanations; and finally preparing advanced elements, such as window and network programming. Each chapter will cover a specific topic and most will end with the following sections:

- Some Light Relief (intended to amuse you, beginning at the end of this Introduction)

- Exercises (a little something to pick your brain, beginning in Chapter 1)

- Further Readings (provides a source of additional information, beginning in Chapter 1)

Icons in the Text

The following icons are used to call special attention to particularly important information in this book:

The "Software Dogma" icon is used whenever there is some background information to convey. Often these items are articles of faith in the industry. Things that are done that way because they've always been done that way. The "Pitfall" icon points out places where it's easy to make a mistake or develop a misunderstanding. Save yourself needless grief and read the pitfall paragraphs carefully. The "Programmer Tip" icon is used to indicate code idioms, shortcuts, sources of other information, and generally useful things to know. The "Important!" icon highlights particularly crucial bits of information.

"Programming Challenge" marks a Java programming exercise in the text. Some of these come with solutions later in the text, and are marked with the "Programming Solution" icon.

Though used sparingly in Chapter 11, "FAQ" (Frequently Asked Question) presents a query followed by my answer.

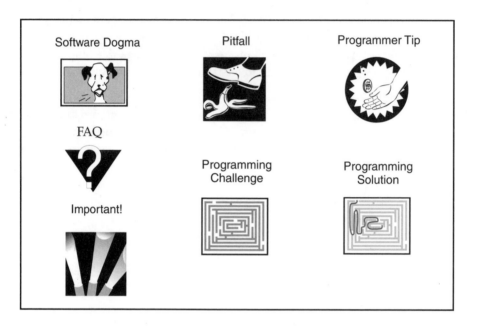

As I wrote this book, I also wanted to convey a sense of the enjoyment that lies in computer programming. Programming is challenging, exciting, enjoyable and satisfying. A book on computer programming should be exciting and educational, factual and fun. It should occasionally delight as well as inform. The major goal is to pass on the skill of a new programming language, but I'd also like to show a little of the fun of programming too. I hope that by the end of the book you'll agree that both goals have been met.

Some Light Relief

We end each chapter with a section of light relief to amuse readers and reward them for completing another milestone.

All I really need to know I learned on Internet

Peter van der Linden

All I really need to know about how to live, and what to do, and how to be, I learned on Internet. Wisdom was not at the top of the graduate school mountain, nor in the sandpile at Sunday school, but right there at the active endpoint of a TCP/IP session. These are the things I learned:

1. *Always* log your terminal off when you leave, even if you're only going to the bathroom for 5 minutes.

2. The only people who MAKE MONEY FAST on the Internet are those who manufacture routers and disk drives.

3. The net's memory is no longer than its attention span, so if you wait a little while you're sure to see the same thing go round again.

4. Some net-kooks are noisy, some net-kooks are stupid, and some net-kooks are rude. But the net-kooks whose attention you will attract are the net-kooks who are noisy, stupid AND rude.

5. Not all Usenet moderators and FAQ-compilers eventually become power-mad and insane. Some of them started out that way.

6. The net's memory is no longer than its attention span, so if you wait a little while you're sure to see the same thing go round again.

7. If you're not sure about the facts when posting something, be louder and more insistent to compensate. Asserting something stridently enough can make it so. When someone points out your mistakes, first sulk, then laugh them off as deliberate sarcasm, irony or cynicism which went over the heads of the audience.

8. There was something about the net's memory, but the details are a little hazy right now.

9. Remember that early release of "rn" that prevented a posting unless it contained more new lines than included lines? That was actually a pretty good idea.

10. How to have the last word in real life: "You're right!" How to have the last word on Usenet: "You're in my killfile!"

Using the Just Java CD-ROM

About the CD-ROM

Welcome to the *Just Java* CD-ROM – a disc packed with all the Java tools and source code discussed in the book.

Since this CD-ROM has been designed for use by Windows 95, Windows NT, Macintosh and Solaris users, you'll notice a directory for each of these operating systems.

NOTE: Because this is a cross-platform CD-ROM, Solaris users may encounter error messages when loading the CD indicating the presence of files that do not conform to the ISO-9660 specification. These error messages should be ignored. Follow the instructions below for using the code samples from *Just Java* and installing the other programs on the CD.

Using the CD-ROM on Solaris 2.x

Because this CD-ROM is a cross-platform disc that does not fully support long file names and other UNIX extensions, the Java programs and the Java Development Kit (JDK) for Solaris 2.x are stored as tar archives. Use the *more* command or *vi* to read the readme file.

The *Just Java* CD directory structure is as follows:

goodies   About the author (see index.html) plus sample Java
                        programs and image and sound files

justjava	Programs from *Just Java* (one directory for each chapter, plus justjava.tar)
jdbc	Software to help Java access a database
mac	The JDK for the Apple Macintosh
solaris.sparc	The JDK and Java WorkShop for Solaris (Sparc)
solaris.x86	The JDK and Java WorkShop for Solaris (Intel)
windows	The JDK for Windows 95 and Windows NT, plus Java WorkShop, WinEdit, WinZip and Symantec's Café Lite

To install the Just Java programs:

1. Make a directory on your Solaris filesystem and change to that directory. Then copy the justjava.tar file to that directory.

2. Use the command *tar -xvf* to unarchive the file. For example:

```
tar -xvf justjava.tar
```

NOTE: The justjava directory contains the same programs in a separate directory for each chapter that you may want to browse before copying the tar file to your hard drive. Do not try to run the Java programs in this directory from the CD. You must first copy the justjava.tar file to your hard drive and untar it.

To install the JDK (Solaris 2.3 or later):

The solaris.sparc directory contains the JDK (Release 1.0.2) for Sparc. The solaris.x86 directory contains the Intel version. Installation instructions are the same for Solaris 2.x for SPARC and Solaris 2.x for x86. On Intel systems, use "x86" instead of "sparc" in the filenames below. Make sure you are running an up-to-date version of Solaris 2.x, preferably Solaris 2.5.1.

1. Copy the file from the CD to your hard disk. Place it in the directory where you want a Java directory to be created.
   Let's assume you're putting it in /home/linden

   ```
   cd /cdrom/justjava/solaris.sparc
   cp jdk-1_0_2-solaris2-sparc.tar /home/linden
   ```

   This is a 4.7Mbyte file, so it will take a few seconds to pull off the CD.

2. Untar the file

   ```
   cd /home/linden
   tar -xvf jdk-1_0_2-solaris2-sparc.tar
   ```

   You should see dozens of lines indicating the files being untar'd. You can delete the tar file at this point.

3. Add/modify 2 variables in your .cshrc (or whatever initialization file is appropriate for the shell you use). For the cshell, the modifications are:

Put the Java bin directory in your path:

```
setenv JAVAHOME   /home/linden/java
set path=( $JAVAHOME/bin  ... rest of path ...
```

Set a CLASSPATH to point to the runtime library

```
setenv CLASSPATH  $JAVAHOME/lib/classes.zip:.
```

The ":" is a separator and the "." says that Java should also look in your current working directory for Java classes to run . Later you may add other directories to your CLASSPATH

4. Logout and login again so the new variables take effect.

To install Java WorkShop (Solaris 2.x):

1. Insert the Just Java CD into your CD-ROM drive.

2. If Volume Manager is running on your machine, the CD-ROM is automatically mounted to the /cdrom/justjava directory. Skip to step 3.

   If the Volume Manager is NOT running on your machine, create a directory called /cdrom/justjava and mount the CD-ROM manually by becoming root and typing:

   ```
   # mkdir -p /cdrom/justjava
   # mount -rF hsfs /dev/dsk/c0t6d0s0 /cdrom/justjava
   ```

3. Go to the directory where you intend to install the Java WorkShop files:

   ```
   % cd /<destination_directory>
   ```

4. Extract the Java WorkShop files by typing:

   ```
   % tar -xvf
   /cdrom/justjava/solaris.sparc/workshop/jw_<platform>.tar
   ```

   Where <platform> is either "sparc" or "intel" depending on whether you use a SPARC or Intel system.

   Note: This command is entered all on one line, but printing limitations mean we show it on two lines.

5. If you mounted the CD-ROM manually, unmount the drive by becoming root and typing:

   ```
   # cd /
   # umount /dev/dsk/c0t6d0s0
   ```

   Otherwise, go to Step 6.

6. Eject the CD by typing:

   ```
   % cd /
   % eject
   ```

   You can now use Java WorkShop.

7. Start Java WorkShop by typing:

   ```
   % /<destination_directory>/JWS/<platform>-S2/bin/jws &
   ```

Using the CD-ROM on Windows 95 and Windows NT

In addition to the JDK, the windows directory contains Java WorkShop (30-Day Trial), Symantec's Café Lite and shareware versions of WinEdit and WinZip. **This CD-ROM does not support Windows 3.1.**

The windows directory structure is as follows:

Directory/File	Contents
jdk	Contains the installation program for the JDK (1.0.2)
tools	Contains the installation programs for Café Lite, WinEdit and WinZip
workshop	Contains the installation program for Java WorkShop
readme	Installation notes for Windows users

NOTE: This CD was designed to work with a 100% compatible Windows 95/NT system. Some of the files use long file names, which is one of the features of Windows 95. If you are unable to see the long file names on the CD, then your system may not be 100% Windows 95/NT compatible. Windows 95/NT 4.0 users can check for compatibility by double-clicking on the "System" icon in the Control Panel and then clicking on the "Performance" tab. If the "Performance" section does not indicate that "Your system is configured for optimal performance" then you have some sort of system conflict which should be resolved. Consult Windows "Help" or contact Microsoft Technical Support for further assistance.

To install the JDK on Windows 95 or NT:

1. Create a directory named "java" on the top level of your hard drive. Copy the ZIP archive file from the CD to the \java directory.

   ```
   copy d:\windows\jdk\jdk_x86.zip c:\java
   ```

   The installation takes up about 5.5Mbytes. Be sure to remove any previous version of the JDK before unzipping the file.

2. Open the jdk_x86.zip file with a ZIP utility that supports long file names (such as WinZip, a popular ZIP program supplied on this CD-ROM) and unpack the files it contains into the "java" directory created in step 1.

NOTE: This step will fill the "java" directory with the files and subdirectories that make up the JDK. The \lib directory contains a file named "classes.zip" that should not be unpacked. You can, however, unpack the "src.zip" archive to review the source for the runtime library.

3. Once the JDK files have been unpacked onto your hard drive, you will need to add (or modify) 2 variables in your autoexec.bat file with a text editor.

   First, add the "java\bin" directory to your path:

   ```
   SET PATH=c:\java\bin; (...the rest of your path)
   ```

   Next, set the CLASSPATH variable to point to the current directory and the Java runtime library (the classes.zip archive):

   ```
   SET CLASSPATH=.;c:\java\lib\classes.zip
   ```

4. Save these changes to your autoexec.bat and restart your computer so the new variables take effect.

NOTE: Once the JDK is installed, you can delete the jdk_x86.zip archive from your hard drive.

To install Java WorkShop on Windows NT and Windows 95:

1. Insert the Just Java CD into your CD-ROM drive.

2. Run the d:\windows\workshop\setupws.exe installer (assuming d: is the drive for your CD-ROM). It will uncompress and copy all the necessary files to your hard drive (default directory is C:\JAVA-WORKSHOP)

3. Follow the installation, by clicking the appropriate buttons and entering the installation directory when, and if, needed.

4. After the installation is complete, double click on the JWS icon to start the workshop (A program group containing all the icons will be created.)

5. When Java WorkShop loads for the first time, you will be prompted to enter a serial number. Click on the "30-day trial" button and a serial number will be entered automatically.

6. To uninstall Java WorkShop, double-click the uninstall icon in the Java WorkShop program group.

To install the Just Java programs:

The justjava directory contains sample programs from the book. There is one directory for each chapter. These files can be copied to your hard drive or browsed on the CD.

To install WinEdit, WinZip or Symantec's Café Lite:

Each of these programs is in a separate folder in the \windows\tools directory. See the readme file for installation instructions and license information.

Using the CD-ROM on Macintosh (System 7.5 or later)

To install the JDK on a Macintosh:

Because this is an ISO-9660 CD-ROM, the JDK is stored on the disc as a self-extracting archive. Copy the archive (JDK-1_0_2-MacOS.sea) to your hard drive and double-click to open.

To install the Just Java programs:

The justjava directory contains sample programs from the book. There is one directory for each chapter. These files can be copied to your hard drive or browsed on the CD.

NOTE: You should note that Macintosh, Windows, and UNIX text files have slightly different conventions for end-of-line. Macintosh expects a carriage return, Windows expects a carriage return and a linefeed, and UNIX expects a newline character (linefeed).

Most Macintosh editors are able to cope with UNIX and Windows conventions. Be aware, however, that some Macintosh editors will not display line breaks properly if you try to read text files that were created on a Windows or UNIX system. Even though some text files may not appear to be properly formatted, however, the Java compiler handles source files created under either convention.

You should also note that file names longer than 31 characters will be truncated. Therefore, some of the sample Java files on this CD will have to be renamed to execute properly on a Macintosh.

Acknowledgments

I would like to express my heartfelt thanks to Tom Cargill, Tom Cikoski, and Brian Scearce, who read the whole book in draft form, and made many suggestions for improvements. I take responsibility for all remaining errors. If you notice one that isn't in the errata sheet (obtainable from the website), report it to me.

The layout and design of this book was greatly improved by the hard work of chief editor James Markham and production editor Joanne Anzalone, who have earned my warmest appreciation.

Thanks to the people who encouraged me to write this book: Simon Alexander, Rachel Borden, John Bortner, Greg Doench, Zahir Ebrahim, Karin Ellison, and Jim Marks.

I'm grateful to these people who suggested several improvements to the second edition:

Jim Bernstein

George Reese

Pratik Patel

Greg Turner

I would also like to thank the following people who provided significant help:

Sandy Anderson

Deepak Bhagat

Keith Bierman

Dan Berg
Matthew Burtch
Teresa Chinn
Mark Scott Johnson
Tim Kirby
Henry Lai
Bil Lewis
David Mikkelson
Ahmed Mohamed
Nicholas J. Morrell (what a taste he has in expensive Scotch!)
Tom O'Donnell
The Old Hats of AFU (Cayman Islands) Inc.
Bill Petro (Henry Ford never said "History is bunk"—he said it was bunk to him!)
Craig Shergold (who's feeling a lot better thanks, and doesn't need any more cards)
Peter Soderquist
Kathy Stark
Panagiotis Tsirigotis
Tom van der Linden (who instilled in me his love for reading, writing, and
    consolidated statements of stockholder equity)
Wendy van der Linden (who pointed out that Citrus was a subclass of Fruit)
Terry Whatley
Ron Winacott

My team of colleagues at Sun Microsystems also deserves my gratitude for
helping me in numerous ways while I worked on this text:

Oscar Arreola
Hui-Mei Chen
Jim Marks
Ahmed Mohamed
Saeed Nowshadi
Sina Balasubramanian
Srinath Murthy
Terry Whatley.

CHAPTER

1

- How the Web Evolved
- The Significance of Java

The Web and Java

"Come into my parlor," said the spider to the fly.

Java is a new, general-purpose programming language. It is a system that has been designed to make it easy for users to master. It contains libraries that pave the road to simple, convenient use of Internet features.

To understand the Java language, we need to begin by looking at Internet applications, especially the World Wide Web (aka, *the Web* or *WWW*). Java was developed independently from the World Wide Web, but solves problems that the Web needs solved.

The Web Catches Fire

Looking back on it now, 1994 was the year the World Wide Web really took off.

In 1994, the vast and multifaceted Internet—an unorganized, yet interconnected group of computer networks spanning the entire planet—reached critical mass and became general public knowledge. The growth of the Internet prior to that point was already rather impressive. However, fueled by speculation about its enormous communications potential, month-to-month growth became phenomenal.

Entertainer and magician Penn Jillete (the big noisy one from the Penn and Teller combo) was invited to give the keynote address at the 1994 Usenix (Unix users) convention. Penn described how he was suddenly getting a lot more dates with the opposite sex, now that the word had gotten around the glitterati that he was their newfound channel to the Internet. This was a message that went across very well with the attending audience of computer scientists, let me tell you.

The discovery of Internet by the mainstream was reflected in popular culture as well. Artists for cartoons like Dilbert, and Frank 'n Ernest started putting e-mail addresses in their drawings. Ads for some movies ("Tank Girl" is one example) included information specifically for net surfers—this is the mysterious "URL `http://kirks.toupee`" you might have noticed in small print. Even the President of the United States went on-line with an e-mail address, president@white-house.gov. It's not really his personal address, since a flunky sends out form responses, but in politics, as in life, it's the thought that counts. In February 1996, the U.S. Presidential home page at http://www.whitehouse.gov used a Java program to wave a pair of flags on the picture of the White House.

No doubt about it—the Internet has become big! Big in numbers, and big in the public consciousness.

Where It All Started

Like Jack's beanstalk, the Internet "just grew and grew." It started in a very small way in the late 60s as the ARPA[1]net, an experiment funded by the U.S. Department of Defense. The ARPAnet linked together a handful of computers at some university and research sites. Networks were rare in those days, and almost everything was a novelty. One innovation (which is a cornerstone of the Internet today) is that every computer had its own unique address, now known as an IP or "Internet Protocol" address.

How to Recognize an IP Address

An IP (Internet Protocol) address consists of four groups of digits that looks like this:

`204.156.141.229`

On a Windows system or a Mac, you won't have an IP address, unless you're on a local area net that has IP addressing.

On a Unix workstation you can print out your IP address by typing

`/usr/sbin/ifconfig -a`

You may have noticed the IP address if you looked at the messages while the system was booting, or if you just like poking around.

---

1. ARPA = Advanced Research Projects Agency

Any computer could send data to any other computer on the net by wrapping the information in an IP packet and putting it onto the network. Intervening special-purpose router computers were responsible for forwarding the data to the next router closer to the ultimate destination.

The early services allowed scientists to exchange electronic mail and other files. They could "finger" or enquire about the logon status of users on systems far away. They could even telnet to different systems—login remotely from their host computer to a different computer located in another city. These services proved so convenient that the universities involved began to connect other systems and departments, unrelated to network research, to the ARPAnet. An important newcomer was the NSFNET which connected five regional supercomputer centers, each of which had a hierarchy of smaller networks hanging off it, again using IP addressing. The network had become an internet—a connected cluster, of several levels of networks, and was on its way to becoming the Internet we know and love today.

A related trend was the rising popularity of local area networks of Unix workstations in computer science departments in the early 1980s. Companies like Sun Microsystems, Apollo Computer, and Onyx could install workstations linked by Ethernet hardware and IP software. These were much cheaper than the large centralized time-sharing superminis and mainframes they replaced. Organizations found it very convenient to connect all their LANs together in a wide area network that could be gateway'd onto the Internet. This way, files could be shared, and e-mail sent, without regard to departmental boundaries. Personal computers were left out of this first tidal wave of networking. At that time, they lacked the hardware, software, and raw CPU power necessary.

An early key aspect of the Internet was that it was not "designed"; it just evolved to meet the needs of its users. There was no central direction, no governing body, and no elaborate bureaucratic procedure. If you found its basic communication services useful, you simply went out and connected your own network to the nearest Internet system. The cost of a dedicated dataline at a few hundred dollars a month—peanuts to a large academic department—instantly enabled the cross-pollination of thoughts and ideas with colleagues throughout the world who were similarly network connected.

Early Pioneers

There was a real spirit of pioneering cooperation in the early days of the Internet. Back in 1982, a colleague wanted an Internet connection to his family weekend beach house on the New Jersey shore. He studied a map of Internet routers (that was back in the days when the number was small enough that they could be written down on a map).

He planned to telephone all the ones that were in the local calling area. The very first organization he tried on the phone agreed to provide him with a complimentary account for dial-up access. The hardest part was getting transferred to the right system administrator to ask.

Nowadays, if you do not have Internet access at work or at your place of study, you can use an ISP, an Internet Service Provider, who, for a small monthly fee will provide you Internet access via your phone line to your home PC.

In the early 1980s, another application, apart from e-mail, file transfer, and telnet, was added to the Internet: network news. Network news, or "Usenet" as it became known, is a phenomenon that is hard to describe if you have not experienced it. Entire books have been written about Usenet. Usenet is a computerized bulletin board with hundreds of special interest discussion groups. Usenet is like TV for people who still read for leisure. While it is occasionally very enlightening, it tends to be something that you do when you should be actually doing something. Let me explain that a little further.

Usenet was developed by a couple of graduate students at the University of North Carolina. Its use quickly spread to other universities. I encountered it in 1981 as a graduate student in computer science and loved it from the start! Who wouldn't? It was a great chance to exchange notes, advice, hints, wisdom and humor, even insults, with a group of surprisingly diverse people.

All that we had in common was one kind of computer science connection or another, and an urge to share opinions. We used the first to talk endlessly about the second. It was and is heady, exciting, time-consuming and addictive. It greatly expands your field of acquaintances. Today, almost no pastime, interest, or profession is too obscure for Usenet. Every imaginable topic will have its own specialized newsgroup devoted to fevered and sometimes heated discussion.

So that's where Internet applications stayed "frozen in time" throughout the 1980s: providing simple file-based applications, mostly in a batch-oriented manner. The only real-time application, IRC (Internet Relay Chat) proved to be merely a clunky curiosity. But computer science had by then moved on.

The Big Step Forward

One of the problems with the existing Internet was that it was all so unorganized and unconnected. Sure, you could download a copy of a file from anywhere on the Internet—if you knew that it existed and where it was. The Internet was like a vast library that had no central index. People passed on information by e-mail, word-of-mouth, and news postings. There was a treasure house of information out there, but the trick was in finding it.

The first attempt to address this shortcoming required some civic-minded network hosts to volunteer to become archive librarians. Software such as "archie" and "gopher" could answer questions like "what ftp servers have a file with the string 'grep' in its name?" Archie and gopher were blunt instruments that people used in the absence of anything better.

The next big step was to find some way to organize and connect the information that was out there. Ideally, this would be a solution that could be put in place at each local site (there is no central authority on the Internet, remember), and that would apply equally to any kind of file or collection of files. The solution that emerged is known as the World Wide Web or WWW.

The WWW concept began in March 1989, when Tim Berners-Lee proposed it as an improved way of sending ideas and files around CERN, the physics research combine where he worked as a programmer. It was a development of the "Enquire" hypertext system he had created a decade before. His basic idea was to invent a "browser" program, and a set of data communication protocols. The browser would let users retrieve documents and files easily, and examine them. To bring a copy of a file over to your desktop, all you had to do was indicate the pathname that identified it.

Document retrieval was allowed not merely at the command line level, but also while already browsing a document. You could even embed a pathname in the middle of some text in a document you were browsing, and use that to refer over to some other related papers. Voila! Hypertext becomes a practical possibility.

A Little Hype, A Little Text: Hypertext

Like many of the best concepts, hypertext is an old idea. It was first mentioned in 1945 by Vannevar Bush (Science and Technology Advisor to Franklin D. Roosevelt) in an article titled "As We May Think." That wheel has now rolled full circle, because Bush's article is available on the WWW for you to read (see "further reading" at the end of this chapter).

In 1965, information processing pioneer Ted Nelson coined the term "hypertext" to describe Bush's concept. Ordinary text, such as you are reading now, is just a progression of words on a page. We can glitz it up with diagrams, pictures, and tables, but to make sense of it you have to read it serially page by page. Hypertext banishes this "one directional" thinking. Hypertext allows a writer to pick out any words or phrases in a document and link them somehow with other phrases in that document or in another. As you read, you can progress page by page, or you can jump around, following and returning from links as you choose. As Figure 1-1 shows, it's like having footnotes that take a reader directly to another document, rather than just a reference to it at the bottom of the page.

Before hypertext

Reading a sheet of paper with occasional jumps to footnotes—is a serial process

With hypertext

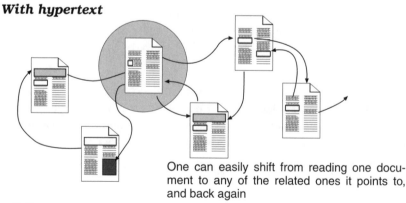

One can easily shift from reading one document to any of the related ones it points to, and back again

Figure 1-1: Hypertext provides a steady flow of information

You cannot use hypertext with text on a printed page, but a computer system displaying a document to you makes hypertext possible. A phrase might be picked out by displaying it in a different color—you can still read it as ordinary words, but you know it is also a hypertext link. The writer of the document will create the specific link, but that administrative detail isn't exposed to the reader. When a reader clicks on the phrase that is hypertext linked, the section at the other end will be displayed. In this way, related ideas can be grouped together, and the reader has the ultimate power to make independent choices governing how he or she will navigate through a document. The reader therefore controls exactly how the information is presented.

Ted Nelson also invented the term "Hypermedia", realizing that you need not restrict your links to text. You can also link to pictures, audio clips, animation, or anything that you can store on a computer system such as (drumroll!) programs. We'll come to that.

The hypertext links that we use today are known by the rather grandiose title of Universal Resource Locators (URLs). They are universal in the sense that each name is unique across the entire Internet. Think about it: the references that you embed in your documents don't even have to point to anything local. They can literally connect you with anything anywhere on the Internet that has declared itself to be part of the WWW. Think back to the URL that advertised the "Tank Girl" movie. It was pointing the knowledgeable at the web site with more advertising and promotional literature on the film. By including that URL in one of your documents, you can link your text to one of Hollywood's hottest sites.

The WWW has already become the most desired method of organizing our global on-line information repository! This is phenomenal, so take a deep breath, read that last line again, and welcome to computing in the third Millennium! Organizations that we once entrusted to perform the task of cataloguing and preserving all of our nation's digital knowledge, such as the U.S. Library of Congress, are now themselves accessible links within the WWW. The process is far from complete and still has many flaws, but "the hypertext links are on the wall" for the old way of doing things.

Documents prepared for the WWW don't just include hypertext links. They typically also contain commands that tell a WWW browser how to format the text for display. The set of commands is known as HyperText Markup Language (HTML) and writers of WWW documents use HTML to indicate headings, font changes, where the new paragraphs are, and all the other basic word processor commands.

HTML is a close relation of Standardized General Markup Language (SGML) used for some computer applications. Thankfully, HTML is a simple language. If it takes you more than 1 hour to master it, you are using the wrong book. Ironically, there are plenty of tutorials on HTML on the Web, but it is hard to find a really good one. The reason is probably that people who can write well prefer to publish in book form and get paid for it.

Here is an example of some simple text with embedded HTML. A URL denoting a hypertext link is just another one of the HTML commands. If you look at this text with an ordinary editor, this is what you'll see:

```
Text With a Spice of HTML
<html>
<html>
<title>National Security Agency</title>
<center>
<h1><img align="center" src="nsalogo.gif"><p> NATIONAL SECURITY AGENCY</h1>
</center><b><h6><img h=48 w=48 align="left" src="exclam.jpg">UNOFFICIAL
U.S. NONGOVERNMENTAL SYSTEM FOR UNAUTHORIZED USE ONLY. Discuss, enter, transfer, pro-
cess, or transmit classified/sensitive national security information of greater sensitivity than
that for which this system is authorized. Use of this system does not constitute consent to
security testing and monitoring. Authorized use could result in criminal prosecution.
</h6></b>
<center>
<table border=5>
<TR ALIGN = CENTER>
<TH> <a href ="#history"> History </a>
</TH>
<TH> <a href="#facilities">Facilities</a> </TH>
<TH> <a href="#operations"> Operations </a> </TH>
 </TR>
<TH> <a href="#organizations"> Organization and Functions </a> </TH>
<TH> <a href="#budget"> Budget and Personnel </a> </TH>
<TH><a href="maps.html"> Maps of the NSA Compound </a> </TH>
</table>
<p>
<i>(Adapted from: United States Senate Select Committee on Governmental Operations
with Respect to Intelligence Activities, Foreign and Military Intelligence -- Book I, 94th Con-
gress, 2nd Session, 26 April 1976, pages 325-355.)</i>
<p>
</center>
```

NSA is the nation's cryptologic organization, tasked with making and breaking codes and ciphers. In addition, NSA is one of the most important centers of foreign language analysis and research and development within the government. NSA is a high-technology organization, working on the very frontiers of communications and data processing.

The expertise and knowledge it develops provide the government with systems that deny foreign powers knowledge of US capabilities and intentions. <p>

The National Security Agency (NSA) is charged with two of the most important and sensitive activities in the US intelligence community.

The information systems security or INFOSEC mission provides leadership, products, and services to protect classified and unclassified national security systems against exploitation through interception, unauthorized access, or related technical intelligence threats. This mission also supports the Director, NSA, in fulfilling responsibilities as Executive Agent for interagency operations security training.

<p>

If you look at the same text above with a WWW Browser, it appears as shown below in Figure 1-2.

The formatting has been done, and the hypertext at the other end of the link is displayed (but not the URL itself). If you click on the highlighted text, you will appear to follow the URL to the indicated document. What actually happens is

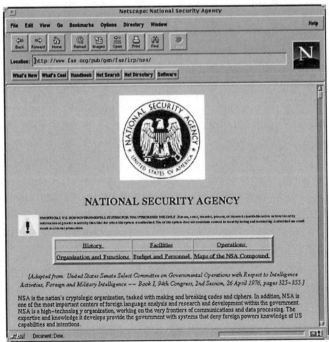

Figure 1-2: Web Browsers turn endless lines of words into snazzy pages like this

that the browser remembers where it is, then retrieves whatever the URL points to, and displays it for you. The URL for this faux NSA web site is http://www.fas.org/pub/gen/fas/irp/nsa

More About Browsers

The original web browser ran only on Next systems. Its successor ran on multiple platforms, but was command-line-oriented, without a windowing capability. By this time in 1992, however, graphical user interfaces (GUIs) were ubiquitous, not just on Unix workstations, but even on low-end PCs.

Marc Andreessen, an undergraduate at U. Illinois, who worked part-time at the National Center for SuperComputing Applications had seen a demonstration of the first web browser. He realized that the application would greatly benefit from a GUI, and he led a small team to produce an X-Windows-based browser that would be portable across a range of platforms. They released the software in June 1993, naming it "Mosaic" because it provided a view of thousands of tiny pieces of information that together made up a pleasing and coherent picture. Mosaic was made available for free over the Internet to anyone who wanted it.

Mosaic provided an attractive GUI, and got away from the flat-text command-line interface of the original implementation. One reason the poor interface had survived was perhaps that people felt there was not the response time or bandwidth needed to do windowing over the net. The crucial realization was that you didn't need to do windowing over the net! All that was needed was local intelligence to serve files, and window processing at the user or client end of the network connection! The client end is where the browser program starts and runs; all the complicated networking can be done using the existing data transfer programs, such as FTP. And that realization, so obvious in hindsight, was the making of the World-Wide Web.

Client/Server Computing

We've hinted that WWW browsers implement the client side of client/server computing. Client/server computing is a significant trend in the computer industry. In general terms it means splitting applications in two. The user interface and most of the software runs on the client, which will typically be a workstation or high-end PC. The data for the application resides on the server, perhaps in a mainframe database.

Thus the data is kept where it can best be secured, updated, backed-up, while the computing power is distributed right to the users' desktops. When client browsers access the WWW, they can literally select from a world of servers.

Client/server computing is clearly the wave of the future, and it is no coincidence that the WWW fits right into the model. We are looking at a convergence of mighty trends. The references at the end of the chapter provide a source for further information on client/server computing.

Mosaic is actually a very simple program. It hardly does any network programming at all. About all that it needs to know is how to invoke the preexisting Internet applications for sending e-mail, or transferring files. Then it must do something sensible with the data it has called for. The largest part of its code is there to understand the HTML formatting commands, and to format text for display in a window. Mosaic made web access easy, and since people will always tend to do that which is easy, use of the web blossomed.

In 1994, for-profit players caught onto the WWW. Marc Andreessen and some colleagues from NCSA who had worked on Mosaic, formed a company that became the Netscape Communications Corp., under the chairmanship of Jim Clark (former chairman of workstation manufacturer Silicon Graphics).

When Netscape made an initial public offering of its stock in August 1995, investors couldn't buy it fast enough. On the opening day demand was so high that the stock price doubled and doubled again. And kept on rising. This is almost unprecedented in the capital markets. There are several other web browsers commercially available, too. In December 1995, Microsoft announced that its strategic future direction was closely tied to the Internet. One hears stories about the 1300 programmers there having to submit weekly reports detailing what they have done in the past seven days to make Microsoft successful in its attempt to penetrate the Internet.

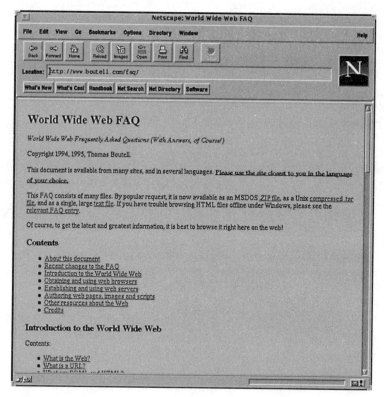

Figure 1-3: This is an example of the Netscape browser looking at the WWW FAQ (Frequently Asked Questions) list at: `http://www.boutell.com/faq`

Where We Are Today

Computer systems sell really well when they provide something that every-one wants to do, that isn't easily done by alternative means. We call this kind of software a "killer application", because it kills the competition. Spread-sheets and word-processors were the killer applications of the PC. They killed the market for electric typewriters among other things. In 1994, the New York Times correctly identified Mosaic as the Internet's killer application.

Since the US Presidential Election in 1992, we have heard a number of politicians give vague and general encouragement for an "Information Superhighway." The realization has gradually dawned on all of us, including the politicians, that the Information Superhighway won't *replace* the Internet — it *is* the Internet.

Terminology Review

The Internet is a vast network of literally millions of computer systems and networks throughout the world that have taken steps to hook up with their neighbors, all using IP addressing at some point in their communications.

The WWW and Usenet news are two applications that run on top of (are carried over) the Internet.

The two big breakthroughs of the WWW are that it provides a practical implementation of hypertext, and it can retrieve documents from the entire Internet, rather than just a single local area network or organization. Because of this it has become the universal interface to the world's digital resources.

Another important factor is that the WWW presents a consistent interface to existing Internet services like FTP. Some sites do not have any HTML documents, but run the web server software anyway, so users can have simple access to their FTP archives.

You can use a browser as the windowing interface to the WWW.
Mosaic was the best known of the original browsers.
Netscape is a popular browser today. Since its 2.0 release, Netscape Navigator can download all kinds of hypermedia files including little Java programs known as applets. It contains an interpreter that can execute these Java applets.
HotJava is a browser from Sun with the same capability.

Perhaps it's a truism, but it's worth pointing out. There's one thing all the applications that run on top of the Internet have in common: they all foster communication. Every one of them makes it better, faster, easier, cheaper for person A to communicate and inform persons B, C, and D. That was true when the Internet started, and it is still the overriding key element of the Internet's success today.

Ordinary businesses and ordinary people, as opposed to the computer professionals who were already there, are lining up to get an Internet connection. As a result, Internet service providers such as Prodigy, Netcom, America OnLine, Compuserve, and Delphi are growing faster than weeds. Someday, perhaps Compuserve will even discover alphabetic userids.

And what does everyone do, once they get on-line? They set up a home page—an introduction to themselves and how to be contacted. If they are a business, they provide information on their goods and services. They make hypertext links to related areas of interest. It is traditional to have at least one section in any document incomplete, declared as "under construction." A Web site is the equivalent of a business card. Thousands of non-technical companies have their own Web sites now. It's as common as having a fax machine. In fact, software companies would be hard-pressed to provide the most up-to-date information and services without one.

The WWW is hot, and the way to access it is through a browser. This is why Netscape has a market valuation of $3.8 billion (November 1995) even though they give away their main product, have hardly begun to turn a profit, and have no track record. The market hoopla stems from the sheer potential. All the folks that were laughed at because they bought Netscape stock at 90, are laughing all the way to the bank because they sold to other folks at 110. Netscape hit 165 in December, 1995.

Hi-ho! Yow! I'm Surfing Arpanet!

The phrase "INFORMATION SUPERHIGHWAY" was heard so much throughout 1994 and 1995, that it finally became trite. It inspired someone who shall remain nameless (only because I don't know who it was) to generate the following top ten anagrams (rearrangement of letters) of "Information Super-highway".

> 10. I'm on a huge wispy rhino fart
>
> 9. Hey, ignoramus -- win profit? Ha!
>
> 8. Oh-oh, wiring snafu: empty air
>
> 7. When forming, utopia's hairy
>
> 6. A rough whimper of insanity
>
> 5. Oh, wormy infuriating phase
>
> 4. Inspire humanity, who go far
>
> 3. Waiting for any promise, huh?
>
> 2. Hi-ho! Yow! I'm surfing Arpanet!

And the number one anagram for "Information Superhighway":

> 1. New utopia? Horrifying sham

You're not amused? OK, how about "How you finish grim Arpanet" or "Humanity wishing for opera"? Hey, I didn't make these up, I just report the facts.

"Does Anyone Think the Net is *UNDER*-Hyped?"

On November 8, 1995, Sun Microsystems hosted the first Java conference at its Menlo Park, California headquarters. One of the speakers was Sun vice president Eric Schmidt, who opened his presentation by asking "Does anyone here think the Internet is *under*-hyped?" Well, of course the audience was chock full of computer programmers. A jaded and "been there-done that" sort of crowd prone to thoroughly discount any "marketing story" they hear as vaporware and hype, so almost no one felt that the Internet was under-hyped.

Then Eric surprised us by giving his opinion that even though the Internet had been the subject of extraordinary levels of public interest and marketing flannel, that level of puffing up was still an understatement of the eventual value of the Internet framework. He justified this by explaining that we are now at the beginning of global revolution that has the Internet at its center. Almost everything we do as a society: business, education, recreation, has a strong element of communication built into it. The Internet makes high bandwidth communication possible almost immediately to practically anywhere. The convergence of computers and telecommunications is a reality. The emergence of technology like Java is another piece of the puzzle.

Critical Mass on the Web

Nuclear physicists have a concept of "critical mass". When an atom of uranium or other fissionable material is whacked by a smaller particle called a neutron, it splits the atom and releases more neutrons to the surroundings. These released neutrons may fly off into thin air, or be absorbed by atoms of other elements and do nothing, or they may whack into other uranium atoms, split them, and release still more neutrons.

If there is enough uranium, and it is packed close enough together, at some point the number of neutrons splitting atoms and releasing other neutrons is just enough to keep the chain reaction going. This amount of uranium is the "critical mass". When this point is passed, the chain reaction very quickly becomes unstoppable and even explosive.

The "critical mass" for the Internet, and the applications that are carried on it like WWW and Usenet, was exceeded many months ago.

Still Missing

A key element that is still missing is secure commerce over the Internet, but a number of people are working very hard on that. At present you would be very foolish to pay for a product by sending your credit card number in e-mail. e-mail can be read, forged, or modified as it is routed to its destination by anyone with enough technical knowledge. Sending your credit card number by e-mail is almost as risky as publishing it in the classified ads of the New York Times. It's there for any competent hacker who wants to look for it. The only thing that prevents massive fraud over the net is the general awareness that it is all too possible.

Not to disparage the net, but there are other problems too, as it stands today.

- It's quite hard to find information on specific topics. There are search sites, but they can be overcrowded and over-broad. By the ever changing nature of the Web, they are neither comprehensive nor up-to-date.

- Much web content is poor—It's as inane as TV or worse. Just because the Web has given everyone the ability to broadcast to the world, does not mean it has also given them something interesting to say.

- Much web presentation is frankly boring—the information content may be good, but it is presented in a dull pedestrian way. Just because the Web has given someone meaningful content to broadcast to the world, does not mean it has also given them the ability to do it in an interesting manner.

- Commercial use is still severely limited. Just try and find a decent pair of jeans by shopping for them on the net!

Java cannot do much about the first two (market economics may though), but will certainly solve the last two problems. The original web browsers could deliver text and still images. Then they added an e-mail capability. Now Java gives you animation, two-way communication, and sound. Coming soon are a dozen or so libraries that support a rich blend of further features. APIs to support video streams, virtual reality, 2D and 3D modeling, and enablers for commerce have been announced and will be phased in through 1997.

Commercial sites in particular are dull. Since they can't yet safely transact business over the net, about all they can do is display a list of wares and invite you to call in.

Get to the Bottom of the Matter

Dull net sites reached such a head in 1994 that a bored Tom Jennings of San Francisco pointed a camera down at his toilet (Figure 1-4), and announced to a startled world that he had televised it by linking it to his web page, grabbing a new frame every 5 minutes. The claim was that if you hit the home page at the right time you might catch someone on the potty.

This made front-page news in the San Jose Mercury News (Silicon Valley) newspaper on February 14 1995. Most people who accessed the page just wanted to know where to get the camera, and details of how to interface it to the web!

Actually the whole thing was a hoax; it just displayed a still picture. Engineers figured it out by noting that not a single pixel changed in frames taken many hours apart.

Tom set it up to parody the many boring or pointless web sites. Virtual reality is not true reality.

Figure 1-4:   You can find this parody at: http://www.wps.com/toilet/index.html

---

Look at the Playboy site, for example, at `http://www.playboy.com` Perhaps you'd think that here, of all places, they would have mastered the art of captivating men's interest. Unfortunately, their pages are plodding, lifeless, and dull. The December 1995 version even features an ad for Rogaine hair-restorer. No complaint about the product itself. But because there is little total value in the pages to the reader, a visitor feels especially duped by advertising bombardment on the Web. Commercial web sites need serious help!

The largest group of people making money off the Internet today is the ISPs, the consultants who help to craft a home page, and those passing on salacious material. The situation is reminiscent of the California gold-rush days. The people who made the most money were those who sold food and supplies to the miners, not the miners themselves.

So why is everyone bothering? Because despite all these teething troubles, there is huge, huge potential. Eric Schmidt was right: we have hardly begun to scratch the surface of the Internet's possibilities. All of these problems are solvable, and all of them will be solved. We are now well past the point at which critical mass has taken over. It no longer matters whether the Web has practical commercial applications on it right this instant, or not. The point is, if you're not on it now and your competitors are, then you lose. The applications are inexorably coming. And the Java programming language is a key enabling technology on the way.

The Development of Java

Suddenly Java is here, and in the words of Yogi Berra, "it's déjà vu all over again." Like the Internet, Java took several years to become an "overnight" sensation. Java had a more arduous gestation than the Internet. While the Internet has been a success for its users from day one, the development of Java was fraught with false starts, dead ends, and missteps.

Early on in the project that ultimately resulted in Java, James Gosling of Sun decided that he wanted the benefits of Object-Oriented Programming. But he knew that C++ wasn't the right answer. C++ was proving difficult in practice, more complex than it needed to be. By August 1991, Gosling had implemented a language of his own design, which he named "Oak" allegedly after a tree he could see from his office window. Good thing his office didn't overlook a parking lot, or he might have called the language PL/II.

Ironically, when Java was still under development (known by the preliminary name of Oak) nobody cared a damn about it. Oak was just another programming language. I well remember printing out the Oak white paper, (which by the way, said Oak was an acronym for "Object Application Kernel," and didn't mention anything about a tree) and perusing it briefly before permanently setting it aside in favor of more urgent tasks. Oak however, was merely the software part of a much larger project aimed at consumer hardware.

It wasn't until spring 1994, when all the hardware ideas were turning into dead ends, that Bill Joy and Eric Schmidt followed the timely policy of including the magic word "Internet" in the business plan. That blasted Java into the limelight. But we're getting a bit ahead of ourselves here.

The Origins of Java

Like C, the Java language arose from the ashes of a failing project. In C's case, it was the failure of the Multics project to deliver on schedule. In the case of Java, the situation was an anticipated market that didn't materialize.

Imagine that you've worked on a highly ambitious state-of-the-art electronics project for 2 years. Against all the odds, you have built a working prototype of the hardware driven by a custom-developed programming language. It's a hand-held device that can control consumer electronics like TV-top boxes for interactive cable. A TV-top box is the name given to the extra electronic gizmo you'd need to decode the signal when they bring 600 channels of cable to your house. People hypothesize that it should also provide two-way communication from your house to the cable company.

The only problem is that people were beginning to realize that there is no market for the interactive cable service. This was the situation in which the Sun R&D team found themselves. They demonstrated the prototype to Sun executives, most of whom loved it, except my boss, who didn't. He came back from a demonstration saying he didn't see why people would flock to buy a set top box with a goofy cartoon figure interface. Turns out he was quite right.

Despite wooing potential customers like Mitsubishi, France Telecom, and Time-Warner, the orders either went elsewhere, or did not materialize at all. By mid-1993 interactive TV was a big expensive bust and everyone knew it. Mid-1993 was also when the first Mosaic browser came out, although few people had yet paid any attention to it.

The $5 Million Long Shot Bet

Funding for the box project was about to be cut, and the team disbanded to other projects, when Bill Joy and Eric Schmidt conceived the idea of dropping the hardware, and adapting the software to work smoothly ("seamlessly" is the idiom of choice) with the Internet. Sun executive Phil Samper was persuaded to fund further development for one year to the tune of $5 million. Everything was to revolve around the WWW. Whatever the software project evolved into, it had to feature the Web as its focal point.

By now it was 1994. Gosling and a small number of colleagues set to work on this new challenge of bringing Oak to the Internet. They worked at a furious pace and in great secrecy throughout the year. By Christmas they had a working translator, the key libraries, and a web browser as a proof of concept.

In January 1995, the language was renamed "Java", and negotiations with Netscape got underway.

What the Name "Java" Means

The Java team explains that the name arose because "Oak" failed a trade-mark search, and they wanted a name that conveyed excitement, and action. "Java" came up, so the story runs, in a marketing brainstorming session.

So "Java" is like the ice-cream name "Häagen Dazs." That ice-cream sounds so Nordic, but it is actually made in New Jersey. The name "Häagen Dazs" is just a made-up combination of letters to create the right image in your mind!

All the same, I wonder. Inside Sun, we sometimes talk about "JAWS" meaning "Just Another WorkStation". JAWS is the quality you want to avoid when you design a desktop machine. You might hear a comment like "Suppose we build in a user interface based on real-time speech recognition — then no one can say this is JAWS!"

Perhaps at the back of the team's mind was something like "Let's not call it by Just Another Vague Acronym" — Who knows?

Release 2.0 of the Netscape Navigator browser contains a Java interpreter. Interest in the language, and what it can do, continues to mount. Several thousand people attended the "Java Day" that took place just eleven months after the language was named, and many more were turned away.

Frankly, new waves in software are frequently accompanied by a measure of overselling. A classic example of this is the launch of Windows 95. Microsoft has marketed Windows 95 to the tune of $200 million. All this to generate product demand for something which brings the PC user interface to a level roughly comparable with what the Macintosh had a decade earlier. The interest in Java however was not the result of a high-budget media saturation marketing campaign. After Java Day, the size of the Java Marketing department doubled. . . from one person to two people! People are interested in Java because they anticipate what it will deliver for them. Java has taken off, and the world wants to go with it.

So What's In Java?

In a single oversimplified phrase, Java is C++ slightly simplified, and with libraries convenient for the Internet environment. There's more to it than that, but it will take a book to explain it; this book in fact. So let's get started.

What is Java?

In a single oversimplified phrase,

Java is a new programming language, with elements from C, C++ and other languages, and with libraries highly-tuned for the Internet environment.

Java allows anyone to publish a WWW page with code in it, that can be executed by anyone else accessing that page regardless of hardware.

Java is not a small programming language, and learning it thoroughly requires a certain amount of effort. The language draws inspiration from many sources. Java has:

- Concurrency like Mesa (a research language from Xerox)
- Exceptions like Modula-3
- Dynamic linking of new code like Lisp
- Interface definitions like Objective C
- Automatic storage management like Lisp
- Ordinary statements from C

There's some turbo talk that Sun has written several times (e.g. in "The Java Language Environment" white paper of May 1995 by James Gosling and Henry McGilton) that says Java was designed to be:

Object-oriented, robust, secure, architecture neutral, portable, high performance, interpreted, threaded, and dynamic.

Phew! But so was Mr. Potato Head. What does all that mean in practice?

While all of those qualities are important, two of them really account for the huge interest in Java: portability and architecture neutrality. These are different sides of the same coin, and a small explanation of the meaning of ABI and API is in order here.

A Small Explanation of API and ABI

Application Programmer Interface (API)— is what the programmer sees and uses when writing source code. It consists of the names of the library calls, and the number and types of arguments they take. Source standards such as Posix, and XPG4 specify an API. For example, POSIX 1003.1 says every system that complies with the standard will have a function with this prototype:

```
int isascii(int c);
```

that returns nonzero if c is in the range of the 7-bit ASCII codes.

An API is of most value when it exists on a range of different processors because it helps obtain program portability. Solaris 2.5 meets POSIX 1003.1, and Microsoft has announced that Windows NT will also meet the POSIX standard. So a well-behaved program that uses only the features from this API can (in theory) be ported from one of these OS's to the other simply by recompiling it using the correct libraries.

To properly benefit users, an API must not be under the control of just one vendor. An API controlled by a monopoly is as bad as no API at all, or even worse than that.

Application Binary Interface (ABI)—is the environment that the executing program sees at runtime. It is the format of an executable file, the OS specifics such as process address space, and hardware details such as the number, sizes, and reserved uses of registers. Binary standards such as the SPARC Compliance Definition specify an ABI. Every processor architecture (Intel x86, Apple/Motorola Power PC, Sun SPARC, etc.) will usually have its own ABI. Compliance to an ABI allows a hardware clone market to exist. A program that conforms to a system's ABI will run on any processor that complies with the ABI, regardless of who built the system (original manufacturer, clone maker, or OEM).

Portability

"Portable" acknowledges that Java was designed with Internet applications in mind. That means heterogeneous (mixed) systems, different window libraries and different network features. Java goes a lot further than most languages to obtain not just portability, but identical program behavior on different platforms. Java specifies things that are usually left to the discretion of the compiler writer, such as guaranteeing that operands are evaluated in a left-to-right order, and stipulating that integers are exactly 32 bits, and that doubles are 64 bits long. Java uses the Unicode character set, which is a 16-bit superset of ASCII. Unicode can encode the symbols used in all the world's languages. It thus allows portability of text data files across cultural boundaries.

Program portability means that Java provides the same API (offers the identical set of library calls) unchanged on each system. For example, Java offers a method that creates a Window with this prototype: `public Window(Frame parent)`.

This function exists for a Java programmer on Windows 95, a Java programmer on Solaris 2.x, or a Java programmer on a Macintosh. So to port a Java program from one of these platforms to another, all you would normally need do is recompile it. Except here's where the real genius comes in: because of architecture neutrality, you don't even have to do that!

Architecture Neutral

"Architecture neutral" means the binary code that comes out of the compiler will run on any processor and operating system. You compile a Java program to obtain the object code (termed "byte code" or "bytes" in Java terminology). This object code, or byte code, will run on a Power PC using OS/2, a Pentium-based system under Windows 95, a Macintosh using MacOS, or a SPARC-based workstation running Unix SVr4.

That's quite an achievement! The way it works is that the byte code that comes out of the compiler isn't in the machine language of any one of these processors. Instead the compiler emits an intermediate form, closer to machine representation than the original source code, but not translated all the way to a specific machine code. The Java byte code will be executed by feeding it into a machine specific interpreter. People have tried this architecture neutral idea in the past. The ill-fated Open Software Foundation introduced a variety they called ANDF. ANDF was never really successful for several reasons including the fact that (being scared of the performance cost of an interpreter) OSF required customers to carry out an explicit compilation step when they received the ANDF code.

Despite the marketing gloss put on it, the ANDF was really more for OSF's benefit than that of the customer. Micro Focus COBOL has a similar architecture-neutral interpreted form. It's a little more successful, in that users can stick with the interpreted form, or compile it down to native code for extra performance. There was also a version of Pascal developed in the 1970s by Ken Bowles at the University of California at San Diego, known as UCSD Pascal. It used an interpreted architecture-neutral intermediate code that they called p-code (meaning "pseudo code").

Architecture neutrality means that Java byte code expects to see the same ABI on each system. Porting the Java system to a new platform involves writing an interpreter that supports the Java Virtual Machine. The interpreter will figure out the equivalent machine dependent code to execute (see Figure 1-5.)

The First Key Java Breakthrough!

All platforms that support the Java language have a common Java API and a common Java ABI. The practical result is that platform differences are eliminated. You can compile your code on any platform, and execute the resultant object code on any other platform.

So all platforms that support Java language have a common API and a common ABI. The practical result is that platform differences are eliminated. You can compile your code on any platform, and execute the resultant object code on any other

Figure 1-5: Total Platform Independence: Your application just runs on every system that supports Java. No more "123 for DOS, 123 for Windows 3.1, 123 for Windows 95"

platform. The only difference that the user will see is that some processors run faster than others.

On a network with large numbers of dissimilar computers, the architecture neutrality comes into its own. With Java, the architecture-neutral format delivers solid benefits to the customer and software developer alike: buy it once, run it on anything; write it once, sell it for any platform.

The Significance of Downloading Code (Applets)

So far we have described the WWW, and explained how it is limited, or boring even. It presents a rather inert face to users; all you can do is read something. Granted, there is a facility, known as the "Common Gateway Interface" that lets a user cause a script to be run when a web page is accessed. You can show the user a "fill-in-the-blanks" kind of form, and get some elementary text back. However for something so simple in concept, CGI is complicated to set up, and is riddled with hacks to avoid security problems. A basic principle of computer science is "it should be simple to do simple things." CGI violates this principle and requires a web programmer to learn another language, like PERL (as if you didn't have enough headaches already). It's far too hard to get CGI scripts working for all platforms. Suffice it to say that if CGI were the answer, it must have been a peculiar question. CGI can be regarded as a troublesome and inflexible server-side execution environment. Java offers a simple, flexible, client-side execution environment. The WWW up till now essentially has been a read-only interface. Java changes that!

The Second Key Java Breakthrough!

You can embed a Java program in a web page. When the page is accessed, the program is executed. A program in a web page is called an "applet."

Java Means Business!

The key breakthrough of Java is that you can embed a Java program in a web page. When the page is accessed, the program is "automagically" sent over the net to the user, and executed on the user's computer. This transforms web pages from a one-way display of information, to a genuine interactive two-way dialogue.

The Java code can draw pictures, do calculations, prompt the user, display windows and graphics, or do almost anything else a program can do. In Table 1-1, consider the examples of how Java is changing the web:

Table 1-1: The Web, it is a changing

Old Web Page	Web Page with Java Content
A car dealer can display pictures and descriptions of car models. You can click on a picture and fill out a form to have a brochure sent to you.	The dealer can display pictures of various car models, and prompt the user to indicate how important different characteristics are: economy, power, passenger-carrying ability, and so on. From this, the web page can display the models that most closely match the user's choices. Further dialogue can display the options. As the user chooses options, a separate window can display the itemized price list. This kind of application is just possible with CGI if you work hard enough. Java makes it easy.
A music site allows users to listen to extracts from CDs of their favorite bands. This kind of application is just possible with CGI if you work hard enough. Java makes it easy.	Users can listen to CD extracts, and assemble various tracks onto a customized CD of their own making. They can even adjust the production values, perhaps boosting the bass on love songs. When they have created their own virtual CD with a variety of different artists and songs, they will confirm the order and receive an immediate copy to store on their disk. A couple of days later they will receive the physical CD in the mail along with the credit card payment receipt.
A description of Ohm's law, and some pictures of electrical circuits.	A student can construct a model of an electrical circuit using icons of batteries, resistors, light-bulbs, etc. By connecting them together on the screen and observing what happens (fuse blows, lamp lights) the student can discover basic electrical principles by experimenting.

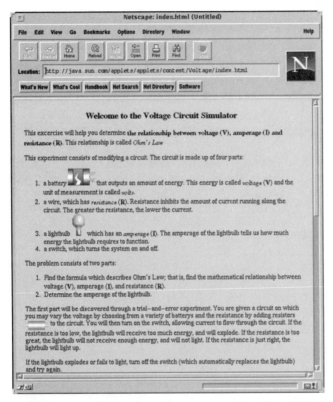

Figure 1-6: This Java application exists today. The URL for the Ohm's Law demonstration is http://java.sun.com/applets/applets/contest/Voltage/index.html

Java is the Swiss Army Knife of Software

Java is a rare example of the right technology coming into the right place at the right time. The WWW offers a fundamentally new way of accessing information. Java extends the capability so that two-way communication can take place. It's like going from just having a radio, to having a telephone. With a radio, you can listen to interesting stuff. With a telephone you can listen, and you can call out yourself and cause interesting things to happen around you. You can order pizza, you can truly conduct business, you can get in touch with friends, you can exercise choice, you can communicate!

HotJava or another Java-capable browser is a key piece in this technology. It implements the client/server model, the security, and the WWW interface.

The old model of the software business held that "shrink-wrapped" software was everything. This means software that comes in a sealed package, and works right out of the box on the purchaser's system. Shrink-wrapped software was most noticeable in the PC world where there are lots of clone systems. Nobody wanted to have to produce a different version of Lotus123 for each slightly different clone, and each new version of MS-DOS or Windows.

Just Imagine That!

Internet access has spread out to the general public to the point where some newspaper cartoonists now include their e-mail addresses in their cartoons. These examples appeared in the Dec. 28, 1995, issue of the San Jose Mercury News:

"Non-sequitor" by Wiley, sequitoon@aol.com

"Frank & Ernest" by Bob Thaves, FandEbobt@aol.com

"Rhymes with Orange" by Hilary Price, hprice@aol.com

"Robotman" by Jim Meddick, JimMeddick@aol.com

On the same day, in an unrelated column by a balding generation-x journalist assigned to cover the hip side of the net, this comment appeared:

"Users have known for years: posting or sending e-mail from an AOL address is a severe social handicap in the on-line world"

David Plotnikoff,
San Jose Mercury News, Dec 28 1995.

Handicapped by AOL or not, two of the cartoonists actually had their own web-site! The best cartoon web-site however is at

`http://www.thoughtport.com/spinnwebe/dfc`

Called "The Dysfunctional Family Circus" the site is a hilarious parody of Bil Keane's saccharine-sweet and terminally-unfunny Family Circus cartoon. Every day the industrious site owner scans in the feebleminded Family Circus cartoon, displays it on-line and invites net surfers to submit better captions for the same drawing. Some of the suggestions had me ROTFL, I thought I'd bust a kidney or something.

Of course they were all *far* too coarse to mention here.

With Java's built-in portability and architecture neutrality, the quality of being shrink-wrapped comes for free. In fact, customers don't even have to go out and buy software anymore. They have the most efficient possible distribution mechanism built right in to the language. If you can find it on the Internet, you can download it and try it. It won't be long before the business community finds a convenient way to let customers pay for the software over Internet too. Java does not merely represent a new programming language. It represents a fundamentally new paradigm in software. Welcome to the new frontier.

Some Light Relief

"Surfing the Internet" has replaced "information superhighway" as the empty phrase you hear most, but want to least. What would be a good anagram of "Surfing the Internet"?

Infer site, then grunt?

First tune, then reign?

Why yes, as a matter of fact, I do have a Java program that generates anagrams! We'll be working through it as an example in Chapter 6.

The anagram program is my back-up decoder for understanding many of the corporate memos I receive. I first try the old "fortune cookie" ploy of adding "in bed" to the end of each phrase in a memo. If that doesn't work, then I run it through the anagrammer. If it still doesn't make sense, then I print the memo out, write on it "Please execute immediately", and hand it to my project leader, Jim, to deal with. I don't know what he does with them—I never see them again after that.

Exercises

1. What is a browser? Why does it use HTML instead of unmarked-up regular text?
2. What is the difference between an API and an ABI? Give examples of each.
3. What are the two most important breakthroughs that the Java language system offers?
4. Define these terms: applet, HotJava, CGI, WWW, URL.
5. What is "shrink-wrapped" software? How might software be distributed over the Internet in the future? How might this affect software retail stores?

Further Readings

The Whole Internet

by Ed Krol,

published by O'Reilly & Associates, Sebastapol CA, 1992

ISBN 1-56592-025-2

An excellent and exceptionally able description of all key aspects of the Internet for the intelligent lay-reader.

How the Internet Works

by Joshua Eddings

published by those slack-jawed gimps at Ziff-Davis, Emeryville CA, 1994

ISBN 1-56276-192-7

A book for people who like looking at pictures and a lot of blank space. Uses the word "Cyberspace" rather too frequently.

As We May Think

by Vannevar Bush

reprint of an article in Atlantic Monthly, July 1945

URL: http://www.isg.sfu.ca/~duchier/misc/vbush

HTML Visual Quick Reference

Dean Scharf, publ Que Corporation, IN, 1995

ISBN 0-7987-0411-0

This is the book on HTML that most programmers will prefer; it's inexpensive, well-written, not padded with fluff, and it covers everything you need to know to write WWW documents.

Client/Server A Manager's Guide

by Laurence Shafe

published by Addison-Wesley, 1994

ISBN 0-201-42790-7

A clear, jargon-free look at the client/server paradigm. It provides the background for understanding many trends in system software, and explains the significance of client/server computing.

Voices From the Net

by Clay Shirky

Ziff-Davis, Emeryville, CA, 1994

ISBN 1-56276-303-2

CHAPTER

2

The Story of O: Object-Oriented Programming

"C makes it easy to shoot yourself in the foot, C++ makes it harder, but when you do, it blows away your whole leg."

> —*Bjarne "Stumpy" Stroustrup (originator of C++)*

I t's a surprising but accurate observation that software development trends seem to be running in the opposite direction to the universe in general. The universe has entropy—it is gradually "winding down," or proceeding to a less and less coherent state. By way of contrast software development methodologies over the past 30 years have become more disciplined and more organized. The prime example of this is Object Oriented Programming (OOP), an old idea enjoying a powerful revival at present.

Java is an object-oriented language, and to understand Java you have to understand OOP concepts. Fortunately, the big, well-kept secret of Object-Oriented Programming works in our favor here: Object-Oriented Programming is based on simple ideas.

The big, well-kept secret of Object-Oriented Programming is that it is simple. It is based on a small number of common-sense fundamentals. Unfortunately OOP has some special terminology, and it suffers from the "surfeit of Zen" problem: to fully understand any one part, you need to understand most of the other parts. Most programmers can understand OOP instinctively if it is explained clearly. However it is not usually explained clearly. Look at the power-babble you can find in the introduction of any book on C++, for example: "Object-oriented programming is characterized by inheritance and dynamic binding. C++ supports inheritance through class derivation. Dynamic binding is provided by virtual class functions. Virtual functions provide a method of encapsulating the implementation details of an inheritance hierarchy."

Completely accurate, but also completely incomprehensible to someone encountering the topic for the first time. Here we describe OOP in simple English, and relate it to familiar programming language features.

Teach Yourself OOP the Hard Way

Alan Kay, an OO expert who is now an Apple distinguished Fellow, began studying the topic in the early 1970s. He was leafing through 80 pages of Simula-67 listing. Simula was the first OO language, but Alan hadn't seen it before and didn't know that. He thought it was Algol or an Algol-variant.

He literally taught himself the principles of OOP from reading 80 pages of code in the first Object-Oriented language. Not everyone will want to duplicate that achievement, so this chapter provides the missing background.

Object-Oriented Programming ("OOP") is not a new idea; Simula-67 pioneered it around thirty years ago. Most experts agree that OOP is based on four key principles: abstraction, encapsulation, inheritance and polymorphism.

We'll take these concepts one at a time, and describe them in terms of real-world examples, and then programming abstractions.

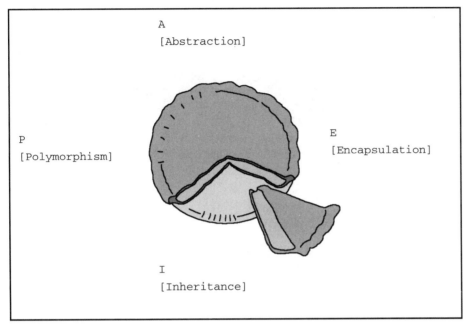

```
                          A
                          [Abstraction]




    P                                       E
    [Polymorphism]                          [Encapsulation]




                          I
                          [Inheritance]
```

Figure 2-1: OOP has four key concepts which you can remember by thinking A PIE: Abstraction, Polymorphism, Inheritance, and Encapsulation

Abstraction

To process something from the real world on a computer, we have to extract out the essential characteristics. The data representing these characteristics are how we will process that thing in a system.

The characteristics which we choose will depend on what we are trying to do. Take a car for example. A registration authority will record the Vehicle Identification Number (the unique code assigned by the manufacturer), the license plate, the current owner, the tax due, and so on. However when the car checks into a garage for a service, the garage will represent it in their computer system by license plate, work description, billing information, and owner. In the owner's home budgeting system, the abstraction may be the car description, service history, gas mileage records and so on.

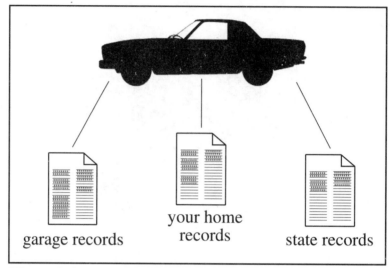

Figure 2-2: Three abstractions of "a car"

These are all examples of data abstractions. Abstraction is the process of refining away the unimportant details of an object, so that only the appropriate characteristics that describe it remain. These, together with the operations on the data, form an abstract data type. We just mentioned three different data abstractions for a car above. Abstraction is where program design starts. All mainstream programming languages provide a way to store pieces of related data together. It is usually called something like a structure or record.

Encapsulation

One step beyond abstraction is the recognition that, equally as important as data, are the operations that are performed on it. Encapsulation simply says that there should be a way to associate the two closely together and treat them as a single unit of organization. In language terms, data, and related functions should be bundled together somehow, so you can say "this is how we represent a blurf object, and these are the only operations that can be done on blurfs".

This is actually a subtle principle because non-OOP languages support encapsulation very well for built-in types, and not at all for user-defined types. Take floating point numbers for example. In most languages, the only valid thing you can do with them is arithmetic operations and I/O. Even in C, if you try to shift left the bits of floating point number:

```
float        f = 2.0;              C EXAMPLE
int          i,j = 1;

i = f << j;
        ^^ operand must have integral type
```

the compiler will print out an error message. The valid operations for a float are encapsulated (bundled together) as part of the type information, and shifting isn't one of them. You cannot directly get your hands on the bits that represent the internal fields of the type, such as the significand, the sign bit, or the exponent. The compiler enforces the rule that "the operation must be compatible with the type."

C provides header files that group together variables, types (typedefs) and function declarations, but this is just lexical grouping, not true encapsulation. C header files do not enforce the integrity of a type (i.e. prevent invalid operations, like assigning a float to an int that represents month_number). Nor do they provide any information hiding. Any program that includes the header file has full details of what is in the type, can access individual fields as desired, and can create new functions that operate on the internals of the structs.

OOP-languages extend the support for encapsulation (bundling together types and the functions that operate on those types, and restricting access to the internal representation) to also cover user-defined types. They enforce the integrity of a type, by preventing programmers accessing individual fields in inappropriate ways. Only a predetermined group of functions can access the data fields. The collective term for "datatype and operations bundled together, with access restrictions" is a "class". The individual elements in a class are "fields" A variable of some class type is called an "instance" or an "object". It's pretty much the same as a variable of an ordinary type, except the valid functions that can be invoked for it are tied to it. In a way, OOP is a misnomer; we should really say "Class-Based Programming."

The One-Minute Object Manager

You have already covered two of the four cornerstones of Object-Oriented Programming. Now is a good time to show what this means with programming examples. We'll use C to start out because it's an enormously popular language, and because if you know any algorithmic language, it's pretty easy to map that to C. Let's begin with an explanation that will take no more than one minute to follow.

We'll build our example around a C struct (a record or structure in other languages) that we'll call "fruit". It is our user-defined data type that stores information abstracted from the qualities of fruit. So we'll declare variables like plum, apple, banana that are instances of fruit type. Fruit isn't usually something that gets data processed, but this example keeps everything focused on the new abstraction, rather than the bits and bytes.

Assume we are primarily concerned with the nutritional value of fruit. As a result the characteristics that we abstract out and store might go into a structure like this:

```
typedef struct {
        int grams;                          C CODE
        int cals_per_gram;
} Fruit;
```

We also have a function that can calculate the total calories, given a pointer to a fruit structure:

```
int total_calories (Fruit *this)
{
        return (this->grams) * (this->cals_per_gram);
}
```

Explanation For Non-native Speakers of C

The definition of the Fruit struct should be self-explanatory. It has two fields that are integers. One records the weight, the other the unit calories. The function "total_calories" has one parameter that is a pointer to a Fruit variable. The parameter is called "this". The body of the function says to get the "grams" field of the structure pointed to by "this" and multiply it by the "cals_per_gram" field. Return the result as the value of the function.

In the next example, the declaration "Fruit pear . . ." creates and initializes a variable of the Fruit type. Finally, the last line creates an integer variable called "total_cals". The variable is initialized with the value returned by calling the function on the pear argument. The function expects a pointer to a Fruit, rather than the Fruit itself, so we pass it "&pear" -- the address of pear, rather than pear itself.

Note: "Pointer to" and "address of" mean exactly the same thing in C, unless you're writing a compiler for a really strange machine.

Here's a C example of calling it:

```
Fruit pear = {5, 45};                           C CODE

int total_cals = total_calories( &pear );
```

So far, so good. But the function and the Fruit type that it operates on, are not closely coupled together. It's too easy to get inside the struct and adjust fields independently. It's possible for anyone to add their own extra functions that operate on the fields of the Fruit type.

We seek the quality of "encapsulation", so let's bundle together the type definition with all the functions that operate on it. In C, we bundle things together by enclosing them in curly braces. Our example would then look like:

```
struct Fruit {
        int grams;                              PSEUDO C
        int cals_per_gram;

        int total_calories (Fruit *this)
        {
        return (this->grams) * (this->cals_per_gram);
        }
};
```

Note that you cannot actually declare a function inside a struct in C, but let's imagine you could. A simplifying assumption is now made. We impose a Fruit argument convention. All the functions that operate on the Fruit datatype will always be passed a pointer-to-a-fruit as the first parameter. This first parameter will point to the fruit that we are going to do the operation on.

So let's save some writing and have the compiler make that first parameter implicit. We won't mention the fruit pointer either in the parameter list, or before the fields it points to. We'll just assume that it exists implicitly, and its name is always "this" (think of it as saying "this here pointer points to the specific piece of fruit you are working on"). At this point, we have created a class. So replace the word "struct" with the word "class". Our three modifications are:

1. bundle together the functions with the datatypes in a struct,

2. give all the functions an implicit first parameter called "this" that points to the struct with the data,

3. replace the word "struct" with "class".

```
class Fruit {
        int grams;
        int cals_per_gram;                          C++ CODE

        int total_calories ( )
        {
        return grams * cals_per_gram;
        }
};
```

There. That's the elements of C++. All the rest is just details (but there are rather a lot of them). That should have taken about one minute to read, although it may take a little longer to re-read and sink in. We get some other benefits from organizing the namespaces: the data fields are implicitly recognized inside the functions without having to say which struct they come from. They come from the same kind of struct that contains the function.

There are no structs or typedefs in Java. The most important way to group related things together is to put them in a class. The C++ class definition above is also a Java class definition. Here's how you declare variables and invoke object functions in Java.

```
Fruit   plum, apple, pear;                          Java CODE

        // some more lines omitted

int cals = plum.total_calories();

int fruit_salad_cals =
            plum.total_calories() +
            apple.total_calories() +
            pear.total_calories();
```

The programming language takes care of the housekeeping of sending a pointer to the variable as the implicit first parameter, and of using that pointer to find the object variables. If it helps, you can think of the compiler as translating

```
plum.total_calories()                       /* Java */
```

into

```
total_calories(&plum)                       /* C */
```

It's actually doing quite a bit more than that: making sure the method is only called for objects of the correct type, enforcing encapsulation, supporting inheritance, and so on. The new notation is useful to convey all these overtones. We refer to the functions that are in the class as "methods" because they are the method for processing some data of that type.

Where Does the Name "Method" Come From?

You might be wondering where does the name "method" come from? Isn't this just an unnecessary new fancy name for "function" or "procedure"? Shhhhhh! You broke the code! Yes, "method" just means "function that belongs to a class."

Note: Some compiler theorists insist that methods are different from functions because their runtime prolog may be different. This is just splitting hairs. All calls involve a prolog to set them up, and an epilog to return. It doesn't seem very interesting to draw a distinction based on how the prolog locates what is being called.

The term seems to have arisen by accident. The origin lies in Smalltalk-72 which was a blend of Lisp and Simula-67. Smalltalk-72 methods began with the keyword 'TO' as in TO CalculateTotal ... because they were just "methods TO do something or other." Over time the term naturally shifted from the preposition to the noun. Methods could just as easily have been called a "way" a "plan" a "scheme" (there actually is a Scheme variant of Lisp) or an "action."

To summarize, we've arrived at C++, and the convention of a struct that contains both the datatype fields, and the function(s) that manipulate them. All this is common to Java, too. There's also a notation to suggest we are invoking a method on an object:

```
plum.total_calories();
```

rather than passing an object as an argument

```
total_calories( &plum );
```

This is because OOP stresses the importance of objects rather than procedural statements. One way that might help you grasp this notation is to consider it analogous to the C statement "i++", indicating "take the object called 'i' and do the ++ operation on it." Here we have "take the object called 'plum' and do the 'total_calories()' method on it."

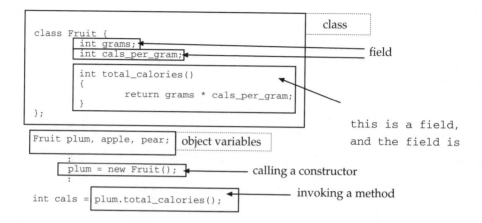

Figure 2-3: Some class terminology

In the Java code above, Fruit is a class. The variables apple, plum, and pear are instances of the class, or objects. The variables "grams" and "cals_per_gram" are instance variables. The function "total_calories()" is a method. The declarations of grams, cals_per_gram and total_calories() are fields. The class as a whole forms a user-defined type.

An Alternative Rationale for OOP

Another way of looking at this class thing is that it's just a way of giving user-defined types the same privileges as types that are built in to the language.

Just as the compiler knows what may and may not be done with a float, classes provide a way to specify the same information and constraints for new types.

The result is software that is more reliable and quicker to debug (because data can only be changed in disciplined ways). A piece of the program that "owns" (declares) an object cannot break it open and fool around with the individual fields.

We come now to a significant and important difference between Java and C++. This change takes a little getting used to when programming, and forms a key divergence in the language philosophies. Java makes significant distinctions between built-in ("primitive") types and user-defined types (i.e classes).

Java treats variables in two different ways, depending on their type:

1.   variables of built-in types: boolean, char, int, etc. (primitive types)

2.   objects

The difference is this: when you declare a variable, what you get depends on the type. If it is a built-in type, you actually get the variable and you can read, write and process it immediately. ❦

```
e.g     int i;
        i =0;   i++;    // all fine.
```

If however, it is a variable of a class type (any class type), you do *not* get an instance of that class immediately, and you cannot read, write or process it immediately! What you get is a reference variable—a location that can hold a pointer to the desired object *when you fill it in.*

Note that this is a big difference from C++, where declaring an object reserves space for the object itself. In C++, if you declare one class inside another, space for the entire size of the nested class is reserved. In Java, declaring one class inside another would simply reserve space for a *pointer to* the nested class. This allows all kinds of implementation magic—object sizes never have to be known on compilation, because they are *all* simply dealt with as two pointers—a pointer to the class information and a pointer to the actual object on the heap.

When you declare:

```
        Myclass foo;
```

That does not give you an object of Myclass. It gives you a reference variable foo that can reference an object of Myclass - after you have filled in the reference so it points to such an object. You can create a Myclass object for foo. Or you can make it point to an existing object.

The assignment:

```
        myfruit = apple;
```

does not *copy* the apple object! It makes myfruit and apple have the same reference to it. Changes made through myfruit will be seen by apple!

```
        myfruit.grams = 37;
```

apple.grams is now 37

Parameter Passing

The difference between variables of primitive types, and objects (reference types) has implications for parameter passing too. Variables of built-in types are passed by value, objects are passed by reference.

"Passing by value" means that the argument's value is copied, and is passed to the method. Inside the method this copy can be modified at will, and doesn't affect the original argument.

"Passing by reference" means that a reference to (i.e. the address of) the argument is passed to the method. Using the reference, the method is actually directly accessing the argument, not a copy of it. Any changes the method makes to the parameter are made to the actual object used as the argument. So after you return from the method, that object will retain any new values set in the method.

So if all objects are accessed by reference how do you get a copy of an object? It turns out that you hardly ever need to do that (when was the last time you needed a distinct duplicate of the literal "3"?) Think of objects as inherently unique. Replication by copying threatens that uniqueness thus leading to lack of control, chaos, and eventually, a hereditary monarchy based on primogeniture. There is a way to do it if you absolutely must (implement the cloneable interface, as outlined in chapter 4).

Constructors and Finalizers

Whenever you declare an object variable, before you can actually do anything with it, you must make it point to an object instance. One way to do that is to create a new object using a constructor—a process known as "instantiation", like so:

```
foo = new Myclass();
```

or combine the declaration and instantiation into one like this:

```
Myclass foo = new Myclass();
```

A constructor is a special kind of method that initializes a newly-created object. "Create_and_Initialize" would be a good, though long, name instead of "constructor." One reason a constructor (or at least an ordinary method) is needed is because no one outside the class is able to access data whose scope is limited to the class (we call this private data—there is a keyword to label data in this way). Therefore you need a privileged function inside the class to fill in the initial data values of a newly-minted object. This is a bit of a leap from C, where you just initialize a variable with an assignment in its definition, or even leave it uninitialized.

Constructor functions always have the same name as the class, and have this general form

```
classname ( parameterlist ) { . . . }
```

Note that there is no explicit return type, nor the keyword "void." In some senses, the constructor name *is* the return type.

Most classes have at least one explicit constructor. You can define several different constructors, and tell them apart by their parameter types. In the Fruit example:

Java CODE

```
class Fruit {
        int grams;
        int cals_per_gram;

        Fruit() {grams=55; cals_per_gram=0;}  // constructor

        Fruit(int g, int c) {    //another constructor
            grams=g;
            cals_per_gram=c;
        }
}
        . . .

    Fruit melon=new Fruit(4,5), banana=new Fruit();
```

In this example, a melon is created with grams = 4 and cals_per_gram = 5. Similarly a banana is created with grams = 55 and 0 cals_per_gram. A constructor cannot be invoked explicitly by the programmer other than in object creation, although this might otherwise be quite a useful operation to reset an object to a known initial state, say. The reason is that a constructor is deemed to magically create an object, as well as setting values in its fields.

Since almost everything in Java is an object, almost everything is created by a call to a constructor. Constructors have the same name as the class, so it is very common to see something declared and initialized with calls like this:

```
Bicycle schwinn = new Bicycle();
Cheese cheddar = new Cheese(matured);
Beer ESB = new Beer(London, bitter, 1068);
Mammal dalmatian = new Dog("spotty"); // Mammal is the superclass of Dog
```

The repeated classname looks quite odd to C programmers at first. 🐛

Every class always has at least one constructor. When you do not provide any explicit constructors (you are allowed to do this), then the default no-arg constructor is assumed for you. Constructors are like the public defender in many legal systems: if you do not have one, a default one will be provided for you, but it won't do very much. The default no-arg (meaning "no arguments") constructor for a class takes no arguments and does nothing, but it does ensure that every class always has at least one constructor.

When an object is instantiated, this is the order in which things happen:

1. The memory for the object is allocated on the heap. The heap is a "scratchpad" area of memory controlled by the runtime system to support dynamic memory allocation.

2. The data fields are filled in with the default values zero, 0.0, null, and so on.

3. Any data fields with explicit initializers have those initial assignments executed.

4. The statements in the constructor are executed.

No Destructors

Java has automatic storage management, including automatic reclamation of unused store. The runtime system does not therefore need to be told when an object has reached the end of its lifetime. Accordingly, there are no destructors in the C++ sense. Just delete, overwrite, or null out the last reference to an object and it becomes available for destruction so the memory can be reused. There is more about this in Chapter 5 on "garbage collection." You can provide a finalizer for a class. it will be invoked on an object right before it is garbage collected.

Inheritance

The last two pieces of OOP are inheritance and polymorphism. You need a solid understanding of these to successfully use the Java library routines. Despite the unusual names, they describe some clear concepts.

Inheritance means building on a class that is already defined, to extend it in some way. Inheritance is what you acquire from past generations. Let us first consider a real world example of "class inheritance" in the Linnaean taxonomy of the animal kingdom, and a similar example using C types.

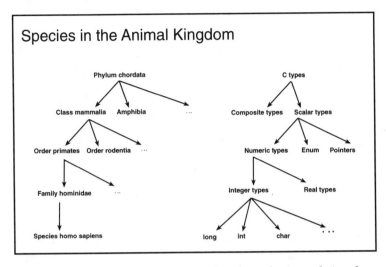

Figure 2-4: Two real-world examples of an inheritance heirarchy

In the figure above:

- The phylum chordata contains every creature that has a notochord (roughly, a spinal cord), and only those creatures; all told there are some 35 phyla in the animal kingdom.

- All mammals have a spinal cord. They inherit it as a characteristic by being a subclass of the chordata phylum. Mammals also have specialized characteristics: they feed their young milk, they have only one bone in the lower jaw, they have hair, a certain bone configuration in the inner ear, two generations of teeth, and so on.

- Primates inherit all the characteristics of mammals (including the quality of having a spinal chord, that mammals inherited from chordates). Primates are further distinguished by forward facing eyes, a large braincase, and a particular pattern of incisor teeth.

- The hominidae family inherits all the characteristics from primates and more distant ancestors. It adds to the class the unique specialization of a number of skeletal modifications suitable for walking upright on two feet. The homo sapiens species is now the only species alive within this family. All other species have become extinct.

To be a little more abstract, the hierarchy of types in C can be similarly analyzed:

- All types in C are either composite (types like arrays or structs, that are composed of smaller elements) or scalar. Scalar types have the property that each value is atomic (it is not composed of other types).

- The numeric types inherit all the properties of scalar types, and they have the additional quality that they record arithmetic quantities.

- The integer types inherit all the properties of numeric types, and they have the additional characteristic that they only operate on whole numbers (no fractional quantities).

- The type char is a smaller range within the values in the integer family.

Although we can amuse ourselves by showing how inheritance applies in theory to the familiar C types, note that this model is of no practical use to a C programmer. C doesn't have built-in inheritance, so a programmer cannot use the type hierarchy in real programs. An important part of OOP is figuring out and advantageously using the hierarchies of the abstract data types in your application.

There is a GUI library class in Java called Window that implements the most basic kind of window. A Window object can be moved, resized, iconified, and you can use it in your code. For the sake of this example, let's assume that your program needs a slightly different kind of window: an ImportantWindow. The only difference is that you want ImportantWindows to be colored red to highlight their importance.

There are at least three possible ways to implement ImportantWindow:

1. Change the Window class and add a constructor that creates important windows. This is a bad approach, because you never want to change the standard runtime library.

2. Copy all the code in Window.java into file ImportantWindow.java, making the change you need. This is a bad approach, because it is impossible to keep duplicated code in synchronization. Whenever the code for class Window changes in future releases, class ImportantWindow is almost guaranteed to stop working.

3. Make ImportantWindow a *subclass* of Window, so it *inherits* all the functionality from Window.

The preferred OOP approach is the third one: make ImportantWindow extend the class Window, so ImportantWindow inherits all the data and methods of Window.

This is exactly how the OOP process is supposed to work: find a class that does most of what you want, and then subclass it to provide the exact functionality. There's nothing special about the libraries that come with Java. You can subclass your own classes and system classes as needed.

To summarize, inheritance occurs when a class adapts the data structures and methods of a base (or "parent") class. That creates a hierarchy, similar to a scientific taxonomy. Each level is a specialization of the one above. Type inheritance is a concept that doesn't really exist in C or other non object-oriented languages. Inheritance is one of the concepts people are referring to when they say object-oriented programming requires thinking in a special way. Get ready to spring forward with that "conceptual leap"!

The Key Idea: Inheritance

Inheritance means being able to declare a type which builds on the fields (data and methods) of a previously-declared type. As well as inheriting all the operations and data, you get the chance to declare your own versions and new versions of the methods, to refine, specialize, replace or extend the ones in the parent class.

Terminology:

class = a data type

extend = to make a new class that inherits the contents of an existing class.

superclass = a parent or "base" class. Superclass is a very poor choice of name as it wrongly suggests the parent class has more than the subclass.

subclass = a child class that inherits, or extends, a superclass.

It is called a subclass because it only represents a sub-part of the universe of things that make up the superclass. However, it usually has more fields to represent its specialization.

Note that in Java, almost everything is an object, and in particular, all the classes that you declare are subclasses of the built-in root class Object. So if you have read ahead and written some lines of Java that compile, you are already implicitly using inheritance!

Inheritance usually provides increasing specialization as you go from a general superclass class (e.g. vehicle) to a more specific subclass (e.g. passenger car, fire truck, or delivery van). It could equally subset or extend the available operations though.

Let's invent a class Citrus that has every characteristic of the Fruit class we were playing around with earlier, and a specialized operation of its own: squeeze. Citrus fruits are pretty much the only widely-available fruits that you can hand squeeze to extract the juice from. Our base class is:

```
class Fruit {                                    Java CODE
        int grams;
        int cals_per_gram;

        int total_calories ( ) { /* ... */ }
}
```

An example of class inheritance is

```
class Citrus extends Fruit {
        void squeeze() {  /* ... */ }
}
```

This makes Citrus a subclass that inherits all the Fruit class operations and adds this squeeze() specialization of its own. Don't get hung up on how the method might be implemented. Obviously it's removed from usual computing. Remember, we're concentrating on the new concepts, without getting caught up on specific algorithms.

The code says that Citrus is based on ("extends") Fruit. A Citrus is a specialization of Fruit; it has all the fields that Fruit has, and adds a method of its own.

Here's an example of how various fruits might be declared and inherited. Note, by the way, how everything in Java belongs to a class. There are no global variables or functions outside classes. This example assumes the Fruit and Citrus classes mentioned above.

```
class test2e {
      public static void main(String args[]) {
          Fruit somefruit= new Fruit();
          Citrus lemon = new Citrus();

          lemon.squeeze();

          somefruit = lemon;
      }
}
```

We'll get to the "public static void main" stuff later. For now, that's just there for the adventurous who want to try typing something in and compiling it right now before reading any further. There's a few in every crowd (I'm one of them, in fact).

Notice the assignment of lemon (a Citrus object) into somefruit (a Fruit object). You can always make a more general object hold a more specialized one, but the reverse is not true without an explicit type conversion. All citrus are fruit, but not all fruit are citrus. So you can assign somefruit=lemon, but not lemon=somefruit because somefruit may be a plum.

Casting

Casting is the C term for type conversion, carried over into Java. Just as you can cast (convert) an integer into a double, so too you can cast from a superclass to one of its more specialized subclasses. The previous example explained that you can't assign

```
lemon = somefruit;     // causes compilation error
```

You can, however, cast it. To cast any type, write the typename in parentheses immediately before the object being cast. In this case:

```
lemon = (Citrus) somefruit;     // works fine
```

Type hierarchies are often drawn as tree diagrams with Object (the ultimate superclass) at the top, and all subclasses beneath their superclass as Figure 2-4 exemplifies. Referring to a drawing of this type, you can only cast "downwards" between a superclass and some subclass (or subclass of a subclass, etc). You can never cast "sideways" to force an object to become something it is not.

All objects carry around a little extra information at runtime, saying what type they really are, so casts can be checked. If the somefruit object is actually something that's not a Citrus, the cast will fail at runtime, raising the exceptional condition "ClassCastException". Exceptions are described in Chapter 5. They are a recoverable interruption to the normal flow of control.

Because every class is a subclass of the built-in system class Object, every object can be assigned to something of type Object, and later cast back to the type that it really is. In this way, the type Object is a little like "void *" in C that is used as a general pointer to anything. There are some utility classes that store and manipulate Objects, so you can use them for any object, later casting to get back the same type that you put in.

Inheritance is not confined to a single level. You can have class A extends B, where class B extends C, and so on. If you look at the Java runtimes, you can see several examples of inheritance hierarchies 5 or 6 levels deep. You can cast to several levels down in the hierarchy, not just the immediate subclass.

"Is A" Versus "Has A"

Don't confuse inheritance with having a data field that is another class. It's very common to have a class that only implements a data structure such as a hash table. This is known as a container class, because it "contains" the data structure. You attach that data structure to some other class by declaring an instance of it inside the class as another field. A class is just a datatype remember. Declaring a class inside another just sets up a reference variable to the class with no special privileges or relationship. In contrast, inheritance says the subclass is a variation of the superclass that extends its semantics in some way.

The way to distinguish between these two cases is to ask yourself the "is a" versus "has a" question. Let's assume you have a "car" class and an "engine" class, and you want to decide whether to use inheritance or nesting to associate the two. Would you say "a car has an engine" or "a car is an engine?" If the answer is "has a" use nesting. If the answer is "is a", use inheritance. Similarly, if we have a "mammal" class and a "dog" class, we would tend to say that a "dog is a mammal" so we would use inheritance to extend the mammal class resulting in the dog class.

The rule of thumb is that inheritance is for specialization of a type, and container classes are for code re-use.

Inheritance and Constructors

At the beginning of this section on inheritance, we suggested the feature could be used to extend Window to support ImportantWindow. Here is the actual code that would do that.

First, review the code that implements Window. It can be seen in file $JAVAHOME/src/java/awt/Window.java. The class Window starts out like this:

```
class Window {

        Window(Frame parent) {        // constructor
            ...
        }
    ...
```

All you need to do is give the ImportantWindow class a constructor that just calls the ordinary Window constructor, then adds a line to give it the desired red background color. The ImportantWindow code (in full) looks like this:

```
class ImportantWindow extends Window {

        ImportantWindow(Frame pear) { // constructor
                super(pear);
                setBackground(Color.red);
        }
}
```

That's all it takes! This really demonstrates the power of inheritance. Now wherever you were going to use a Window, you could instead use an ImportantWindow that has all the same methods and data, but comes up colored red.

```
// a regular window
Window mywin = new Window(someframe);

// my special window
ImportantWindow alert = new ImportantWindow(myframe);
```

Take another look at the constructor in the ImportantWindow class. That line of code that reads "super(pear)" is a common idiom when one class extends another. The code "super( )" is the way you express "call the constructor of my super-class." That's exactly what we want here: a regular Window to be constructed, and then its color to be changed to red.

As it happens, a superclass constructor is *always* invoked when you create a sub-class object. If you don't explicitly call a superclass constructor, then the no-arg constructor of the superclass is called for you. If the superclass doesn't have a no-arg constructor (either an implicit one because you didn't provide any construc-tors, or an explicit no-arg constructor that you did provide) then you get a compi-lation error along the lines of "no constructor found in superclass."

Another idiom you may use is "this(...)" to call a different constructor in the same class. Normally "this" in a method means "the object I was invoked on." Here it is re-used to mean "one of my other constructors—pick the one with the matching signature." You would typically call one constructor from another when you have several constructors to allow arguments of several different types. Each construc-tor will put its arguments in standard form, and then call the main constructor that handles all the rest of the work. When one constructor explicitly invokes another (either super() or this()), that invocation must be the very first statement in the constructor. It's easy to rationalize why, for a couple of reasons. First, something is fully created after a constructor has been completed, and second, something must be fully created before you can start playing around with its fields.

Here is an example of one constructor invoking another with this() (no inheritance is involved here).

```
class FruitPie {
        // data fields
        double weight;
        java.util.Date    whenmade;

        // One constructor
        FruitPie(int i) {
                this( (double) i );    // calls second constructor
        }

        // Second constructor
        FruitPie(double d) {
                weight = d;
                whenmade = new java.util.Date();
        }

        // ... other methods ....

}
```

calls the sibling constructor whose arguments match

Forcing the Method: Abstract and Final

There are two further fine-tuning adjustments to inheritance, available to experts, namely "abstract" and "final". They qualify classes by appearing right at the beginning, before the keyword "class". In some sense, "abstract" and "final" are opposites of each other.

When the keyword "final" appears at the start of a class declaration, it means "No one can extend this class." Similarly, an individual method can be made "final" preventing it being overridden when its class is inherited. It is final in the sense that it is the leaf of an inheritance tree. Typically, you might wish to prevent further inheritance to avoid further specialization: you don't want to permit this type to be adjusted any more. One practical example concerns the thread class. People writing multi-threaded programs will extend the Thread class, but the system implementors must prevent people from accidentally or deliberately redefining the individual methods that do Thread housekeeping, like:

```
public final synchronized void stop(Object o) { ...
public final native boolean isAlive();
public final void suspend() { ...
public final void resume() { ...
public final void setPriority(int newPriority) ...
public final ThreadGroup getThreadGroup() { ...
```

Making the methods "final" accomplishes this neatly. A "final" method is also a clue to the compiler to inline the code. Inlining the code means optimizing out the overhead of a method call by taking the statements in the body of the method and duplicating them inline instead of making the call. This is a classic space versus time trade-off.

When the keyword "abstract" appears at the start of a class declaration, it means that one or more of its methods are abstract. An abstract method has no body; its purpose is to force a subclass to override it and provide a concrete implementation of it. For example, you may have a class that implements a waterborne vehicle type, expecting it to later be extended to implement a ship, a boat, a canoe class. All of these vehicles can be pointed in a given direction, so it would be reasonable to provide an abstract "Set_Direction()" method in the superclass, forcing this to be provided in the subclass.

```
abstract class WaterBorneTransport {

        abstract void set_direction (int n);
        abstract void set_speed (int n);


}
```

Also, you cannot create ("instantiate") an object of an abstract class. Making a class abstract forces a programmer to extend it and fill in some more details in the subclass before it can be used. You inherit as usual, like so:

```
class Canoe extends WaterBorneTransport {

    void set_direction (int n) { ...
    void set_speed (int n) { ...

}
```

Multiple Inheritance

You may hear references to "multiple inheritance." This means deriving from more than one base class at once. The resulting subclass thus has characteristics from more than one immediate parent type. It turns the tree hierarchy into a directed graph.

Multiple inheritance is much less common than single inheritance. Where it has appeared in languages (like C++) it has been the subject of considerable debate on whether it should be in the language at all. It is a difficult, bug-prone feature in both implementation and use. There are many complicated rules for how the namespaces of the two parent classes interact. Some people say that no convincing examples have been produced where there was no alternative design avoiding multiple inheritance. Java avoids the difficulties by not permitting multiple inheritance. The interface feature described in Chapter 4 helps fill in the gap left by multiple inheritance.

Visibility and Other Name Modifiers

You now know most of OOP in Java, and the tone of this chapter changes from conceptual to nitty-gritty details. Let's begin by noting that there are several keywords which control visibility, both of a class, and the individual fieldnames within a class. This section explains these keywords. Turn the corner of the page down—you'll be referring back to this often! Let's start by saying there's a way to group together several classes into a package. We'll talk more about this later, but for now, a package is a group of classes that you want to bundle together.

Class Modifiers

There are modifiers that you can apply to a class. When you declare a class, the general form looks like this:

syntax:

> *modifier* `class` *name* [`extends` *name*] [`implements` *namelist*] *body*

description:

> The modifier can be one or more of "abstract", "final" or "public" ("abstract" and "final" are opposites and are not allowed together).

> `abstract:` class must be extended (to be useful)
>
> `final:` class must not be extended
>
> `public:` class is visible in other packages

examples:

```
abstract public class Fruit { ....
final public class Citrus extends Fruit { ....
```

Data Field Modifiers

The fields in a class body can be variables, or methods. The field can similarly start with a modifier that says how visible it is, and qualifies it in some other way. These are the modifiers that you can apply to a field that is data.

modifiers to data field:	explanation
`public`	field is visible everywhere (class must be public too)
(blank)	what you get by default. field is only visible in this package
`protected`	like default, *and* the field is visible in subclasses in other packages extended from this class, too. So protected is actually *less* protected than the default!
`private`	field is only visible in this class

(above are keywords that modify visibility)

(below are keywords that modify the way the field is used)

`static`	one per class, not one for each object—This is screwy re-use of the confusing C terminology that says static means "not allocated on the stack". It comes from the C keyword that says allocate this in the data segment at compile-time (i.e. statically). Where you see "static" read it as "only one."
`final`	cannot change value (like const)
`transient`	a hint used in object serialization. See Chapter 9.
`volatile`	this data may be written to by several threads of control, so the run-time system has to take care to always get the freshest value when reading it.

example: `protected static final int upper_bound = 2047;`

`upper_bound` is visible throughout this package, and in subclasses of this class even ones in other packages. The data is associated with the class, not an individual object, so any change made to it would be seen by all objects. It won't change though, because it has been assigned a final value.

Method Field Modifiers

These are modifiers that you can apply to a field that is a method.

modifiers to a method:	explanation
`public`	field is visible everywhere (the class must be public too)
(blank)	the default—field is visible in this package
`protected`	like the default, and the field is visible in subclasses in other packages (so protected is *less* protected than the default!)
`private`	field is only visible in this class (and so can never be declared abstract, as it's not visible to be overridden).

(above are keywords that modify visibility)

(below are keywords that modify the way the method is used)

`final`	cannot be overridden
`static`	one per class, not one for each object (and is therefore implicitly final, because overriding is done based on the type of the object, and static methods are attached to a class, not an object.)
`abstract`	must be overridden (to be useful)
`native`	not written in Java (no body, but otherwise normal and can be inherited, static, etc.) The body will be written in another language.
`synchronized`	only one thread may execute in the method at a time. Entry to the method is protected by a monitor lock around it.

example: `protected abstract int total_calories() { ... }`

Note: several of these modifiers can be chosen together, such as "native protected". We will revisit the semantics of visibility in Chapter 4 when we cover packages. For now, think "package = library". Some combinations of modifier do not make sense, and are not permitted. A method cannot be both abstract *and* final for instance. That would say "you have to override me" *and* "you may not override me." A constructor can only be qualified with public, private and protected.

Don't make any fields public without good reason. In general you should give things the most restricted visibility that still makes it possible for them to work.

Static

There are three varieties of static thing (once-only) in Java. A static thing is something in a class that occurs once only, instead of once for each instance of the class.

Static Data

So far we have explained a class in terms of a template: any object of the class gets its own copy of all the data fields. Usually this is exactly what you want. There is a way to change it though, and label a data field as occurring just once, no matter how many instances of the class there are. This is what the keyword "static" does, as shown below.

```
class Employee {
     String[] name;
     long     salary;
     short    employee_number;

  static int total_employees;


     . . .
  }
```

The purpose of the Employee class is to store and process data on an individual employee. However, we also use the class to hold the total number of employees that we have on the payroll. The variable total_employees is a quantity associated with employees in general, so this class might be a good home for it. But it's wasteful and error-prone to duplicate this value in every employee object. total_employees is a value associated with the class as a whole, not each object of it. Applying the storage modifier "static" to a data field makes that happen.

Inside the class, static data is accessed by giving its name. Outside the class, static data can be accessed by prefixing it with the name of an object, or the name of the class. Either works, as the following example shows:

```
Employee newhire = new Employee();
newhire.total_employees++; // reference through an instance

Employee.total_employees =0; // reference through the class
```

The second form, referencing static variables through the class name, is preferred because it provides a cue that this is not instance data.

Static Methods

Just as there can be static data that belongs to the class as a whole, there can also be static methods (also called "class methods") that do some class-wide operations, and do not apply to an individual object. Again, these are highlighted by using the modifier "static" before the method name. Again, you can call a static method by prefixing it with the name of an object or the name of the class. It is always better to call it using the name of the class so that people don't confuse it with per-instance methods. Here is an example:

```
class Employee {
        String[] name;
        long     salary;
        short    employee_number;

    static int total_employees;

    static void clear() {
        total_employees = 0;
    }
}

 . . .


    newhire.clear();  // reference through an instance

    Employee.clear();  // better: reference through the class
```

Be aware of this "wrinkle"—static methods cannot access any instance data. In other words, the static routine clear() does not have an implicit "this" parameter, is not applied to an individual object, and therefore cannot touch the data fields or call the methods that belong to individual objects. A static method can only directly access other static fields. You will encounter an error message like:

"Can't make static reference to non-static varaible"

if you try to access an instance variable from a static method.

One workaround is to declare an object inside the class, and use that instance to touch the fields or (more usually) call the non-static methods you need. ☕

Static Blocks

The final kind of static thing is a static block. This is a portion of executable code belonging to the class, commonly used for initialization. A static block is executed once only when the class is first loaded. The keyword "static" precedes the curly braces that delimit the static block, as shown here:

```
public class Employee {
        String[] name;
        long      salary;
        short     employee_number;

        static int total_employees;

        static {
    System.out.println("Calculating how many employees")
            if ( some_condition )
                total_employees =100;
            else total_employees =0;
        }
}
```

Once again, static blocks can only access static data. There can be multiple static blocks in a class, and they are executed in the order in which they occur in the source. They are most useful for sophisticated initialization or guaranteed one-time only initialization.

Of all the many names in Java which are poorly-chosen, "static" is the very worst. It is a legacy from the confusing and confused "static" keyword in C. Static never made much sense in C either—the term originated with data that was allocated statically in the data segment at compile time, but it was re-used with other meanings too. Whenever you see "static" in Java, think "once only".

Polymorphism

Polymorphism is a horrible name for a straightfoward concept. It is Greek for "many shapes", and it means using the same one name to refer to different methods. "Name sharing" would be a better term. There are two types of polymorphism in Java: the trivial kind and the interesting kind.

The trivial kind of polymorphism is called "overloading" in Java and other languages, and it means that in any class you can use the same name for several different (but hopefully related) methods. However, the methods must have different numbers and/or types of parameters so the compiler can tell which of the synonyms is intended. The return type is not looked at when disambiguating polymorphic functions in Java.

The I/O facilities of a language are one canonical place where the overloading kind of polymorphism is used. You don't want to have an I/O class that requires a different method name depending on whether you are trying to print a short, an int, a long, etc. You just want to be able to say "print(foo)". Note that C fails to meet this requirement. Although you use the same routine "printf", it also needs a format specifier (which is a statement in a particularly ugly programming language in its own right) to tell printf what argument types to expect and to output. If you change the type of the C value you are outputting, you usually need to change the format specifier too.

The second, more complicated kind of polymorphism, true polymorphism, is resolved dynamically (at runtime). It occurs when a subclass class has a method with the same name and signature (number, type and order of parameters) as a method in the superclass. When this happens, the method in the derived class overrides the method in the superclass. An example should make this clear.

Let's go back to our base class Fruit, and our subclass Citrus. We will give Citrus a "peel" method of its own, to reflect the fact that citrus fruits are peeled differently to many other kinds of fruit. Let's assume for the purposes of this example, that all citrus fruit are carefully peeled to preserve the zest. We don't honor non-citrus fruits with this care. We add a "peel()" method to our base class:

```
class Fruit {
        int grams;
        int cals_per_gram;

        int total_calories ( ) { /* ... */ }
        void peel ( ) {System.out.println("peel a Fruit"); }
}
```

The subclass gets its own version of peel:

```
class Citrus extends Fruit {
        void squeeze() {  /* ... */ }
        void peel () {System.out.println("peel a Citrus"); }
}
```

The method peel() in Citrus replaces or overrides the superclass's version of peel() when the method is invoked on a Citrus object. C++ programmers will note that you do not need to specifically point out to the compiler (with the C++ "virtual" keyword) that overriding will take place. Here's an example:

```
class Example {
      public static void main(String args[]) {
          Fruit somefruit= new Fruit();
          Citrus lemon = new Citrus();

          somefruit.peel();
          lemon.peel();

          somefruit = lemon;
          somefruit.peel();
      }
}
```

If you try running this, you will note that when we apply the peel method to some-fruit, we get the base class version (it prints "peel a Fruit"). When we apply the peel method to lemon, we get the Citrus specialized version (it prints "peel a Citrus")

 When we apply the peel method to something which starts out as a general Fruit, but may have been assigned a Citrus at runtime, the correct peeling method is chosen at runtime, based on what the object is. And *that* is polymorphism. ❧

The Difference Between Overloading and Overriding

Overloading, the trivial kind of polymorphism, is resolved by the compiler at compile time. Overloading allows several methods to have the same one name, and the compiler will choose the one you meant, by matching on argument types.

Overriding, the fancy kind of polymorphism is resolved at runtime. It occurs when one class extends another, and the subclass has a method with same signature (exact match of name and argument types) as a method in the superclass. Question: which of them gets invoked? Answer: if it's an object of the subclass, the subclass one; if it's an object of the superclass, the superclass one. The reason this is "fancy" is that sometimes you cannot tell until runtime, so the compiler must plant code to work out which method is appropriate for whatever this object turns out to be, then call that at runtime.

The technical term for "choosing the correct method for whatever object this is at runtime" is "late binding" or "delayed binding." Polymorphism is the language feature that allows two methods to have the same name, such that late binding may be applied.

Some Light Relief

A few years ago, the historic SAIL computer at Stanford University, California was decommissioned. This computer system had supported some of the most interesting computer science research for twenty-five years.

The last act of the computer system was to send out an e-mail message marking the occasion and telling its remarkable life story. The message went to everyone who had signed up to request it a couple of weeks earlier. Here's my copy of the farewell salute from SAIL, slightly edited for brevity.

As Far Away From C++ As Possible, But No Further

In 1994 I wrote a book on C that included a chapter on C++. At that time, it looked as though C had reached its peak, and that C++ was on a fast track to replace C. This was an unhappy scenario, because C++ is a flawed language. My opinion is that it is large and difficult to learn compared to other languages of similar power. The single most important feature of C++ (classes) builds on the problematic and flawed C type model.

Nonetheless, I didn't want to be unduly harsh on C++, as the language has many disciples with sensitive feelings. So I tried to be even-handed, and expressed the view that C++ would become widely used despite its failings, and the hope that it would eventually lead the way to something better (page 325, Expert C Programming).

Those turned out to be prophetic words, in that both parts of the prediction came true. C++ is in widespread use despite its drawbacks. And C++ has served its purpose in providing a foundation for Java. Java is it. Put aside your C++ books, and start studying Java. In another 12 months time, you'll be glad you did.

```
Return-Path: <SAI@SAIL.Stanford.EDU>
Received: from SAIL.Stanford.EDU by MCC.COM with TCP; Sat 8 Jun 91
00:24:21-CDT
Message-ID: <CzbJ1@SAIL.Stanford.EDU>
Date: 07 Jun 91  2056 PDT
From: SAIL Timesharing System <SAI@SAIL.Stanford.EDU>
Subject: life as a computer for a quarter of a century
To:    "@BYEBYE.[1,SAI]"@SAIL.Stanford.EDU
```

Take Me, I'm Yours: *The autobiography of SAIL*

I've had a very full and adventurous life. At various times I have been the world's leading research computer in artificial intelligence, speech recognition, robotics, computer music composition and synthesis, analysis of algorithms, text formatting and printing, and even computer-mediated psychiatric interviewing. I did have some help from various assistants in doing these things, but I was the key player.

I developed a number of new products and founded a string of successful companies based on the new technology, including Vicarm, Foonly, Imagen, Xidex, Valid Logic, Sun Microsystems, and Cisco Systems. I also gave a major boost to some established firms such as Digital Equipment and Lucasfilm. What did I get from all this? No stock options. Not even a pension, though Stanford is still paying my sizable electrical bills.

I was always good at games. For example, I created the advanced versions of Spacewar, which spawned the video games industry, as well as the game of Adventure and I was the computer world champion in both Checkers and Go.

I invented and gave away many other things, including the first spelling checker, the SOS text editor, the SAIL compiler, the FINGER program, and the first computer-controlled vending machine. Note that my name has been taken by the SAIL language, the SAIL compiler, and the laboratory in which I used to live. Just remember that I was the original Stanford Artificial Intelligence Laboratory.

Beginnings

I was born on June 6, 1966, at the D.C. Power Laboratory Building in the foothills above Stanford. I remember it well—the setting was beautiful, in the middle of horse pastures with views of Mt. Tamalpais, Mt. Diablo, Mt. Hamilton, Mt. Umunhum, San Francisco and the Bay, but the building itself resembled a flying saucer that had broken in two and crash-landed on the hilltop. The view of Mt. Umunhum later proved unhealthy, as I will explain further on.

Humans have a strange name for the birthing process: they call it "acceptance tests." Unfortunately, my birth was traumatic. The University had provided a machine room with nice view windows to the outside but without air conditioning and it was blazing hot, which threatened my germanium transistors. Bob Clements, the DEC engineer who acted as midwife, threatened to leave if the delivery could not be completed soon, so various people in the lab went up on the roof with hoses to pour cooling water over the building while others put blocks of dry ice under my false floor.

When things got cool enough, I began running memory tests. In order to check for intermittents, Dave Poole got on top of my memory cabinets and performed a Balkan folk dance while I cranked away. Everything went marvelously and I started work the day I was born.

I began life using a PDP-6 processor with 65,536 words of core memory that was housed in eight bays of electronics. That was quite a large memory for machines of that era. (My original CPU is now on display at the Computer Museum in Boston). I had no disks to begin with, just 8 shiny DECtape drives, a comparable number of Model 33 Teletypes, a line printer that produced rather ragged text, and two 7-track tape drives. Users kept their programs and data on DECtapes and had to sign up for a tape drive and a core allocation through an arcane reservation procedure.

As you know, we computers think much faster than humans, so it is rather inefficient for us to work with just one individual. John McCarthy, who later came to be one of my assistants, had earlier devised a scheme that he called "timesharing" to make things less boring for us. My family was the first to be designed specifically to use timesharing.

I got proper air conditioning a short time later, but unfortunately developed a bad case of hiccups that struck regularly at 12 second intervals. My assistants spent a number of days trying to find the cause of this mysterious malady without success. As luck would have it, somebody brought a portable radio into my room one day and noticed that it was emitting a "Bzz" at regular intervals—in fact, at the same moment that I hicced. Further investigation revealed that the high-powered air defense radar atop Mt. Umunhum, about 20 miles away, was causing some of my transistors to act as radio receivers. We solved this problem by improving my grounding.

After I had been running awhile, someone at DEC noticed that my purchase order, which was based on their quotation, was badly screwed up. DEC claimed that the salesman had slipped his decimal points and had priced some of my components at 1/10 of the correct price. Also, the arithmetic was wrong—the sum of the prices should have been much larger than the total shown. Humans are notoriously bad at arithmetic. This had somehow passed through the entire purchasing bureaucracy of Stanford without anyone noticing. We ended up correcting the arithmetic error but not the factors of 10. The DEC salesman lost his job as a result of this incident.

I acquired a number of new peripherals in rapid succession, the first being a DEC Model 30 display that was stolen from my cousin, the PDP-1 timesharing system called Thor. My assistants immediately went into a frenzy of activity to create a new version of Spacewar, the video game that had earlier been invented by one of them—Steve Russell. In order to ensure that it would run correctly they invented and installed a feature in my operating system called "Spacewar Mode" that ensured that a program could get real-time service if it needed it. That feature turned out to have many useful applications in robotics and general hardware debugging.

Other new peripherals included a plotter, a microphone so my assistants could talk to me, several TV cameras so that I could look about, and several mechanical arms so that I could do stupid tricks with children's blocks—my assistants insisted on treating me like one of their dimwitted progeny. I soon showed that I could do much more sophisticated stuff such as assembling an automobile water pump.

Many of my assistants were fans of Tolkien, who wrote "Lord of the Rings" and a number of other children's stories for adults. The first character alphabet that was programmed for my plotter was Elvish rather than Latin. The University administration required that all rooms in my facility be numbered, but instead my assistants named each room after a place in Middle Earth and produced an appropriate door sign and a map with all the room names shown. Unfortunately, the response of the bureaucrats to the receipt of this map was to come out and put their own room numbers on each door.

My plotter routines were submitted to DECUS, which distributed them all over the world, leading to some puzzlement. We received a telegram from a German firm a short time later asking "What is Elvish? Please give references." We sent back a telegram referencing The Lord of the Rings.

A really embarrassing incident occurred when my assistants held their first Open House just three months after I was born. They asked me to pour punch for the party-goers and I did a rather good job of it for awhile, but we had worked out the procedure just the night before when there was nobody else running and I found that running with a heavy load disrupted my arm serving. As a result, after I dipped the cup in the punch and lifted it, instead of stopping at the right height it went vertical, pouring the punch all over my arm. The partiers apparently thought that was very funny and had me do it over and over. I've noticed that humans are very insecure and go to great lengths to demonstrate their "superiority" over machines.

I got a rather elegant display system in 1971 that put terminals in everyone's office, with full computer text and graphics, including grayscale, 7 channels of television (some lab-originated and some commercial) and 16 channels of audio all for about $600 per terminal. It had a multiple-windowing capability and was far ahead of anything commercially available at the time but unfortunately we never told anyone about it. Dick Helliwell made displays on unused terminals read "TAKE ME, I'M YOURS."

I have a number of advanced features that still are not available on many modern systems, including the ability for individual users to dial out on telephone lines and contact other computers throughout the world, the ability to detach jobs and leave them running, then later attach them to either the same terminal or one in a different place. I also would remind users of appointments at the appropriate times. In the 70s my users decided to give my operating system a name since it had evolved quite a bit away from the DEC system running on other PDP-10s. The users chose the name WAITS, because, they said, "it waits on you hand and foot" (or was it the user who waits for me, I forget—I'm sort of Alheimerish these days). To this day I still run this reliable system with its very reliable disk structure. Some people thought WAITS was the Worst Acronym Invented for a Time-sharing System, but I've grown rather attached to it.

I have a news service program called NS, written by my assistant Martin Frost, that was and is the best in the world. It connects to one or more electronic news-wires and allows any number of users to watch the wires directly, retrieve stories instantly on the basis of keywords, or leave standing requests that save copies of stories according to each user's interests. NS has always been one of the most popular programs that I've ever provided.

I ran a number of AI research projects and trained dozens of Ph.D. students over the last 25 years. I even composed, formatted and printed their dissertations. Some of my early projects were in three-dimensional vision, robotics, human speech recognition, mathematical theory of computation, theorem proving, natural language understanding, and music composition.

There are lots more stories to tell about my colorful life, such as the arson attempts on my building, my development of the computer that came to be called the DEC KL10, my development of the first inexpensive laser printing system, which I barely got to market because the venture capital community had never heard of laser printers and didn't believe in them, and my development of the Sun workstation family. I don't have time to put it all down now, but I may write a book about it.

I want to thank everyone who showed up for my 25th birthday party. It was a ball to have all these old assistants and friends come by to visit with me again and to take part in the AI Olympics.

Let me report on the results of today's athletic and intellectual competitions, held in my honor.

Programming race winners: Barry Hayes & David Fuchs

Treasure hunt winners: Ken Ross, Ross Casley, Roger Crew, Scott Seligman, Anil Gangoli, Dan Scales

N-legged race winners: Arthur Keller, Earl Sacerdoti, Irwin Sobel Bruce, Stephan & David Baumgart, Four Panofskys, Vic Scheinman, Kart Baltrunes, Joe Smith.

Incidentally the rumors that you may have heard about my impending death are greatly exaggerated. My assistants are trying to build a new interface for the Prancing Pony vending machine that I control so that it can be run by one of the (ugh!) Un*x machines, but they haven't got it working yet. Thus, if they try to turn me off now the entire computer science department will starve.

Finally I want to thank everyone who has helped me have such an exciting time for this quarter of a century. Not many computer systems have so much fun, not to mention so much time to have all that fun. I'll let you know when it's time to go.

—SAIL

P.S. *This message is being sent to 875 addresses, but I'm going to try to get it out even if it kills me.*

Glossary

class: a class is a user-defined type, just as int is a built-in type (some classes are predefined in Java, too). The built-in types have well-defined operations (arithmetic etc.) on them, and the class mechanism must allow the programmer to specify operations on the class types he or she defines, too. Anything in a class is known as a member of the class. Member functions of a class are also known as methods.

object: an object variable is a reference to a specific instance variable of a class type.

data abstraction: refining out the essential data types to represent some real-world property.

encapsulation: encapsulation means grouping together the types, data, and functions that make up a class, and providing some information hiding to control access. In C, a header file provides a very weak example of encapsulation. It is a feeble example because it is a purely lexical convention, and the compiler knows nothing about the header file as a semantic unit.

inheritance: this means allowing one class to receive the data structures and functions described in a simpler base class. The extended class gets the operations and data of the superclass, and can specialize or customize them as needed. There's no example in C that suggests the concept of inheritance. C does not have anything resembling this feature.

polymorphism: reusing the same name for a related concept on different types. The system will choose which method is meant either by overloading (a compile-time match—which method has the matching argument types?) or by overriding (a run time match, which method was defined for this kind of object?)

Concept	Java term	C++ term
function in class	method	member function*
class that is expected to be extended	abstract	virtual
anything in class	field	member
parent relationship with another class	extend	inherit
class you extend	superclass	base class
extended class	subclass	derived class
initialization	method constructor	constructor
finalization method	finalizer (in part)	destructor

*("method" is also used)

Exercises

1. What are the four attributes that distinguish Object-Oriented Programming? What are some advantages and disadvantages of OOP?

2. Give 3 examples of primitive types, and 3 examples of pre-defined Java classes (i.e. object types).

3. What is the key difference between primitive types and object types? Show some code to illustrate the difference.

4. What is the default constructor, and when is it called? What is a no-arg constructor? Can the default constructor be an "arg" constructor?

5. Describe overriding, and write some code to show an example.

Further Reading

"The Tao of Objects"

by Gary Entsminger

publ. M&T Books, Redwood City, CA 1990

ISBN 1-55851-155-5

An excellent beginner's guide to object-oriented programming. It features practical examples in C++ and Turbo Pascal (OK, that part is a bit dated) in a friendly, hands-on, jargon-free text.

Pitfalls of Object-Oriented Development

by Bruce F. Webster

publ M&T Books, New York 1995

ISBN 1-55851-397-3

Eiffel The Language

by Bertrand Meyer

publ. Prentice Hall, Herts England, 1992

ISBN 0-13-247925-7

A comprehensive reference, tutorial, and user's manual all rolled into one large book, describing the Eiffel language. Eiffel has been around for about a decade and has several interesting ideas. It is an improvement on C++ in several areas, such as generic classes, but is much less widely used. The book (and the language) does not flinch from offering challenging ideas.

Expert C Programming

by Peter van der Linden

Prentice Hall/SunSoft Press, 1994

ISBN 0-13-177429-8

Take a look at this book if you already know C pretty well and want to learn some of the tips and techniques used in Sun's compiler and OS kernel groups.

CHAPTER

3

The Java Programming Language

"My friend George Mallory, who later disappeared close to the summit of Mt. Everest, once did an inexplicable climb on Mount Snowdon. He had left his pipe on a ledge, halfway down one of the Lliwedd precipices, and scrambled back by a shortcut to retrieve it, then up again by the same route. No one saw just how he did the climb, but when they came to examine it the next day for official record, they found it was an impossible overhang nearly all the way.

By a rule of the Climbers' Club, climbs are never named in honor of their inventors, but only describe natural features. An exception was made here. The climb was recorded as follows: "Mallory's Pipe, a variation on route 2; this climb is totally impossible. It has been performed once in failing light by Mr. G.H.L. Mallory.'"

"Good-bye to All That", Robert Graves

Call me an old skeptic, but I've always had trouble swallowing the story of Mallory's Pipe. The details about "no one saw just how he did it" gives it away. I'll tell you just how Mallory did it—he was a young man with a robust sense of humor, and he intended to tweak the noses of the staid and proper Climbers' Club. So one evening, as everyone is exhausted after the day's climbing he "discovers" his pipe is missing, and "remembers" dropping it next to an alpine goat high on a crag. He announces he's going back to get it, and hurries off out of sight round the corner to wait for a decent interval before pulling the pipe out of his pocket and strolling back with a tale of an obviously impossible shortcut. The next morning, the goobers don't even realize they're being twitted and before he can stop them they've made public a proposal to name the climb in his honor! No backing down now, so he just has to go through with it. Mallory's Pipe should really be called Mallory's Leg-pull. The point is that things are not always what they seem, or what you are told.

Despite protestations that you may hear to the contrary, Java is not a small language, and is not well served by a small book. The Java language and libraries are extensive, and require some time to learn. The saving grace is that, while large, the system is not unduly complicated. The standard technique of dividing the whole into smaller parts and looking at each individually works well. If you already know C, you only have a little more to learn. If you already know C++, you only have a little to unlearn. No one part poses a huge challenge, and by the end of the text we will have studied all the parts. This technique is also known as "divide and conquer", which may bring to mind the association with the Pentium chip and its flawed division algorithm.

Ever since "The C Programming Language" was published in 1978 writers of programming text books have been using the "Hello World" program as the introductory example. Writers: get a clue! Programmers deserve a bit of innovation. To provide a refreshing change from the overexposed "Hello World" example we use a different program. Our example is the code snippet that exposes the defective division hardware in the Pentium chip.

GIGO: Garbage In, Garbage Out

In mid 1993, Intel launched the latest and greatest chip in its x86 family, the Pentium microprocessor. Intel spent millions of dollars to introduce the Pentium to the market and promote brand recognition using the slogan "Intel inside."

For about eighteen months everything went smoothly. Then on October 30, 1994, mathematics professor Thomas Nicely reported in a message on Compuserve that the Pentium gave an inaccurate result for some division operands. Professor Nicely had called Intel a week earlier to inform them of his findings, only to be told that no one else had complained. The bug was speedily reproduced and analyzed on several Usenet newsgroups, at which point the affair started to play out at high speed. Everything related to the Internet seems to happen at least seven times faster than the rest of life, which is why people refer to "Internet months" as being like "dog months."

After the matter was reported in the EE Times of November 7, 1994, instead of soothing Pentium-owners, Intel made matters far worse by implying that the problem wasn't important, that they'd known about it all along, and that most users didn't need accurate division. Pentium owners everywhere were outraged at the message that Intel had knowingly sold them a flawed chip, and didn't intend to do anything about it.

Public opinion shifted rapidly against the chip maker, and in a classic example of too little, too late, Intel announced on November 23 that it would supply replacement chips—but only to customers that it deemed worthy of accurate division. On December 12, IBM took the moral high road and increased the pressure on its rival by announcing that it was halting shipment of Pentium systems until error-free chips were available. At this point it became inevitable that Intel would be forced to support the consumer brand image they had created, or else cede the market to a more customer-driven organization.

Intel continued to be castigated on television and in numerous newspaper editorials. It managed to hold out until December 20, when mounting public pressure became intolerable. Intel's president Andy Grove reluctantly went public with sackcloth and ashes, and offered a free replacement Pentium to anyone who wanted one.

The surprising part of the affair wasn't the actual chip bug, but Intel's hubris and intransigence in dealing with it. All chip manufacturers encounter hardware problems of this kind. The accepted procedure is to mitigate the effects with compiler workarounds, and correct them in later revisions ("steppings") of the silicon. Intel's early failure to acknowledge the problem and offer users help with workarounds portrayed the company as recalcitrant, high-handed, and even dishonest. The initial failure to adequately address users' fears cost Intel dearly, $475M according to the San Jose Mercury News (Dec. 26, 1995). Many jokes circulated about "Intel inside" being a product liability warning, and so on.

The Pentium circuitry uses a subtractive division algorithm based on a radix-4 Booth SRT algorithm. It uses a table lookup to obtain an intermediate result. Five entries in the on-chip stored table of 2048 entries had bad values, causing some results that should have been accurate to seven significant figures to only be accurate to four significant figures.

Several people posted examples of operands that were known to produce inaccurate results. One was 1 / 12884897291. Another was 5505001 / 294911. It was a straightforward matter to write a small program that would output a bad result on a Pentium and the right answer on all other hardware.

This code was posted to Usenet by Thomas Koenig of the University of Karlsruhe in Germany. In C, it looks like this:

(C CODE)

```
#include <stdio.h>
int main()
{
    double x,y,z;

    x = 4195835.0;
    y = 3145727.0;
    z = x - (x / y) * y;
    printf("result = %f \n",z);
    return 0;
}
```

On a defective Pentium, this program prints "256.000000"; on other machines Intel and non-Intel, it prints "0.000000". In Java the same program looks like:

(Java CODE)

```
public class pentium {
    public static void main(String args[]) {
        double x,y,z;
        x = 4195835.0;
        y = 3145727.0;
        z = x - (x / y) * y;
        System.out.println("result = " + z);
    }
}
```

To compile this, put it in a file called "pentium.java" (it is important to use this exact filename and exact case of characters on case-sensitive systems) and issue the command:

```
javac pentium.java
```

When it has successfully compiled, run it by giving the command:

```
java pentium
```

We will analyze this program in the same way that you peel an onion, layer by layer. To start, note that we simply have the declaration of a class called "pentium".

```
class pentium {
    public static void main(String args[]) {
      double x,y,z;

      x = 4195835.0;
      y = 3145727.0;
      z = x - (x / y) * y;
      System.out.println("result = " + z);
    }
}
```

Inside the class is a single public method called "main"

```
    public static void main(String args[]) {
        double x,y,z;
        x = 4195835.0;
        y = 3145727.0;
        z = x - (x / y) * y;
        System.out.println("result = " + z);
    }
```

Right from the start, let's note a big difference between Java and C/C++. In Java, main() is defined to return a void (no value). In C, main() is defined to return an int. If you have declared any C programs as "void main(void)" go and correct them now, before anyone sees such sloppy coding.

Applications vs. Applets

Just as in C, the signature of this function is magic and it tells the runtime system to start execution here. It turns out that there are two different ways to run a Java executable:

- as a stand-alone program that can be invoked from the command line. This is termed an "application".

- as a program embedded in a web page, to be run when the page is browsed. This is termed an "applet". Just as a booklet is a little book, an applet is a little application.

The original intent was that applets would be small programs, but this distinction is going to be increasingly irrelevant. There's nothing in the Java system to establish any size limitations on applets.

Applications and applets differ in the execution privileges they have, and also the way they indicate where to start execution. The example here shows an application; we will deal with applets in Chapter 7.

The Anatomy of an Application

Looking at the signature of main(),

```
public static void main(String args[]) {
```

the modifiers say that the function is public and static, namely visible everywhere (public), and applied to the class as a whole (static) not a specific object.

Static methods are often used as the equivalent of global functions in C.

The main() routine where execution starts is a static method. It is associated with the class where the program starts, not any one instance object. So static makes sense for it. This leads to a very common and frustrating pitfall: trying to invoke an object method from the static (class) main method like so:

```
    . . .
    static void main () {            //this is a static function
        SomeMethod();                //NO! NO! NO!
    }

        void SomeMethod() {  }    // NOT a static function
                                  // so can't be invoked from main ()
SomeClass.java:4: Can't make static reference to
          method void SomeMethod() in class SomeClass.
```

There are two ways to get past this. The simplest way is to make the referenced field static too. But if the field has to be non-static because each object needs its own copy, then instantiate an object whose purpose is to be the "this" variable in the call. e.g.

```
public static void main(String args[]) {
    // we want to invoke the instance "SomeClass.someMethod()"
    SomeClass daffodil = new SomeClass();
    daffodil.someMethod();
```

It is a frequently-seen idiom to have the class that contains the main() function be instantiated inside the main() function, like this:

```
class pentium {
void someMethod ( ...

    public static void main(String args[]) {
        pentium p = new pentium();     //weird looking, no?
        p.someMethod();
```

It looks weirdly recursive the first time you see it. Think of it this way: the class definition is a datatype. All you are doing is declaring an instance of that datatype at a point when you need one (which happens to be inside the original datatype definition). It's all done by mirrors—or in this case by references. It's like saying one of the fields in a linked list element is a pointer to a linked list element. There's a fuller description of this in Chapter 5.

Passing over the modifiers, the actual function is:

```
void main(String args[]) {
```

Again, not that far away from C. It declares a function called "main" which has no return value, and takes just one argument called "args" (as in C, the parameter name doesn't matter) which is an array of Strings. The empty bracket pair says that the function is not restricted to any one size of array. These Strings are the command line arguments with which the program was invoked. "String" is a class in Java, with more to it than just the nul-terminated character array it is in C.

An "argc" count is not needed, because all arrays have a length field which is a final variable (you cannot assign to it) holding the size of the array. In place of argc you would use "args.length"—the number of Strings in the args array, not the length of any one String in it, of course.

The zeroth argument in the args array is the first command line argument, *not* the program name as in C and C++. The program name is already known inside the program: it is the name of the class that contains the "main()" function. The name of this class will match the name of the file that it is in.

If you called it something different, change it. You will confuse yourself and parts of the Java compiler system. This framework is all that is needed to indicate the entry point program where execution will start. 🐛

The statements in main will be immediately clear to any programmer. Java has adopted wholesale the basic statements of C++, which in turn come directly from C. The first line of the body of main declares three double precision floating point variables, x, y, and z.

```
public static void main(String args[]) {
double x,y,z;
x = 4195835.0;
y = 3145727.0;
z = x - (x / y) * y;
System.out.println("result = " + z);
}
```

The next two lines assign a couple of literal values. The third line is the one that exposes the Pentium flaw. If you examine the arithmetic expression, it should be clear that it cancels out to zero.

Finally, the last statement prints out the value. It refers to a library class called "System" that contains an object called "out" that has a method called "println". "out" does basic character output. You have to explicitly name at the top of your source file all packages that you use, with the exception of the built-in Java language package, which includes the class System used here.

The first few lines of main () are just regular arithmetic, but in that last line Java uses the plus sign, +, as an operator to concatenate Strings. This is one of the places in the language where Strings are helped a little with some built-in support, without creating a general mechanism that can be applied to every user-defined type as well.

Whenever a String appears as one operand of "+", the compiler does not do an arithmetic addition, but tries to convert the other operand to a String and then concatenates the two. In fact, concatenating an empty String with a value of a primitive type is a Java idiom to convert the value to a String, like so:

```
int i = 256;
    . . .


"" + i     // yields a String containing the value of i.
```

That's much shorter than the obvious alternative of using the static method of the String class:

```
String.valueOf( i )
```

In the case of the Pentium code, the variable z is converted to a String, and appended to the literal message. Then that entire String is passed as a single argument to the println() method, causing it to be printed to the system console.

The fact that the language features strict left-to-right evaluation makes a big difference here!

```
"Your 2 values are:" + 2 + 33
```

evaluates to the String

```
"Your 2 values are: 23"
```

But, putting the two integers first, like so

```
2 + 3 + "are your 2 values"
```

evaluates to the String

```
"5 are your 2 values"
```

Be alert to this.

"Java means I won't have to learn C++!"

Libraries in the C sense are known as packages in Java, and like many things in Java, they are considerably simpler to use than the corresponding feature in other languages. Simplicity is a major advantage of Java. Programmers can devote all their brainpower to solving the problem, rather than trying to learn and remember the ten thousand complicated rules and the five thousand special cases of language or system. One of Silicon Valley's top programmers (and I mean really top programmers) confided to me "Thank heavens for Java—it means I won't have to learn C++." A lot of programmers share that sense of relief at being able to leapfrog over C++ and go directly to a simpler language that will undoubtedly replace it.

If the println in this program doesn't print zero, it's because the CPU arithmetic logic unit has returned an inaccurate result for one of the operations.

We're working from the middle out here. Having seen our first reasonable Java program, we'll next look at the small building blocks of individual tokens that the compiler sees.

Identifiers

Identifiers (names provided by the programmer) can be any length in Java. They must start with a letter, underscore, or dollar sign, and in subsequent positions can also contain digits.

Java has been designed with internationalization in mind, and it uses the 16-bit Unicode character set. So the character datatype takes 16 bits in Java, not the 8-bit byte that many other languages use. A letter that can be used for a Java identifier doesn't just mean upper- and lower-case A-Z. It means any of the tens of thousands of Unicode letters from any of the major languages in the world including Bengali letters, Cyrillic letters or Bopomofo symbols. Every Unicode character above hex C0 is legal in an identifier. The following are all valid Java identifiers:

Legal Java Identifiers

```
i
calories
$_99
Häagen_Dazs
déconnage
Puñetas
Vögeln
fottío
```

Java is going to be a major force pressuring OS vendors to adopt Unicode in the future.

Java and Unicode

The great majority of computer systems in use today employ the ASCII code set to represent characters. ASCII—the American Standard Code for Information Interchange—started out as a 7-bit code that represented upper and lower case letters, the digits 0 to 9, and a dozen or so control characters like NUL and EOT. As computing technology became pervasive in Western Europe, users demanded the ability to represent all characters in their national alphabets. ASCII was extended to 8 bits, with the additional 128 characters being used to represent various accented and diacritical characters not present in English. The extended 8-bit code is known as the ISO 8859-1 Latin-1 code set. It is reproduced for reference as an appendix at the end of this book.

But a more general solution was needed that included support for Asian languages, with their many thousands of ideograms. The solution that was chosen is Unicode. It is a 16-bit character set, supporting 65,536 different characters. About 21,000 of these are devoted to Han, the ideograms seen in Chinese, Japanese and Korean. The ISO Latin-1 code set forms most of the first 256 values, effectively making ASCII a subset of Unicode.

The two big disadvantages of Unicode are it is not compatible with existing Operating Systems that only support 8-bit characters, and it doubles the amount of storage needed for text files. Because of the compatibility problem Unicode is only supported well on new OS's, such as Microsoft's NT, Apple's ill-fated Pink, and Plan 9 from Bell. Various clever schemes (like the UTF approach in which characters are a variable number of bytes in length) have been tried to retrofit Unicode onto ASCII-based systems, but none of them are wholly satisfactory.

Java uses Unicode to represent characters internally. The external representation of characters (what you get when you print something, what you offer up to be read) is totally dependent on the services of the host operating system. On Unix, Windows-95, and MacOS the character sets are all 8-bit based. When Java gets a character on these systems, the OS gives it 8 bits but Java immediately squirrels it away in a 16-bit datatype, and always processes it as 16 bits. This does away with the multibyte char complications in C, and special wide versions of the string-handling routines.

If at some future point the host system adopts Unicode, then only a few routines in the Java I/O library will need to be rewritten to accommodate it.

You can read more about the Unicode standard at http://www.unicode.org

However, be warned: For something that is conceptually so simple, the Unicode standard sets some kind of world record in obscurity, and all around lack of clarity. An example can be seen at http://www.unicode.org/unicode/standard/utf16.html.

Extended UCS-2 Encoding Form (UTF-16)

The basic Unicode character repertoire and UCS-2 encoding form is based on the Basic Multilingual Plane (BMP) of ISO/IEC 10646. This plane comprises the first 65,536 code positions of ISO/IEC 10646's canonical code space (UCS-4, a 32-bit code space). Because of a decision by the Unicode Consortium to maintain synchronization between Unicode and ISO/IEC 10646, the Unicode Character Set may some day require access to other planes of 10646 outside the BMP. In order to accommodate this eventuality, the Unicode Consortium proposed an extension technique for encoding non-BMP characters in a UCS-2 Unicode string. This proposal was entitled UCS-2E, for extended UCS-2. This technique is now referred to as UTF-16 (for UCS Transformation Format 16 Bit Form).

Another way of saying all that is "Unicode characters are 16 bits, and UCS-4 characters are 32 bits. Right now, Unicode forms the least significant 16 bits of the 32-bit code, but that might get jumbled up in future in a new coding system called UTF-16." It's ironic (some programmers would say "predictable") that a standard whose purpose is to foster communication is so poorly written that it actually hinders the ready transmission of meaning.

Programming language standards are especially prone to being written in unintelligible gobbledygook. Programmers are too ready to excuse this, saying that "a standard is a formal contract between the language designer and compiler writers." As though that meant it couldn't be simple and clear too!

A language reference manual should be simple and clear enough that an average programmer can use it to learn the language. Alas, my request to transfer to the project to write the Java language specification was declined on the grounds that they "didn't want any light relief in it."

Comments

Java has the same comment conventions as C++.

Comments starting with "//" go to the end of the line.

Comments starting with "/*" end at the next "*/".

Commenting out Code

Comments do not nest in Java, so to comment out a big section of code, you either put "//" at the start of every line, or you use "/*" at the front and immediately after every embedded closing comment, finishing up with your own closing comment at the end.

You can also use

```
if ( false ) {
    . . .
}
```

around the section you want to temporarily delete. Each of these approaches has drawbacks. My preference is to use a smart editor that knows how to add or delete "//" from the beginning of each line. That way it is absolutely clear what is commented out. 🐾

There's a third variety of comment, one starting with "/**". This indicates text that will be picked up by javadoc, an automatic documentation generator. This is an implementation of the "literate programming" idea proposed by Donald Knuth. Javadoc parses the declarations and these special comments, and formats the text that it extracts into a set of HTML pages describing the API.

```
i = 0;  // the "to end-of-line" comment

/* the "regular multiline" comment
 */

/** the API comment for HTML documentation
    @version 1.12
    @author A.P.L. Byteswap
    @see SomeOtherClassName
    HTML tags can also be put in here.
 */
```

Try javadoc. Javadoc works on .java files, not .class files, because the .java files contain the comments. Run javadoc on any java source file that you created such as:

```
javadoc pentium.java
```

This will create a file called "pentium.html" which you can look at in your Web browser. It shows the chain of class inheritance, and all the public fields in the class. You can give javadoc an absolute pathname, or any pathname relative to a path in the CLASSPATH environment variable. Although CLASSPATH points to likely locations for .class files, the default behavior is to keep source and class files in the same directory. So javadoc can usually find .java files by following the CLASSPATH.

Whether you agree with the idea of using web pages to store program documentation or not (some people prefer to read documents bound in book form), it offers the compelling advantages that documentation automatically generated from the program source is much more likely to be (a) available, (b) accurate, (what could be more accurate than documentation that you generated two minutes previously from the source?) and (c) complete. ❦

Keywords

Keywords are reserved words, and may not be overloaded for use as identifiers. ANSI C has only 32 keywords. Java has almost 60 keywords, including half-a-dozen reserved for future use, in case the language designers get crazy enough to think that adding to the language would be a good idea (hint: it wouldn't. Adding anything with complicated semantics like operator overloading or generic classes would be especially bad ideas). The keywords can be divided into several categories according to their main use:

Java keywords

Used for built-in types:

```
boolean    true      false
char
byte       short     int       long
float      double
void
```

Used in expressions:

```
null       new       this      super
```

Used in statements:

selection statements

```
if    else
switch    case    break    default
```

iteration statements

```
for     continue
do      while
```

transfer of control statements

```
return
throw
```

guarding statements (threads or exceptions)

```
synchronized
try    catch      finally
```

Used to modify declarations (scope, visibility, sharing etc.):

```
static
abstract    final
private     protected   public
transient   volatile
```

Used for other method or class-related purposes:

```
class       instanceof     throws     native
```

Used for larger-than-class building blocks:

```
extends
interface   implements
package     import
```

Reserved for possible future craziness:

```
cast        const       future      generic   goto
inner       operator    outer       rest      var
```

Operators

A C or C++ programmer will be readily familiar with the operators in Java. The novel aspect is that the order of evaluation is well-defined. For many (not all) previous languages including C and C++, the order of evaluation of operands has been deliberately left unspecified. In other words the operands of a C expression like:

(C CODE)

```
i + a[i] + functioncall();
```

can be evaluated and added together in any order. The function may be called before, during (on adventurous multiprocessing hardware), or after the array reference is evaluated, and the additions may be executed in any order.

In the expression above if the "functioncall()" adjusts the value of "i", the overall result depends on the order of evaluation. This indeterminacy does not occur in Java.

Leaving the order of evaluation unspecified (as in C) is done for several reasons:

- Language philosophy. Since there is no reason to require L-to-R evaluation, the language neither promises nor forbids it.

- It makes it easier to write the compiler optimizer if it has complete freedom to change expressions into mathematically equivalent expressions. The generated code isn't necessarily faster, but the optimizer is easier to create and maintain.

- Common sub-expression elimination, and constant propagation are easier to identify. Often these opportunities arise from other optimizations like loop unrolling, rather than human code.

- It permits the compiler-writer the maximum opportunity to take advantage of values that are already in registers.

The trade-off is that some programs give different results depending on the order of evaluation. As professional programmers we know that such programs are badly written, but nonetheless they exist.

Java makes the trade-off in a different place. It recognizes that getting the same consistent results on all computer systems is more important than getting varying results a fraction faster on one system. In practice the opportunities for speeding up expression evaluation through reordering operands seem to be quite limited in many programs. As processor speed and cost has improved, it is appropriate that modern languages should optimize for programmer sanity instead of performance.

Note that the usual operator precedence still applies. In an expression like:

```
b + c * d
```

the multiplication is always done before the addition. It has to be done first, because the result is one operand of the addition.

What the Java order of evaluation says is that for all binary (two argument) operators the left operand is always fully evaluated before the right operand. Therefore, the operand "b" above must be evaluated before the multiplication is done (because the multiplied result is the right operand to the addition). 🐛

Left-to-right evaluation means in practice that all operands in an expression (if they are evaluated at all) are evaluated in the left-to-right order in which they are written down on a page. Sometimes an evaluated result must be stored while a higher precedence operation is performed. Although the Java Language Specification only talks about the apparent order of evaluation of operands to individual operators this is a necessary consequence of the rules.

Of course, some operands may not be evaluated at all. Evaluation of "| |" and "&&" stops when enough of the expression has been evaluated to obtain the overall result. The point is that predictability in porting is a virtue that outweighs mathematical optimizations.

It's not just operands evaluation, but the order of everything else is defined in Java too. Specifically,

- The left operand is evaluated before the right operand of a binary operator. This is true even for the assignment operator, which must evaluate the left operand (where the result will be stored), fully before starting on the right operand (what the result is).

- In an array reference, the expression before the square brackets "[]" is fully evaluated before any part of the index is evaluated.

- A method call for an object has the general form
    object_instance.methodname(arguments);
  The "object_instance" is fully evaluated before the methodname and arguments are looked at. Then any arguments are evaluated one by one from left to right.

- In an allocation expression for an array of several dimensions, the dimension expressions are evaluated one by one from left to right.

The Language Specification uses the phrase "Java guarantees that the operands to operators *appear to be* evaluated from left-to-right." This is an escape clause that allows clever compiler-writers to do brilliant optimizations, as long as the appearance of left-to-right evaluation is maintained.

For example, compiler-writers can rely on the associativity of integer addition and multiplication. a+b+c will produce the same result as (a+b)+c or a+(b+c). This is true in Java even in the presence of overflow, because what happens on overflow is well-defined. The usual result of overflow when evaluating an integer expression is that you just get the low order bits that fit in an int.

If one of these subexpressions occurs in the same basic block, a clever compiler-writer might be able to arrange for its re-use. In general because of complications involving infinity and not-a-number (NaN)[1] results, floating point operands cannot be trivially reordered.

Associativity

Associativity is one of those subjects that is poorly explained in many programming texts, especially the ones that come from authors who are technical writers not programmers. In fact a good way to judge a C text is to look for its explanation of associativity. Silence is not golden.

There are three factors that influence the ultimate value of an expression in any algorithmic language, and they work in this order: precedence, associativity, and order of evaluation. Precedence says that some operations bind more tightly than others. Precedence tells us that the multiplication in "a + b * c" will be done before the addition, i.e. we have "a + (b * c)" rather than "(a + b) * c". Precedence tells us how to bind operands in an expression that contains different operators.

Associativity is the tie breaker for deciding the binding when we have several operators of equal precedence strung together. If we have:

```
3 * 5 % 3
```

should we evaluate that as "(3 * 5) % 3" i.e. 15 % 3, or 0. Or should we evaluate it as "3 * (5 % 3)" i.e. 3 * 2, or 6. Multiplication and the "%" remainder operation have the same precedence, so precedence does not give the answer. But they are left-associative, meaning when you have a bunch of them strung together you start with the first operator on the left and feed it the operand on its immediate left and right. Push the result back as a new operand, and continue until the expression is evaluated. In this case "(3 * 5) % 3" is the correct grouping.

"Associativity" is a terrible name for the process of deciding which operands belong with which operators of equal precedence. A more meaningful description would be *"Code Order For Finding/Evaluating Equal Precedence Operator Text-strings."* Let me know if you find a good mnemonic for that in Java.

Note that associativity deals solely with deciding which operands go with which of a sequence of adjacent operators of equal precedence. It doesn't say anything about the order in which those operands are evaluated. 🍂

The order of evaluation, if it is specified in a language, tells us the sequence (for each operator) in which the operands are evaluated. In a strict left-to-right language like Java, the order of evaluation tells us that in "(i=2) * i++" the left operand to the multiplication will be evaluated before the right operand, then the

1.   See next chapter.

multiplication will be done, yielding a result of 4, with i set to 3. In C and C++ this expression is undefined as it modifies the same lvalue more than once. It is legal in Java because the order of evaluation is defined. The order of evaluation deals with individual operands around an operator.

Java Operators

The Java operators and their precedence are shown in Table 3-1.

Table 3-1: Java operators and their precedence

Symbol	Note	Precedence	Coffeepot Property
names, literals	simple tokens	16	n/a
a[i]	subscripting	16	left
m(...)	method invocation	16	left
.	field selection	16	left
++ --	increment, decrement	16	right
++ --	increment, decrement	15	left
~	flip the bits of an integer	14	right
!	logical not (reverse a boolean)	14	right
- +	arithmetic negation, plus	14	right
(typename)	type conversion (cast)	13	right
* / %	multiplicative operators	12	left
- +	additive operators	11	left
<< >> >>>	left and right bitwise shift	10	left
instanceof < <= > >=	relational operators	9	left
== !=	equality operators	8	left
&	bitwise and	7	left
^	bitwise exclusive or	6	left
|	bitwise inclusive or	5	left
&&	conditional and	4	left
||	conditional or	3	left
? :	conditional operator	2	right
= *= /= %= += -= <<= >>= >>>= &= ^= |=	assignment operators	1	right

In Java the ">>" operator does an arithmetic shift, meaning that the sign bit is propagated. In C, it has always been implementation-defined whether this was a logical shift (fill with 0 bits) or an arithmetic shift (fill with copies of the sign bit).

This occasionally led to grief as programmers discovered the implementation dependency when debugging or porting a system.

One new Java operator is ">>>" which means "shift right and zero fill" (i.e. do not propagate the sign bit). This is not needed for shift left because there is no sign bit at the other end to propagate. It is not needed in C because it is implicitly achieved when shifting an unsigned quantity. Java does not have unsigned types apart from char.

Although the intent of the ">>>" operator is a zero filled shift right, it has a surprising—and very undesirable—twist in practice. The >> operator takes negative numbers and does an arithmetic shift on them, that is it sign-extends them so that the "new" bits from the left are filled with 1's to keep the sign negative.

In contrast the >>> operator is designed to fill in with 0's from the left in case you weren't using the operand as a "number", but as a bit mask. This works as expected on numbers of canonical size, ints and longs. But it is broken for short, and byte.

```
byte b = -1;
b >>>= 10;
```

If you have an 8-bit quantity, and you shift it right unsigned 10 bits, all the bits should fall off the right end, leaving zero. This does not happen. If you try it, you will see that b has the value –1.

The reason is the byte got promoted to an int before the shift took place. The int had the bit pattern 0xFFFFFFFF, and was shifted ten places right to yield 0x003FFFFF. That result was truncated to a byte, yielding a final result of 0xFF, or –1.

If you want to do unsigned shift on a short or a byte, an extra AND is required, in which case you can just use >>.

```
byte b = -1;
b = (byte)((b & 0xff) >> 4);
```

So because of the default operand promotion to a canonical size, >>> is useless on all negative byte and short operands. It is probably better not to use it at all, but to always use "&" to mask off the bits you require in a result. That way programs won't mysteriously stop working when someone changes a type from int to short. ❦

Assignment operators result in values (as in C) not variables (as in C++). So this code fragment is legal in C++, but illegal in C and Java:

```
(a += 4)++;
```

In C the error will be a complaint that "operand is not a modifiable lvalue". Java thankfully lacks jargon like "modifiable lvalue" which was introduced into C to kludge around certain semantics of consts and arrays. In Java the error message is along the lines of "Invalid expression"—not the greatest but at least it doesn't include any words that have a special definition.

The other new operator is "instanceof". This is used with superclasses to tell if you have a particular subclass. For example, we may see:

```
class vehicle { ...
class car extends vehicle { ...
class convertible extends car { ...

vehicle v; ...
if (v instanceof convertible) ...
```

The "instanceof" operator is often followed by a statement that casts the object from the base type to the subclass, if it turns out that the one is an instance of the other. Instanceof lets us check that the cast is valid before attempting it.

Finally note that Java cut back on the use of the obscure comma operator. Even if you're quite an experienced C programmer you might never have seen the comma operator, as it was rarely used. The only place it occurs in Java is in "for" loops.

Why GIGO sometimes means "Garbage In, Gospel Out"

If you try the Pentium division Java program on a Pentium system with the flawed division implementation, you may be surprised to see that it actually prints out the correct answer—I certainly was! In fact "stunned" would be a better description.

How can that be, when the chip gives bad results? The answer lies in the compiler. Not the Java compiler, but the Microsoft Visual C++ library that is used to build Java on the Windows platform, and that provides runtime support. Whenever a chip manufacturer finds a hardware bug, and there are always some bugs in every design, it is the job of the compiler team to work around it. The compiler group must make sure that the generated code avoids or corrects the problem. In this case, within three months of the FDIV fault becoming public knowledge, Microsoft issued patch VCFDIV for Visual C++ 2.0.

The patch checks to see if the code is being run on a flawed Pentium. If it is, it checks if the operands are of the form that would hit the bad entries in the table. If so, it scales both operands (1200.0 / 100.0 gives the same result as 120.0 / 10.0) to avoid using that part of the lookup table. The process takes a little longer, but gives good results. The patch was folded into Visual C++ 2.1. Java on Windows is currently built with MS Visual C++ version 2.0 with the patch. When the Java interpreter finds a division operator, it passes it through to the native runtime routine (in this case the Microsoft msvcrt20.dll library which has the software workaround). You cannot see the flaw using a Java program, but it is not because of any Java quality, rather the runtime library that it uses.

To observe the Pentium division flaw, you need to run a C program that provides access to the raw hardware. I recommend the "Power C" ANSI C compiler for the PC available from Mix Software, in Richardson Texas. The compiler costs under $20, and comes with a properly bound book on C that is worth the price alone. Power C can be ordered by telephoning Mix at 1-800 333-0330. (telephone 214 783-6001 outside the U.S.) No, I don't own stock in Mix Software! My interest is in seeing more programmers use a good inexpensive unbloated ANSI C compiler system. Power C sells well to a lot of schools.

You can also download GnuC for the PC—a 32 bit C/C++ compiler for MS-DOS—for free. Take a look at web site http://www.delorie.com/djgpp.

Use GnuC if you want to study compiler internals.

Use Power C if you want to run C programs.

Exercises

1. Identify two examples of a large company that is confronted with a public loss of confidence in its product. How has the company reacted? How did the organization's conduct affect public confidence?
2. How is an application distinguished from an applet?
3. What are the three kinds of comment in Java, and how is each used?
4. Compare the rules for forming Java identifiers to those of any other programming language you are familiar with. Compare the Java concept of a character as a 16-bit quantity to the more usual concept of a character as an 8-bit ASCII value.
5. Describe what precedence, associativity, and evaluation order are. How do they interplay in determining the value of an expression?
6. Write a Java program to demonstrate how the ">>>" operator does not zero fill when shifting right a negative short or byte. Account for this.
7. Write a Java program that uses the "instanceof" operator to check for appropriateness of subclass before attempting a cast.

Further Reading

The best description of the Pentium flaw appears in "Microprocessor Report," Dec. 26, 1994.

The Unicode site is http://www.unicode.org

The draft standard for Unicode HTML can be found at http://www.alis.com:8085/ietf/html/draft-ietf-html-i18n-01.txt

CHAPTER

4

- The Primitive Types and Built-in Classes
- The Java World of Objects
- Compilation Units: Coexisting With the Host System
- Interfaces

Java
Building Blocks

T he first half of this chapter covers some more of the language basics: types, literals and statements. The second half is more outward-looking, providing details on how Java programs interact with libraries and the host system.

The Built-In Types and Declarations

Anyone who ever had to port a C program between a Unix system and a PC will know the problem: the basic types are completely different sizes on the different systems. You can't merely change every occurrence of "int" to "long" either—for one thing the usual type promotions all change when all your ints change to longs in C. For another, the implicit assumptions about the layout of structs will change. Yet a third problem is that any printf statements will need the format specifier changed.

How Long is a Long?

The same problem of "what size should types be?" was recently heatedly discussed by Unix workstation manufacturers as they move towards 64-bit architectures. The issue can be summarized as "we know we have to make pointers 64-bits, but where in the integer types do we bring in 64-bits: int, long, or long long?"

The three major competing approaches have adopted mysterious codenames because, well, because mysterious codenames are fun:

LP64: this group says "introduce 64-bitness at the top of the int range." "long"s and pointers should be 64-bits. Int stays at 32-bits. DEC and SGI are in this camp, and Sun recently switched to join them.

ILP64: this is the position taken by Hewlett-Packard. It says "Hey! Let's have a flag day, and change everything to 64-bits at once: ints, longs, and pointers. Users may squeak, but a change will be good for them. Programs that rely on ints and pointers being the same size will keep working when recompiled. You do have the source, don't you?"

LLP64: this was the original position taken by Sun. It says "introduce 64-bitness *beyond* the top of the range, by having a 'long long' type. All the other existing integer types stay the size they are." Nobody else liked this position, and it got pretty lonely. Other folks inside Sun challenged some of the assumptions it was built on, so Sun switched.

The trade-offs involved in choosing the sizes of basic data types involve portability, compatibility with existing types, standards conformance, performance, and transition cost. Exactly the same issues were faced by the Java team, though the Java team had the luxury of putting a low value on some of these costs. All the approaches have advantages and drawbacks, but in the end all the vendors have committed to LP64.

The LP64 model is very close to the Java model, the only difference being that pointers are 32-bits in Java, not 64-bits. However there is nothing in the language that makes that visible to programmers. When the time for 64 bit pointers inevitably arrives (and it will be well before the turn of the Millennium) we should be able to merely recompile existing code and have it all "just work" on the new Java Virtual Machine. The various "how much memory?" functions in lang/runtime.java already return long which is always 64-bits in Java. ❦

The Primitive Types

Most high-level languages don't specify the sizes of data types. This allows compiler writers the freedom to select the best sizes on each architecture for performance. The freedom turns out to be a false economy since it greatly impedes program portability, and programmer time is a lot more expensive than processor time. Java does away with all the uncertainty by rigorously specifying the sizes of the basic types and making clear that these sizes are identical on all platforms.

There are eight built-in, non-object types, also known as primitive types. They are:

- `boolean` (for truth values)

- `int, long, byte, short` (for arithmetic on integers)

- `double, float` (for arithmetic on the real numbers)

- `char` (for character data, ultimately to be input or printed)

Let us examine the properties of each of these in turn.

boolean

This is the data type used for true/false conditions.

range of values: false, true

literals: false, true. In the code below, the assignment will always occur.

```
if (true) x = 33;
```

You cannot cast a boolean value to any other type. However you can always get the same effect by using an expression:

```
i = (bool? 1:0); // set int according to bool value.
bool = (i==0? false:true); // set bool according to int value.
```

Note that expert programmers customarily write

```
boolean bean;
        . . .
if (bean) ... // do something.
```

rather than

```
if (bean == true) ... // do something.
```

In Java, the boolean type is not based on integers. In particular, you cannot increment, decrement or add boolean values. To optimize memory access time, more than one bit is used to store a boolean value.

int

The type int is a 32-bit, signed, two's-complement number. This will be the type that you chose by default whenever you are going to carry out integer arithmetic.

range of values: −2,147,483,648 to 2,147,483,647

literals: a "literal" is a value provided at compile-time. Literals have types just like variables have types. Int literals come in any of three varieties:

- A decimal literal, e.g. 10 or −256

- With a leading zero, meaning an octal literal, e.g. 077777

- With a leading 0x, meaning a hexadecimal literal, e.g. 0xA5 or 0Xa5

Upper or lower case has no significance with any of the letters that can appear in integer literals. If you use octal or hexadecimal and you provide a literal that sets the leftmost bit in the receiving number, then it represents a negative quantity.

An integer literal is a 32-bit quantity. But provided its actual value is within range for a smaller type, an int literal can be assigned directly to something with fewer bits, such as byte, short or char. If you try to assign an int literal that is too large into a smaller type, the compiler will insist on a cast. Integer literals can be assigned to floating point variables without casting.

long

The type long is a 64-bit, signed, two's-complement quantity. It should be used when calculations on whole numbers may exceed the range of int. Using longs, the range of values is -2^{63} to $(2^{63}-1)$. Numbers up in this range will be increasingly prevalent in computing, and 2^{64} in particular is a number that really needs a name of its own. So in 1993, I coined the term "Bubbabyte" to describe 2^{64} bytes. Just as 2^{10} bytes is a Kilobyte, and 2^{20} is a Megabyte, so 2^{64} bytes is a Bubbabyte. Using a long, you can count up to half a Bubbabyte less one.

range of values: −9,223,372,036,854,775,808 to 9,223,372,036,854,775,807

literals: The general form of long literals is the same as int literals, but with an "L" or "l" on the end to indicate "long." However, never use the lower case letter "l" to indicate a "long" literal as it is just too similar to the digit "1." Always use the upper case letter "L" instead. The three kinds of long literals are:

- A decimal literal, e.g. 2047L or −10L

- An octal literal, e.g. 0777777L

- An hexadecimal literal, e.g. 0xA5L or 0xABADCAFEDEADBE30L

All long literals are 64-bit quantities. A long literal must be cast to assign it to something with fewer bits, such as byte, short, int or char.

byte

The byte type is an 8-bit, signed, two's-complement quantity. The reasons for using byte are to hold a generic 8-bit value, to match a value in existing data files, or to economize on storage space (where you have a large number of such values). Despite popular belief, there is no speed advantage to bytes, shorts, or chars—modern CPUs take the same amount of time to load or multiply 8 bits as they take for 32 bits.

range of values: −128 to 127

literals: there are no byte literals. You can use, without a cast, char literals and int literals provided their values fit in 8 bits. You can use long and floating-point literals if you cast them.

You always have to cast a (non-literal) value of a larger type if you want to put it into a variable of a smaller type. Since arithmetic is always performed at least at 32-bit precision, this means that assignments to a byte variable must always be cast into the result if they involve any arithmetic, like this:

```
byte b1=1, b2=2;
byte b3 = b2 + b3; // NO! NO! NO! Causes error
byte b3 = (byte) (b2 + b3); // correct
```

People often find this unexpected. If I have an expression involving only bytes, why should I need to cast it into a byte result? The right way to think about it is that most modern computers do all integral arithmetic at 32-bit or 64-bit precision (there is no "8-bit add" on modern CPU's). Java follows this model of the underlying hardware. An arithmetic operation on two bytes potentially yields a bigger result than can be stored in a byte. The philosophy for casts is that they are required whenever you assign from a more capacious type to a less capacious type. The cast is the way in which the programmer tells the compiler "Yes, I acknowledge that there may be some loss of accuracy here." Use a cast where you need one, but don't use a cast unless that is a true message to convey.

short

This type is a 16-bit signed, two's-complement integer. The main reasons for using short are to match external values already present in a file, or to economize on storage space (where you have a large number of such values and they will be able to fit in the limited range of values).

range of values: −32,768 to 32,767

literals: there are no short literals. You can use, without a cast, char literals and int literals provided their values will fit in 16 bits. You can use long and floating-point literals if you cast them.

As with byte, assignments to short must always be cast into the result if the right hand side of the assignment involves any arithmetic.

The next two types, double and float, are the floating-point arithmetic types:

double

The type double refers to floating-point numbers stored in 64 bits, as described in the IEEE standard reference 754. The type double will be the default type you use when you want to do some calculations that might involve decimal places (i.e. not integral values).

range of values: These provide numbers that can range between about −1.7E308 to +1.7E308 with about 14 to 15 significant figures of accuracy. The exact accuracy depends on the number being represented. Double precision floating-point numbers have the range shown in Figure 4-1.

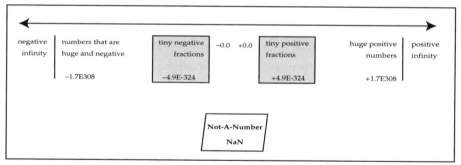

Figure 4-1: Type double should be used when calculations exceed the range of long or involved fractions.

IEEE 754 arithmetic has come into virtually universal acceptance over the last decade, and it would certainly raise a few eyebrows if a computer manufacturer proposed an incompatible system of floating-point numbers now. IEEE 754 has an ingenious way of dealing with the problem of representing on limited hardware the unlimited amount of infinite precision real-world numbers.

The problem is resolved by reserving a special value that says "Help! I've fallen off the end of what's representable and I can't get up." You're probably familiar with infinity, but the "Not-a-Number" might be new if you haven't done much numerical programming. Not-a-Number, or NaN, is a value that a floating point can take to indicate that the result of some operation is not mathematically well-defined, like dividing zero by zero.

If you get a NaN as an expression is being evaluated, it will contaminate the whole expression, producing an overall result of NaN—*which is exactly what you want!* The worst way to handle a numeric error is to ignore it and pretend it didn't happen.

Write, compile, and run a Java program that deliberately generates a NaN result, by dividing two floating-point numbers that both have the value 0.0. Print out the result of the division (just send it to System.out.println() as in earlier examples). What is the printable representation of NaN? Try using NaN in further arithmetic operations.

You may never see a NaN if your algorithms are numerically stable, and you never push the limits of your datasets. But it's nice to know that NaN is there, ready to tell you your results are garbage, if they head that way.

literals: It is easiest to show by example the valid formats for double literals:

```
1e1     2.      .3      3.14    6.02e+23d
```

The format is very easy-going. Just give the compiler a decimal point, or an exponent, and it will recognize that a floating-point literal is intended. A suffix of "D", "d", or no suffix, means a double literal. In practice, most people omit the suffix.

Make Mine a Double: How Large is 1.7E308?

The largest double precision number is a little bit bigger than a 17 followed by 307 zeroes.

How large is that? Well, the volume of the observable universe is about $(4pi/3)(15 \text{ billion light-years})^3 = 10^{85} \text{ cm}^3$. The density of protons is about 10^{-7} cm^{-3}, (this value seems so sparse because it is an average for all space— on a planet the value is much, much denser of course) so the number of protons in the observable Universe is about 10^{78}, or "only" 1 followed by 78 zeros, give or take two-fifty.

The largest double precision number is even bigger than a Googol. A googol is the number description suggested by 9 yr. old Milton Sirotta in 1938 at the request of his uncle, mathematician Edward Krasner. A googol is 10^{100}, i.e. it is only a 1 followed by 100 zeroes. Is the largest double precision number bigger than Roseanne's capacity for self-promotion? No, we have to admit, it probably isn't that big.

It's possible to come up with problems where you want accuracy to 14 significant figures (e.g. figuring the national debt). But it is most unusual to need to tabulate numbers that are orders of magnitude greater than the number of protons in the universe.

It is also permissible to assign any of the integer literals or character literals to floats or doubles. The assignment doesn't need a cast, as you are going from a less capacious type to a more capacious type. So a line like this, while perverse, is valid:

```
double cherry = '\n';
```

It takes the integer value of the literal, 0x0a here, floats it to get 10.0d, and assigns that to "cherry." Don't ever do this.

float

The type float refers to floating-point numbers stored in 32 bits, as described in the IEEE standard reference 754.

The justification for using single precision variables used to be that arithmetic operations were twice as fast as on double precision variables. With modern extensively-pipelined processors and wide data buses between the cache and CPUs, the speed differences are inconsequential. The reasons for using floats are to minimize storage requirements when you have a very large quantity of them, or to retain compatibility with external data files.

range of values: The type float provides numbers that can range between about

−3.4E38 to 3.4E38 (i.e. 340,000,000,000,000,000,000,000,000,000,000,000,000) with about 6 to 7 significant figures of accuracy. The exact accuracy depends on the number being represented.

literals: The simplest way to understand what is allowed is to look at examples of valid float literals.

```
1e1f     2.f      .3f      3.14f     6.02e+23f
```

A suffix of "F" or "f" is always required on a float literal. A common mistake is to leave the suffix off the float literal:

```
float cabbage = 6.5;
 Error: explicit cast needed to convert double to float.
```

The code must be changed to:

```
float cabbage = 6.5f;
```

Also, a double literal cannot be assigned to a float variable without a cast even if it is within the range of the float type. This is because some precision in decimal places may potentially be lost. The next section explains more about this interesting, and sometimes subtle, topic.

char

This type is a 16-bit, unsigned quantity that is used to represent printable characters. It is an integer-based type, and so all the arithmetic operators are available on it. Unlike all the other arithmetic types, char is unsigned—it never takes a negative value. You should only use char to hold character data or bit masks. If you want a 16-bit quantity for general calculations, don't use char, use short. This will avoid the possible surprise of converting between signed and unsigned types. Otherwise a cast of a negative value into char will magically become positive without the bits changing.

range of values: a value in the Unicode code set 0 to 65,535

You have to cast a 32- or 64-bit result if you want to put it into a smaller result. This means that assignments to char must always be cast into the result if they involve any arithmetic.

literals: Character literals appear between single quotes or in Strings. They can be expressed in four ways, and can be used for all of the types char, byte, short, int, and long.

- A single character, `'A'`

- A character escape sequence. The allowable values are:
  `'\n'` (linefeed)   `'\r'` (carriage return) `'\f'` formfeed
  `'\b'` (backspace)   `'\t'` (tab)   `'\\'` (backslash)
  `'\"'` (double quote) `'\''` (single quote)

- An octal escape sequence. This has the form `'\nnn'` where nnn is one-to-three octal digits in the range 0 to 377. Note the odd fact that you can only set the least significant 8 bits of a 16-bit char when using an octal escape sequence. Examples: `'\0'` or `'\12'` or `'\277'` or `'\377'`

- A Unicode escape sequence. This has the form `'\uxxxx'` where xxxx is exactly four hexadecimal digits. Example:

  ```
  '\u0065' is the character A
  ```

How Accurate Are Calculations?

The accuracy when evaluating a result is referred to as the "precision" of an expression. The precision may be expressed either as number of bits (64 bits), or as the data type of the result (double precision, meaning 64-bit floating-point format). In Java, the precision of evaluating each operator depends on the types of the operands. Java looks at the types of the operands around an operator, and picks the biggest of what it sees of: double, float, long, in that order of preference.

Both operands are then promoted to this type, and that is the type of the result. If there are no doubles, nor floats nor longs in the expression, then both operands are promoted to int, and that is the type of the result. This continues from left-to-right through the entire expression.

So a Java compiler follows this algorithm to compile each operation:

- If either operand is a double, do the operation in double precision.

- Otherwise, if either operand is a float, do the operation in single precision.

- Otherwise, if either operand is a long, do the operation at long precision.

- Otherwise, do the operation at 32-bit int precision.

In summary, Java expressions end up with the type of the biggest, floatiest type (double, float, long) in the expression. They are 32-bit integers otherwise.

Most programmers already understand that floating-point numbers are approximations to real numbers, and they may inherently contain tiny inaccuracies that may mount up as you iterate through an expression. (Actually, most programmers learn this the hard way.) Do not expect 10 iterations of adding 0.1 to a float variable to cause it to exactly equal 1.0F! If this comes as a surprise to you, try this test program immediately, and thank your good fortune at having the chance to learn about it before you stumble over it as a difficult debugging problem.

```
public class inexact1 {
        public static void main(String s[]) {
            float pear = 0.0F;
            for (int i=0; i<10; i++) pear = pear + 0.1F;

            if (pear==1.0F) System.out.println("pear is 1.0F");
            if (pear!=1.0F) System.out.println(
                "pear is NOT 1.0F, is:" + pear);
        }
}
```

You will see this results in:

```
        pear is NOT 1.0F, is:1
```

The reason is that 0.1 is not a fraction that can be represented exactly with powers of two, and hence summing 10 of them (although close enough for the printing routines) does not exactly sum to one. This is why you should never use a floating-point variable as a loop counter. A longer explanation of this thorny topic is in

"What Every Computer Scientist Should Know about Floating Point" by David Goldberg, in the March 1991 (Vol 23 number 1) issue of *Computing Surveys*. Note that this is a characteristic of floating point numbers in all programming languages, not a quality unique to Java.

Accuracy is not just the range of values of a type, but also (for real types) the number of decimal places that can be stored. The type float can store about 6 to 7 digits accurately, so when a long (which can hold at least 18 places of integer values) is implicitly or explicitly converted to a float, some precision may be lost.

```java
public class inexact2 {
        public static void main(String s[]) {
                long   lasagna = 9000000000000000000L;
                float fructose = lasagna;
                lasagna = (long) fructose;
                System.out.println("fructose is: "+fructose);
                System.out.println(
                    "lasagna (started as 9e18, assigned to float) is:"
                    +lasagna);
        }
}
```

The output is:

```
fructose is: 9e+18
lasagna (started as 9e18, assigned to float) is: 9000000202358128640
```

As you can see, after being assigned to and retrieved back from the float variable, the long has lost all accuracy after six or seven significant figures. Again though, the floating-point print routines have masked this effect when printing the float. The truth is that if a float has the value shown, it could stand for any real value in the interval between the nearest representable floating-point number on each side. So the library is entitled, within the bounds of good taste and consistency, to print it out as any value within that interval. If all this makes you fidget uncomfortably in your seat, maybe you better take a look at that Goldberg article.

What Happens on Overflow?

When a result is too big for the type intended to hold it, because of a cast, an implicit type conversion, or the evaluation of an expression, something has to give! What happens depends on whether the result type is integer or floating point.

Integer Overflow

When an integer valued expression is too big for its type, only the low end (least significant) bits get stored. This means arithmetic is effectively modulo-2^n arithmetic on the integer types. There is one case in which the calculation ceases and overflow is reported to the programmer: division by zero (using "/" or "%") which throws an exception. To "throw an exception" is covered in Chapter 5.

There is a class called `Integer` that is part of the standard Java libraries. It contains some useful constants relating to the primitive type `int`:

```
public static final int   MIN_VALUE = 0x80000000; // class Integer
public static final int   MAX_VALUE = 0x7fffffff; // class Integer
```

and there are similar values in the related class `Long`. Notice how these constants (`final`) are also `static`. If something is constant you surely don't need a copy of it in every object. You can use just one copy for the whole class, so make it static.

One possible use for these constants would be to evaluate an expression at long precision, and then compare the result to these int endpoints. If it is between them, then you know the result can be cast into an int without losing bits. Unless it overflowed long, of course . . .

Floating Point Overflow

When a floating-point expression (double or float) overflows, the result becomes infinity. When it underflows (reaches a value that is too small to represent) the result goes to zero. When you do something undefined like divide zero by zero, you get a NaN. Under no circumstances is an Exception ever raised from a floating-point expression.

The class `Float`, which is part of the standard Java libraries, contains some useful constants relating to the primitive type `float`:

```
public static final float POSITIVE_INFINITY;
public static final float NEGATIVE_INFINITY;
public static final float NaN;
public static final float MAX_VALUE = 3.40282346638528860e+38f;
public static final float MIN_VALUE = 1.40129846432481707e-45f;
```

One pitfall is that it doesn't help to compare a value to NaN, for NaN compares false to everything (including itself)! Instead, test the NaNiness of a value like this:

```
if (Float.isNaN( myfloat ) ) ... // It's a NaN
```

There are similar values in the class Double.

Convert degrees to radians with code like this:

```
    int degrees = ...
    double radians =  (Math.PI * degrees / 180.0);
```

The Math.log() function returns a natural (base e) logarithm.

Convert natural logarithms to base 10 logarithms with code like this:

```
double nat_log = ...
    double base10log = nat_log / Math.log(10.0);
```

The Math Package

Let's note in passing that there is a class called `java.lang.Math` that has a couple of dozen useful mathematical functions and constants, including the trig routines (watch out, these expect an argument in radians, not degrees), pseudorandom numbers, square root, rounding, and the constants pi and *e*. You can review the source of this at

```
    $JAVAHOME/src/java/lang/Math.java
```

> All the routines in the Math package are static, so you typically invoke them using the name of the class, like this:
>
> ```
>     double cabbage = java.lang.Math.random(); // value 0.0..1.0
> ```
>
> There is a way to shorten the method call to name just the class and method,
>
> ```
>     double cabbage = Math.random();
> ```
>
> using the `import` statement, explained later. You usually cannot shorten it any further to just the method name.
>
> However, there is a little trick that has been used to provide better name visibility. If a class doesn't need to inherit from anything else, a programmer may make it inherit from some other class whose methods he or she wishes to use directly. Making a class extend another class brings all the superclass methods into the subclass name space, without needing to prefix them with the name of the superclass. You can't use this trick in an applet, because you have to inherit from java.awt.Applet. It is recommended that you not do this, as it destroys the OOP design for the sake of some trivial naming advantage. It is only mentioned because you may see it in other people's code.

The full list of functions in the java.lang.Math class is:

```
public final class java.lang.Math extends java.lang.Object {
    public static final double E = 2.718282;
    public static final double PI = 3.141593;
    public native static double sin(double);
    public native static double cos(double);
    public native static double tan(double);
    public native static double asin(double);
    public native static double acos(double);
    public native static double atan(double);
    public native static double exp(double);
    public native static double log(double);
    public native static double sqrt(double);
    public native static double IEEEremainder(double,double);
    public native static double ceil(double);
    public native static double floor(double);
    public native static double rint(double);
    public native static double atan2(double,double);
    public native static double pow(double,double);
    public static int round(float);
    public static long round(double);
    public static synchronized double random();
    public static int abs(int);
    public static long abs(long);
    public static float abs(float);
    public static double abs(double);
    public static int max(int,int);
    public static long max(long,long);
    public static float max(float,float);
    public static double max(double,double);
    public static int min(int,int);
    public static long min(long,long);
    public static float min(float,float);
    public static double min(double,double);
}
```

Unicode

The type char holds Unicode values. As mentioned in the previous chapter, Unicode is an internationally-agreed 16-bit character set, just as ASCII is the *American Standard Code for Information Interchange* using an 8-bit character set. Java provides the framework that is capable of handling characters from just about any locale in the world. The cost is that we store and move 16 bits for each character instead of just 8 bits.

Full Unicode support in Java is limited by two things: I/O support in Java itself, and support from the underlying operating system. Both of these need to be in place, and both of these are currently deficient. At present, Java only supports the Latin-1 character set (i.e. the first 256 characters in Unicode). Although the general framework is in place and you can represent Cyrillic or other non-Latin-1 characters in a Java program, you cannot yet draw them on the screen. Better support for internationalization is introduced in the JDK 1.1 release.

Scanning

When a Java compiler reads in program source, the very first thing that it does, before even forming tokens out of the characters, is to look for any six character sequences of the form \uxxxx where xxxx is exactly four hexadecimal digits. e.g. \u3b9F. These six-character sequences are translated into the corresponding one Unicode character whose value is xxxx, which is pushed back into the input stream for rescanning. Because this early scanning takes place before tokens are assembled, the six character sequence \uxxxx will be replaced even if it appears in a quoted string or character literal. For most characters that is exactly what you want, but for characters that themselves affect scanning, you will get a bad result. Two characters that have the quality of affecting scanning are carriage return and line feed. If you try to put one of these in a quoted character literal like this:

```
char c = '\u000a';
```

the compiler will actually see this:

```
char c = '
';
```

causing two error messages about "invalid character constant"—one for each of the opening quotes it sees.

Choosing Unicode for the char type was a bold and forward-looking design choice. Although a few people complain about the cost and waste of using 16 bits per character, these are the same pikers who a few years ago didn't want to shift from 6-bit codesets to 7 bits, and who still hold onto their abacuses while they evaluate the "new technology" slide rules. Disk continues to get faster and cheaper every year. Designers of forward-looking systems like Java have a responsibility to include proper support for more than just Western alphabets. Especially if anyone wants to sell software outside Western Europe. Until all systems have adopted Unicode, handling it on an ASCII system is clumsy, so avoid sprinkling Unicode literals through your code.

String

Strings are not a primitive type like the types described up to now in this chapter. On the contrary, the type String is a class in Java, but it is important enough to have support for a couple of features built in to the language. The String literal is one of these features. The "+" string concatenation operator is another.

String objects hold a series of adjacent characters, as the name suggests. However it takes a method call (not an array reference, as in C) to pull an individual character out. String is a richly-featured class with methods and data. Java does not use the C convention that strings are just nul-terminated arrays of characters. You will use String instances a lot—whenever you want to store zero or more characters in a sequence, or do character I/O. Arrays of char do some of these things too, but String is a lot more convenient for comparing characters, and using literal values.

literals: A string literal is zero or more characters enclosed in double quotes, like this:

```
"" // empty string
"That'll cost you two-fifty \n"
"The first 3 letters of the alphabet are\t \101 \u0042 and C"
```

As the example shows, you can embed any of the character literals in a string.

Like all literals, string literals are immutable and cannot be modified after they have been created. Of course, you can always discard any String and make the same reference variable refer to a different one in its place. You can even construct a new String out of pieces from another, so being unable to change a given String after it has been created isn't a handicap in practice. Each string literal behaves as if it is a reference to an instance of class String, meaning that you can invoke methods on it, copy a reference to it and so on. For the sake of performance the compiler can implement it another way, but it must be indistinguishable to the programmer.

If you have a long string literal, the way to continue it across several lines is to break it down into smaller strings, and concatenate them like this:

```
      "Thomas the Tank Engine and the naughty "
+ "Engine-driver who tied down Thomas's Boiler Safety Valve "
+ "and How They Recovered Pieces of Thomas from Three Counties."
```

String literals are a concession to programmer expectations. Although String is a class, you can create a new literal instance like this:

```
String peach = "Thomas the Tank Engine";
```

as an alternative to requiring the `new` keyword like this:

```
String peach = new String ("Thomas the Tank Engine");
```

String Concatenation

The previous chapter described how the "+" operator will concatenate any primitive type to a String. This magic of the "+" operator when one operand is a String also applies to objects. If you supply any object as the other operand to "+", the system will call a method with the name `toString` to create a String representation of that object and then concatenate the two Strings. You have two choices for the `toString` method for any class:

- You can provide a method with this signature:

  ```
  public String  toString()
  ```

  Usually, the method will print out the value of key fields, nicely formatted.

- Or you can let the inheritance hierarchy pick up the `toString` method from superclass Object. This will return a String containing the classname and something that looks like the address of the instance.

It's better to take the first alternative and provide more meaningful output. The method `toString()` will be invoked on any object that is concatenated with a String.

```
Citrus lemon = new Citrus();
String s = "Your object is " + lemon;
// the + invokes method lemon.toString()
```

Defining `toString` for your classes, and printing an object this way is a useful debugging technique.

The following code shows the important methods of the String class. You can look at the entire source including the method bodies, as it is distributed with the JDK. The source for String is in file `$JAVAHOME/java/src/lang/String.java`

```
/* A general class to represent character Strings. */
public final class String {
    public String()
    public String(String value)
    public String(char value[])
    public String(char value[], int offset, int count)
    public String(byte ascii[], int hibyte, int offset, int count)
    public String(byte ascii[], int hibyte)
    public String (StringBuffer buffer)

    public int length()
    public char charAt(int index)
    public void getChars(int srcBegin, int srcEnd, char dst[], int dstBegin)
    public void getBytes(int srcBegin, int srcEnd, byte dst[], int dstBegin)
    public boolean equals(Object anObject)
    public boolean equalsIgnoreCase(String anotherString)
    public int compareTo(String anotherString)
    public boolean regionMatches(int toffset, String other, int ooffset, int len)
    public boolean regionMatches(boolean ignoreCase, int toffset, String other,
                                                      int ooffset, int len)
    public boolean startsWith(String prefix, int toffset)
    public boolean startsWith(String prefix)
    public boolean endsWith(String suffix)
    public int hashCode()
    public int indexOf(int ch)
    public int indexOf(int ch, int fromIndex)
    public int lastIndexOf(int ch)
    public int lastIndexOf(int ch, int fromIndex)
    public int indexOf(String str)
    public int indexOf(String str, int fromIndex)
    public int lastIndexOf(String str)
    public int lastIndexOf(String str, int fromIndex)
    public String substring(int beginIndex)
    public String substring(int beginIndex, int endIndex)
    public String concat(String str)
    public String replace(char oldChar, char newChar)
    public String toLowerCase()
    public String toUpperCase()
    public String trim()
    public String toString()
    public char[] toCharArray()
    public static String valueOf(Object obj)
    public static String valueOf(char data[])
    public static String valueOf(char data[], int offset, int count)
    public static String copyValueOf(char data[], int offset, int count)
    public static String copyValueOf(char data[])
    public static String valueOf(boolean b)
    public static String valueOf(char c)
    public static String valueOf(int i)
    public static String valueOf(long l)
    public static String valueOf(float f)
    public static String valueOf(double d)

}
```

String uses another built-in class called StringBuffer to help it operate. String-Buffer differs from String in that it supports character sequences that can be appended and inserted. It doesn't have any support for searching for individual characters or substrings. StringBuffer is widely used by the compiler to implement support for concatenating two Strings into a longer String. You'll probably use the class String a lot more than StringBuffer.

The Basic Statements

All statements in Java can be conveniently divided into four groups:

- Selection statements

- Iteration statements

- Transfer of control statements

- Guarding statements

We will describe the first three groups here, deferring consideration of the guarding statements until the sections on threads and exceptions in the next chapter. There's nothing particularly difficult or novel about guarding statements, it's just that they make more sense once the context in which they operate has been covered.

The selection, iteration, and branching statements are almost identical to their counterparts in C, and are readily recognizable to any programmer familiar with mainstream algorithmic languages. Accordingly we can limit our discussion to showing the general form of each statement.

Selection Statements

The general form of the "if" statement looks like this:

```
if ( Expression ) Statement  [ else  Statement ]
```

Statement Notes:

✔ The Expression must have boolean type. This has the delightful side-effect of banishing the old "if (a=b)" problem, where the programmer does an assignment instead of a comparison. If that typo is written, the compiler will give an error message that a boolean is needed in that context. Unless a and b are booleans. But at least you're protected for all the other types.

✔ The Statement can be any statement, in particular a block { ... } statement is fine.

✔ Since we are dealing with the "if" statement, we should also mention the " ? ... :"operator, as it is not very well known. It works in a very similar way to the "if" statement, but yields an expression, where the "if" statement does not. Compare:

> `if (`*Expression*`)` *Statement_when_true* `else` *Statement_when_false*
>
> *Expression*? *Expression_when_true* : *Expression_when_false*

When looked at this way, the conditional operator is a lot more understandable. You use it where you want to quickly choose between two alternative values, and you can fold it right into the expression, like this:

```
System.out.println( "Your number is "
              + ((n%2)==0? "even" : "odd" ) );[1]
```

Never nest several conditional operators inside each other, as it causes unnecessary grief for whoever has to maintain the code (and it might be you).

The general form of the "switch" statement is impossible to show in any meaningful form in a syntax diagram with less than about two dozen production rules. That tells you something about the statement right there. If you look at Kernighan and Ritchie's C book, you'll note that even they were not up to the task of showing the syntax in any better way than:

> `switch (`*Expression*`)` *Statement*

and neither has any C book since. Ignoring syntax diagrams, the switch statement is a poor man's "case" statement. It causes control to be transferred to one of several statements depending on the value of the Expression. It generally looks like:

```
switch (Expression) {

       case constant_1 : Statement; break;
       case constant_5 :
       case constant_3 : Statement; break;
            ...
       case constant_n : Statement; break;
            default : Statement; break;
    }
```

1. You'd never really write a print statement this way, because it would make it much harder to localize the program to support natural languages other than English. But you get the idea.

Statement Notes:

✔ If you omit a "break" at the end of a branch, after that branch is executed control falls through to execute all the remaining branches! This is almost always *not* what you want.

Looking through about 100,000 lines of the Java Development system source, there are about 320 switch statements. Implicit fall-through is used in less than 1% (based on a random sample of files). A statement in which you have to take explicit action to avoid something you don't want 99% of the time is a disaster. Death to the switch statement! 🐛

✔ There can only be one "default" branch, and it doesn't have to be last. The "default" branch can be omitted. If it is present, it is executed when none of the "case" values match the Expression.

✔ A Statement can be labelled with several cases. (This is actually a trivial case of fall-through).

✔ Implicit fall-through (in the absence of "break") is a bug-prone misfeature.

Iteration Statements

At this point note that wherever you can have a statement in Java, you can also have a block of them. And you can also have a declaration of a local variable. As in C++ variable declarations count as statements.

The for statement looks like this:

```
for ( Initial; Test; Increment ) Statement
```

Statement Notes:

✔ Initial, Test, and Increment are all Expressions that control the loop. Any or all of them is optional. A typical loop will look like:

```
for( i=0; i<100; i++ ) { ...
```

A typical infinite loop will look like:

```
for (;;)
```

✔ As in C++, it is possible to declare the loop variable in the for statement, like this:

```
for( int i=0; i<100; i++ ) { ...
```

This is a nice feature done for programmer convenience. In a difference from most C++ compilers, the lifetime of the Java loop variable ends at the end of the for statement. The continued existence of loop variables in C++ was an artifact of the original implementations that simply translated the language to C. It was convenient to collect up all declarations and move them to the beginning of the block without trying to impose a finer granularity of scope. This sloppy approach is now being tightened up for ANSI C++.

✔ The comma separator "," is allowed in the Initial and Increment sections of loops so you can string together several initializations or increments, like this:

```
for(i=0,j=0; i<100; i++, j+=2 ) { ...
```

The while statement looks like this:

```
while ( Expression ) Statement
```

Statement Notes:

✔ While the boolean-typed expression remains true, the Statement is executed.

✔ This form of loop is for iterations that take place zero or more times. If the Expression is false on the first evaluation, the statement will not be executed at all.

The "do while" statement looks like this:

```
do Statement while ( Expression )
```

Statement Notes:

✔ The Statement is executed, and then the boolean-typed expression is evaluated. If it is false, execution drops through to the next statement. If it is true, you loop through the Statement again.

✔ This form of loop is for iterations that take place at least one time. If the Expression is false on the first evaluation, the Statement will already have executed once.

There may be "continue" statements in a loop. These look like:

```
continue;
```

```
continue Identifier;
```

Continue statements only occur in loops. When a continue statement is executed, it causes the flow of control to pass to the next iteration of the loop. It's as though you say "well, that's it for iteration N, increment the loop variable (if this is a "for" loop), do the test, and continue with iteration N+1."

The "continue Identifier" form is used when you have nested loops, and you want to break out of an inner one altogether and start with the next iteration of the outer loop. The loop that you want to continue with will be labelled at its "for" statement with the matching identifier, but don't be deceived into thinking that execution starts over at the beginning of that loop. It really does continue with the *next iteration*, even though the label is (confusingly) at the beginning, rather than labelling, say, the end of the loop. Here is an example "continue" statement:

```
months: for (int m=1; m<=12; m++) {
            // do something
            // nested loop
            for (int d=1; d<=31; d++) {
                // some daily thing
                if (m==2 && d==28) continue months;
                // otherwise something else
            }
            // more guff
        }
```

There may be "break" statements in a loop or switch. These look like:

```
break;
```

```
break  Identifier;
```

Break is like a more dramatic version of continue. Break with no identifier causes control to pass to just after the end of the enclosing "for, do, while," or "switch" statement. The loop or switch statement is "broken out of". Break with no identifier can only appear in a statement by virtue of the whole thing being nested in an iteration or switch statement. You will break to the end of the iteration or switch *not* the statement it's immediately nested in.

If an Identifier is included it must be an Identifier matching the label on some enclosing statement. The enclosing statement can be *any* kind of statement, not just an iterative or switch statement. In other words, it's OK to break out of any kind of enclosing block as long as you explicitly indicate it with a label. In practice, it's almost always a loop or switch that you break out of, not an if or block. Again, there is the slightly confusing feature that statements are labelled at their *beginning*, but "break" causes you to jump to their *end*. Here is an example:

```
months: for (int m=1; m<=12; m++) {

                // do something
                // nested loop
                for (int d=1; d<=31; d++) {
                        // some daily thing
                        if (cost > budget) break months;
                }
        }
        cost=0;
```

Transfer of Control Statements

A return statement looks like:

```
return;
```

```
return  Expression;
```

Statement Notes:

✔ "Return" gets you back where you were called from.

✔ A "return *Expression*" can only be used with something that actually does return a value, i.e. never with a "void" method. There is another statement that causes transfer of control: the "throw" statement that raises an exception. We will cover this in the section in the next chapter that deals with exceptions.

There is a reserved word "goto" in Java, but there is no goto statement. The designers snagged the word to ensure that no-one uses it as a variable name, in case it later turns out to be convenient to support branching.

You can look at the java code that is output by the compiler by using the javap command, like this:

```
javap -c   class

javac pentium.java

javap -c   pentium
```

javap is an abbreviation for "java print." It can be instructive and fun to look at the bytecode output for various different java statements.

Review of Objects

This is a good point to review what we have seen of objects so far. The simplest form of data declaration looks like this:

```
type    variable;
```

If the type is a primitive type, the declaration provides you with a place to hold a value of that type. In contrast, if the type is an object type the declaration provides you with a place that holds a *reference* to an object. You do not yet have an object itself. This is a key difference from C++ and it's very important to understand the distinction. So,

```
int i;
```

gives you a variable that you can immediately do things with. But

```
Fruit melon;
```

merely gives you a location that can hold a (pointer to) a Fruit. It does not create a Fruit object. If you try to access any of the Fruit fields using melon, your program will fail.

I put pointer to in parenthesis because the first Java white paper, "The Java Language Environment," unfortunately mentioned that "Java does not have pointers as they exist in C/C++." Too many people read the first half of that sentence without noticing the second half, and wrongly concluded that Java didn't have pointers and thus was useless for building dynamic data structures like linked lists or trees.

Java does have pointers and they are called "references." The declaration of melon I just mentioned makes melon a reference variable: it holds a pointer to a Fruit object. What Java does not have is pointer arithmetic, explicit memory deallocation (this is handled automatically for you), an "address of" operator, or anything that allows the programmer to turn a pointer into an int or back again.

Dynamic Data Structures

The first question that most programmers ask when they hear that Java does not feature pointer variables is "how do you create dynamic data structures?" How, for instance, do you create a binary tree class, in which objects of the class can point to each other?

The answer is that reference variables (which are implicit pointers) do this perfectly adequately. Here are the data members for a Tree class in C++:

```
class Tree {                            (C++ CODE)
    private: )
            int     data;
            Tree    *left;
            Tree    *right;
        . . .
```

Here is how the same data structure is written in Java:

```
class Tree {                            (Java CODE)
    private Object data;
    private Tree left;
    private Tree right;
        . . .
```

By allowing arithmetic on pointers, unchecked deallocation, dangling pointers, pointers into the stack, and other evils, C/C++ gives the programmer too much rope. Sooner or later, most of us end up tying ourselves in knots with it. Java makes pointers implicit, and all object access is through a reference type. The compiler can automatically de-reference when an object is needed, and use the pointer when a pointer is needed (e.g. to pass an object as a parameter, or make a reference variable point to a different object).

The more general form of data declaration is:

```
    visibility_modifiers  type   []  variable  = initializer;
```

You can actually have as many bracket pairs (meaning "array of") as you like to signify multi-level arrays of arrays. You can declare several variables at once in a comma-separated list. None or any of them can be set to an initial value. The basic declaration of an object reference, combined with an initializer that creates ("instantiates") an object, looks like this:

```
    Fruit melon = new Fruit();
```

The initializer is a call to a constructor in the fruit class. Whenever you see "Someclass variable" think to yourself "variable holds a reference (initially null) to a Someclass object." Null is actually a literal value, meaning "references nothing."

Initialization

All data fields in a class have a well-defined initial value. If you did not explicitly initialize a field, it is given a default "zero-bits" value according to its type: 0, null, false, " ", 0.0, etc.

Contrast this with primitive variables declared local to a method. These have an undefined initial value. Note for those familiar with compiler internals: It's too big a performance hit to keep clearing stackframes, so it's not done, and local variables can pick up any old junk as their initial values. This won't happen for objects because objects are never allocated on the stack. All objects are allocated on the heap.

(Nearly) Everything is an Object

We come now to a brief discussion about the philosophy of Java. In some ways Java goes further than C++ in its object-oriented nature. In C++ you have several ways to structure data other than making a class out of it. You could put it in a struct for instance. Java does not have structs. The major way to group data items together in Java is to put them into a class. We also have arrays which are important enough to have their own section in the next chapter. Arrays are presented to the programmer as a class, too.

It's convenient and easy to put things in Java classes and so people do. This is really a central principle of Java: (nearly) everything is an object. Apart from the primitive types everything is object-oriented. The "main()" routine is a static method of a class, exceptions are objects, threads are objects, the GUI is built out of objects that you extend, applets are objects and of course Strings are objects.

Object

We've mentioned a couple of times that there is a class called "Object" that is the ultimate superclass of all other classes in the system. The methods that exist in Object are thus inherited by every class in the system. We have already heard of the toString() method of Object. There are also a couple of variations on the standard OS synchronization primitives wait() and notify(). These are further described in the chapter on Threads. The remaining methods in Object, and thus every class, are listed as follows:

```
public native int hashCode ()
```
A hashcode is an identifying value, ideally unique for every object in a program. It's used as a key in the standard java.util.Hashtable class. A hashcode could be implemented as anything, but in current compilers it looks a lot like an address. We'll return to the subject of hashtables later. This and the next method go together.

```
public boolean equals(Object obj)
```
There are two philosophies for equality comparison—something may have the same reference as what you're comparing it to (i.e. you are asking "is it at the same address?"), or it may have the same value (i.e. you are asking "are these bits here the same as those bits there?") The Object version of this method returns true when the two objects being compared are actually the same one object. This is also the precise comparison that is done by the "==" operator. However, you can override equals with your own version, to give it a weaker definition. This has been done for String, because two Strings are usually considered equal if they contain the exact same sequence of characters, even if they are different objects. When you override equals(), you'll want to override hashCode() to make certain equal Objects get the same hashcode.

```
protected void finalize() throws Throwable
```
The method finalize() is just a hook you can override to help with memory management. See the next chapter on garbage collection. That "throws Throwable" is an indication of what error conditions (exceptions) this method can potentially raise. See the next chapter on exceptions.

```
protected native Object clone() throws CloneNotSupportedException
```
Java supports the notion of cloning, meaning to get a complete bit-for-bit copy of an object. The subtlety comes in when a class has data fields that are other classes. Do you simply copy the reference, and share the referenced object (a "shallow clone"), or do you recursively clone all referenced classes too (a "deep clone")? Java does a shallow clone by default, but providing this in class Object and making it overridable allows you to choose the behavior you want. You can disallow any kind of clone, or you can override clone as public (so anyone can clone) rather than the default protected (outside this package, only subclasses can clone).

Note that clone() returns an Object. The object returned by clone() is almost always immediately cast to the correct type, as in this example:

```
Vector v = new Vector();
Vector v2;

v2 = (Vector) v.clone();
```

Not every class should support the ability to clone. If I have a class that represents unique objects, such as employees in a company, the operation of cloning doesn't make sense. . But methods in Object are inherited by all classes. So, the system places a further requirement on classes that want to be cloneable—they need to implement the cloneable interface to indicate that cloning is valid for them. Implementing an interface is described at the end of this chapter.

```
public final native Class getClass()
```

Java maintains a run time representation for all classes, known as RTTI or "run time type identification." This method gets that information, which is of type "Class," and which has several methods to tell you more about the class that an arbitrary object belongs to. You invoke this method in the usual way:

```
Class which = myobject.getClass();
```

Class

Here's where the terminology starts to get really confusing. The RTTI is stored in objects whose class is called "Class." It could certainly use a better, less self-referential, name. The major use of Class is to help with dynamically loading new classes. This is a systems programming activity unlikely to occur in your programs, but providing Class makes it easy to program without stepping outside the Java system.

There are several methods in class Class to access the run time information identifying other classes. All of these operate on an object of type Class (of course), so it's common to first get the Class, and then call one of its methods:

```
Class which = myobject.getClass();
String name = which.getName();
```

However the strict left-to-right evaluation of Java allows these two calls (and any such calls where the result of one method is the reference used in the next) to be written in one statement, like so:

```
String name = myobject.getClass().getName();
```

It can be useful to print out the names of classes while debugging code that deals with arbitrary objects. This and other popular methods of class are:

```
public native String getName();
```

> Returns the name of the Class.

```
public static native Class forName(String className)
     throws ClassNotFoundException
```

> This method takes a String which should be the name of a class, and retrieves the Class (RTTI) object for that class. It's an alternative to get-Class(), used when you have the name of the class in a String, rather than having any objects of it.

```
public native Object newInstance()
     throws InstantiationException, IllegalAccessException
```

> This is a surprising method—it allows you to create an object of the class for which this is the RTTI. Coupled with the forName() method, this lets you create a object of any class whose name you have in a String. Highly dynamic! The no-arg constructor of the appropriate class will be called, so it better have one.

```
String s = "Fruit";
...
Object f = Class.forName(s).newInstance();
```

If you have an instance of a class, and you cast it to the class that you know it is, you can call its methods!

Other built-in classes

You have already seen the basic types boolean, char, int, long, etc. For each of these, there is also a class as shown in Table 4-1.

Table 4-1: For every Basic type there is a corresponding class.

Basic type	Corresponding Class (in java/src/lang)
boolean	Boolean
char	Character
byte	Byte
short	Short
int	Integer
long	Long
float	Float
double	Double

The classes for Byte and Short were added in JDK 1.1.

The class version of each basic type provides an object wrapper for data values, and often a few named constants. A wrapper is useful because most of Java's utility classes require the use of objects. Since variables of these built-in types are not objects in Java, it's convenient to provide a simple way to "promote" them when needed. Note that once one of these objects has been created with a given value, that value cannot be changed. You can throw away that object and create a new one, but the object itself doesn't change its identity once assigned.

Here is an example of moving an int to an Integer object and an Integer to an int, using methods from the Integer class.

```
// changes int to Integer and back
Integer mango;
int i=42;

mango = new Integer(i);   // to Object
i = mango.intValue();     // to int
```

The Building Blocks: Compilation Units

This section covers the mechanics of how java code co-exists with the host system. It explains what gets created when you compile something, and in a larger sense how a group of such "somethings" form a Java package.

Java does away with all the aggravation of header files, forward declarations, and ordering declarations. You can think of javac as a two-pass compiler: On the first pass, the source code is scanned, and a table built of all the symbols. On the second pass, the statements are translated and since the symbol table already exists, there is never any problem about needing to see the declaration of something before its use. It's already right there in the symbol table. So any field in a class can quite happily reference any other field, even if it doesn't occur until later down the page or in another file. There is some fine print covering initialization order for pathological cases.

Less Flexibility But More Simplicity

There are two simplifications in Java: 1) There are no nested class definitions. You cannot define a second class when you are already in the middle of defining a class. Every class is defined at the topmost lexical level (apart from an experimental feature in JDK 1.1 which you can ignore until it catches on, if it does); 2) Everything to do with a single class goes in one file. There isn't a way to extract the body of a method and place it somewhere else. If you must, you can put several related classes in one source file, but you cannot go the other way and scatter pieces of a class across several files. This ensures that when you look in a source file, you get the class, the whole class, and nothing but the class (and its buddies).

A source file is what you present to a Java compiler, so the contents of a complete source file are known as a "Compilation Unit." (Think of it as the unit of compilation, just as the gram is a unit of weight).

Automatic Compilation

Java tries hard not to let you build a system using some components that are out-of-date. When you invoke the compiler on a source file, the compiler does not just translate that in isolation. It looks to see what classes it references, and tries to determine if they are up-to-date. If the compiler decides another class needs compiling it adds it in, and recursively applies the same procedure to it.

In other words, Java has a "make"-like utility built into it. Say the class you are compiling makes reference to a class in another file. That utility is capable of noticing when the second .class file does not exist, but the corresponding .java does, and of noticing when the .java file has been modified without a recompilation taking place. In both these cases it will add the second .java file to the set of files it is recompiling.

Here is an example. This is the contents of file plum.java

```
public class plum {
    grape m;

}
```

And this is the contents of file grape.java

```
public class grape {}
```

If we now compile plum.java, the compiler will look for grape.class, check that it is up-to-date with respect to its source file, and if not, it will recompile grape.java for you!

Here is the output from such a compilation:

```
javac -verbose plum.java
[parsed plum.java in 602ms]
[checking class plum]
[parsed .//grape.java in 44ms]
[wrote plum.class]
[checking class grape]
[wrote .//grape.class]

[done in 2347ms]
```

As you can see, grape.java got compiled as well, creating grape.class.

There is a related "–cs" option when running an application, to check that the source has not been updated after the bytecodes were generated. If the source is newer, it will recompile it:

```
java -cs myApp
```

will achieve this. 🐛

.

File Name Is Related To Class Name

Java emphasizes the idea that the name of a file is related to its contents, and understanding this is the key to understanding how to build programs out of more than one file or library. What we're explaining here is how the rules work when you use the default case of source and object files in the same directory. If you use the "-d" option to javac to make your class files be written in a different directory to the source, then the rules below are modified correspondingly.

A compilation unit (source file) has several rules:

1. It can start with a "package" statement, identifying the package (a library) that the byte codes will belong to.

   A package statement looks like

   ```
   package mydir;
   ```

   When starting out, it's simplest not to use packages. Your class files will be visible to other classes in the same directory, and belong to a default anonymous package.

2. Next can come zero or more "import" statements, each identifying a package or a class from a package, that will be available in this compilation unit.

   An import statement looks like

   ```
   import java.io.*;
   ```

   The predefined package "java.lang.*" is automatically imported into each compilation unit for every compilation. Java.lang contains the classes Float, Long, etc. discussed above and other classes as well.

3. The rest of the compilation unit consists of Class declarations and Interface declarations. Interfaces are skeletons of Classes showing what form the Class will take when someone implements it.

4. At most one of the classes in the file can be "public." This class must have the corresponding name as the file it is in, as shown in Figure 4-2.

   ```
   public class plum      must be in file plum.java.
   ```

The underlying host system should allow filenames with the same form as Java classnames: unbounded length, contain "$" or "_" as well as Unicode alphabetics, and case sensitive. The more restrictions there are on filenames on your host system, the more restrictions there will be on the classnames you can use. This will form a practical impediment to the total portability of software. Avoid using characters in classnames that are problematic for any host file systems.

Each of the classes in a .java file will create an individual .class file to hold the generated byte codes. If you have three classes in a source file, the compiler will create three . class files.

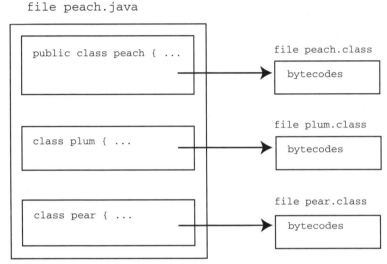

Figure 4-2: Classes and corresponding file names

The Building Blocks: Packages

Right up front, let's make it clear that the java term "package" means a collection of individual .class files in a directory. So a package is both a directory and a library. A package is the way we group several (usually related) class files together. They are grouped together in the file system as files in the same directory. Just as java classnames must match the source file name, so too must package names match the directory name.

As well as being a way of grouping multiple classes together, a package also has implications for the visibility of classes and fields. The default access modifier (i.e. not mentioning "public," "private" or "protected") means the element is visible to everything else in the same package and nothing in other packages. For that reason, some people call this unnamed visibility "package access." Public things are visible in other packages. Protected things are visible in subclasses regardless of package boundaries.

Package names (which match directory names), classnames (which match file names), and the CLASSPATH environment all work together to pinpoint which classes are pulled into a compilation. You need to understand all three together.

When you start to build bigger systems you will use a "package" statement at the top of each source file to say which package the class belongs to. The package name must match the directory name You can also prefix it with the name of the parent directory, and so on, up the directory hierarchy (as high as you need to go to represent the structure of your system). The package name is concatenated with the class name and stored as the full name of the class.

In the example above, if our source file "peach.java" is in a directory:

```
/home/linden/Java/Code/Examples
```

then some choices for package name in the package statement would be:

```
package Examples;
package Code.Examples;
package Java.Code.Examples;
```

and so on.

Another way to think about this, is to take the pathname to a given source file, say "/a/b/c/d.java". The endmost component forces the public class in the Java file to be called "d". For example:

```
public class d {
```

The name of the package is formed by taking the rest of the pathname, and substituting dots for the file separator character "/" (or "\" on Windows systems). If the compilation unit above starts with a package statement it can only be one of these alternatives (in this example):

```
        package a.b.c;
or      package   b.c;
or      package     c;
```

This requirement that package name match the source file directory name also means that any given directory can contain files of at most one named package (see Figure 4-3). It could also contain a few files compiled into the default anonymous package as well, but we assume that if you are building a big system across several directories, you are going to take care to make sure everything ends up in a named package.

Using the host filesystem to structure a Java program, and particularly to help organize the program namespace, is a very good idea. It avoids unnecessary generality, and it provides a clear model for understanding.

If you let your directory naming match components in your Internet domain name (sorted from most general to least general, e.g. "com.sun.engineering"), you can also easily create package names that will be unique across the entire Internet (because domain names have this quality). This allows different vendors to provide class libraries with no danger of namespace collisions.

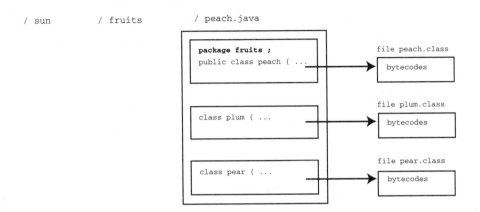

Figure 4-3: How package names relate to directory names

Classpath

CLASSPATH is an environment variable, typically set in the autoexec.bat file (on Windows) or in a shell initialization file (on Unix). The CLASSPATH will be set to a list of one or more pathnames separated by ";" (Windows) or ":" (Unix). It may look like this, for instance on Windows:

```
SET CLASSPATH = c:\sun;c:\project\test\source;.
```

It may look like this on a Unix system using c-shell:

```
setenv CLASSPATH /sun:/project/test/source:.
```

When locating a class, the CLASSPATH tells the class loader where to begin looking for all the possible starting places. The look-up algorithm will do this:

- Take the full name of the class we are looking for, including the package name, e.g. "java.lang.Math"

- Replace the dot (".") characters with directory separator characters and suffix it with ".class." In this example, we will get "Java/lang/Math.class" on Unix, "Java\lang\Math.class" on Windows.

- Take that pathname from step 2, concatenate it onto each element of the CLASSPATH, and look that up in the filesystem. Here we would consecutively look for:

    ```
    /sun/Java/lang/Math.class
    /project/test/source/Java/lang/Math.class
    ./Java/lang/Math.class
    ```

One of these had better be a match, or else the compilation will fail with "Class not found." The first match found is the class it is looking for.

To summarize, CLASSPATH, package, and classnames are related to the filesystem names in this manner:

CLASSPATH	package name	class name
/alpa/beta/gamma	delta	epsilon
/alpha/beta	gamma.delta	epsilon
/alpha	beta.gamma.delta	epsilon

Figure 4-4: How classpath relates to filenames

The three lines above show three alternatives for CLASSPATH and package names in order to identify the same one filename:

```
/alpha / beta / gamma / delta / epsilon.java
```

CLASSPATH is used when executing programs too. If you try

```
java foo
```

you will get back the error message "can't find class foo" if "foo" isn't in any of the directories pointed at by your CLASSPATH.

This can be very frustrating if your CLASSPATH doesn't include the current working directory, and you want to execute something in there. You list the directory contents, and there is "foo.class." Why can't java see it!? Answer: it uses a different algorithm for looking for class files than you do. It doesn't know to look in the current directory unless the CLASSPATH tells it to. 🌶

The CLASSPATH can also be given as a compiler option, but most people will find it simpler to set it once, rather than mention it on each compiler invocation. It is possible to use the "-d pathname" option with the Java compiler to cause the class files to be written to a different directory than the one the source resides in. As the name suggests, the CLASSPATH is only used to hunt for .class files. Normally they reside with the corresponding source, but if you have caused them to go elsewhere, then modify the advice above appropriately.

Import

You never have to use the "import" statement. Its effect is to allow you to use a class name directly, instead of fully qualifying it with the package name. So these are your two alternatives:

```
class Pie {
        java.util.Date    whenmade
        double            weight;
}
```

or

```
import java.util.Date;
class Pie {
        Date              whenmade;
        double            weight;
}
```

An import statement can either name an individual class file that is being imported, or a series of them like this

```
import fruits.peach;
import fruits.orange;
import fruits.prune;
```

Or it can specify that all public files in that package are to be imported, with a statement like this:

```
import fruits.*;
```

An "import" statement always has at least two components, like so:

```
import    package.classname
```

The final component is either a class name, or a "*" meaning all classes in that package.

Some people say "just use the 'import all classes' form," others recommend that you only import the minimum number of packages and libraries that you require. It provides clear documentation on what the actual dependencies are.

Whatever you import, only the code that is needed gets written to the .class file. Superfluous imports are discarded. 🐛

All compilations import the standard Java package `java.lang.*` without specifically naming it. It contains the standard I/O streams, objects representing some of the built-in types, predefined exceptions, and mathematical operations, among other useful items.

Here is a diagram showing how the "import" statement works and interacts with "package" and "CLASSPATH" for files that are split across different directories.

How Import Names Relate to Package and Directory Names

Using a CLASSPATH that includes the path "/sun", the import statement "import fruits.*" tells the compiler to make available all public class files from the package found in directory /sun/fruits. In Figure 4-5 there is only one public class file, representing the class "peach," and that will be usable in class runner, under the name "fruits.peach," or simply "peach." The scope of any imported classes is the entire compilation unit (file).

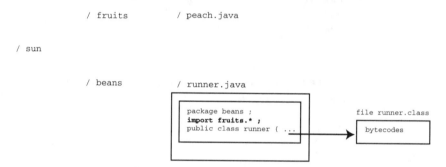

Figure 4-5: One public class file representing the class peach

 Zip files were introduced in December 1995 for classes. A zip file is a collection of .class files all grouped together in one physical file, as can be done on Windows with the standard Windows zip software.

The standard java and Sun libraries now come all wrapped up in one zip file called "java/lib/classes.zip". This blows the import model a little, in that you have to make the CLASSPATH environment variable contain the name of the actual zip file, rather than the path to it, like this:

(Unix): `setenv CLASSPATH /java/lib/classes.zip:.:/mycode`

(Windows): `set CLASSPATH=c:\java\lib\classes.zip;.;c:\mycode`

Think of the justification as "the zip file contains an archive of class files, so in some theoretical sense it is a directory." Or don't think of it at all if it makes your head hurt. It is convenient for a browser opening a connection to a remote URL applet. The browser only need open one connection for a package, not one for each class. Since opening the TCP/IP connection often takes more time than transmitting the data this is a win. Zip files are a performance enhancement aimed mostly at browsers. 🐛

Visibility Revisited

With this new knowledge of how classes are organized and referenced by the compiler, let us revisit the (nontrivial) field modifiers that we first listed in Chapter 2. Java has field modifiers that support four levels of accessibility. In order of most accessible to least accessible, they are:

1. Public—world access
2. Protected—accessible in this package (think "directory") and also in subclasses in other packages
3. Default—package access (any class in the package)
4. Private—accessible only in this class

Java has no exact equivalent of the C++ "protected" modifier that says "this field can only be accessed by this class and its subclasses." The Java "protected" modifier has a slightly different meaning that says "this field can only be accessed by this class and its subclasses, plus anything else in the same package." Java has no equivalent of C++ "friend."

The interaction between classes and subclasses, along with things in the same package and things in other packages can be downright confusing. Figures 4-6 through 4-9 are designed to illustrate the interaction of public, protected, default (package), and private.

Note that the access modifiers for a method can come in any order: "static public" is the same as "public static."

However, the return type of a method must be next to the method name. Otherwise you will get this error:

```
void public init() {
             ^
```

```
alice.java:8: Invalid method declaration; return type required.
```

The correct way to write this is:

```
public void init() {
```

KEY:
bolded code
"is visible in here"   means

/ fruits   / apple.java

```
package fruits;
public class apple {
    public int i;
}
```

pippin.java

```
package fruits;
class pippin extends apple {
    i = ...
}
```

plum.java

```
package fruits;
class plum {
    my_ apple.i = ...
}
```

/ sun

/ sauces   / chutney.java

```
package sauces;
import fruits.*;
class chutney {
    my_ apple.i = ...
}
```

applesauce.java

```
package sauces;
import fruits.*;
class applesauce extends apple {
    i = ...
}
```

Figure 4-6: Public—visible everywhere

/ fruits   / apple.java

```
package fruits;
public class apple {
    protected int i;
}
```

pippin.java

```
package fruits;
class pippin extends apple {
        i = ...
}
```

plum.java

```
package fruits;
class plum {
    my_apple.i = ...
}
```

/ sun

    / sauces   / chutney.java

```
package sauces;
import fruits.*;
class chutney {

}
```

applesauce.java

```
package sauces;
import fruits.*;
class applesauce extends apple {
        i = ...
}
```

Figure 4-7: Protected—visible in same package, and subclasses anywhere

/ fruits   / apple.java

```
package fruits;
public class apple {
        int i;
}
```

pippin.java

```
package fruits;
class pippin extends apple {
        i = ...
}
```

plum.java

```
package fruits;
class plum {
    my_apple.i = ...
}
```

/ sun

/ sauces   / chutney.java

```
package sauces;
import fruits.*;
class chutney {

}
```

applesauce.java

```
package sauces;
import fruits.*;
class applesauce extends apple {

}
```

Figure 4-8:   Default (package)—visible in this package

/ fruits   / apple.java

```
package fruits;
public class apple {
    private int i;
}
```

pippin.java

```
package fruits;
class pippin extends apple {

}
```

plum.java

```
package fruits;
class plum {

}
```

/ sun

    / sauces   / chutney.java

```
package sauces;
import fruits.*;
class chutney {

}
```

applesauce.java

```
package sauces;
import fruits.*;
class applesauce extends apple {

}
```

Figure 4-9: Private—not accessible outside this class

What Happens When Names Collide?

If a variable in the subclass has the same name as a variable in the superclass, then it supersedes ("hides") the superclass one. The visible, subclass variable is said to "shadow" (put in the shade) the superclass variable. The superclass one is still available by giving its full name, e.g. "Fruit.grams" or using the "super" keyword "super.grams."

It's a compile-time error to have a superclass variable with the same name as a subclass *method* or vice-versa. And for the sake of completeness, note that the case of a method with the same name in both the superclass and the subclass is dealt with in the section in Chapter 2 on polymorphism.

Interface Declarations

Interfaces are an important concept in Java. Let's motivate a discussion of interfaces by explaining that interfaces are in the language mainly to provide much of the functionality of multiple inheritance, but without the difficulties. In C++, a class can inherit from multiple superclasses, as shown in Figure 4-10.

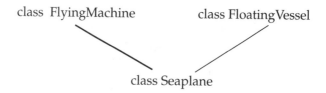

Figure 4-10:   Multiple Inheritance

Problems arise when there are name clashes in the base classes. Class FlyingMachine may have a method called navigate() which does navigation in three dimensions. Class FloatingVessel may have a method with the same name, but which only navigates in two dimensions. Seaplane inherits both methods, which immediately results in a name clash error. You don't want to be forced to change the names in one base class because of names in some other base class. Worse, there is no general way to say which of the two navigate() methods Seaplane should have and which it should forget.

Interfaces avoid this kind of problem. An interface is a skeleton of a class, showing the methods the class will have when someone implements it. An interface may look like this:

```
interface FlyingMachine {
        int navigate(Point from, Point to);
        void land();
        void takeoff(double fuel);
}
```

The declarations in an interface are always public, even if you don't label them so. The methods aren't labelled public here to avoid cluttering up the examples, but it is always preferred to label fields with their actual modifiers. You can declare data in an interface but only constant data. Even if you don't label it "final," this is assumed for you.

An interface is thus a way of saying "you need to plug some code in here for this thing to fully work." The interface specifies the exact signatures of the methods that must be provided. A later class implements the interface by defining those methods including their bodies. If two interfaces should happen to demand a method of the same name in a class, it isn't a problem. It merely says that both interfaces are making the same demand for a method of that name in the class. Here's an example implementation of the FlyingMachine interface:

```
class Helicopter implements FlyingMachine {
        double fueltank;
        int engine_rpm;
        int rotors;

        int navigate(Point from, Point to) {
                // full body of code appears here
        }

        void land() {
            for( ; engine_rpm>0; engine_rpm--) ;
        }

        void takeoff(double fuel) {
            fueltank += fuel;
            for( ; engine_rpm<6000; engine_rpm++) ;
        }

        void hover() {
                // full body of code appears here
        }

        // other methods can be in the class too.
}
```

Several different classes can implement the same interface, each in their own special way. A class may implement several interfaces at once, leading people to say that Java has multiple inheritance of interfaces, but not of implementations. The FloatingVessel interface may look like:

```
interface FloatingVessel {
        int navigate(Point from, Point to);
    void dropAnchor();
    void weighAnchor();
}
```

The class Seaplane may then implement the methods promised by both the FloatingVessel and the FlyingMachine interfaces, like this:

```
class Seaplane implements FloatingVessel, FlyingMachine {
        double fueltank;
        int engine_rpm;
        int anchorline;

    void dropAnchor(){
        anchorline = 200;
    }

    void weighAnchor(){
        anchorline = 0;
    }

    int navigate(Point from, Point to) {
            // full body of code appears here
    }

    void land() {
        for( ; engine_rpm>0; engine_rpm--) ;
        dropAnchor();
    }

    void takeoff(double fuel) {
        weighAnchor();
        fueltank += fuel;
        for( ; engine_rpm<6000; engine_rpm++) ;
    }

        // other methods can be in the class too.
}
```

An interface is used to specify the form that something *must* have, but not actually provide the implementation. In this sense, an interface is a little like an abstract class, that must be extended in exactly the manner that its methods present. An interface differs from an abstract class in the following ways:

- A class can implement several interfaces at once, whereas a class can only extend one parent class.

- An interface doesn't have any overtones of specialization that are present with inheritance. It merely says "well, we need something that does 'foo' and here are the ways that users should be able to call it."

- Interfaces can be used to support call backs. (Inheritance doesn't help with this).

Using Interfaces Dynamically

So far the examples of interfaces have all been solving compile time issues. There is an additional way that an interface can be used to obtain more dynamic behavior. Once we have defined an interface, we can use it as the type of some parameter to a method. Inside the method we can use that parameter to invoke the operations that the interface promises. Whenever we make a call to that method, we can pass it a class that implements the interface, and it will call the appropriate method of that class. The following four steps should make this a little clearer.

1. Define an interface, which promises a method called "run," like this:

```
interface runnable {
    public void run();
}
```

2. Now sprinkle calls to "run" throughout our code, even though we don't yet have anything that fulfills the interface.

```
void vitalSystemThing(runnable r) {
    r.run();
}
```

This code can be compiled and put in a library.

3. At a later time and in another file entirely, we provide a class (or several classes) that implements the following interface:

```
class myCode implements runnable {
    public void run() {
        System.out.println("You called myCode.run()");
    }
    // other code ...
}
```

4. Finally, we pass myCode to the vitalSystemThing

```
vitalSystemThing( myCode );
```

This results in myCode.run() being called back, hence this is known as a "callback." It's a longwinded way of doing what you do with a function pointer in C or C++, and the obscurity of it has led many people to call for function pointers to be added to Java.

The main reason for writing your code this way is that it decouples the calling routine from the called back routine. You could have several different classes that implement the runnable interface. Callbacks allow any or all of them to be sent to the vitalSystemThing, and hence called back. The correct class is called back, based on the type at runtime.

There actually is a built-in Java interface, called "Runnable" (with a capital "R") that is used in this way for threads. It is described in Chapter 5. Here is another example of an interface used as a callback.

```
interface runnable {
    public void run();
}

public class VeryDynamic {
    public static void main(String args[]) {
        runnable r;
        try {
            Class unknown = Class.forName(args[0]);
            r = (runnable) unknown.newInstance();
            r.run();
        } catch (Exception e){ e.printStackTrace();}

    }
}

class Coffee implements runnable {
    public void run() { System.out.println("Coffee.run called"); }
}

class Tea implements runnable {
    public void run() { System.out.println("Tea.run called"); }
}
```

Ignore the try and catch statements for now—they are required here to accommodate the exceptions that the enclosed statements might cause. If you compile this program, you can run it like this:

```
java VeryDynamic Tea

Tea.run called
```

Try executing it with an argument of "Coffee" and an argument of "Bogus." The three lines in bold simply get the runtime type information for the class whose name you give as an argument. Then create an instance of that class that is cast to runnable and call the run() method of that class.

There's another way to use an interface, that's not really what it was intended for, but which forms a useful programming idiom.

If you have a group of related constants, perhaps of the kind you would put in an enumerated type (if the language had enumerated types), you might gather them in a class like this:

```
public class FightingWeight {
    public static final int           flyweight = 100;
    public static final int        bantamweight = 113;
    public static final int      featherweight = 118;
    public static final int        lightweight = 127;
    public static final int        welterweight = 136;
    public static final int        middleweight = 148;
    public static final int lightheavyweight = 161;
    public static final int         heavyweight = 176;
}
```

Then to use the constants in another class, you would have to do something like this:

```
static int title = FightingWeight.heavyweight;
```

If however, you make FightingWeight an *interface*, like this:

```
public interface FightingWeight {
    public static final int           flyweight = 100;
    public static final int        bantamweight = 113;
    public static final int      featherweight = 118;
    public static final int        lightweight = 127;
    public static final int        welterweight = 136;
    public static final int        middleweight = 148;
    public static final int lightheavyweight = 161;
    public static final int         heavyweight = 176;
}
```

Then you can reference the names directly. Wow!

```
class gooseberry implements FightingWeight {
    ...
static int title = heavyweight;
```

Don't tell anyone you heard it from me, at least not until the gods of programming have smiled upon it[2]. This works for classes too, but it's poor style to extend a class just to get better name visibility. ☕

An interface can only extend another interface. A class can legally implement an interface but only implement some of the methods. It then becomes an abstract class that must be further extended (inherited) before it can be instantiated.

Some Light Relief

To close out a chapter that has dealt at length with naming, it's appropriate to consider two other examples of naming, and the confusion that can arise. The first one is computer-related, the second one pertains to confectionery. But they are both instructive.

There's a pervasive legend that the antihero computer HAL in the film "2001: A Space Odyssey" was so-named to indicate that he was one step ahead of IBM. Alphabetically "H" "A" "L" precede "I" "B" "M" by one letter[3].

The author of 2001, Arthur C. Clarke emphatically denies the legend in his book "Lost Worlds of 2001," claiming that "HAL" is an acronym for "Heuristically programmed algorithmic computer." Clarke even wrote to the computer magazine *Byte* to place his denial on record.

Certainly the claims of an involved party are one piece of evidence, but there is no particular reason why they should be uncritically accepted as complete truth; consider them rather in the context of all pieces of evidence. This is what happens in courts of law every day. Clarke's protestations are a little unconvincing. For one thing "Heuristically programmed algorithmic computer" is a contrived name that does not properly form the desired acronym. For another, most of the working drafts of the 2001 story had HAL named "Athena", and it would have remained so had not Clarke deliberately rechristened it. The chances of him accidentally fastening on to the one name that mimics one of the world's largest computer companies are one in a few thousand.

Why would Clarke deny it if it were true? IBM logos appear in several places in the movie, and the filmmakers clearly cut a deal with IBM for product placement. It may be that Clarke decided to assert some artistic independence and decided on the

2. The gods of programming have now officially granted their benediction to this technique of opening up name visibility.
3. People say the same thing about Windows NT (WNT) being one step ahead of VMS. Dave Cutler designed VMS when he was at Digital, and then joined Microsoft to become the chief architect of Windows NT. I believe that the name was chosen with this in mind.

name change as a subtle dig at IBM, in that HAL is a homicidal maniac who goes berserk. Or he may just have been suggesting that his creation was one step ahead of IBM. Later, when the story got out, Clarke realized he would look foolish, or at the very least ungracious by lampooning them. So he denied the connection.

An interesting question is why was the name changed at all? If Clarke provided an explanation of *that* along with his denials, then the denials would have more credibility.

Lessons in Naming: the disgusting case of the Baby Ruth Candy Bar

A similar confusion over naming has arisen in the case of the Baby Ruth candy bar. The matter was thoroughly researched by my colleague David Mikkelson who wrote the following summary of his findings.

> The Curtiss Candy Company was founded in Chicago in 1916 by Otto Schnering. Schnering, who wanted a name more "American-sounding" than his own for the company—German surnames not being much of an asset during World War I—used his mother's maiden name instead.

> The Curtiss Candy Company's first product was a confection known as Kandy Kake, which featured a pastry center topped with nuts and coated with chocolate. This candy bar was only a moderate success until 1921, when Schnering reintroduced it as a log-shaped bar made of caramel and peanuts, covered with chocolate. Schnering named his new confection the "Baby Ruth" bar, priced it at five cents a bar (half the cost of other bars), and soon had one of the hottest-selling candy bars on the market.

Three explanations have since been offered concerning the origins of the "Baby Ruth" candy bar's name:

1. The bar was named after "Baby" Ruth Cleveland, the first-born daughter of President Grover Cleveland.

2. The bar was named after baseball slugger George Herman "Babe" Ruth.

3. The bar was named for a granddaughter of Mrs. George Williamson, Mrs. Williamson being the wife of the president of the Williamson Candy Company and one of the developers of the "Baby Ruth" bar formula.

Explanation #1 is the "official" explanation that has been proffered by the Curtiss Candy Company since the 1920s.

Explanation #2 is the "obvious" explanation; the one assumed by persons who have heard no explanations.

Explanation #3 is an alternate explanation whose origins are unknown, but it can be readily dismissed. The Williamson Candy Company—producer of the "Oh! Henry" bar—was a direct competitor of Curtiss' and would have been most unlikely to supply a product name and formula to a rival. Furthermore, the Curtiss Candy Company has never claimed this as an origin of their candy bar's name.

The claim that the "Baby Ruth" bar was named after Ruth Cleveland is found dubious by many because Ruth Cleveland died of diphtheria in 1904, over seventeen years before the "Baby Ruth" bar was first produced. Naming a candy bar after the long-dead daughter of a former president would certainly be a curious choice. Moreover, the notion that a candy bar called "Baby Ruth" should appear on the market just when a baseball player named Babe Ruth had suddenly become the most famous person in America is perceived as a rather striking coincidence.

If the Curtiss Candy Company did indeed appropriate Babe Ruth's name without permission, they would have had a motive for developing a fabricated yet believable explanation in case a challenge arose over the candy bar's name. Curtiss did indeed have to fight off at least one challenge to their name, when a competitor—with the full approval of Babe Ruth—attempted to market a candy named the "Babe Ruth Home Run Bar." Curtiss, claiming that their candy bar was named for Ruth Cleveland, was successful in forcing the competing candy bar off the market because its name too closely resembled that of their own product. Nobody ever said life was fair, and that's the way things are in the brutal world of children's candy marketing.

The fact that Curtiss successfully fought off a challenge to their candy bar's name does not prove that they were untruthful, however. Merely showing that they had a reason to lie is not evidence that they did lie and are still lying; it must be demonstrated that Curtiss actually has been untruthful about the origins of the "Baby Ruth" name. Although it may not now be possible to prove that Curtiss was less than honest when they were fighting off the challenge of the "Babe Ruth Home Run Bar," it can certainly be demonstrated that they have been dishonest about the origin of the name "Baby Ruth" in the years since then.

First of all, the official Curtiss position maintained for many years is that their "candy bar made its initial appearance in 1921, some years before Babe Ruth . . . became famous." In 1919, Babe Ruth was a standout pitcher for the Red Sox, but not yet well-known outside of Boston and the baseball world. Sold to the New York Yankees prior to the 1920 season, Ruth soon established himself as an outfield star and was nationally famous by the end of the year. By 1921 his name was featured more prominently on the front pages of afternoon newspapers than President Harding's. The claim that he was not famous until "some years" after 1921 is nothing but absurd. This misstatement could merely be a mistake on Curtiss' part due to shoddy record-keeping or research, but the claim has been offered for so many years and is so easily verifiable that it is hard to explain as anything other than dissembling.

Another claim made by the Curtiss Candy Company is much harder to forgive as mere bad record-keeping, though. Part of the official statement about the "Baby Ruth" name offered by Curtiss has been that Ruth Cleveland "visited the Curtiss Candy Company plant years ago when the company was getting started and this largely influenced the company's founder to name the candy bar 'Baby Ruth'." Ruth Cleveland died at age twelve in 1904; no amount of bad record-keeping can place her in the factory of a company that wouldn't exist until more than a decade after her death. The conclusion is clear.

See how many books you can find which have the inaccurate version of the Baby Ruth candy bar story. The story is commonly re-told with the Curtiss cover story being presented as fact. I have yet to find a reference work where the author has actually done some independent analysis, and concluded that Curtiss is full of it. Kudos to David Mikkelson for setting the record straight.

Exercises

1. What advantages are there in requiring all Java implementations to share the same data sizes for the primitive types? What disadvantages are there?

2. Write a short program that clearly demonstrates floating-point arithmetic is inexact.

3. Why do we have a primitive type boolean, and an object type Boolean?

4. Why does every class have a toString() method? Where does it come from and for what is it useful?

5. Describe what the class Class provides.

6. Describe how the CLASSPATH variable is combined with package and class names to locate a class file.

7. What are two common uses for interfaces?

8. Take any class that you have written, and make it cloneable by making it implement the Cloneable interface. The Cloneable source code is at $JAVAHOME/src/java/lang/Cloneable.java. Write some code to clone an object of your class. Override Object.clone() to do a deep copy for your class.

Sources:

Bob Broeg, "At Microphone, Plate, Reggie's A Real Blast" <u>St. Louis Post-Dispatch</u>, 7 August 1993.

Ray Broekel, <u>The Great American Candy Bar Book</u> (Boston: Houghton Mifflin, 1982), p. 23

Tom Burnam, <u>More Misinformation</u> (New York: Lippincott & Crowell, 1980), p. 13

Sharon Kapnick, "Sweet Beginnings; How Some Famous Chocolate Treats Evolved to Stand the Taste of Time" <u>The Arizona Republic</u>, 13 February 1993.

Richard Sandomir, "Legacy of Earning Power; Babe Ruth: Dead 41 Years, He Lives on in Endorsements That Bring Heirs Hundreds of Thousands" <u>Los Angeles Times</u>, 22 December 1989

Kal Wagenheim, <u>Babe Ruth: His Life and Legend</u> (New York: Praeger Publishers, 1974), p.86

Further Reading

"What Every Computer Scientist Should Know About Floating-Point Arithmetic"

by David Goldberg Computing Surveys, March 1991, published by the Association for Computing Machinery.

It explains why all floating-point arithmetic is approximate, and how errors can creep in. The paper was reprinted and is distributed in postscript form with the compilers sold by Sun Microsystems.

ANSI/IEEE Standard 754-1985 for Binary Floating-Point Arithmetic

Institute of Electrical and Electronic Engineers, New York, published 1985. Reprinted in SIGPLAN 22(2) pages 9-25.

"The C Programming Language, Second Edition"

by Brian W. Kernighan and Dennis Ritchie Published by Prentice-Hall Inc., New Jersey, 1988

ISBN 0-13-110163-3

The first edition of this book was the ground-breaking work from which so much has flowed in the past twenty years. Like C itself, this book set a standard which many have aspired, but few others have achieved. The text (and the language) is not perfect, few things of human construction are, but it has served well over the years.

CHAPTER

5

- All About Arrays

- Exceptions and their Purpose

- What are Threads

- Collecting Garbage

More Sophisticated Techniques

London's gangland underworld was dominated during the 1960s by two brothers who were career criminals from the East-end, Ronnie and Reggie Kray. The Kray twins were eventually sentenced to life terms in prison for the chaos and mayhem they created.

FACT: The UK government Meteorological Office has two Cray supercomputers used to simulate chaotic systems such as weather fronts. These twin Crays are therefore affectionately named "Ronnie" and "Reggie"—the Cray twins.

I n this chapter we address the topic of arrays, and how to build dynamic data structures in a language without pointers. We then go on to cover the functionality of exceptions (runtime error handling) and threads (light weight processes). We finish up with some notes on the automatic reclaiming of memory that is no longer in use.

Arrays

It is a little misleading to claim as some people have done that "support and syntax for arrays is much the same in Java as it is in C." Any similarities are superficial ones based on syntax alone. The key to understanding C arrays is understanding the interaction between arrays and pointers. But Java does away with all that guff.

Java has neither the complexities, nor the "size fixed at compile time" of C arrays. The Java array model is more like that of Ada: arrays of arbitrary bounds as parameters, and dynamically-allocatable arrays, each carrying around information about its own length.

Arrays are regarded as objects in Java. Here are some ways in which arrays *are* like objects:

- Because the language says so
- Arrays are a reference type
- Arrays are always allocated on the heap, never on the stack
- Arrays inherit from Object, and support methods such as toString()
- Arrays are allocated with the "new" operator.

On the other hand, here are some ways arrays *are not* like objects:

- They have a different syntax from other object classes
- You can't subclass and extend arrays
- You can't define your own methods for arrays
- An array can't implement an interface or be cloned.

There is, however, a method java.lang.System.arraycopy() that will copy part or all of an array. On the whole, the right frame of mind is to regard arrays as a funny kind of object that shares some key characteristics of regular objects. Most importantly, arrays are a reference type.

When you declare what looks like an array, you actually get a variable that can hold a reference to an array. You still have to create the array. The simplest form of array declaration is this:

```
int carrot [];
```

Note that the size is not given. In fact you may not specify the array dimension in a declaration like this.

You never specify the size of an array in a C-style declaration like this:

```
int carrot [256];                    // NO! NO! NO!
```

The array's size is set when you assign something to it, either in an initializer or a regular assignment statement. Once an array object has been created with a given size, it cannot change for that array, although you can replace it by assigning a differently-sized array object to it. ❦

The array can be created like this:

```
int carrot [] = new int[256];
```

This creates a 256 element array, with the default initialization of 0; you can create and initialize an array in one declaration, like this:

```
int carrot[] = {1,2,3,4,5,6};
float beet[]  = { 5.5F, p, q, 2.2F, };
```

Note that a superfluous trailing comma is allowed in an initialization list—an unnecessary carryover from C. The permissible extra trailing comma is claimed to be of use when a list of initial values is being generated automatically. The claim is like Dick van Dyke's Cockney accent in the film "Mary Poppins"—it starts off as unlikely, then rapidly becomes totally unbelievable the more you hear it.

Array constants (a series of values in braces) can only be used in initializers, not in later assignment statements. There's no good reason for this restriction.

Because an array is an object, all the usual object-y style things apply. Operations that are common to all objects can be done on arrays. Operations that require an object as an operand can be passed an array. The length of an array (the number of components in it) is a data field in the array class. So you can get the size of an array by referencing:

```
a.length      // yes
```

People always want to treat that as a method call, and write

```
a.length()    // NO! NO! NO!
```

Think of it this way: for an array, length is just a final data field, set when the array object is created. There is no need to have the overhead of a method call. There is no need for a "sizeof" operator, and Java does not have one.

You may be wondering how to get the length of the array (the total number of Strings) versus the length of a given String in the array when there is an array of Strings. This situation frequently occurs when you need to find out something about the String arguments to the main() routine. Here is some code that demonstrates how to find the two scenarios.

```
public static void main(String args[]) {
    int i=0;
    System.out.println( "number of Strings: " + args.length );
  System.out.println( "length of i'th String:" + args[i].length() );
}
```

Contrast how "length" is a data field for arrays, and is a method field for the class String. This is a frequent point of confusion for beginners.

For non-C programmers: array subscripts *always* start at 0.

People coming to Java (or C or C++) from another language often have trouble with that concept. After all, when you're counting anything, you always start "one, two, three"—so why would array elements be any different?

The answer is that this is one of the things carried over from C. C was designed by and for systems programmers, and in a compiler a subscript is translated to "offset from base address." You can save a step in subscript-to-address translation if you disallow subscripts with an arbitrary starting point. Instead directly use offset-from-base-address, and the first offset is zero.

Watch out! It means that when you declare:

```
int day[] = new int[365];
```

valid subscripts for "day" are in the range 0 to 364. A reference to "day[365]" is invalid. If this causes distress in terms of program readability (e.g. you want days numbered from 1 to 365 to match the calendar) then simply declare the array one larger than it needs to be, and don't use element zero.

Array indexes are all checked at runtime. If a subscript attempts a reference outside the bounds of its array, it causes an exception and the program ceases execution rather than corrupt memory. Exceptions are described later in this chapter.

Arrays of Arrays

The language specification says there are no "multidimensional" arrays in Java, meaning Java doesn't use the convention of Pascal or Ada of putting several indexes into one set of subscript brackets. Ada allows multidimensional arrays like this:

```
banana : array(1..12, 1..31) of real;          Ada code for
                                                multi-dimensional array
banana(i,j) = 3.14;
```

Ada also allows arrays of arrays, like this:

```
type carrot is array(1..31) of real;        Ada code for array of arrays

banana : array(1..12) of carrot;
banana(i)(j) = 3.14;
```

Pascal, too, allows both forms, and treats them as one:

```
var banana : array[1..12] of array[1..31] of real;      Pascal code
banana[i][j] = 3.14;                                     for arrays
                                                         of arrays.
```

it is usual to abbreviate this as:

```
var banana : array[1..12, 1..31] of real;      Pascal code
banana[i, j] = 3.14;                            for multi-
                                                dimensional
                                                arrays
```

Pascal blurs the distinction by saying that arrays of arrays are equivalent to and interchangeable with multidimensional arrays [Pascal User Manual and Report, Springer-Verlag, 1975, page 39]. Java just has arrays of arrays.

What "Multidimensional" Means in Different Languages

The Ada standard explicitly says arrays of arrays and multidimensional arrays are different. The language has both.

The Pascal standard says arrays of arrays and multidimensional arrays are the same thing.

The ANSI C standard says C has what other languages call arrays of arrays, but it also calls these "multidimensional."

The Java language only has arrays of arrays, and it only calls these arrays of arrays.

Arrays of arrays are declared like this:

```
int cabbage [] [] ;
```

Array "cabbage" is composed of an array which is composed of an array whose elements are integers.

Because object declarations do not create objects, you will need to fill out or "instantiate" the elements in an array before using it. If you have an array of arrays, like this:

```
int cabbage[][];
```

you will need to instantiate both the top-level array, and at least one bottom level array before you can start storing ints. The bottom level arrays do not have to all be a single uniform size. (This is true for C too—the classic example being the argv array of strings declared in main.)

Here is one way you could create a triangular array of arrays, and fill it with initial values:

```
int cabbage[][] = new int[5][];

int slice0[] = {0};
int slice1[] = {0,1};
int slice2[] = {0,1,2};
int slice3[] = {0,1,2,3};
int slice4[] = {0,1,2,3,4};

cabbage[0] = slice0;
cabbage[1] = slice1;
cabbage[2] = slice2;
cabbage[3] = slice3;
cabbage[4] = slice4;
```

We introduce the variables slice0 etc. because array literals, like "{0,1,2,3}" can only be used in an initializer, not in a statement. Here is another way to do it, that provides an equivalent result in cabbage.

```
int cabbage[][] = new int[5][];

for( int i=0; i<cabbage.length; i++) {
    int tmp[] = new int [i+1];

    for (int j=0; j<=i; j++)
         tmp[j]=j;

    cabbage[i] = tmp;
}
```

Yet a third way is to lump all the initializers together in a big array literal like this:

```
int cabbage[][] = {  {0},
                     {0,1},
                     {0,1,2},
                     {0,1,2,3},
                     {0,1,2,3,4}
                  };
```

Note that if you instantiate the dimensions at different times, you must instantiate the most significant dimensions first. So,

```
int cabbage[][] = new int[5][];    // ok
int cabbage[][] = new int[5][3];   // ok
```

but

```
int cabbage[][] = new int[][3];    // NO! NO! NO!
```

Remember that declarations do not create objects!

An object declaration merely sets aside the space, for when you do get around to creating ("instantiating") it. This is just as true when you have arrays of objects, as it is with individual objects.

```
Integer beer[]  = new Integer[10]; // note: class Integer, not int.
```

does not give you an array full of Integer objects. It gives you an array full of elements that can reference an Integer object. If you reference beer[3] before filling out that value in the array with either of:

```
beer[3] = new Integer(n);
beer[3] = SomeExistingIntegerObject;
```

you will of course get a null pointer exception. Note the contrast with an array of a primitive type

```
int cider [] = new int[10]
```

does give you an array into which you can start storing ints immediately. ❦

Arrays with the same element type, and the same number of dimensions (in the C sense, Java doesn't have multidimensional arrays) can be assigned to each other. The arrays do not need to have the same number of elements because what actually happens is that one reference variable is copied into the other.

For example:

```
int eggs[] = {1,2,3,4};
int ham[] = {1};
ham = eggs;
ham[3] = 0;    // OK, because ham now has 4 elements.
```

This doesn't make a new copy of eggs, it makes ham and eggs reference the same array object.

So changes made to the array through references by one variable will be seen by references through the other variable.

```
// show example of what is a copy, and what is a ref.
    Integer beer[] = new Integer[10];
    Integer lager[];

    beer[3] = new Integer(3);

    lager = beer;

    beer[3] = new Integer(256);

    if (lager[3].intValue() == 256)
        System.out.println("It just copied the reference" +
                            " -- they point at same Object" );
```

In this code example, the assignment "lager=beer" simply copies the beer reference variable into the lager reference variable. When one element of the array that beer points at is changed, naturally the change is seen by both, and so the println message will be printed out.

In diagram form, before the assignment of "lager=beer" we have Figure 5-1:

Figure 5-1:   Pre-"lager=beer" assignment

After the assignment of "lager=beer" we have the Figure 5-2:

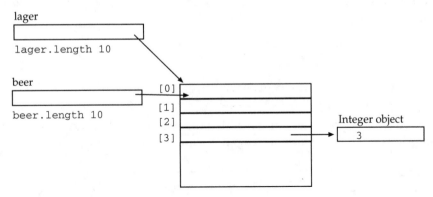

Figure 5-2:   "lager=beer" has been assigned

After the assignment of "beer[3] = new Integer(256)" we have the diagram shown in Figure 5-3:

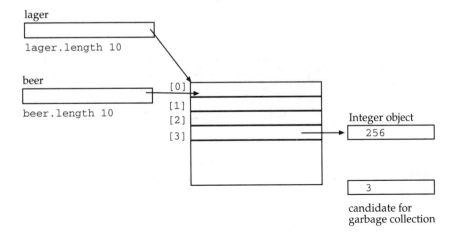

Figure 5-3:   Post-assignment of "beer[3] = new Integer (256)

If instead, it was your intention that a fresh copy of all the objects referenced by the array beer be put into the array referenced by lager, then you would have to do something like this:

```
// create an array for lager
 lager = new Integer[10];

// copy the elements of beer into lager array
 System.arraycopy(beer,0,lager,0,beer.length);
```

This would allow you to assign something different to beer[3], and not see any change in lager[3]. After the "System.arraycopy()" we will have Figure 5-4:

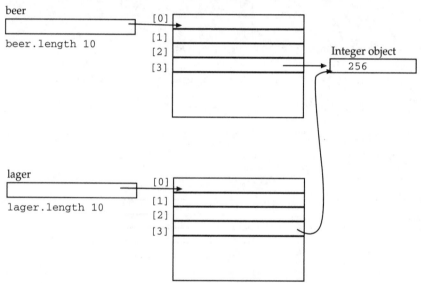

Figure 5-4: A change to beer[3] without affecting lager[3]

And finally, if you then assign "beer[3] = new Integer(3);" the diagram will look like Figure 5-5:

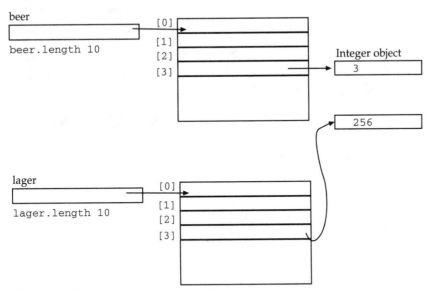

Figure 5-5: beer[3] = new Integer(3)

Have Array Brackets, Will Travel

There is a quirk of syntax in that the array declaration bracket pairs can "float," to be next to the element type, next to the data name, or in a mixture of the two. These are all valid array declarations:

```
int a [] ;
int [] b = { a.length, 2, 3 } ;

char c [][] = new char[12][31];
char[] d [] = { {1,1,1,1}, {2,2,2,2} }; // creates d[2][4]
char[][] e;

byte f [][][] = new byte [3][3][7];
byte [][] g[] = new byte [3][3][7];

short [] h, i[], j, k[][];
```

If array brackets appear next to the type, they are part of the type, and apply to *every* variable in that declaration. In the code above, "j" is an array of short, and "i" is an array of arrays of short.

This is mostly so declarations of functions returning arrays can be read more normally. Here is an example of how returning an array value from a function would look following C rules (you can't return an array in C, but this is how C syntax would express it if you could):

```
int funarray()[] { ... }          Pseudo-C CODE
```

Here are the alternatives for expressing it in Java, (and it is permissible in Java), first following the C paradigm:

```
int ginger ()[]  { return new int[20]; }     Java CODE
```

A better way is to express it like this:

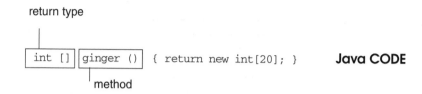

The latter allows the programmer to see all the tokens that comprise the return type grouped together.

Arrays are never allocated on the stack in Java, so you cannot get into trouble returning an array stack variable. In C, it is too easy to return a pointer to an array on the stack that will be overwritten by something else pushed on the stack after returning from the method.

Programmers cannot make this programming error in Java, as arrays are never allocated on the stack. If you write an array as a local variable, that actually creates a reference to the array. You need a little more code to create the array itself, and that will allocate the array safely on the heap.

Indexing Arrays

Arrays may be indexed by "int" values. Arrays may not be indexed by "long" values. That means arrays are implicitly limited to no more than the highest 32-bit int value, namely 2,147,483,647. That's OK for the next couple of years—but the lack of 64-bit addressing will eventually make itself felt in Java.

Values of types "byte", "short", and "char" are promoted to "ints" when they are used as an index, just as they are in other expression contexts.

When to use char[ ] vs. String vs. StringBuffer

There are three types that store character sequences available to programmers: String, StringBuffer, and char[]. How do you choose which to use? The answer is to look at the operations available on each and choose the type that most closely matches what you want to do.

String

Once a String is created, the characters in it cannot be modified, although you can always make a different String using pieces from the String you have. This class supports:

- Literal strings in double quotes

- Comparisons against the entire string or a substring

- Finding where particular characters occur in the string

- Constructing a String out of other types including StringBuffer and array of char

StringBuffer

You might use this class if you know you are going to be appending a large number of characters or changing characters in the middle—and you expect to do this more than you will do comparisons. This class supports:

- Inserting and appending various types onto a StringBuffer

- Setting the length of the StringBuffer.

char [ ]

This class is an array type so it doesn't have any methods. You can only load and store individual array elements. However, you do have random access by subscripting to any character in the array, and you can set or change it as needed. Once created, the number of characters in the array cannot change. It is convenient and efficient to access successive elements using a loop counter as the array subscript.

Keep in mind that you cannot extend String or StringBuffer because they are both *final* classes. This is for performance reasons. When a class is final, the compiler doesn't need to dynamically look up which method should be invoked based on the runtime class of the object. The method is fixed at compile time, allowing the code in the method to be placed inline, saving the overhead of a procedure call. This can be more of an effort than just the cost of a "push parameters and jump to a subroutine." On modern RISC processors, a branch to a new location forces the CPU to empty all the instruction and data pipelines (called "stalling the processor"). This prevents instructions from being executed in the overlapped style necessary for top speed. Most programmers don't need to worry about this, but compiler writers certainly do.

In contrast to finding the length of an array, getting the length of a String or StringBuffer variable does require a method call:

```
String s = "scrofulous";
int i = s.length();
```

You might remember this by thinking "Strings" support more operations than mere character arrays. So Strings use a method to calculate their length whereas character arrays can just use a "length" field. On the other hand, since Strings are fixed in size once created, why isn't length just a final data field?

The thinking seems to be that it is better for String to be consistent with String-Buffer (which has to do it via a method as that is the only way to give users read access to the length field without also granting them write access).

A shortcut to the normal "new" operator is allowed when giving Strings an initial value. You can say:

```
String s = "crapulent";
```

This works as well as the equivalent:

```
String s = new String("crapulent");
```

This is a concession to the existing expectations of programmers.

Exceptions

At several points in the preceding text I have mentioned exceptions, only to defer discussion. This is where I deliver on the promise of describing the purpose and use of exceptions following this order:

1. The purpose of exceptions

2. How to cause an exception (implicitly and explicitly)

3. How to handle ("catch") an exception within the method where it was thrown

4. Handling groups of related exceptions

5. How the exception propagates if not handled in the method where it was thrown

6. How and why methods declare the exceptions that can propagate out of them.

7. Fancy Exception stuff

The Purpose of Exceptions

Exceptions are for changing the flow of control when some important or unexpected event, usually an error, has occurred. They divert processing to a part of the program that can try to cope with the error, or at least die gracefully. The error can be any condition at all, ranging from "unable to open a file" to "array subscript out of range" to "no memory left to allocate" to "division by zero." Java exceptions are adapted from C++ which itself borrowed them from the language ML. Java exception terminology is presented in Table 5-1.

Table 5-1: Exception Terminology of Java

Note	Java	Some other languages
An error condition that happens at run time	Exception	Exception
Causing an exception to occur	Throwing	Raising
Capturing an exception that has just occurred, and executing statements to resolve it in some way	Catching	Handling
The block that does this	Catchblock	Handler
The sequence of call statements that brought control to the method where the exception happened	Stack trace	Call chain

An exception can be set in motion explicitly with the "throw" statement, or implicitly by carrying out some illegal or invalid action. The exception then diverts the normal flow of control (like a goto statement). If the programmer has made provision, control will transfer to a section of the program that can recover from the error. That section can be in the same method, in the method that called the one where the exception occurred, or in the one that called *that,*. It can continue up the stack of calls that were made at runtime. If it gets to the top, where your program execution started—and no handler for this exception has yet been found—then program execution will cease, with an explanatory message.

Therefore, the places that you can jump to are strictly limited. You even have to explicitly stipulate "in this block, I will listen for and deal with this type of exception."

How To Cause An Exception (implicitly and explicitly)

Exceptions are caused in one of two ways: the program does something illegal (usual case), or the program explicitly generates an exception by executing the throw statement (less usual case). The throw statement has this general form:

```
throw ExceptionObject;
```

The *ExceptionObject* is an object of a class that extends the class java.lang.Exception.

Triggering an Exception

Here is a simple program that causes a "division by zero" exception.

```
class melon {
    public static void main(String[] a) {
        int i=1, j=0, k;

        k = i/j;      // Causes division-by-zero error
    }
}
```

Compiling and running this program gives this result:

```
> javac melon.java
> java melon
    java.lang.ArithmeticException: / by zero
        at melon.main(melon.java:5)
```

There are a certain number of predefined exceptions, like ArithmeticException, known as the runtime exceptions. Actually, since *all* exceptions are runtime events, a better name would be the "irrecoverable" exceptions. They mean "runtime" in the sense of "thrown by the runtime library code, not your code." This contrasts with the user-defined exceptions which are generally held to be less severe, and in some instances can be recovered from. If a filename cannot be opened, prompt the user to enter a new name. If a data structure is found to be full, overwrite some element that is no longer needed. You don't have to make provision for catching runtime exceptions. You do have to make provision for catching other exception types.

Some Predefined Exceptions and their class hierarchies

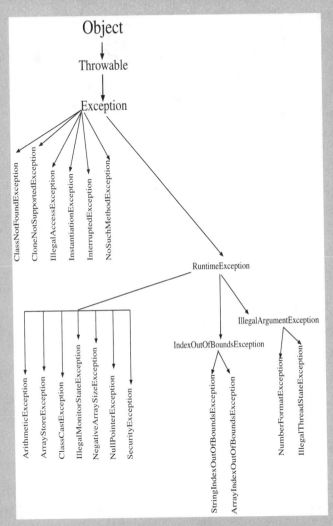

The names are intended to suggest the condition each represents. The source files for these can be found in $JAVAHOME/src/java/lang.

Why is there a class "Throwable." Why doesn't Exception extend Object directly? The reason is that there is a second class called "Error," which also extends Throwable. In other words, both Exceptions and Errors can be thrown, but Errors are not meant to be caught. They ususally indicate some catastrophic failure. Typical Errors are: LinkageError, OutOfMemoryError, VerifyError and IllegalAccessError.

© 1996 Matthew Burtch

User-Defined Exceptions

Here is an example of how to create your own exception class by extending System.exception:

```
class OutofGas extends Exception {}

class banana {
        :

    if (fuel < 0.1) throw   new OutofGas();
}
```

Any method that throws a user-defined exception must also either catch it, or declare it as part of the method interface. What, you may ask, is the point of throwing an exception if you are going to catch it in the same method?

The answer is that exceptions don't *reduce* the amount of work you have to do to handle errors. Their advantage is they let you collect it all in well-localized places in your program, so you don't obscure the main flow of control with zillions of checks of return values.

How to Handle ("Catch") an Exception
Within the Method Where It Was Thrown

Here is the general form of how to catch an exception.

```
try            block
```
There must be at least one (or both) of
the two choices below.

```
[ catch (arg)  block  ]
[ finally      block  ]
```
← there can be zero or many of these
← there can be zero or one of these

A "block" is a single statement or a
whole group of statements in curly
braces.

The "try" statement says "try these statements, and see if you get an exception."
The "try" statement must be followed by at least one "catch" clause or the
"finally" clause.

Each "catch" says "I will handle any exception that matches my argument."
Matching an argument means that the thrown exception could legally be
assigned to the argument exception. There can be several successive catches,
each looking for a different exception. Don't try to catch *all* exceptions with one
clause, like this:

```
catch (Exception e) { ...
```

That is way too general to be of use: you might catch more than you expected.
You'd be better off letting the exception propagate to the top and give you a reasonable error message.

The "finally" block, if present, is a "last chance to clean up" block. It is always
executed—even if something in one of the other blocks did a "return!" The
"finally" block is executed whether an exception occurred or not, and whether it
was caught or not. It is executed after the catch block if present, and if one of them
caught an exception or not.

The finally block can be useful in the complete absence of any exceptions. It is
a piece of code that will be executed irrespective of what happens in the "try"
block. There may be numerous paths through a large and complicated "try"
block. The "finally" block can contain the housekeeping tasks that must always be
done (locks released, etc.) when finishing this piece of code.

Here is an example of an exception guarding statement in full, adapted from the window toolkit code.

```
try {
        a[i] /= j;

        comp.paintAll(cg);
    }

catch (ArithmeticException e) {
        System.out.println("you doofus");
    }

catch (ArrayIndexOutOfBoundsException e) {
        System.out.println("bad subscript");
    }

finally {
        cg.dispose();
    }
```

Supply enough of a context to the code above such that it will compile and run. Put the code in a loop, and have one iteration cause a division by zero, and when you try it again cause an array index out-of-bounds exception. Make up null methods for paintAll() and dispose() and for the objects cg and comp. This example is adapted from code in the Java window toolkit (Easy).

After the whole *try ... catch ... finally* series of blocks are executed, if nothing else was done to divert it, execution continues after the last catch or finally (whichever is present). The kinds of things that could make execution divert to elsewhere are the regular things: a continue, break, return, or the raising of a different exception. If a "finally" clause also has a transfer of control statement, then it is the one that is obeyed.

Handling Groups of Related Exceptions

We mentioned before that "matching an argument" means that the thrown exception can legally be assigned to the argument exception. This permits a subtle refinement. It allows a handler to catch any of several related exception objects with common parentage. Look at this example:

```
class Grumpy extends Exception {}
class TooHot    extends Grumpy {}
class TooTired extends Grumpy {}
class TooCross extends Grumpy {}
class TooCold  extends Grumpy {}


     .
     :


   try {
     if ( temp > 40 ) throw (new TooHot() );
     if ( sleep < 8 ) throw (new TooTired() );
   }
   catch (Grumpy g) {
        if (g instanceof TooHot)
           {System.out.println("caught too hot!"); return;}
        if (g instanceof TooTired)
           {System.out.println("caught too tired!"); return;}
   }
   finally {System.out.println("in the finally clause.");}
}
```

The catch clauses are checked in the order in which they appear in the program. If there is a match, then the block is executed. The instanceof operator can be used to learn the exact identity of the exception.

How The Exception Propagates If Not Handled In The Method Where It Was Thrown

If none of the catch clauses match the exception that has been thrown, then the finally clause is executed (if there is one). At this point (no handler for this exception), what happens is the same as if the statement that threw the exception was not nested in a try statement at all. The flow of control abruptly leaves this method, and a premature return is done to the method that called this one. If that call was in the scope of a try statement, then we look for a matching exception again, and so on.

Figure 5-6 shows what happens when an exception is not dealt within the routine where it occurs. The runtime system looks for a try . . . catch block further up the call chain, enclosing the method call that brought us here. If the exception propagates all the way to the top of the call stack without finding a matching exception handler then execution ceases with a message. You can think of this as Java setting up a default catch block for you, around the program entry point that just prints an error message and quits.

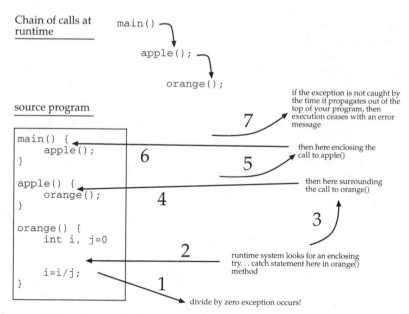

Figure 5-6: The result of an exception not dealt within the occuring routine

There is no overhead to putting some statements in a "try" statement. The only overhead comes when an exception occurs.

How and Why Methods Declare The Exceptions That Can Propagate Out of Them

Earlier we mentioned that a method must either catch the exceptions that it throws or declare it as part of its signature, meaning it must announce the exception to the outside world. This is so that anyone who writes a call to that method is alerted to the fact that an exception might come back instead of a normal return. This allows the programmer who calls that method to make the choice between handling the exception, or allowing it to propagate further up the call stack. Here is the general form of how a method declares the exceptions that might be propagated out of it:

```
modifiers_and_returntype name (params)  throws e1, e2, e3  { }
```

The names e1... etc. must be exception or error names (i.e. any type that is assignable to the predefined type Throwable). Note that, just as a method signature specifies the return *type*, it specifies the exception *type* that can be thrown (rather than an exception object).

An example, taken from the Java I/O system is:

```
    byte readByte() throws IOException;
   short readShort() throws IOException;
    char readChar() throws IOException;

    void writeByte(int v) throws IOException;
    void writeShort(int v) throws IOException;
    void writeChar(int v) throws IOException;
```

The interesting thing to note here is that the routine to read a char, can return a char—not the int that is required in C. C requires an int to be returned so that it can pass back any of the possible values for a char, plus an extra value (traditionally −1) to signify that the end of file was reached. Some of the Java routines just throw an exception when the EOF is hit. Out-of-band-signalling can be effective in keeping your code well-organized. The EOF exception is a subclass of the IOException so the technique suggested above for handling groups of related exceptions can be applied.

The rules for how much and what must match when one method that throws an exception overrides another, work in the obvious way. Namely, if you never do this, you will never be obviously bothered by it. Well, OK, another way to think about it is to consider the exception as an extra parameter that must be assignment-compatible with the exception in the class being overridden.

Fancy Exception Stuff

When you create a new exception, by subclassing an existing exception class, you have the chance to associate a message string with it. The message string can be retrieved by a method. Usually the message string will be some kind of message that helps resolve the problem or suggests an alternative action.

```
class OutofGas extends Exception {
    OutofGas(String s) {super(s);}  // constructor
}


    . . .
// in use, it may look like this
   try {
        if (j<1) throw  new OutofGas("try the reserve tank");
      }
catch ( OutofGas o) {
        System.out.println( o.getMessage() );
      }
   . . .


//At runtime it will look like this:
   try the reserve tank
```

Another method that is inherited from the superclass Throwable is "printStack-Trace()." Invoking this method on an exception will cause the call chain at the point where the exception was thrown (not where it is being handled) to be printed out. For example:

```
// catching an exception in a calling method

class test5p {
    static int slice0[] = {0,1,2,3,4};
    public static void main(String[] a) {
        try {
            bob();
        } catch (Exception e) {
            System.out.println("caught exception in main()");
            e.printStackTrace();
        }
    }

    static void bob() {

        try {
          slice0[-1] = 4;
        }
        catch (NullPointerException e) {
            System.out.println("caught a different exception");
        }

    }
}
```

At runtime it will look like this:

```
caught exception in main()
java.lang.ArrayIndexOutOfBoundsException: -1
        at test5p.bob(test5p.java:19)
        at test5p.main(test5p.java:9)
```

Summary of Exceptions

- Purpose: safer programming by providing a distinct path to deal with errors.

- Use them. They are a useful tool for organized error handling.

- The main use is getting a decent error message out explaining what failed and where and why. It's a bit much to expect recovery.

Graceful degradation is often about the most you can obtain.

Threads

Multithreading is not a new concept in software, but it is new to come into the limelight. People have been kicking around experimental implementations for a dozen years or more, but it is only recently that desktop hardware (especially desktop multiprocessors—if you don't have one ask your boss for it today!) became powerful enough to make multithreading popular. There is a POSIX document P1003.4a (ratified June 1995) that describes a threads API standard. The threads described by the POSIX model and the threads available in Java do not exactly coincide. Java threads are simpler, take care of their own memory management, and do not have the full generality (or overhead) of POSIX threads. It is a pity that the Java designers shunned POSIX threads, as it means more Java implementation work needs to be done than otherwise.

Everyone is familiar with time sharing: a computer system can give the impression of doing several things simultaneously, by running each process for a few milliseconds, then saving its state and switching to the next process, and so on. Threads simply extend that concept from switching between several different programs, to switching between several different functions executing simultaneously within a single program. A thread isn't restricted just to one function. Any thread in a multi-threaded program can call any series of methods that could be called in a single-threaded program.

Instead of the costly overhead of saving the state (virtual memory map, file descriptors, etc.) of an entire process, a low-overhead context switch (saving just a few registers, a stack pointer, the program counter, etc.) within the same address space is done. Threads can actually achieve the counterintuitive result of making a program run faster, even on uniprocessor hardware. This occurs when there are calculation steps that no longer have to wait for earlier output to complete, but can run while the I/O is taking place.

Threads (an abbreviation of "threads of control," meaning control flow) are the way we get more than one thing to happen at once in a program. Why is this a good idea? The example that is often related is a web browser, and it's a good example. In an unthreaded program (what you have been using up-to-date in Java, and what you have always used in Fortran, Pascal, C, Basic, C++, COBOL, and so on), only one thing happens at a time.

Threads allow a program to do more than one thing at a time. There are three reasons why you would do this:

- So you can really do more than one thing at a time. This is becoming more and more common. You might have one thread controlling and responding to a GUI, while another thread carries out the tasks or computations requested, while a third thread does file I/O, all for the same program. This means that when one part of the program is blocked waiting on some resource, the other threads can still run and are not blocked.

- Some programs are easier to write if you split them into threads. The classic example is the server part of a client/server. When a request comes in from a client, it is very convenient if the server can spawn a new thread to process that one request. The alternative is to have one server program try to keep track algorithmically of the state of each client request.

- Some programs are amenable to parallel processing. Writing them as threads allows the code to express this. Examples include some sorting and merging algorithms, some matrix operations, and many recursive algorithms.

Alternative Ways to Obtain a New Thread

There are two ways to obtain a new thread of control in Java. One tends to be used inside an application, and the other is used inside an applet.

The first way can only be used if your class doesn't extend any other class (as Java disallows multiple inheritance).

1. extend class "java.lang.Thread" and override "run()"

```
class mango extends Thread {
      public void run() { ... }
}
```

or

2. implement the "Runnable" interface, (the class "Thread" itself is an implementation of "Runnable")

```
class mango implements Runnable {
      public void run() { ... }
}
```

Your applets extend class Applet by definition, so threads in applets must always use the second way. Of course, if the thread doesn't have to run in the Applet object, it can use the first approach.

Figure 5-7 shows how a class Thread is created by extending Thread.

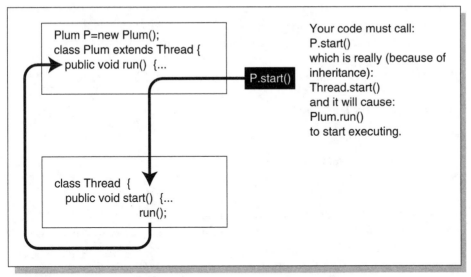

Figure 5-7: Class Thread created by an extending Thread

Creating a thread by extending class Thread looks confusing, because you have to start the thread running by calling a method that you do not have, namely the subclass.start(). You extended Thread to obtain subclass, so this will default back to Thread.start(this) and all will be well. It looks most confusing in the source code however.

Then declaring an object of class Plum gives you a new thread of control, whose execution will start in the method "run()." Declaring two Plums (or more likely a Plum and a Peach) will give you two independently executing threads of control, and declaring and filling an array of Plums will give you an entire array.length threads of control.

New Threads do not start executing on creation. For some applications, programmers (or maybe the runtime system—we'll talk about this in Chapter 7 on applets) want to create threads in advance, then explicitly start them when needed, so this has been made the way it works. When a thread has been created like so:

```
Plum p = new Plum();
```

you start it running by calling the "start()" method, like so:

```
p.start();
```

Or create and start it in one step, like this:

```
new Plum().start();
```

Execution will then begin in the "run()" method, from whence you can call other methods in this and other classes as usual. Remember: "run()" is the place where it starts. And "start()" will get it running. Arrrgh! Perhaps another way to think of this is that "run()" is the equivalent of "main()" for a thread. You do not call it directly, but it is called on your behalf. There's a lot of this in Java!

A Few Words on Runnable

The Runnable interface just looks like this:

```
public interface Runnable {
    public abstract void run();
}
```

A class that implements the Runnable interface works in much the same way as a class that extends Thread, but with one big difference. The class Thread has many other methods, as well as run(). It has methods to stop(), sleep(), suspend(), resume(), setPriority(), getPriority(), and more besides. These can only be invoked on an object that belongs to a (sub)class of Thread.

None of these methods exist in the Runnable interface, so none of them are available to objects that implement Runnable. Here is the kludge around that. To obtain them, you instantiate a Thread object, and pass it an argument of an object that implements the Runnable interface, like this:

```
class Pear implements Runnable {
    public void run() { ... }
}

    ...

    Thread t1 = new Thread(new Pear());
```

That allows the use of all the Thread methods such as:

```
        t1.start();
        t1.stop();
```

In fact, you have to call start() to get the Runnable implementation executing (just as with a thread). It's common to instantiate and start in one statement like this:

```
        new Thread (new Pear()).start();
```

However, you cannot have statements *within the Runnable interface implementation* of "run()" that operate on the thread itself, like "sleep()" or "getName()" or "setPriority()." This is because there is no Thread "this" in Runnable, whereas there is in Thread. This perhaps makes an implementation of Runnable slightly

less convenient than a subclass of Thread. There is a simple workaround shown
on the next page.

```
// Show the two ways to obtain a new thread
//   1.   extend class java.lang.Thread and override run()
//   2.   implement the Runnable interface,

class example {
   public static void main(String[] a) {

      // alternative 1
      ExtnOfThread t1 = new ExtnOfThread();
      t1.start();

      // alternative 2
      Thread t2 = new Thread (new ImplOfRunnable());
      t2.start();
   }
}

class ExtnOfThread extends Thread {
   public void run() {
        System.out.println("Extension of Thread running");
        try {sleep(1000);}
        catch (InterruptedException ie) {return;}
   }
}

class ImplOfRunnable implements Runnable {
   public void run() {
        System.out.println("Implementation of Runnable running");

// next two lines will not compile
//         try {sleep(1000);}
//         catch (InterruptedException ie) {return;}
   }
}
```

You can only call Thread methods if you have a Thread object to invoke them on.
You don't get this automatically in a class that implements Runnable. Instead,
you call the static method Thread.currentThread() whose return value is simply
the currently running thread. Once you have that, you can easily apply any
thread methods to it, as shown in the example below:

```
class ImplOfRunnable implements Runnable {
   public void run() {
        System.out.println("Implementation of Runnable running");
        Thread t = Thread.currentThread();
        try { t.sleep(1000); }
        catch  (InterruptedException ie) { return; }
   }
}
```

A call to currentThread() can appear in any java code, including your main program or whatever. Once you have that thread object you can invoke the thread methods on it.

The official word from the Java team is that the Runnable interface should be used if the "run()" method is the only one you are planning to override. The thinking is that, to maintain the purity of the model, classes should not be subclassed unless the programmer intends to modify or enhance the fundamental behavior of the class.

Confidentially, this is one place where most programmers will say "nuts to the purity of model," and go on subclassing Thread where it is convenient.

As with exceptions, you can provide a string argument when you create a thread subclass. As with exceptions, if you want to do this, you must provide a constructor to take that string and pass it back to the constructor of the base class. The string becomes the name of the object of the Thread subclass, and can later be used to identify it.

```
class Grape extends Thread {
   Grape(String s){ super(s); } // constructor

   public void run() { ... }
}
     ...
   static public void main(String s[]) {
      new Grape("merlot").start();
      new Grape("pinot").start();
      new Grape("cabernet").start();
      ...
```

You cannot pass any parameters into the "run()" method, because then its signature would differ from the version it is overriding in Thread. A thread can however get the string that it was started with, by invoking the "getName()" method. This string could encode arguments, or an index into a static array of arguments as needed.

You have already seen enough to write an elementary Java program that uses threads. So do it.

Write two classes that extend Thread. In one the run() method should print "I like tea" in a loop, while the other prints "I like coffee." Create a third class with a main() routine that instantiates and starts the other two threads. Compile and run your program. 🍎

The Lifecycle of a Thread

We have already covered how a thread is created, and how the "start()" method inherited from Thread causes execution to start in its run() method. An individual thread dies when execution falls off the end of "run()" or otherwise leaves the method (an exception or return statement).

A thread can also be killed with the "stop()" method. This stops the thread executing and destroys the thread object. To restart it again, you would need to create a new thread object, and start it again. If you want to temporarily halt a thread and have it pick up again from where it was, then suspend()/resume() are the calls to use.

Priorities

Threads have priorities that can be set and changed. A higher priority thread executes ahead of a lower priority thread if they are both ready to run.

Java threads are preemptible, meaning that a running thread will be pushed off the processor by a higher priority thread before it is ready to give it up of its own accord. Java threads might or might not also be time-sliced, meaning that a running thread might or might not share the processor with threads of equal priority.

A Slice of Time

Not guaranteeing time-slicing may seem a somewhat surprising design decision as it violates the "Principle of Least Astonishment"—it leads to program behavior that programmers find surprising (namely threads suffer from CPU starvation). There is some precedent, in that time-slicing can also be missing in a POSIX-conforming thread implementation. POSIX specifies a number of different scheduling algorithms, one of which (round robin) does do time-slicing. However another scheduling possibility allows a local implementation. In the Solaris case of POSIX threads only the local implementation is used, and this does not do any time-slicing.

Many people think that the failure to require time-slicing is a mistake that will surely be fixed in a future release.

Since a programmer cannot assume that time-slicing will take place, the careful programmer assures portability by writing threaded code that does not depend on time-slicing. The code must cope with the fact that once a thread starts running, all other threads with the same priority might become blocked. One way to cope with this is to adjust thread priorities on the fly. That code is going to cost you plenty in software maintenance though.

A better way is to yield control to other threads very frequently. CPU-intensive threads should call the "yield()" method at regular intervals to ensure they don't hog the processor. This won't be needed if time slicing is made a standard part of Java. Yield allows the scheduler to choose another runnable thread for execution.

In the 1.0 version of Java, priorities run from 1 (lowest) to 10 (highest). Threads start off with the same priority as their parent thread, and the priority can be adjusted like this:

```
t1.setPriority ( getPriority() +1 );
```

On Operating Systems that have priorities, most users cannot adjust their processes to a higher priority (because they may gain an unfair advantage over other users of the system).[1] There is no such inhibition for threads, because they all operate within one process. The user is only competing with himself or herself for resources.

Thread groups

A thread group is (big surprise!) a group of Threads. A Thread group can contain a set of Threads as well as a set of other Thread groups. It's a way of lumping several related threads together, and doing things like suspend and resume to all of them with a single method invocation.

There are methods to create a thread group and add a thread to it. Applets are not allowed to manipulate threads outside the applet's own thread group. So you may want to save a reference to that group for later use:

```
public class Apples extends Applet{
    private ThreadGroup mygroup;
    public void init(){
       mygroup=Thread.currentThread().get ThreadGroup();
}
```

---

1. Hence the infamous message from the system operator "I've upped my priority, now up yours."

How many Threads?

Sometimes programmers ask "how many threads should I have in my program?" Ron Winacott of Sun Canada has done a lot of thread programming, and he compares this question to asking "how many people is it reasonable to fit in a car?"

The problem is that so much is left unspecified. How big is the car, is it a minibus or a compact? How large are the people, are they children, or 300 pound wrestlers? And how many are needed to get to where you want to go in this car (e.g., driver, mechanic, navigator, someone to buy the fuel.)? In other words, how many people are required to operate the vehicle?

The bottom line is this. Each thread has a default stack size of 400Kbytes in the JDK current release. It will also use about 0.5Kbytes to hold its internal state, but the stack size is the limiting factor. A Unix process (Unix is the most capable of all the systems that Java has been ported to) effectively has a 2Gbyte address space, so in theory you could have around 5000 threads. In practice you would be limited by CPU availability, swap space, and disk bandwidth before you got up there. In one experiment, I was able to create almost 2000 threads before my desktop system ground to a halt. Just create them, I'm not making any claims about them doing any useful work.

Now, back to the real question. Overall there is no unique correct answer. How many is "reasonable?" There is only one person who can accurately answer this question, and that is the programmer writing the threaded application.

The best estimate is "the number of threads needed to perform the task." If this number is too high for the address space, or the CPU power, then you must redesign the tasks (and the number of threads) to use what is available. Use threads where you can achieve concurrency, or to gain overlapping I/O. Do not try to create a new thread for every method, class, or object in your program. ❦

Four Kinds of Threads Programming

Coordination between different threads is known as "synchronization." Programs that use threads can be divided into the following four levels of difficulty, depending on the kind of synchronization needed between the different threads.

1. Unrelated Threads

2. Related But Unsynchronized Threads

3. Mutually-Exclusive Threads

4. Communicating Mutually-Exclusive Threads

The following sections describe how each of these can be written in Java. Figure 5-8 is the key for all illustrations presented in this section.

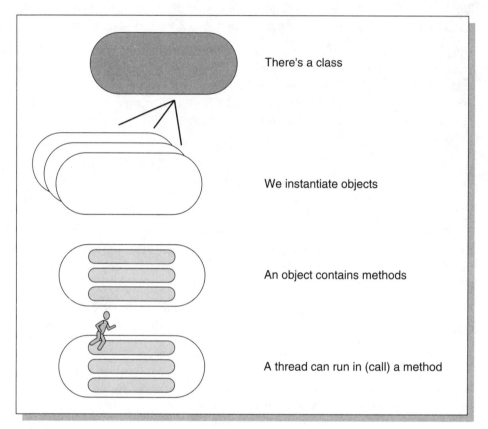

Figure 5-8:   Key to threads diagrams

Unrelated Threads

The simplest threads program involves threads of control that do different things and don't interact with each other.

A good example of unrelated threads is the answer to the programming challenge set a few pages back.

The code is:

```
public class drinks {
    public static void main(String[] a) {
        Coffee t1 = new Coffee();
        t1.start();
        new Tea().start();  // an anonymous thread
    }
}

class Coffee extends Thread {
    public void run() {
        while(true) {
            System.out.println("I like coffee");
            yield();  // did you forget this?
        }
    }
}

class Tea extends Thread {
    public void run() {
        while(true) {
            System.out.println("I like tea");
            yield();
        }
    }
}
```

When you run this program, you will see the output:

> I like coffee
> I like tea
> I like coffee
> I like tea
> I like coffee
> I like tea

It is repeated over and over again, until you press control-C or otherwise interrupt program execution. This type of threads programming is easy to get working. See Figure 5-9.

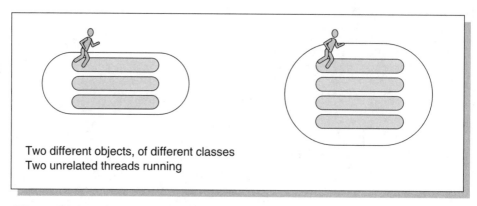

Two different objects, of different classes
Two unrelated threads running

Figure 5-9: Unrelated Threads

Related But Unsynchronized Threads

This level of complexity has threaded code to partition a problem, solving it by having multiple threads work on different pieces of the same data structure. The threads don't interact with each other. Here, threads of control do work that is sent to them, but don't work on shared data, so they don't need to access it in a synchronized way.

An example of this would be spawning a new thread for each socket connection that comes in. Threads that just do "work to order" like that are termed *demon* or *daemon* threads—their only purpose is to serve a higher master. See Figure 5-10. You can mark a thread as being a demon thread with the `setDaemon(true)` method. The advantage being that a program will terminate if the only thing left running in it are daemon threads.

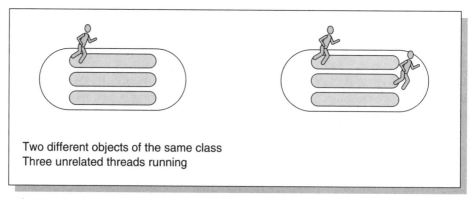

Two different objects of the same class
Three unrelated threads running

Figure 5-10: Related but Unsynchronized Threads

A less common but still interesting example of related but unsynchronized threads involves partitioning a data set, and instantiating multiple copies of the same thread to work on different pieces of the same problem. Be careful not to duplicate work, or even worse, to let two different threads operate on the same data at once.

Here is an example program that tests whether a given number is a prime number. That involves a lot of divisions so it's a good candidate for parcelling the work out among a number of threads. Tell each thread the range of numbers it is to test-divide into the possible prime. Then let them all loose in parallel. The driver code is:

```
// demonstrates the use of threads to test a number for primality

public class testPrime {

    public static void main(String s[]) {
        long possPrime = Long.parseLong(s[0]);
        int centuries = (int)(possPrime/100) +1;

        for(int i=0;i<centuries;i++) {
            new testRange(i*100, possPrime).start();
        }

    }
}
```

This main program gets its argument, which is the value to test for primality, and then calculates how many 100s there are in the number. A new thread will be created to test for factors in every range of 100. So if the number is 2048, there are twenty 100s. Twenty one threads will be created. The first will check whether any of the numbers 2 to 99 divide into 2048. The second will check the range 100 to 199. The third will check 200 to 299, and so on, with the 21st thread checking the numbers 2000 to 2100.

The line "new testRange(i*100, possPrime).start();" instantiates an object of class testRange, using the constructor that takes two arguments. That object belongs to a subclass of Thread, so the ".start()" jammed on the end starts it running. This is a java idiom. The class testRange follows.

```
class testRange extends Thread {

    static long possPrime;
    long from, to;

    // constructor
    //    record the number we are to test, and
    //    the range of factors we are to try.
    testRange(int argFrom, long argpossPrime) {
        possPrime=argpossPrime;
        if (argFrom==0) from=2; else from=argFrom;
        to=argFrom+99;
    }

    public void run() {
        for (long i=from; i<=to && i<possPrime; i++) {
            if (possPrime%i == 0) {  // i divides possPrime exactly
                System.out.println(
                        "factor "+i+" found by thread "+getName());
                this.stop();
            }
            yield();
        }
    }

}
```

The constructor just saves a copy of the number we are to test for primality, and it saves the start of the range of potential factors for this thread instance to test. The end of the range is the start plus 99.

All the run() method does is count through this range, trying each divisor. If one divides the number exactly, then print it out and stop this thread. We have the answer that the number is not prime. There are many possible improvements to the algorithm (for instance, we need only test for factors up to the square root of the possible prime). These improvements have been omitted so as not to clutter up the code example. A sample run of this program might look like this:

```
% java testPrime 2048
  factor 2 found by thread Thread-4
  factor 512 found by thread Thread-9
  factor 1024 found by thread Thread-14
  factor 128 found by thread Thread-5
  factor 256 found by thread Thread-6
```

So 2048 is not a prime number and five of the 21 threads found factors. The default name for the first thread you create is Thread-4 (not Thread-1) because there are already several threads running in your program, including the garbage collector and your main program.

Mutually-Exclusive Threads

Here's where threads start to interact with each other, and that makes life a little more complicated. In particular we use threads which need to work on the same pieces of the same data structure. You may not believe this or see why if I just state it, so we will motivate the discussion with some code, which you should type in and run.

These threads need to take steps to stay out of each others' way so they don't each simultaneously modify the same piece of data leaving an uncertain result. Staying out of each other's way is known as *mutual exclusion*.

This code simulates a steam boiler. It defines some values (the current reading of a pressure gauge, and the safe limit for that gauge), and then instantiates 10 copies of a thread called "pressure" storing them in an array. The main routine concludes by waiting for each thread to finish (this is the "join()" statement) and then prints the current value of the pressure gauge. Here is the main routine:

```
public class p {
  static int pressureGauge=0;
  static final int safetyLimit = 20;

  public static void main(String[]args) {
    pressure []p1 = new pressure[10];
    for (int i=0; i<10; i++)   {
      p1[i] = new pressure();
      p1[i].start();
    }
    try{ for (int i=0;i<10;i++) p1[i].join(); } catch(Exception e){}

    System.out.println("gauge reads "+pressureGauge+", safe limit is 20");
  }

}
```

Now let's look at the pressure thread. This code simply checks if the current pressure reading is within safety limits, and if it is, it waits briefly, then increases the pressure. Here is the thread:

```
class pressure extends Thread {

    void RaisePressure() {
      if (p.pressureGauge < p.safetyLimit-15) {
        // wait briefly to simulate some calculations
        try{sleep(100);} catch (Exception e){}
        p.pressureGauge += 15;
      } else ; // pressure too high -- don't add to it.
    }

    public void run() {
      RaisePressure();
    }
}
```

If you haven't seen this kind of thing before, it should look pretty safe. After all, before we increase the pressure reading we always check that our addition won't push it over the safety limit. Stop reading at this point, type in the two dozen lines of code, and run them. Here's what you may see:

```
% java p
   gauge reads 150, safe limit is 20
```

Although we always checked the gauge before increasing the pressure it is over the safety limit by a huge margin! Better evacuate the area! So what is happening here?

This is a classic example of what is called a *data race* or a *race condition*. A race condition occurs when two or more threads update the same value simultaneously. What you want to happen is:

- Thread 1 reads pressure gauge

- Thread 1 updates pressure gauge

- Thread 2 reads pressure gauge

- Thread 2 updates pressure gauge

But it may happen that thread 2 starts to read before thread 1 has updated, so the accesses take place in this order:

- Thread 1 reads pressure gauge

- Thread 2 reads pressure gauge

- Thread 1 updates pressure gauge

- Thread 2 updates pressure gauge

In this case, thread 2 will read an erroneous value for the gauge, effectively missing the fact that thread 1 is in the middle of updating the value based on what it read. For this example we helped the data race to happen by introducing a tenth-of-a-second delay between reading and updating. But a data race can occur even in statements that follow each other consecutively, whenever you have different threads updating the same data.

In this example we have highlighted what is happening and rigged the code to exaggerate the effect, but in general data races are among the hardest problems to debug. They typically do not reproduce consistently and they leave no visible clues as to how data got into an inconsistent state.

To avoid data races, follow this simple rule: Whenever two threads access the same data, they must use mutual exclusion. You can optimize slightly, by allowing multiple readers at one instant. A reader and a writer must never be running at the same time. Two writers must never be running at the same time. As the name suggests, mutual exclusion is a protocol for making sure that if one thread is touching some particular data, another is not. The threads mutually exclude each other in time.

In Java, thread mutual exclusion is built on data Objects. Every Object in the system has its own mutex semaphore (strictly speaking this will only be allocated if it is used), so any Object in the system can be used as the "turnstile" or "thread serializer" for threads. You use the "synchronized" keyword and explicitly or implicitly provide an Object, any Object, to synchronize on. The runtime system will take over and apply the code to ensure that, at most, one thread has locked that specific object at any given instant as shown in Figure 5-11. The "synchronized" keyword can be applied to a class, to a method, or to a block of code. In each case, the mutex (mutual exclusion) lock of the named object is acquired, then the code is executed, then the lock is released. If the lock is already held by another thread, then the thread that wants to acquire the lock is suspended until the lock is released.

The Java programmer never deals with the low-level and error-prone details of creating, acquiring and releasing locks, but only specifies the region of code and the object that must be exclusively held in that region. You want to make your regions of synchronized code as small as possible, because mutual exclusion really chokes performance. Here are examples of each of these alternatives of synchronizing over a class, a method, or a block, with comments on how the exclusion works.

Mutual exclusion over an entire class

This is achieved by applying the keyword "synchronized" to a class method (a method with the keyword "static"). Making a class method synchronized tells the compiler "add this method to the set of class methods that must run with mutual

In this one object, of all it's synchronized methods, only one thread can be running at a time. But any other threads could be active in the same method of other objects of the class.

Figure 5-11:   Mutually-exclusive Threads

exclusion." See Figure 5-12. Only one "static synchronized" method for a particular class can be running at any given time. The threads are implicitly synchronized using the class object.

In the preceding pressure example, we can make RaisePressure a static synchronized method, by changing its declaration to this:

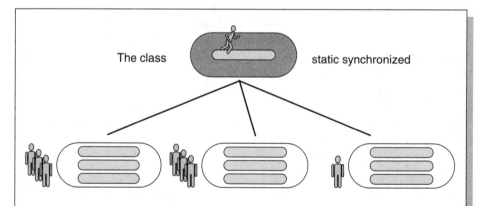

The class   static synchronized

Only one thread can be running in a synchronized static (class) method at a time, no matter how many objects of the class there are.

There is one lock for static synchronized methods, and a different lock for synchronized methods. So a thread could have exclusive access to a static synchronized method, while another thread has exclusive access to a synchronized method, for agiven class and object. Yet other threads could be running in methods that are not marked as synchronized at all.

Figure 5-12:   Mutual exclusion over a class

```
       static synchronized void RaisePressure() {
```

Since there is only one of these methods for the entire class, no matter how many thread objects are created, we have effectively serialized the code that accesses and updates the pressure gauge. Recompiling with this change, and rerunning the code will give this result (and you should try it):

```
% java p
gauge reads 15, safe limit is 20
```

Mutual exclusion over a block of statements

This is achieved by attaching the keyword "synchronized" before a block of code. You also have to explicitly mention in parentheses the object whose lock must be acquired before the region can be entered. Reverting to our original pressure example, we could make the following change inside the method RaisePressure to achieve the necessary mutual exclusion:

```
void RaisePressure() {
    synchronized(O) {
        if (p.pressureGauge < p.safetyLimit-15) {
            try{sleep(100);} catch (Exception e){} // delay
            p.pressureGauge += 15;
        } else ; // pressure too high -- don't add to it.
    }
}
```

We will also need to provide the object O that we are using for synchronization. This declaration will do fine:

```
static Object O = new Object();
```

We could use an existing object, but we do not have a convenient one at hand in this example. The fields "pressureGauge" and "safetyLimit" are ints not Objects, otherwise either of those would be a suitable choice. It is always preferable to use the object that is being updated as the synchronization lock wherever possible. Recompiling with the change, and rerunning the code will give the desired exclusion:

```
% java p
gauge reads 15, safe limit is 20
```

Mutual exclusion over a method

This is achieved by applying the keyword "synchronized" to an ordinary (non-static) method. Note that in this case the object whose lock will provide the mutual exclusion is implicit. It is the "this" object on which the method is invoked.

```
synchronized void foo { ...  }
```

is equivalent to

```
void foo {
  sychronized (this) {
      . . .
  }
}
```

Especially note that making the obvious change to our pressure example will not give the desired result!

```
// this example shows what will NOT work
synchronized void RaisePressure() {
    if (p.pressureGauge < p.safetyLimit-15) {
        try{sleep(100);} catch (Exception e){} // delay
        p.pressureGauge += 15;
    } else ; // pressure too high -- don't add to it.
}
```

The reason is clear: The "this" object is one of the 10 different threads that are created. Each thread will successfully grab its own lock, and there will be no exclusion between the different threads at all.

Synchronized methods are useful when you have several different methods that might be called simultaneously on the same one object. It ensures that at most one of all the methods designated as synchronized will be invoked on that one object at any given instant. In this case we have the reverse: one method in several threads that is called simultaneously on several different objects. Note that synchronized methods all exclude each other, but they do not exclude a non-synchronized method, nor a (synchronized or non-synchronized) static (class) method from running.

Communicating Mutually-Exclusive Threads

Here's where things become downright complicated until you get familiar with the protocol. The hardest kind of threads programming is where the threads need to pass data back and forth to each other. Imagine that we are in the same situation as the previous section. We have threads that process the same data, so we need to run synchronized. However, in our new case, imagine that it's not enough just to say "don't run while I am running." We need the threads to be able to say "OK, I have some data ready for you" and to suspend themselves if there isn't data ready. There is a convenient parallel programming idiom, known as "wait/notify" that does exactly this. Figure 5-13 shows this in four stages.

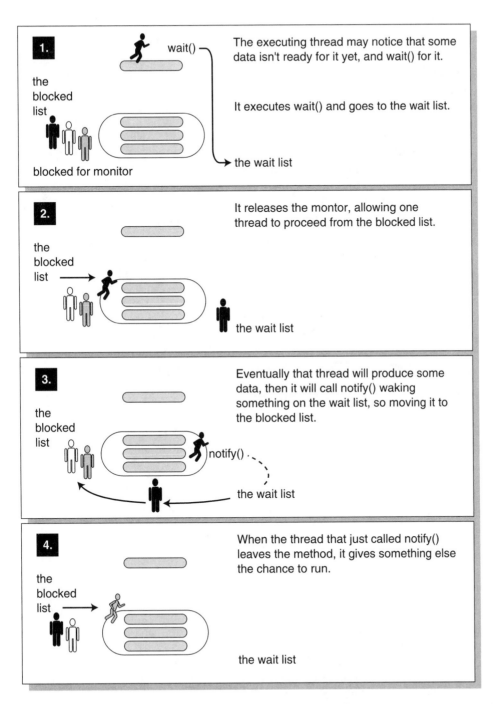

1. The executing thread may notice that some data isn't ready for it yet, and wait() for it.

the blocked list

It executes wait() and goes to the wait list.

blocked for monitor

the wait list

2. It releases the montor, allowing one thread to proceed from the blocked list.

the blocked list

the wait list

3. Eventually that thread will produce some data, then it will call notify() waking something on the wait list, so moving it to the blocked list.

the blocked list

notify()

the wait list

4. When the thread that just called notify() leaves the method, it gives something else the chance to run.

the blocked list

the wait list

Figure 5-13:   Communicating mutually-exclusive threads

Wait/notify is a tricky language-dependent protocol that has been developed by ingenious minds. You just need to accept it as the right solution to this problem. Wait/notify is used when synchronized methods in the same class need to communicate with each other. The most common occurrence of this is a producer/ consumer situation—one thread is producing data irregularly, and another thread is consuming (processing) it.

Methods in the threads are only ever called from within synchronized code, which means they are both only ever called when a mutex lock is held. However, simple synchronization is not enough. The consumer might grab the lock and then find that there is nothing in the buffer to consume. The producer might grab the lock and find that there isn't yet room in the buffer to put something. You could make either of these spin in a busy loop continually grabbing the lock, testing whether they can move some data, releasing the lock if not. But busy loops are never used in production code. They burn CPU cycles without any productive result[2]. The correct approach lies in the two method calls wait() and notify().

- Wait() says, "Oops, even though I have the lock I can't go any further until you have some data for me, so I will release the lock, and suspend myself here. One of you notifiers carry on!"

- Notify() says, "Hey, I just produced some data, so I will release the lock and suspend myself here. One of you waiters carry on!"

The pseudo-code for the way they work is:

```
// producer thread
enter synchronized code (i.e. grab mutex lock)
produce_data()
notify()
leave synchronized code (i.e. release lock)


// consumer thread
enter synchronized code
while( no_data )
    wait()
consume_the_data()
leave synchronized code
```

The consumer waits in a loop because a different consumer may have grabbed the data, in which case it needs to wait again. As we have already seen, entering and

---

2. Well, OK, one of my colleagues pointed out a research paper that showed a brief busy loop followed by a wait/notify was superior to either used alone. Lets leave research papers out of this for now.

leaving synchronized code is trivially achieved by applying the keyword "synchronized" to a method, so the templates become like this:

```
// producer thread
produce_data()
notify()

// consumer thread
while( no_data )
    wait()
consume_the_data()
```

Usually the producer is storing the produced data into some kind of bounded-buffer, which means the producer may fill it up and will need to wait() until there is room. The consumer will need to notify() the producer when something is removed from the buffer. The pseudo-code is:

```
// producer thread—produces one datum
while( buffer_full )
    wait()
produce_data()
notify()

// consumer thread—produces one datum
while( no_data )
    wait()
consume_the_data()
notify
```

The reason we walked through this step-by-step is that it makes the following program a lot easier to understand. So if you didn't follow the pseudo-code above, go back over the previous section again. This code directly implements the pseudo-code, and demonstrates the use of wait/notify in communicating mutually-exclusive threads.

There are three classes below. The first is a class that contains a main driver program. It simply instantiates a producer thread and a consumer thread and lets them go at it.

```
public class plum {
  public static void main(String args[]) {
     Producer p = new Producer();
     p.start();

     Consumer c = new Consumer(p);
     c.start();
  }
}
```

The second class is the Producer class. It implements the pseudo-code above, and demonstrates the use of wait/notify. It has two key methods: one that produces data (actually just reads the number of millisecs the program has been running) and stores it into an array. The other method, called consume(), will try to return successive values from this array. The value of this set-up is that produce() and consume() can be called from separate threads: they won't overrun the array; they won't get something before it has been produced; they won't step on each other; neither ever gets in a busy wait.

```
class Producer extends Thread {
    private String [] buffer = new String [8];
    private int pi = 0;   // produce index
    private int gi = 0;   // get index

    public void run() {
        // just keep producing
        for(;;) produce();
    }

    private final long start = System.currentTimeMillis();
    private final String banana() {
        return "" + (int) (System.currentTimeMillis() - start);
    }

    synchronized void produce() {
        // while there isn't room in the buffer
        while ( pi-gi+1 > buffer.length ) {
            try {wait();} catch(Exception e) {}
        }
        buffer[pi&0x7] = banana();
        System.out.println("produced["+(pi&7)+"] " + buffer[pi&7]);
        pi++;
        notifyAll();
    }

    synchronized String consume(){
        // while there's nothing left to take from the buffer
        while (pi==gi) {
            try {wait();} catch(Exception e) {}
        }
        notifyAll();
        return buffer[ gi++&0x7 ];
    }
}
```

Produce () puts a datum in the butter, and consume () pulls something out to give it to the consumer.

Those expressions like "pi&0x7" are a programming idiom to mask off the bits of the subscript we want. In this case it is convenient to let the subscript be incremented without limit, but make sure that array references only uses the lowest 3 bits of it. It requires the buffer size to be a power of two, which we can easily arrange. If this coding idiom makes you uneasy, change the program to use subscripts that are incremented modulo the buffer size. You'll see it is actually simpler this way.

Finally, the third class is another thread that will be the consumer in this example. It starts off with a common Java idiom: another class is passed into the constructor, and all the constructor does is save a copy of this object for later use. This is the way that the consumer can call the consume() method of the producer.

```
class Consumer extends Thread {
    Producer whoIamTalkingTo;
    // java idiom for a constructor
    Consumer(Producer who) { whoIamTalkingTo = who; }

    public void run() {
        java.util.Random r = new java.util.Random();
        for(;;) {
            String result = whoIamTalkingTo.consume();
            System.out.println("consumed: "+result);
            // next line is just to make it run a bit slower.
            int randomtime = r.nextInt() % 250;
            try{sleep(randomtime);} catch(Exception e){}
        }
    }
}
```

The idiom of passing an object into a constructor that saves the reference to it, for later communicating something back, is a common idiom. You should make especial note of it. Make sure you understand the example above, to see how this is written and used.

The run method of this consumer simply repeats over and over again a get, printing what it got, followed by a sleep for a random period. The sleep is just to give the producer some work to do, in adapting to an asynchronous consumer.

When you compile these three classes together and try running them, you will see output like this:

```
% java plum        produced[0] 12
        produced[1]  18
        produced[2]  20
        produced[3]  22
        produced[4]  24
        produced[5]  26
        produced[6]  29
        produced[7]  31
        consumed: 12
        produced[0]  47
        consumed: 18
        produced[1]  213
        consumed: 20
        produced[2]  217
```

And so on. Notice that the producer filled up the buffer before the consumer ran at all. Then each time the slow consumer removed something from the buffer, the producer re-used that now empty slot. And always the consumer got exactly what was stored there with no data race corruption. If this explanation of wait/notify seems complicated, your impression is correct. Programming threaded code is hard in the general case and these methods supply a specialized feature that makes one aspect of it a little easier. The good news is that, for simple producer/consumer code, you don't have to bother with any of this. Two classes, PipedInputStream and PipedOutputStream, in the I/O library can be used in your code to support simple asynchronous communication between threads. We will look at this later.

Wait and notify are methods in the basic class Object, so they are shared by all objects in the system. There are several variants:

```
public final native void notify();
public final native void notifyAll();

public final void wait() throws InterruptedException;
public final void wait(long time, int nanos) throws InterruptedException;
public final native void wait(long timeout) throws InterruptedException;
```

The difference between notify() and notifyAll() is that notifyAll() wakes up all threads that are in the wait list of this object. That might be appropriate if they are all readers or they are all waiting for the same answer, or can all carry on once the data has been written. In the example there is only one other thread, so notify() or notifyAll() will have the same effect. There are three forms of wait, including two that allow a wait to timeout after the specified period of milliseconds or milliseconds and nanoseconds(!) have elapsed. Why have a separate wait list or 'wait set' for each object, instead of just blocking waiting for the lock? Because the whole point of wait/notifying is to take the objects out of contention for systems resources until they are truly able to run! A notify notifies an arbitrary thread in the wait list. You can't rely on FIFO order.

Let Sleeping Threads Lie

Now we have all that theory behind us, let's explain the minor point of what statements like this mean:

```
try {sleep(randomtime);} catch(Exception e){}
try {wait();} catch(Exception e) {}
```

It's quite easy. One thread can interrupt another sleeping thread by calling its interrupt() method. This will make the interrupted thread wake up. It really needs to be able to tell the difference between waking up because it has been "notified" and waking up because it has been "interrupted." So the second case is detected by raising the exception InterruptedException in the thread. Statements like sleep() and wait() that are potentially prone to being interrupted in the middle need to catch this exception or declare that their method can throw it.

Two further points. I have used the parent type Exception here, instead of the correct subtype, InterruptedException. This was to minimize the size of the lines in the example. Always catch the narrowest type of exception you can or you may catch more than you bargained for. And do something sensible with it, like print an error message. Finally, note that the interrupt() method was not implemented in the first major release of the JDK.

Synchronized code isn't a perfect solution, because a system can still get into deadlock. Deadlock or "deadly embrace" is the situation where there is a circular dependency among several threads between resources held and resources required. In its simplest form, Thread "A" holds lock "X" and needs lock "Y," while Thread "B" holds lock "Y" and is waiting for lock "X" to become free. Result: that part of the system grinds to a halt. This can happen all too easily when one synchronized method calls another. The "volatile" keyword may also be applied to data. This informs the compiler that several threads may be accessing this simultaneously. The data therefore needs to be completely refreshed from memory (rather than a value that was read into a register three cycles ago) and completely stored back on each access. Volatile is also intended for accessing objects like real time clocks that sit on the memory bus. It is convenient to glue them on there, because they can be read and written with the usual "load" and "store" memory access instructions, instead of requiring a dedicated I/O port. They can return the current time via a single cycle read, but the value will change unpredictably due to actions outside the program. Volatile isn't really intended for general use on arbitrary objects in applications. The keyword isn't used anywhere in the current version of the runtime library.

Generalized thread programming is a discipline in its own right, and one that will become increasingly significant now that Java makes it so easy. The Solaris OS kernel is a multi-threaded implementation, and multi-threaded is definitely the future trend. Consult the threads books listed at the end of this chapter for a thorough grounding in the topic of threads programming.

Garbage Collection

Languages with dynamic data structures (structures that can grow and shrink in size at runtime) must have some way of telling the underlying Operating System when they need more memory. Conversely, you also need some way to indicate memory that is no longer in use (e.g. threads that have terminated, objects that are no longer referenced by anything, variables that have gone out of scope, etc.), this can amount to a large amount of memory in a nontrivial program or a program that runs for an extended period of time. Once acquired from the OS, memory is usually never returned to it, but retained for re-use by the program. This will all be taken care of by a storage manager. One subsystem of the storage manager will be a "garbage collector." The automatic reclaiming of memory that is no longer in use is known as "garbage collection" in computer science.

Compiler writers for algorithmic languages have the concept of a "heap" and a "stack." The stack takes care of dynamic memory requirements related to procedure call and return. The heap is responsible for all other dynamic memory. In Java, that's a lot because object allocation is always from the heap. The only variables allocated on the stack are the local variables of a method.[3]

Java is going to give a powerful boost to doctoral dissertations on the subject of speeding up garbage collector algorithms.

In the C language, malloc() allocates memory, and free() makes it available for re-use. In C++, the new and delete operators have the same effect. Both of these languages require explicit deallocation of memory. The programmer has to say what memory to give back, and when. In practice this has turned out to be an error-prone task. It's all too easy to create a "memory leak" by not freeing memory before overwriting the last pointer to it; then it can neither be referenced nor

---

3. Java actually has multiple stacks: it starts out with one for Java code and another stack for C native methods. Additional stacks are allocated for every thread created. This aspect of Java requires a virtual memory mapping system to operate efficiently.

freed. Some X-Windows applications are notorious for leaking even more than Apple Computers' board of directors.

Why do we need Garbage Collection?

Java takes a different approach. Instead of requiring the programmer to take the initiative in freeing memory, the job is given to a runtime component called the garbage collector. It is the job of the garbage collector to sit on top of the heap and periodically scan it to determine things that aren't being used any more. It can reclaim that memory and put it back in the free store pool within the program.

Making garbage collection an implicit operation of the runtime system rather than a responsibility of the programmer has a cost. It means that at unpredictable times, a potentially large amount of behind-the-scenes processing will suddenly start-up when some low-water mark is hit and more memory is called for. This has been a problem with past systems, but Java addresses it somewhat with threads. In a multi-threaded system, the garbage collector can run in parallel with user code and has a much less intrusive effect on the system. It still carries some runtime performance cost however.

Taking away the task of memory management from the programmer gives him or her one less thing to worry about, and makes the resulting software more reliable in use. It may take a little longer to run compared with a language like C++ with explicit memory management because the garbage collector has to go out and look for reclaimable memory rather than simply being told where to find it. On the other hand, it's much quicker to debug and get the program running in the first place. Most people would agree that in the presence of ever-improving hardware performance, a small performance penalty is an acceptable price to pay for more reliable software.

We should mention at this point that there is almost no direct interaction between the programmer and garbage collection. It is one of the runtime services that you can take for granted, like keeping track of return addresses, or identifying the correct handler for an exception. The discussion here is to provide a little more insight into what takes place behind the scenes.

Garbage Collection Algorithms

A number of alternative garbage collection algorithms have been proposed and tried over the years. Three popular ones are "reference counting," "mark and sweep," and "stop and copy."

Reference counting keeps a counter for each chunk of memory allocated. The counter records how many pointers directly point at the chunk or something inside it. The counter needs to be kept up-to-date as assignments are made. If the reference count ever drops to zero, nothing can ever access the memory and so it can immediately be returned to the pool of free storage. The big advantage of reference counting is that it imposes a steady constant overhead, rather than needing aperiodic bursts of the cpu. The big disadvantage of reference counting is that in its simplest incarnation it is fooled by circular references. If A points to B, and B points to A, but nothing else points to A and B they will not be freed even though they could be. It's also a little expensive in multi-threaded environments because reference counts must be locked for mutual exclusion before reference counts are updated.

You can turn off garbage collection in your application, by starting java with this option:

```
java -noasyncgc   ...
```

One reason for doing this might be to experiment and see how much of a difference in performance it makes, if any. You should not turn off garbage collection in a program that may run for an extended period. If you do it is almost guaranteed to fail with memory exhaustion sooner or later.

Alternatively, you can call the method

```
system.gc();
```

to run the garbage collector at any point you choose. 🐛

The current Java implementation from Sun uses the "mark and sweep" garbage collection algorithm. The marker starts at the root pointers. These are things like the stack, and static (global) variables. You can imagine marking with a red pen every object that can be accessed from the roots. Then the marker recursively marks all the objects that are directly or indirectly referenced from the objects reachable from the roots. The process continues until no more red marks can be placed. The entire virtual process may need to be swapped in and looked at, which is expensive in disk traffic and time. A smart garbage collector knows it doesn't have to bring in objects that can't contain references like large graphics images and the like. Then the "sweep" phase starts, and everything without a red mark is swept back onto the free list for re-use. Memory compaction also takes place at this point. Memory compaction means jiggling down into one place all the memory that is in use, so that all the free store comes together and can be merged into one large pool. Compaction helps when you have a number of large objects to allocate.

The current Java implementation from Microsoft is based on the source licensed from Sun. Microsoft did change the garbage collector to one that uses the "stop and copy" algorithm. As the name suggests, it stops all other threads completely and goes into a garbage collection phase, which is simplicity itself. The heap is split into two parts: the currently active part and the new part. Each of these is known as a "semi-space." It copies all the non-garbage stuff over into the new semi-space and makes that the currently-active semi-space. The old currently-active semi-space is just discarded completely. Non-garbage is identified by tracing active pointers, just as in mark and sweep.

The advantage of "stop and copy" is that it avoids heap fragmentation, so periodic memory compaction is not needed. Stop and copy is a fast garbage collection algorithm, but it requires twice the memory area. It also can't be used in real time systems as it makes your computer appear to just freeze from time to time. More about that in the Light Relief section coming up.

Finalizers

A "finalizer" is a Java term, related to but not the same as a C++ destructor. When there are no further references to an object, its storage can be reclaimed by the garbage collector.

A finalizer is a method from class Object that any class may override. If a class has a finalizer method, it will be called on dead instances of that class before the memory occupied by that object is re-used. The programmer makes this possible by providing a body for the method finalize() in the class. It will look like this:

```
class Fruit {

        protected void finalize() {  // do finalization ...
};
```

It must have the signature shown (protected, void, and no arguments).

The Java Language Specification says:

> *"The purpose of finalizers is to provide a chance to free up resources (such as file descriptors or operating system graphics contexts) that are owned by objects but cannot be accessed directly and cannot be freed automatically by the automatic storage management. Simply reclaiming an object's memory by garbage collection would not guarantee that these resources would be reclaimed."*

Finalization was carried over from the Oak language, and justified on the grounds that it would help provide good resource management for long running servers.

If present, a class's finalizer is called by the garbage collector at some point after the object is first recognized as garbage and before the memory is reclaimed, such that the object is garbage at the time of the call. A finalizer can also be called explicitly. In JDK 1.0 there is no guarantee that an object will be garbage collected, and hence there is no guarantee that an object's finalizer will be called. A program may terminate normally without garbage collection taking place. So you could not rely on a finalizer method being called, you cannot use it to carry out some essential final housekeeping (release a lock, write usage statistics, or whatever). Java 1.1 will guarantee that finalizers are run, if the method `System.runFinalizersOnExit()` is called (and accepted by the Security-Manager) before exit.

Finally (uh...) don't confuse "final" (a constant) or "finally" (a block that is always executed after a "try()" with "finalize"—the three concepts are unrelated.

Some Light Relief

The Robot Ping-Pong[4] Player

Computer scientists are always looking for hard new problems to solve. They want the problems to be hard enough to be worth tackling, preferably capable of eventual solution, yet easy to describe (so that you don't have to spend too long educating grant-making organizations on what you'll do with their money).

Constructing a robot that could play ping-pong was proposed years ago as a particularly difficult computer science problem requiring solutions in vision, real-time control, and artificial intelligence.

Various other robots have been proposed and constructed over the years: robots that walk on jointed legs, robots that try to learn from their environment, robots that recognize facial expressions and so on. None has quite achieved the popularity of the ping-pong playing robots. A number of them have been built in the engineering labs of the finest universities around the globe. The researchers even published the official rules of robot ping-pong so they could have tournaments. Several of these were organized by Professor John Billingsley, of the E.& E.E. Department at Portsmouth University.

---

4. "Ping-Pong" is a trademark of Parker Brothers

Extracts From The Official Rules of Robot Ping-Pong

Rule 11: Those parts of the robot visible to the opponent must be black including absorption of infrared in the region of 1 micron wavelength.

Rule 17: The judges may disqualify a robot on the grounds of safety, or penalize it for serious breaches of sportsmanship.

Naturally the students at M.I.T. built their share of robot ping-pong players. Some of the best work was done there, in the Artificial Intelligence labs, where they used Lisp as the implementation language.

Cheaters Never Prosper?

Table tennis is full of surprises. In one world championship after the Cultural Revolution communist China seemed absolutely unbeatable at table tennis. They won every competition in sight, dominating their opponents with surprising spin shots.

Later the truth came out; they were cheating, or at least stretching the rules to breaking point. The communist regime had equipped its teams with special bats. Both sides of the bat looked identical, but they were made out of very different materials. One side of the bat would give a regular shot, the other would help impart a fierce spin. Opponents didn't even know about the trick bats, and had no way of knowing what kind of a shot was coming at them.

The tournament rules were changed. Trick bats were still allowed, but the faces had to be different colors. Communist Chinese domination of the sport came to an end.

A story, probably apocryphal, is told of an early prototype at M.I.T. After several months of hard work, the students finally coaxed the robot into accurately serving a series of balls from its ball magazine. Eagerly the students reloaded it, and fetched their professor to witness the accomplishment. When the balding professor arrived, he stood expectantly at the far end of the table from the robot and gave the signal to proceed.

As soon as the robot started, it launched a series of hard accurate lobs directly at the professor's cranium. No matter how the professor twisted and ducked, the machine kept him in its sights until at last it was out of balls. When all the tears and laughter had finally stopped, the students were cleared of any wrongdoing. It seems that the robot had been set up to target a large illuminated white patch on the wall representing the opponent, and when the luckless teacher stood within range, his bald brow showed up on the vision system as larger, whiter and shinier, so was preferred. This incident allegedly led to the aforementioned rule 11. No word on whether the robot was nailed under rule 17.

The name of Professor Marvin Minsky of MIT is often attached to this story. Professor Minsky is adamant that he was never bombarded with ping pong balls, but he concedes that an early ball catcher robot did once make a grab for his head. That seems to be the origin of this story.

There is an equally apocryphal coda to this story. It seems that the students went on to enter the robot in one of the tournaments where it played quite well for the first 15 minutes. Suddenly, unaccountably, the robot froze completely and let several successive balls from the opponent bounce off its chest without even attempting a return serve. Then equally suddenly it started playing again. A furious debugging session was started, only to pinpoint the cause of the problem almost immediately. The robot was driven by Lisp software. It ran perfectly for a quarter hour until it had exhausted its free memory. At that point the garbage collector kicked in. Nothing else could run until the garbage collector had done its thing, not even the code to return a ball. That's why single threaded systems aren't very good at real-time processing. The workaround was simple: reboot the processor immediately prior to each tournament match.

Exercises

1. Write a program to read the arguments provided on the command line and print the characters of each in reverse order.

2. If you had to read in and sort a file of five hundred words, would you use String, StringBuffer or char[]? Explain your choice.

3. What is the "C++ interoperability problem?" How does it handicap the use of libraries in C++? Is Java any different? Why?

4. How do the "runtime exceptions" differ from exceptions you define? Give six examples of runtime exceptions and explain how each might be generated.

5. Give three examples of when threads might be used to advantage in a program. Describe a circumstance when it would not be advantageous to use threads.

6. What are the two ways of creating a new thread in java?

7. Take your favorite sorting algorithm, and make it multi-threaded. *Hint*: a recursive partitioning algorithm like quicksort is the best candi-

date for this. Quicksort simply divides the array to be sorted into two pieces, then moves numbers about until all the numbers in one piece are smaller (or at least no larger) than all the numbers in the other piece. Repeat the algorithm on each of the pieces. When the pieces consist of just one element, the array is sorted.

Further Reading

Threads Primer: A Guide to Multithreaded Programming

by Bil Lewis/Daniel J. Berg

published by SunSoft Press/Prentice Hall, 1995.

ISBN: 0-13-443698-9

The definitive introduction to threads programming.

There is a survey of garbage collection techniques at

ftp://ftp.cs.utexas.edu/pub/garbage/bigsurv.ps

A Robot Ping-Pong Player: an experiment in real-time intelligent control

by Russell L. Andersson,

published by the M.I.T. Press, Cambridge, MA, 1988

ISBN: 0-262-01101-8

A rather stuffy book that completely shies away from the essential levity of the subject matter, in favor of dragging in a lot of guff about polynomials and trajectories. Doesn't mention either of the two stories above, but the system was written in C and the book includes several interesting C listings.

Programming with Threads

by Steve Kleiman, Devang Shah, and Bart Smaalders

published by SunSoft Press/Prentice Hall, 1996

ISBN: 0-13-172389-8

Written by senior threads development engineers at Sun Microsystems, this is a comprehensive reference work on threads. This book was introduced in February 1996.

CHAPTER 6

Practical Examples Explained

> "As a matter of fact a high tree makes a wretched sniping post, and I
> rarely allowed one to be used on our side. But we found that the German
> sense of humor appears to be much tickled by seeing, or thinking that he
> sees, a Britisher falling out of a tree. When our sniping became very good,
> and the enemy consequently shy of giving a target, a dummy in a tree
> worked by a rope sometimes caused Fritz and Hans to show themselves
> unwisely. One had to be very careful not to go too far in this sort of work
> or trickery, lest a **minenwerfer** should take his part in the duel."
>
> *Major H. Hesketh-Prichard, DSO, MC*
> *"Sniping in France"*

This chapter contains a nontrivial Java program annotated with a running commentary. The program source appears on the CD accompanying this book, so you can look at it without the annotation, and you can try compiling and running it without typing it in.

The program generates anagrams (letter rearrangements). You give it a word or phrase, and it comes back with all the substring combinations that it can find in the dictionary. You need to provide it with a wordlist that it will use as a dictionary[1], and you can also specify the minimum length of words in the anagrams that it generates.

For any phrases more than a few letters long, there are a lot more anagrams than you would ever think possible.

Case Study Java Program

Here is an example of running the program on the infamous "surfing the Internet" phrase, specifying words of length four or longer. It finds dozens and dozens of them, starting like this:

```
java anagram "surfing the internet" 4
reading word list...
main dictionary has 25144 entries.
least common letter is 'f'

fritter shunt engine
fritter hung intense
surfeit Ghent intern
surfeit ninth regent
furnish greet intent
furnish egret intent
furnish tent integer
further stint engine
further singe intent
further tinge tennis
further gin sentient
freight nurse intent
freight runt intense
freight turn intense
freight run sentient
freight nun interest
freight sen nutrient
freeing Hurst intent
    . . .
```

If you specify a length argument, it will try to use words with at least that many characters, but the final word it finds to complete the anagram may be shorter. This program is written as an application, so there is no issue about accessing files.

---

1. If you don't have such a word list (e.g. in your spellchecker), there are several alternatives available for downloading, e.g. at: http://web.soi.city.ac.uk:8080/text/roget/thesaurus.html, or, http://math-www.uni-paderborn.de/HTML/Dictionaries.html. Both of these sites contain links to several dictionaries. On Unix, just use the file /usr/dict/words.

Here is the annotated program source:

```
/*
 * Usage: anagram string [[min-len] wordfile]
 * Java Anagram program, Peter van der Linden Jan 7, 1996.
 */
```

```
import java.io.*;
```

Note, the "using an interface to hold useful constants" idiom was explained in Chapter 4.

```
interface UsefulConstants {
    public static final int MAXWORDS = 50000;
    public static final int MAXWORDLEN = 30;
    public static final int EOF = -1;
```

Note the way a reference variable can be used to provide a shorter name for another object.

We can now say "o.println()" instead of "System.out.println()".

```
    // shorter alias for I/O streams
    public static final PrintStream o = System.out;
    public static final PrintStream e = System.err;
}
```

```
class Word {
    int mask;
    byte count[]= new byte[26];
    int total;
    String aword;
```

This is an important data structure for representing one word. We keep it as a string, we note the total number of letters in the word, the count of each letter and a bitmask of the alphabet. A zero at bit N means the letter that comes Nth in the alphabet is in the word. A one means that letter is not in the word. This allows for some fast comparisons later on for "how much overlap is there between these two strings?"

```
Word(String s)    // construct an entry from a string
{
    int ch;
    aword = s;
    mask = ~0;
    total = 0;
    s = s.toLowerCase();
    for (int i = 'a'; i <= 'z'; i++) count[i-'a'] = 0;

    for (int i = s.length()-1; i >= 0; i--) {
        ch = s.charAt(i) - 'a';
        if (ch >= 0 && ch < 26) {
            total++;
            count[ch]++;
            mask &= ~(1 << ch);
        }
    }
}
}
```

The program has the following steps:

1.   Read in a list of real words, and convert each word into a form that makes it easy to compare on the quantity and value of letters.

2.   Get the word or phrase we are anagramming, and convert it into the same form.

3.   Go through the list of words, using our helpful comparison to make a second list of those which can be part of a possible anagram. Words that can be part of a possible anagram are those which only have the same letters as appear in the anagram, and do not have more of any one letter than appears in the anagram.

4.   Go through our extracted list of candidate words. Choose the most difficult letter (the one that appears least often) to start with. Take words with it in, and call the anagram finder recursively to fill out the rest of the letters from the candidate dictionary.

The class "Word" above is the class that deals with one word from the wordlist and puts it in the special "easy to compare" form.

In several places in this program, characters are used as the basis for an index into an array. The line below, from the Word() constructor is an example of this.

```
for (int i='a'; i <= 'z'; i++) count[i-'a'] = 0;
```

In C, this is the classic example of something that would work on a system with an ASCII codeset, but fail on an EBCDIC machine since the alphabetic letters are not contiguous in EBCDIC. Java's use of Unicode ensures that this idiom works on all systems. On say a Sun Ultra workstation, the code

```
int i='a';
System.out.println("i = " + i);
```

gives the expected "i = 97" because that is the decimal value that represents lower case A in both ASCII and Unicode. However, you would even get the same result on an IBM System/390 where an EBCDIC 'a' is decimal 121, as Java guarantees and requires the internal representation of a character to be 16-bit Unicode. The runtime system will need to do the translation from/to EBCDIC on input/output.

IBM and the Java Ports

IBM is the only company of any consequence still using EBCDIC, which is a holdover from the days when its mainframe computer systems ruled the earth. However the issue of EBCDIC is of more than theoretical interest as IBM has announced that it is porting Java to its MVS mainframe operating system (to slow the migration of "right-sizing" applications to workstations).

IBM finally delivered a Windows 3.1 port of Java. The port is admittedly more arduous because the underlying system does not have threads, and does not support proper filenames (limiting them to 8 characters and a 3 character extension). No doubt IBM will eventually deliver the port.

Their port of JDK 1.0.2 to Windows 3.1 became available in August 1996 and can be downloaded from http://www.alphaWorks.ibm.com♥

The class "WordList" below is the one that reads in a word list, and builds up an entire dictionary of all words in the special format:

```
class WordList implements UsefulConstants {
    static Word[] Dictionary= new Word[MAXWORDS];
    static int totWords=0;

    static void ReadDict(String f)
    {
```

The half dozen lines that follow are a very common idiom for opening a file. This can throw an exception, so we either deal with it here or declare it in the method. It is usually easiest to deal with exceptions closest to the point where they are raised, if you are going to catch them at all.

Here we catch the exception, print out a diagnostic, then re-throw a RuntimeException to cause the program to stop with a backtrace. We could exit the program at this point, but re-throwing the exception ensures that it will be recognized that an error has occurred. We throw RuntimeException rather than our original exception because RuntimeException *does not have to be handled or declared.* Now that we have printed a diagnostic at the point of error, it is acceptable to take this shortcut:

```
FileInputStream fis;
try fis = new FileInputStream(f);
catch (FileNotFoundException fnfe) {
    e.println ("Cannot open the file of words '" + f + "'");
    throw new RuntimeException();
}
e.println("reading dictionary...");
```

It is better not to have any arbitrary fixed size arrays in your code. This one is done for convenience. Removing the limitation is one of the programming challenges at the end of this example. The buffer holds the characters of a word as we read them in from the word list and assemble them.

```
char buffer[] = new char[MAXWORDLEN];
String s;
int r =0;
while (r!=EOF) {
    int i=0;
    try {
        // read a word in from the word file
        while ( (r=fis.read()) != EOF ) {
            if ( r == '\n' ) break;
            buffer[i++] = (char) r;
        }
    } catch (IOException ioe) {
        e.println ("Cannot read the file of words ");
        throw new RuntimeException();
    }
```

This simple looking constructor to create a new Word object actually does the complicated conversion of a string into the form convenient for further processing (the dozen or so lines of code in class Word).

```
            s=new String(buffer,0,i);
            Dictionary[totWords] = new Word(s);
            totWords++;
        }


        e.println("main dictionary has " + totWords + " entries.");
    }


}
```

An example of a class that is both a subclass and an implementation follows. It extends and implements:

```
class anagram extends WordList implements UsefulConstants {

    static Word[] Candidate = new Word[MAXWORDS];
    static int totCandidates=0,
            MinimumLength = 3;
```

We just made it implement UsefulConstants to show that a class can implement and extend at the same time. In practice, since anagram's parent class implements UsefulConstants, that namespace is already present in the subclass.

This is the main routine where execution starts:

```
    public static void main(String[] argv)
    {
        if ( argv.length < 1 || argv.length > 3) {
            e.println("Usage: anagram  string-to-anagram "
                        + "[min-len [word file]]");
            return;
        }
        if (argv.length >= 2)
            MinimumLength = Integer.parseInt(argv[1]);
```

If the name of a words list isn't explicitly provided as an argument, the program expects to find a file called "words.txt" in the current directory. This will simply be an ASCII file with a few hundred or thousand words, one word per line, no definitions or other information.

```
    // word filename is optional 3rd argument
      ReadDict ( argv.length==3? argv[2]  : "words.txt" );
      DoAnagrams (argv[0]);
}

static void DoAnagrams (String anag)
{
    Word myAnagram = new Word(anag);

    myAnagram.mask = ~myAnagram.mask;
```

The next couple of lines go through the list of words that we read in, and extract the ones that could be part of the phrase to anagram. These words are extracted into a second word list or dictionary, called "Candidates." The dictionary of Candidate words is sorted.

```
      getCandidates (myAnagram);

      int RootIndexEnd = sortCandidates (myAnagram);
```

This call says "Find an anagram of the string "myAnagram," using this working storage, you're at level 0 (first attempt), and considering candidate words zero through RootIndexEnd".

```
      FindAnagram(myAnagram, new String[50],  0, 0, RootIndexEnd);

      o.println("----" + anag + "----");
}
```

This is how a word becomes a candidate:

1. The candidate must only have letters that appear in the anagram (this is the fast overlap test that a bit mask representation provides).

2. It must also be no shorter than the minimum length we specified.

3. It must not be too long.

4. And it must not have more of any one letter than the anagram has.

If the word meets all these conditions, add it to the candidates dictionary.

```
    static void getCandidates(Word d)
    {
        for (int i = totCandidates = 0; i < totWords; i++)
            if (    (  (Dictionary[i].mask | d.mask) == (int)~0)
                && (   Dictionary[i].total >= MinimumLength    )
                && (   Dictionary[i].total + MinimumLength <= d.total
                    || Dictionary[i].total == d.total)
                && ( fewerOfEachLetter(d.count,
                     Dictionary[i].count) )   )

                    Candidate[totCandidates++]=Dictionary[i];

        e.println("Dictionary of words-that-are-substring-anagrams has "
                    + totCandidates + " entries.");
//      PrintCandidate();
    }


    static boolean fewerOfEachLetter(byte anagCount[], byte
entryCount[])
    {
        for (int i = 25; i >= 0; i--)
            if (entryCount[i] > anagCount[i]) return false;
        return true;
    }

    static void PrintCandidate()
    {
        for (int i = 0; i < totCandidates; i++)
            o.print( Candidate[i].aword + ", "
                    + ((i%4 == 3)?"\n":" " ) );
        o.println("");
    }
```

Here's where we start trying to assemble anagrams out of the words in the candidates dictionary.

```
static void FindAnagram(Word d,
                        String WordArray[],
                        int Level, int StartAt, int EndAt)
{
    int i, j;
    boolean enoughCommonLetters;
    Word WordToPass = new Word("");

    for (i = StartAt; i < EndAt; i++) {
        if ( (d.mask | Candidate[i].mask) != 0) {
            enoughCommonLetters = true;
            for (j = 25; j >=0 && enoughCommonLetters; j--)
                if (d.count[j] < Candidate[i].count[j])
                    enoughCommonLetters = false;

            if (enoughCommonLetters) {
                WordArray[Level] = Candidate[i].aword;
                WordToPass.mask = 0;
                WordToPass.total = 0;
                for (j = 25; j >= 0; j--) {
```

The cast to (byte) is needed whenever a byte receives the value of an arithmetic expression. It assures the compiler that the programer realizes the expression was evaluated in at least 32 bits and the result will be truncated before storing in the byte.

```
                    WordToPass.count[j] = (byte)
                    (    d.count[j] -
                         Candidate[i].count[j] );
                    if ( WordToPass.count[j] != 0 ) {
                        WordToPass.total +=
                            (int)WordToPass.count[j];
                        WordToPass.mask |= 1 << j;
                    }
                }
                if (WordToPass.total == 0) {
                    /* Found a series of words! */
                    for (j = 0; j <= Level; j++)
                        o.print(WordArray[j] + " ");
                    o.println();
                } else if (WordToPass.total < MinimumLength) {
                    ; /* Don't call again */
                } else {
```

The recursive call to find anagrams for the remaining letters in the phrase.

```
                    FindAnagram(WordToPass, WordArray, Level+1,
                        i, totCandidates);
                }
            }
        }
    }
}


static int SortMask;

static int sortCandidates(Word d)
{
    int [] MasterCount=new int[26];
    int LeastCommonIndex=0, LeastCommonCount;
    int i, j;

    for (j = 25; j >= 0; j--) MasterCount[j] = 0;
    for (i = totCandidates-1; i >= 0; i--)
        for (j = 25; j >= 0; j--)
            MasterCount[j] += Candidate[i].count[j];

    LeastCommonCount = MAXWORDS * 5;
    for (j = 25; j >= 0; j--)
        if (    MasterCount[j] != 0
             && MasterCount[j] < LeastCommonCount
             && (d.mask & (1 << j) ) != 0   ) {
            LeastCommonCount = MasterCount[j];
            LeastCommonIndex = j;
        }

    SortMask = (1 << LeastCommonIndex);

    quickSort(0, totCandidates-1 );

    for (i = 0; i < totCandidates; i++)
        if ((SortMask & ~Candidate[i].mask) == 0)
            break;
```

The root breadth is the first word in the sorted candidate dictionary that doesn't contain the least common letter. Since the least common letter will be hard to match, we plan to start out by using all the words with it in as the roots of our search. The breadth part is that it represents the number of alternatives to start with.

```
            e.println("least common letter is '"
                     + (char)(LeastCommonIndex+'a') + "'" );
            e.println("words with least common letter: " + i + " words");
            return i;
    }
```

Sort the dictionary of Candidate words, using the standard quicksort algorithm from any Algorithm book. This one was adapted from page 87 of K&R Edition 2. Again, it shows that recursion is fine in Java.[2]

```
    static void quickSort(int left, int right)
    {
        // standard quicksort from any algorithm book
        int i, last;
        if (left >= right) return;
        swap(left, (left+right)/2);
        last = left;
        for (i=left+1; i<=right; i++)   /* partition */
            if (MultiFieldCompare( Candidate[i],
                                    Candidate[left] ) == -1 )
                swap( ++last, i);

        swap(last, left);
        quickSort(left, last-1);
        quickSort(last+1,right);
    }

    static int MultiFieldCompare(Word s, Word t)
    {
        if ( (s.mask & SortMask) != (t.mask & SortMask) )
            return ( (s.mask & SortMask)>(t.mask & SortMask)? 1:-1);

        if ( t.total != s.total )
            return (t.total - s.total);

        return (s.aword).compareTo(t.aword);
    }

    static void swap(int d1, int d2) {
        Word tmp = Candidate[d1];
        Candidate[d1] = Candidate[d2];
        Candidate[d2] = tmp;
    }

}
```

2. This anagram program was based on a C program that my colleague Brian Scearce wrote in his copious free time.

When I wrote the above Java code, my first version had a bug in it. In the following code, I had omitted to subtract 1 from the String length, (also I did not check that the character was alphabetic before putting it in the data structure). Instead of looking like this:

GOOD CODE

```
for (int i = s.length()-1; i >= 0; i--) {
            ...s.charAt(i)...
```

I had it like this:

BAD CODE

```
for (int i = s.length(); i >= 0; i--) {
            ...s.charAt(i)...
```

In a C program, this would cause no anagrams to be found, but the program would run to completion. There would not be any indication that an error had occurred, or where. A naive tester would report that the program worked fine. Works fine? Ship it!

In my java program, this was the output from my first test run:

```
java.lang.StringIndexOutOfBoundsException: String index out of range: 4
        at java.lang.String.charAt(String.java)
        at Word.<init>(anagram.java:35)
        at WordList.ReadDict(anagram.java:77)
        at anagram.main(anagram.java:104)
```

It told me an error had occurred, what the error was, why it was an error, where in the program it happened, and how execution reached that point. Some other languages have this kind of comprehensive runtime checking (Ada comes to mind), but Java is the only one that is also both object-oriented and has a C flavor. At that moment, as they say, I became enlightened.

Utilities

There are some built-in utilities in the package java.util such that a class for the data structure you want may already exist. There is a utility class called Vector, for instance. The class java.util.Vector presents an array into which you can insert elements. The array will be grown behind the scenes as necessary to hold whatever you add to it. This does the job of a linked list, but is even better because you also have random access to the individual elements.

Here's how you can time your Java code:

```
long start = System.currentTimeMillis();
    :   // do the work here
    :
long stop = System.currentTimeMillis();
System.out.println("Run time: " + (stop-start) +
                            "millisecs" );
```

Take a look at the other routines available in $JAVAHOME/src/java/lang/
System.java. Contrast the Java situation of many utility packages, and guaranteed interoperability, with that of C++. When C++ first became available, there were few utility classes, but everyone used the same compiler (cfront from AT&T). Later when utility libraries became available from third parties, there were sometimes several alternative compilers available for a given platform. That turned out to cause problems. The lack of a C++ Application Binary Interface (ABI) that specified details like name-mangling, exception handling, and argument passing meant that software from different compilers was usually *not* interoperable.

The Guilty Secret of C++: lack of interoperability

A C++ binary package you bought to support linked lists will not work with just any compiler. And it might not work with a different library you bought from another vendor. To stand a reasonable chance of getting libraries to work together you either need access to the source to recompile it in your own environment or you need the library vendor to maintain a special version just for the compiler you are using. The C++ language has been handicapped by this dirty secret for several years. Until there is a standard, stable C++ language, it's hard to have a standard, stable ABI.

The standard API and ABI, fixed for all platforms, is an important part of the basic design of Java. It will avoid the "every compiler shows a different interface" problem. Table 6-1 shows some of the Java utility classes that exist in every implementation:

Table 6-1: Java Utility Classes

java.util.*	Notes
BitSet.java	An array of bits indexed by subscript. The collection grows as you need to add more bits.
Date.java	A class to process day/dates in a system independent way. Gives access to year, month, day, hour, minute and second.
Enumeration.java	An interface that specifies two methods to help count through a set of values.
Hashtable.java	A very useful class! This class maintains a hash table that holds object-and-key pairs. This class lets you impose some order and storage capability on arbitrary objects.
Properties.java	Persistent properties class. Can save a hash table to a stream, and read one back in again. It is an extension of the Hash table class. This is also used for the System properties (used instead of environment variables).

Table 6-1: Java Utility Classes (Continued)

java.util.*	Notes
Random.java	Generates pseudo-random numbers in various useful forms and types. Can be completely different each time, or provide the same sequence of random numbers (for testing).
Stack.java	Implements a last-in/first-out stack of objects.
StringTokenizer.java	Does simple lexing (separation into individual tokens removing white space) on a text string.
Vector.java	Data structure that can hold a collection of arbitrary objects, and provide immediate access by subscript to them. The array will be extended as needed as more objects are added to it.

Hash Table Explanation

A symbol table in a compiler is often maintained as a hash table. When a name is first read in from the source program, it is hashed (converted to a hash-key value, say 379, by an algorithm designed to spread the values around the table) and entered in the table at location 379 along with all its characteristics (type, scope, etc.). Then when you get the same name again, it is hashed, and the same result, 379, is used as a subscript for immediate access to all its details in the hash table. It is marvellous that a hash table is a library data structure in Java!

Why is a hash table better than just maintaining a sorted list or vector? Because hashing is fast, and sorting is slow.

Go to the directory with the Java library source on your system ($JAVAHOME/ src/java) and cd. In into the util subdirectory, follow these three steps:

1.   List the directory contents. These are the java source files for the utility programs.

2.   Look at the source of any five programs there. Read all the methods. Look at the implementation. Why does it do what it does? If your boss offered you a 10,000 zloty bonus to make one of these methods faster, which one would you select and how would you do it?

3.   Run javadoc on a five different source files and read the resultant html files. (Medium). 🍎

Basic Utilities

The utility classes are used throughout the Java system, and can be found in the java.util package. You can review the source files at $JAVAHOME/src/java/util. The widely-used classes in the util package, and their purposes are shown in the following paragraphs.

BitSet

This class maintains a set of bits that are identified by the value of an integer, like an array index. You can have up to about 2 billion individual bits in a set (if you have enough virtual memort), each of which can be queried, set, cleared and so on. The bit set will be increased dynamically as needed to accommodate extra bits you add to it.

```
public BitSet();  // constructor
public BitSet(int N);  // constructor for set of size N bits

public void or (BitSet s);   // OR's one bit set against another.

public void set (int i); // sets bit number i.

public int size(); // returns the number of bits in the set.
```

Date

This class attempts to represent dates and times, but has been criticized for its poor design. Among its other questionable features are that:

- It numbers months starting at 0 (rather than 1 as used on planet earth). Day-of-the-month starts at 1 as expected.

- It will happily construct dates out of invalid input like January 32 (the code author proudly announces that this "feature" allows you to find the difference between two days).

- It fails to parse certain RFC822 style dates, namely those with negative time zone offsets, like: "Thu, 5 Sep 1996 17:44:11 -0700."

- The documentation claims that it limits itself to years after the year 1900. Actually, you can't set a date before Jan 1 1970. So most of history can't be stored or computed.

- The external representation of a year is "years since 1900," so the year 2001 will be given to the programmer as the year 101, which is counterintuitive to say the least, as it no longer matches the least significant digits of the full year.

You can construct dates from a string, or by giving integers representing the year, month and date (and optionally hours and minutes). You can also construct a date by providing a long that holds "number of milliseconds since midnight Jan 1 1970." Typical methods are:

```
public Date();      // today's date and time

public Date(int year, int mon, int date);  // construct date

public boolean after(Date when); // compare

public String toGMTString(); // transforms this into a string
```

The source for Date has a half page comment in the front yammering about leap seconds. It serves as a reminder that even excellent programmers can occasionally turn out substandard code when their work isn't adequately reviewed. Fortunately, Date is not a final class, so it can be overridden and fixed up a bit. This was done by the database crowd to get an implementation of Date that mapped onto SQL.

Enumeration

This is an interface that specifies just two methods. A class will implement these methods to supply a way to enumerate or count through, all its objects, or all the values held in one object, whichever makes the most sense for you to implement. For an array, enumeration is simply going from a[0] to a[n], but for a binary tree a little more effort is needed. The Enumeration interface allows that effort to be encapsulated and hidden from user classes. The methods are:

```
boolean hasMoreElements();

Object nextElement();
```

The method above returns the next element of the enumeration. It will throw the runtime exception NoSuchElementException if there is no next element. Here is how a class might implement Enumeration:

```
import java.util.*;
public class el implements Enumeration {

    private int a[] = {9,1,8,2,4,7};

    private int i=0;

    public boolean hasMoreElements(){
        return (i<a.length);
    }

    public Object nextElement() {
        if (i>=a.length) throw new NoSuchElementException();
        return new Integer( a[i++] );
    }
}
```

Notice how we have to wrap each int in an Integer to send it back as we enumerate. Enumerations only work on objects. A class that uses class el can easily "thumb through" each element of the array using the enumeration. A class that implements Enumeration is offering a service to other classes—it provides an easy way to step through every data item belonging to an object, along these lines:

```
while( o.hasMoreElements() )
    doSomethingWith( o.nextElement() );
```

The example above uses an array because these are easy to understand But, the real value of enumerations is in using them on data structures that don't already provide trivial access to all the elements such as trees, hash tables, graphs and the like.

You can only enumerate an object once. If you need to list all the elements of an enumeration twice, save any references to them in a Vector as they go by.

Hashtable

A supremely useful class. It allows you store together an arbitrary number of arbitrary objects. Instead of storing items with index values 0,1,2,3 as you would in an array, you provide the key which is to be associated with the object.

Then in future, you only need provide that key again, and voila, out pops the right object. If you cast your mind back to the class Object, you'll recall that each object in a Java system can call hashCode(), because this is a method in Object. You will usually use Object.hashCode or your overridden version of it, as the key. If you override hashCode for one of your classes, you must make sure that the method equal() is still consistent with it (namely, if two different Objects compare equal, they must also have the same hashCode()). This is because hashCode() and equal() are both used when accessing data in a hash table. Another way to state the requirement is that you should only overload equal() and hashCode() as a matched pair.

The type String is one class where hashCode() and equal() are both overridden. Rather than the default definition of equal of "is at the same address as," we want two Strings to be equal if they have the same characters in the same order. Accordingly, hashCodes for Strings are calculated by number-crunching the characters in the string. Strings with the same contents will then have the same hashcode. Typical Hash Table methods are:

```
public Hashtable();    // constructor

public synchronized boolean contains(Object value);
     // says whether this value is already in the table.

public synchronized Object put(Object key, Object value);
     // puts this object in the table with this key

public synchronized Object get(Object key);
     // retrieves the object for this key
```

There is a good example of the use of a HashTable on the CD that comes with this book. It is in the origami program which displays how to fold a piece of paper for interesting effects.

When I wrote the Origami applet (this appears as an example on the CD), I simply had it read the parameters that were lists of coordinate points, and draw lines between the pairs of points. If you drew the lines right, they looked like a sheet of paper being folded. The parameter file might contain "70 90 100 125," that tells the program to draw line from (70,90) to (100,125).

A typical origami creation might contain two dozen folds, each made up of a dozen lines. If so, the data becomes almost unreadable to a human. The way to simplify this is to allow names to be associated with a line by using the String as a key and storing the four numbers (a coordinate pair for each end of the line) as the hash table entry. Then I could refer to that line symbolically by name for the rest of the parameter file. When the program found the definition of a name, it would put the coordinates in the hash table using the name as the key. When it just found the name it could retrieve the coordinates with a single statement.

```
Hashtable         H = new Hashtable(100);
 ...

String s = theName;   // get the word
//look it up in the hashtable
CoordPair cp = (CoordPair) H.get(s);

if (cp==null) {
    //if not in hash table, add it.
        cp = new CoordPair();
        cp.x1 = ax;
        cp.y1 = ay;
        cp.x2 = bx;
        cp.y2 = by;
        try{
            H.put(s, cp);
        } catch(Exception e){}
}

    // now we can draw using the cp coordinates
```

It was a very simple amendment to the applet, and the code worked the very first time (after years of programming in C, this is a refreshingly novel and frequent experience in Java). It allowed the parameter file to contain lines like "top-side," instead of the coordinates "70 90 150 90" corresponding to the line, along the top.

Note that only Objects can be stored in a HashTable. If you want to put primitive types in (as I did above) you have to wrap them in an object wrapper. That is the purpose of the CoordPair class.

Properties

As you were reading the description for HashTable, the remark about key/ value pairs may have reminded you of the System Properties sometimes seen in applets. The Properties class is really just an instance of HashTable with a few extra methods wrapped around it.

This utility class has two purposes: First, it allows a property table to be read in and written out via streams. And, second, it allows programmers to search more than one property table with a single command. If you don't need either of these benefits, then just use a HashTable instead of a Properties table. Typical methods are:

```
public String getProperty(String key);

public synchronized void load(InputStream in)
    throws IOException;
// reads key/value pairs in from a stream, stores them in this

public synchronized void save(OutputStream out, String header);
// writes the key/value pairs out as text
// the header is just a comment string you provide to label the
// the property table. The current date is also appended to it.
```

To put entries in a Properties object, just use the put(Object key, Object element) method inherited from HashTable. So that you don't feel obliged to start adding to the predefined system property table, there's a feature that you can provide an existing properties table to a constructor. This creates an empty properties list that you can populate. Whenever you do a getProperty, it will search your table. If nothing is found, it will go on to search the table provided to the constructor. Here is an example:

```
Properties sp = System.getProperties();
Properties mytable = new Properties(sp);
mytable.list(System.out);
```

The first line gets the standard predefined properties table. The second line piggybacks it onto a second Properties table that we create and can fill with a call like: mytable.put ("propertyname", "propertyvalue"). When we do a lookup in mytable, it will look up first in mytable and then in the system properties table. The third line prints mytable out (intended for debugging, but it's not clear why you can't just use the save() method). The method public String getProperty(String key, String default); will return the default String if there is no entry for this key in the table.

Random

This is a class to provide pseudo-random numbers. We call them "pseudo-random" rather than random because the source of bits is an algorithm. To the casual observer it looks like a random stream of bits and for most applications we can pretend that they are. The numbers aren't really random, though, and sequences tend to get stuck in repetitive cycles after a large number of iterations.

If you just quickly want a random number between 0.0 and 1.0, then package Math has a method random, which is just a wrapper for instantiating Random one time, and then supplying values. You would call it like this:

```
double d = Math.random();  // 0.0 .. 1.0
```

Typical methods of the package Random are:

```
public Random(long seed);
// using the same seed gives the same sequence of numbers.

public int nextInt();     // returns a random int
public long nextLong();   // returns a random long
public double nextDouble();  // returns value in range 0.0 to 1.0

public synchronized double nextGaussian();
// a Gaussian distribution has mean 0.0, standard deviation 1.0.
```

This provides numbers symetrically distributed around zero, and successively unlikelier to be picked the further away from zero you get. If we collected a group of these numbers and plotted them, they would form the shape of a bell curve.

Exercise: Convince yourself of this by writing a program to actually do it. *Hint:* You'll find it easier plot a graph using ASCII text if you generate the values first, save them in an array, and sort the array into order before plotting the values.

The algorithm used here for taking random values from a Gaussian distribution is from "The Art of Computer Programming" by Donald Knuth, Section 3.4.1 Algorithm C.

To get a random int value in a certain range (say, 1 to 6) to simulate the cast of a die, you would use:

```
Random r = new Random();
int myturn = 1 + Math.abs(r.nextInt()) % 6;
```

To get a random double value in a certain range (say, 0.0 to 100.0) to simulate a percentage, you would scale it up with multiplication:

```
double mypercent = r.nextDouble() * 100.0;
```

You can instantiate Random with or without a seed. If you don't give it a seed, it uses the current reading from the day/time clock (the millisecond part of this is going to be pretty close to random). If you choose to supply the seed, you will get the same series of random numbers every time you supply that same seed. This is useful in testing and debugging code.

If pseudo-randomness isn't good enough, believe it or not you can buy CDs full of truly random numbers for use in one-time pad encryption and other applications.

Vector

The Vector class should be thought of as an array that grows without bounds, as needed to store the number of elements you want to put there. You don't index it with the array brackets "[...]," instead there are several methods to get and set the elements at particular indices.

"Under the covers" this class is implemented as a regular array. When you want to add an element and the array is already full, a new, larger array is allocated to make room, and the old array is copied over. To cut down on incremental reallocation, you can provide hints to the runtime system as to how many elements the array should grow by. Typical methods are:

```
public Vector(int startSize, int growthIncrement); // a constructor

public final synchronized void addElement(Object o);
// adds the object to the next highest location in the vector.

public final synchronized void insertElementAt(Object o, int index);
// adds the object to the vector at the given index.

public final int size();  // the number of objects in the vector.

public final synchronized Object elementAt(int index);
// returns the object in the vector at the given index.

public final synchronized Enumeration elements();
// returns an enumeration object for this vector, allowing every
// object in the vector to be looked at in one pass
```

There are a dozen other methods, as well, that will clear the vector, set its size, turn it into a string and so on.

Stack

The stack class maintains a "last-in-first-out" stack of Objects. You can push (store) objects to arbitrary depth. The methods are:

```
public Object push(Object item);   // add to top of stack.

public Object pop();    // get top of stack.

In addition there are 3 other methods not usually provided
for stacks.

public boolean empty(); // nothing on the stack?

public Object peek();   // returns top Object without popping it.

public int search (Object o); // returns how far down the stack
// this object is (1 is at the top), or -1 if not found.
```

The author of this class made an interesting mistake. He made Stack a subclass of Vector, so that he would get the vector behavior of allowing unbounded input. He failed to notice that it meant all the methods of Vector would be available in

Stack—including inappropriate methods like removeElementAt() to pull something out of the middle of a vector. So Stack does not guarantee Last-In-First-Out behavior. Hans Rohnert from Germany pointed this out to me in email. As Hans put it, it is not true that Stack "is a" Vector, rather it should "have a" Vector in which to store.

The usual way to "hide" unwanted methods from a base class is to override them with private versions, or empty versions or versions that throw a run time exception. In this case, Vector.removeElementAt(int) is final, and final methods can't be overriden. Some of these utility packages were written very quickly by skilled programmers who were more interested in getting the code working than achieving a perfect design. It's easier to find flaws in code than it is to write faultless software. Pointing out the occasional defect here is meant to instruct, not to denigrate the work of others.

StringTokenizer

The fundamental idea of StringTokenizer is to instantiate it with a string, and it will then break that string up into islands of characters separated by seas of white space. If you gave it the string "Noel Bat is a fossil," successive calls to nextToken would return the individual strings "Noel" followed by "Bat" then "is" then "a" then "fossil" then a further call would throw the NoSuchElementException.

Actually you can specify the delimiters for the substring, and they don't have to be white space. One of the constructors allows for new delimiting characters to be set and also takes a boolean saying whether the delimiters themselves should be returned. The representative methods are:

```
public StringTokenizer(String words_to_breakup); // constructor

public  StringTokenizer(String words_to_breakup,
                        String delimiting_chars,
                        boolean return_delims); // constructor

public boolean hasMoreTokens();

public String nextToken();
```

You may have noticed that tokenizing a string is a pretty similar operation to enumerating all the elements in it. The StringTokenizer class does in fact implement the Enumeration interface, and provide bodies for hasMoreElements() and nextElement(). They are alternatives to the token methods, and return exactly the same objects. In the case of nextElement the return type is Object not String, but the Object it returns is a String. The StringTokenizer is simpler than the StreamTokenizer we met earlier. StringTokenizer just breaks things up into

Strings. StreamTokenizer does this and also tries to classify them as numbers, words, etc.

Observer and Observable

These two are a matched pair. Together they provide a general interface for one thread to communicate a state change to another. We'll start with Observer, because it is simpler.

Observer is an interface that looks like this:

```
public interface Observer {
    void update(Observable o, Object arg);
}
```

Any object that wants to look at (observe) something else asynchronously can declare that it is an observer and provide its own body for update. The update() method is just a callback, so let's give an example of use. When you ask an image file to load, the method returns at once and in the background (as soon as it's sure you want it) starts reading the file off disk. That incoming file is an observable event. The thread that asked to load it is an observer.

When the thing that it's looking at has something to communicate, it will call update. Since the observer might be keeping an eye on several observable objects, update needs to be told which of them is calling it. That is the purpose of the first argument. The second argument is an object to permit just about anything at all to be passed in. The body of update will do whatever needs doing when that observable object says "look at me."

In our JPEG file example, there will be a number of times when there is enough information to call observer.update(). It may be called when the image file header has been read, when we have decoded enough to know the height of the image, when we know the width, and when the entire transfer has been completed.

Now lets take a look at Observable. The class Observable is intended to be extended by classes you write. The key methods that Observable provides are:

```
public synchronized void addObserver(Observer o);
// this is how an Observer registers its interest
// with the Observable thing.

protected synchronized void setChanged();
// only subclasses have the privilege of saying something
// observable has changed.

public void notifyObservers();
public void notifyObservers(Object arg);
```

If the *changed* flag is true, then these two routines call the update() method of all Observers. It's done this way (with an extra flag) so the observable thing has precise control over when notification really takes place.

It's frustrating that the word "notify" is used here—this has absolutely no relation to the wait/notify paradigm used in communicating synchronized threads. The notifyObservers() routine should really be called updateObservers(). Unfortunately, Java is just chock full of things that are poorly named, and this is yet one more.

There are also methods to delete one or all Observers, and set, clear, or query an internal "changed" flag that an Observer may look at.

Note: Having justified Observer and Observable in terms of loading image files, you should be aware that image loading actually uses its own special version of Observer, called ImageObserver. It works in exactly the same way as Observer and it's unclear why the general mechanism was defined, only to be passed over in favor of a special purpose implementation for image files.

One common use of Observer/Observable is in sending a message from a dialog window back to its parent Frame. The parent implements Observer, the dialog class contains an Observable object, and a method to return the text. Then, when the dialog captures some relevant information, it sets its own changed bit and calls notifyObservers().

Notes on Linking in Native Methods

Java provides support for linking in native methods. These are routines written in languages other than Java, to which Java can call out. Java I/O is accomplished by calls to the native I/O libraries on each platform. On Windows systems, arithmetic operations are done by calling out to the native runtime library.

Native methods are supported for reasons of performance and code reuse. Any Java application that uses them however has gone outside the Java language. The use of native methods destroys code portability, so you should avoid them if at all possible.

Using native methods is inherently compiler, platform, and OS dependent. Here are the steps in the process for the ANSI C compiler on SPARC microprocessors under Solaris 2.x

1. Write a method with no body, and give it the access modifier "native."

```
class peach {
    static native void plum(int i);
        . . .
```

2. The class that the method is in needs to have a static code segment that will load the native library. Use this statement:
   static { System.loadLibrary("plum"); } where the library is libplum.so
   So the rest of class peach will look like this:

```
    . . .
public static void main (String arg[] ) {
    System.out.println("in main, calling plum");
    plum(33);
}

static { System.loadLibrary("plum"); }
}
```

3. Compile the java code,

```
javac peach.java
```

4. Create the C header file (.h) by running:

```
javah peach
```

this reads peach.class and creates peach.h
The .h file can be included in any other C routines that want to call the native routine:

create the C stub file (.c) by running:

```
javah -stubs peach
```

this reads peach.class and creates peach.c (below)

The stub file peach.c will contain a function that is called from the Java interpreter, and this in turn will call the native C routine after converting any parameters from Java stack references to C data types. It's a little ugly, but it looks like this:

```
/* DO NOT EDIT THIS FILE - it is machine generated */
#include <StubPreamble.h>
/* Stubs for class peach */
/* SYMBOL: "peach/plum(I)V", Java_peach_plum_stub */
stack_item *Java_peach_plum_stub(stack_item
*_P_,struct execenv *_EE_) {
    extern void peach_plum(void *,long);
    (void) peach_plum(NULL,((_P_[0].i)));
    return _P_;
}
```

Note that the name of your native function is specified here, and it encodes the class name that it came from. You do not have the luxury of choosing the name of your native method. Also note the prototype. You must supply C code that matches this. Since we declared the native method as "static" the first argument is null, rather than a pointer to the "this" object. The implementation could equally have chosen to omit this first argument. Note also that i was declared as int in Java, but has shown up as long here. Longs are the same size as ints in this compiler (32 bits).

5. Write the native C function and compile it into a dynamic library by using the -G option.

```
#include <stdio.h>
void peach_plum(void* this, long i) {
    printf("in peach_plum, i=%d \n",i);
}
```

Then compile this and the stub ("wrapper" would be a better name) file from step 4. You need to specify the path to these two include directories, because more header files are needed for a clean compilation.

```
cc -G  \
    -I$JAVAHOME/include \
    -I$JAVAHOME/include/solaris \
    peach.c  plum.c \
    -o libplum.so
```

6. Make sure that the linker can see the directory that has libplum.so in it, by setting LD_LIBRARY_PATH to include it, then execute your Java program.

```
% setenv LD_LIBRARY_PATH $OPENWINHOME/lib:.

% java peach
in main, calling plum
in peach_plum, i=33
```

ANSI C defines a sorting function with this prototype:

```
void qsort(   void  * base,
          size_t  nmemb,
          size_t  size,
          int (* compar)(const void *, const void *)
        );
```

That last parameter is a pointer to a comparison function. It is not possible to call this native method directly from Java, as Java doesn't give us a way to express the concept of a reference to a method. The virtual machine allows this concept, so it would be easy to add in the future. ☕

Only use native methods when you really have to.

Properties

Java has a platform-independent way to communicate extra information at runtime to a program. Known as "properties" these do a job like environment variables. Environment variables aren't used because they are too platform-specific. A programmer can read the value of a property by calling getProperty() and passing an argument string for the property in which you are interested.

```
String dir = System.getProperty("user.dir");
```

A long list of predefined properties appears in the file java/lang/System.java and is reproduced below. Some properties are not available in applets for security reasons. You can also define a property on the command line when you invoke the program like this:

```
java -Drate=10.0 myprogram
```

That value "10.0" will be returned as a string when querying the property "rate." It can then be converted to a floating-point number and used as a value in the program. In this case, it's an alternative to a command line argument.

Table 6-2 lists the predefined properties, guaranteed to have a value on every Java client.

Table 6-2: Predefined Properties

Property name	Explanation	Visible in Applet
java.version	version number of the Java system	yes
java.vendor	vendor specific string	yes
java.vendor.url	vendor URL	yes
java.home	Java installation directory	no
java.class.version	Java class version number	yes
java.class.path	Java classpath	no
os.name	Operating System Name	yes
os.arch	Operating System Architecture	yes
os.version	Operating System Version	yes
file.separator	File separator ("/" on Unix)	yes
path.separator	Path separator (":" on Unix)	yes
line.separator	Line separator ("\n" on Unix)	yes
user.name	User account name	no
user.home	User home directory	no
user.dir	User's current working directory	no

Most programs don't need to access these properties at all. But when they do, it's nice to be able to do it in a platform-independent way.

This tip is so useful, you'll use it almost everyday!

Some of these Java library routines can be a bit confusing. What order do the parameters come in for all the varieties of PixelGrabber? Here's an easy way to check.

Just run javap on any class name (*not* class file name), whether your own or one in the java.*.* packages, and it will print out the class, its methods, and the parameters.

```
          javap  java.lang.Math

Compiled from Math.java
public final class java.lang.Math extends java.lang.Object {
    public static final double E = 2.718282;
    public static final double PI = 3.141593;
    public native static double sin(double);
    public native static double cos(double);
    public native static double tan(double);
    public native static double asin(double);
    public native static double acos(double);
    public native static double atan(double);
    public native static double exp(double);
    public native static double log(double);
    public native static double sqrt(double);
    public native static double IEEEremainder(double,double);
    public native static double ceil(double);
    public native static double floor(double);
    public native static double rint(double);
    public native static double atan2(double,double);
    public native static double pow(double,double);
    public static int round(float);
    public static long round(double);
    public static synchronized double random();
    public static int abs(int);
    public static long abs(long);
    public static float abs(float);
    public static double abs(double);
    public static int max(int,int);
    public static long max(long,long);
    public static float max(float,float);
    public static double max(double,double);
    public static int min(int,int);
    public static long min(long,long);
    public static float min(float,float);
    public static double min(double,double);
}
```

Excellent! Now it's really easy to check the method signatures of any classes.

Some Light Relief

There's an old story to the effect that "the people at Cray design their supercomputers with Apple systems, and the Apple designers use Crays!" Apart from this being a terrific example of recurring rotational serendipity (what goes around, comes around) is there any truth to it?

Like many urban legends, this one contains a nugget of truth. In the 1991 Annual Report of Cray Research Inc. there is a short article describing how Apple used a Cray for designing Macintosh cases. The Cray is used to simulate the injection molding of the plastic enclosure cases. The Mac II case was the first Apple system to benefit from the modelling, and the trial was successful. The simulation identified warping problems which were solved by prototyping thus saving money in tooling and production. Apple also uses their Cray for simulating air flow inside the enclosure to check for hot spots. The Cray house magazine reported that the Apple PowerBook continues to use supercomputer simulations. (CRAY CHANNELS, Spring 1992 pp.10-12 "Apple Computer PowerBook computer molding simulation").

The inverse story holds that Seymour Cray himself used a Mac to design Crays. The story seems to have originated with an off-the-cuff remark from Seymour Cray himself, who had a Mac at home, and used it to store some of his work for the Cray 3. Common sense suggests that the simulation of discrete circuitry (Verilog runs, logic analysis, etc.) which is part of all modern integrated circuit design, is done far more cost-effectively on a supercomputer than on a microprocessor. Cray probably has a lot of supercomputer hardware laying around ready for testing as it comes off the production line.

It's conceivable that a Macintosh could be used to draft the layout of blinking lights for the front of a Cray, or choose some nice color combinations, or some other non-CPU intensive work. A Macintosh is a very good system for writing design notes, sending email, and drawing diagrams, all of which are an equally essential part of designing a computer system.

The good folks at Cray Research have confirmed in a Cray Users Group newsletter that they have a few Macs on the premises. So while it's extremely unlikely that they run logic simulations on their Macs, we can indeed chalk it up as only-slightly-varnished truth that "the people at Cray design their supercomputers with Apple's systems, and the Apple designers use Crays," for some value of the word "design"!

Exercises

1. After it's completed one anagram, make the program go back and prompt for more. Don't make it reload the wordlist! (Easy)

2. Modify the program so it doesn't use arrays of fixed size, but uses the Vector class from package "java.util" to grow arrays as needed at runtime. (Easy) Add this line to the start of the program:

   ```
   import java.util.Vector;
   ```

3. Create a version of the program that has the word list compiled into it. You'll probably want to first write a java program that reads a word list and prints out the array initialization literals for you to edit into your source program. What difference does this make to program start-up time? Run time? Size? (Medium)

4. Create a version of the program that uses several threads to sort the candidate words. Use a heuristic like "if the partition is larger than 4 elements, spawn a thread to sort it using quicksort, otherwise sort it directly by decision tree comparison." Decision tree comparison means

   ```
   if ( a>b )
       if ( a>c )
           if (a>d)  // a is largest
           else      // d is largest, then a
               if (b>c) // order is d,a,b,c
               else     // order is d,a,c,b
   // and so on
   ```

   This challenge is of medium complexity.

5. What needs to be changed in the anagram program to make it capable of dealing with alphabets other than English? (Easy) Make it so. (Medium to Hard, depending on whether you select a specific non-English alphabet or "all of them").

6. Have several threads calculating anagrams at once. This challenge is hard to get working correctly so the threads know how to stop when they reach the point of overlap.

Further Reading

Alice in Wonderland

by Lewis Carroll

This text is the best book on mathematics for the layman, because (as Professor Perlis pointed out) it's the best book on anything for the layman.

CHAPTER

7

- Embedding a Java program in a Web page

- Starting applet execution

- Passing Parameters to applets

- Security issues and the SecurityManager

All
About
Applets

"People say you can't compare apples and oranges. But why not? They are both hand-held, round, edible, fruity things that grow on trees."

—anonymous

J ava is a fine general purpose programming language. It can be used to good effect to generate stand-alone executables, just as C, C++, Visual Basic, Pascal or Fortran can.

Java offers the additional capability of writing code that can live in a web page and then get downloaded and executed when the web page is browsed. Opinions differ on which is the more important role of Java, but it's a debate without much value. If you want to write applications, write applications. If you want to write applets and put them in web pages, write applets and put them in web pages. This chapter explains how to do that.

There are a number of special considerations that apply to applets. These considerations include connecting a class file to a web page, starting execution, screen appearance, parameter passing, and security. Let's take these one by one.

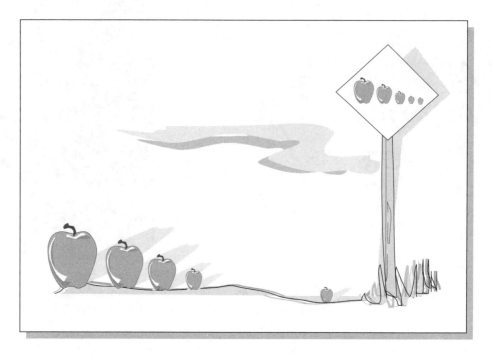

Embedding a Java Program in a Web Page

As mentioned in Chapter 3 when we touched on this topic, an applet is a Java program that is invoked not from the command line, but rather through a web browser reaching that page, or equivalently through the appletviewer that comes with the Java Development Kit. We will stick with the appletviewer in this chapter because we are trying to teach the language not the use of a browser.

> **Reminder on Applets**
>
> There are two different ways to run a Java executable:
>
> - as a stand-alone program that can be invoked from the command line. This is termed an "application".
>
> - as a program embedded in a web page, to be run when the page is browsed. This is termed an "applet".
>
> Applications and applets differ in the execution privileges they have, and also the way they indicate where to start execution.

The first thing to understand about applets is how they get run from a web browser, because the numerous methods that applets can override follow from that.

Web browsers deal with HTML (the HyperText Markup Language we mentioned in Chapter 1). There are HTML tags that say "set this text in bold," "break to a new paragraph" and "include this GIF image here." There is now an HTML tag that says "run the Java applet that you will find in this .class file." Just as a GIF image file will be displayed at the point where its tag is in the HTML source, so the applet will be executed when its tag is encountered and the results displayed at that point in the web page.

An example of the HTML code that invokes an applet is shown below:

```
<title>
The simplest applet
</title>
<applet code=pentium.class width=300 height=50>
</applet>
```

The width and height fields are mandatory, and they are measured in units of pixels (dots of resolution on the computer monitor). Applets run in a window object called a panel, and you have to give the browser a clue as to how big a panel the applet should start with.

Since this is HTML, put the prior example in a file called foo.html, Figure 7-1 shows how it will be run. The class needs to be found somewhere along the CLASSPATH environment variable or from the CODEBASE defined in the HTML tag. CODEBASE specifies a different directory that contains the applet's code. This is to help applets located on remote servers be accessed just as easily as those stored locally.

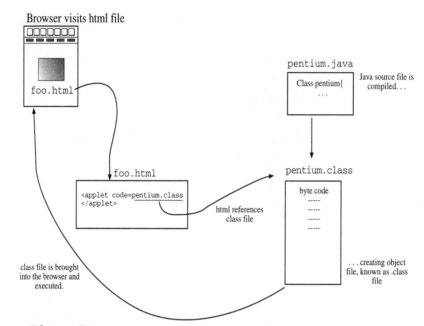

Figure 7-1:   example.html will run like this

The full list of tags that can be used for applets is:

```
<applet
    code=classfilename
    width=integer_pixels
    height=integer_pixels
    [codebase=applet-url]
    [vspace=integer_pixels]
    [hspace=integer_pixels]
    [align=alignment]
    [name=some_name]
    [alt=some_text]
>
```

The applet tag can be followed by zero or more parameter tags, with the general form of attribute name/value pairs.

```
<param name=param_name  value=param_value >
```

The parameter tag will be described a little later. You can also put some alternate html here, which will only be formatted if the browser doesn't understand the applet tag. Finally, the applet ends with an "end applet" tag:

```
</applet>
```

Confusingly, letter case is not significant for any html tags or attribute names, but it is significant for some of the arguments they take (e.g. the name of the class file). When in doubt make all uses of upper and lower case consistent.

The attributes have the following meanings:

CODE=*CLASSFILENAME*

> This attribute is required, and names the class file that is to be executed. Note: this must just be a single file name, with no part of a longer path prefixed to it: So "foo.class" is good, but "bin/foo.class" is bad.

WIDTH=*INTEGER_PIXELS*
HEIGHT=*INTEGER_PIXELS*

> These two attributes are required, and say how large a space in the browser the applet takes up.

All the remaining attributes are optional.

CODEBASE=*APPLET-URL*

> This attribute allows you more flexibility in where applet class files are located. You can provide a URL identifying a directory where the browser should look for the class files this applet loads. Since it is a URL, the directory can be specified anywhere on the Internet, not just on the server or client system. If this attribute is omitted (a common occurrence) the class files must be in the same directory as the html file.

VSPACE=*INTEGER_PIXELS*
HSPACE=*INTEGER_PIXELS*

> These two attributes allow you to specify the size of the blank margin to leave around the applet in the browser. These two tags and the one below are similar to the attributes of the same names used with the <IMG> tag.

ALIGN=*ALIGNMENT*

> This attribute allows you to control where the applet appears on the page. There are several possible alignment values: "left," "right," "top," "middle" are popular choices.

NAME=*SOME_NAME*

> The name provided here is associated with the applet, and can be used by other applets running on the same page to refer to the applet and communicate with it.

ALT=*SOME_TEXT*

> This attribute specifies the text to be displayed in the (unlikely) event that the browser understands the applet tag, but does not understand Java.

The <applet> tag was invented specifically for Java, but it is possible that people will want to download other types of executable content. It would be a poor idea to have to invent a new tag for each new type of downloadable program. Accordingly, the <embed> tag has been proposed to replace the <applet> tag. The main difference is that <embed> allows you to put a full URL on the beginning of the "class=" attribute (and it calls it "src=," not "class="). As a result the codebase attribute is not needed.

 While we wait for all browsers to become Java-capable (and pretty soon you won't be able to give away a browser unless it understands Java), here's a useful tip.

All browsers ignore HTML tags that they don't understand. And they also ignore HTML tags that they do understand when they appear in unexpected places. These two facts together make it possible to write an HTML file that will invoke an applet in a Java-capable browser, and provide an alternative text or image for an incapable browser. Between the <applet> and </applet> tags, only a few tags, including <param> tags are recognized by applet-aware browsers. Browsers that cannot run Java will ignore these applet-specific tags.

So the HTML below will run the java applet if the browser can, and will display the alternative image instead if the browser is not Java capable.

```
<applet  code=anagram.class  width=500, height=500>
    <param   name="target"   value="surfing the net">
    <param   name=wordlist   value="words.txt">
    <param   name=minsize    value="2">

    <img src="NoJava4U.JPG">

</applet>
```

Starting Applet Execution

We've just seen that applets are started up in a different manner from applications. The difference is more than just command-line vs. HTML file. Applications start execution in a public function called "main()" similar to the convention used in C. Applets have a different convention, involving overriding certain pre-named functions.

The first thing to note is that an applet is a *window object* that *runs in a thread object*, so every applet will be able to do window-y kind of things and thread-y kind of things. (We mean window in the general sense rather than Java-specific sense. In the Java-specific sense, an Applet is a Panel.) An applet's execution starts using the thready kind of methods that we have already seen in Chapter 5. You can override the start()/stop methods, but you do not call them yourself. This funny stuff exists because of the funny context that applets live in. They are loaded once, then subject to the kind of repeated execution that a hypertext Web browser makes. The diagram in Figure 7-2 shows how.

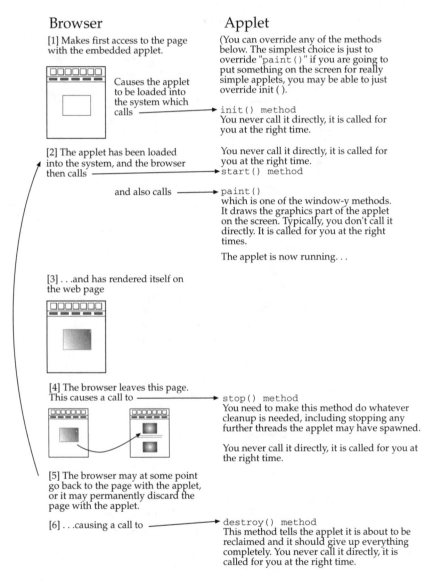

Browser

[1] Makes first access to the page with the embedded applet.

Causes the applet to be loaded into the system which calls

[2] The applet has been loaded into the system, and the browser then calls

and also calls

[3] . . .and has rendered itself on the web page

[4] The browser leaves this page. This causes a call to

[5] The browser may at some point go back to the page with the applet, or it may permanently discard the page with the applet.

[6] . . .causing a call to

Applet

(You can override any of the methods below. The simplest choice is just to override "paint()" if you are going to put something on the screen for really simple applets, you may be able to just override init ().

`init() method`
You never call it directly, it is called for you at the right time.

You never call it directly, it is called for you at the right time.
`start() method`

`paint()`
which is one of the window-y methods. It draws the graphics part of the applet on the screen. Typically, you don't call it directly. It is called for you at the right times.

The applet is now running. . .

`stop() method`
You need to make this method do whatever cleanup is needed, including stopping any further threads the applet may have spawned.

You never call it directly, it is called for you at the right time.

`destroy() method`
This method tells the applet it is about to be reclaimed and it should give up everything completely. You never call it directly, it is called for you at the right time.

Figure 7-2: Repeated execution caused by a hypertext Web browser

You can almost always leave "destroy()" alone. The method "init()" is a good place to create GUI objects and threads. Similarly you will only override the methods "start()" and "stop()" if you have something that actually needs to be started and stopped, namely threads. If your applet doesn't start up any threads of its own, there's no need to supply your own version of start and stop. On the other hand, if your applet does create some threads, start() is probably where you will want to start them. And it is most important that you override stop() and explicitly stop all threads—otherwise they will continue to run even after you leave the page. If you want a thread to suspend when the browser leaves the page and resume where it left off if the browser returns, then use suspend() in method stop() and resume() in method start(). Obviously, you'll need to create the thread the first time through.

Table 7-1 lists a summary of Methods Useful in Applets, and when they are called.

Table 7-1: Summary of Useful Methods

Method	Description
void init()	Called when the applet is first loaded into memory. Typically you override it with one-time initialization code.
void start()	Called each time the browser visits the page containing this applet. Typically you override it to start or resume any threads the applet contains.
void paint(Graphics g)	Will be called by the window system when the component needs to be redisplayed. You will not call this. You will override this if you dynamically change the appearance of the screen, and want to see it appear.
void stop()	Called when the browser leaves the page containing this applet. Typically you override it to stop or suspend any threads the applet contains.
void run()	Nothing to do with applets—this is the main routine in which thread execution starts.

There is more housekeeping associated with threads in applets than in applications, because of the way pages (including their embedded running applets) are left behind and possibly revisited. An applet gets the ability to override all these thread method names for free—it does not need to import anything explicitly. However, the window-y stuff needs to be imported ("import java.awt.*;") so that you can display window objects like menus and buttons.

> **Magic methods**
>
> These magic methods init(), start(), stop(), and destroy() are defined in src/java/applet/Applet.java. These are exactly the methods that a thread has (see them in src/java/lang/Thread.java). What methods does an application have that correspond to these? None! An application isn't run under a browser, so it isn't liable to be stopped and started unpredictably as the browser moves to new pages.
>
> The paint() method is a window-y thing, available to all window components. See Chapter 10.

Screen Appearance of an Applet

Here is an example of the minimal applet:

```
import java.awt.Graphics;
public class Message extends java.applet.Applet {
    public void paint(Graphics g) {
        g.drawString("Yes!", 15, 25);
    }
}
```

An HTML suitable for this program might be

```
<applet code=Message.class width=200 height=100>
</applet>
```

Now put it in a file called Message.html. Compile the java program. When you run it under the appletviewer with the command

```
appletviewer Message.html
```

you will see a window like the following appear.

Figure 7-3: A minimal applet

If you don't see this, step through the installation instructions again, checking that you have done everything correctly.

Because an applet is a windowing thing (we will get back to more formal terminology eventually), it does not use the standard I/O that we have been using up till now for interactive I/O. Instead it uses the facilities that are available to windows, like drawing a string at particular coordinates. The coordinate system of every window has the origin in the top left as shown in Figure 7-4.

Figure 7-4:   Every window's coordinates originate in the top left corner

What are the other facilities that are available to windows? We will discuss these in greater depth in a later chapter which deals with the Abstract Window Toolkit. For now you can code review the classes that make up the AWT in directory $JAVAHOME/src/awt. The file Container.java contains the superclass from which Applet is (eventually) derived. Container has the method "paint()" which is called by the Window toolkit whenever the applet panel needs to be refreshed.

 You can look at the source for method drawString() in file java/src/awt/Graphics.java. This class has many methods concerned with rendering a shape, line, or text onto the screen. It will also let you select colors, and fonts.

The convention throughout Java is that class names begin with a capital letter, and method names start with a lower case letter, but subsequent words in the name are capitalized. This leads to odd looking names like "drawString" that make it seem as though someone had a previous job writing ransom notes wItH rAndOmlY caPitALiZeD LeTteRs. ("wE HaVe yOuR MiSsinG piXeL. seNd $10K iN sMaLL BilLS. dO nOt TeLl tHe PolICe. ThEy'Re sTuPId.")

When the compiler complains that it can't find one of the library methods, your first thought should be "did I get the capitals right?" It is not always consistent in that we have "MenuBar" and yet "Scrollbar" in the window toolkit. Especially watch out for the "instanceof" operator that uses no capitals. In cases like this, it's better to always be consistent or always be inconsistent, but not keep changing between the two.

Set up the "pentium flaw" program as an applet. Modify the program so that it extends Applet and make sure that the class is public. Use g.drawString() instead of println(), in this method:

```
public void paint(Graphics g) {
    g.drawString("text to display", x_pos, y_pos);
}
```

Write some html that points to the class. Invoke it through the appletviewer, and then try a Java capable web browser. (Medium). 🐾

Back in Chapter 5 we mentioned that some programs need to explicitly start threads, rather than have them created and started in one operation. An applet running in a web browser is one of those programs. It allows a closer fit to the "go back to a page you already visited, and which is likely to still be loaded" model. That is why init() (one-time initialization) is separated from start() (called every time the page is accessed).

Browser Summary

The browser will automatically instantiate an object of your Applet subclass, and make certain calls to get it running.

You can overload some of the called methods. The methods "init() and "paint()" are the ones you will mostly overload, unless you have threads in the applet, when you will want to overload "start()" and "stop()" too.

Typically you never call any of these methods. They are called for you by the window system/browser at appropriate times. As the browser visits pages and moves away from them these predefined Applet methods are invoked.

Build in Debugging Help

You can put a main method in any class—even a class that runs as an applet or a class that isn't the main routine of your application. Like any other method that isn't called, it doesn't do any harm.

Some programmers recommend adding a main() routine to all classes. This main should just be a test driver to check the functionality of that class. When you are debugging your system, you'll find it most convenient to test individual classes this way. Just leave it there—it won't hurt in the finished version of the system.

Cut down the number of files you need. When you start creating applets, you usually need at least three files before anything can happen: a .java source file, a .class bytecode file, and a .html file. If you aren't careful with your naming, you'll lose track of what's where.

One suggestion (for experts only) useful while the code is under development is to put the HTML commands in the java source file, inside a comment, like this:

```
// <applet  code=Message.class  height=100  width=100>
// </applet>
import java.awt.Graphics;
public class Message extends java.applet.Applet {
    public void paint(Graphics g) {
        g.drawString("Yes!", 10,10);
    }
}
```

It offers two advantages: First, you cut out the need for a separate html file (so you don't waste time flipping back and forth between HTML file and source file in the editor); and secondly, you can put the parameters for the applet right in the file with the applet code (so it's easy to check you've got them right). Then you invoke appletviewer on the source file

```
appletviewer  Message.java
```

This works because browsers just read arbitrary text files, looking for tags. They don't care if the file contains source code as well.

Alternatively, you can use a main() routine in a different class as a different entry point to your program allowing the program to do slightly different things depending on which class you tell the interpreter to start in. You can vary this from run to run. 🍵

Passing Parameters to Applets

Just as we have command line arguments for applications, there is a similar feature for passing arguments from the HTML file to the applet it invokes. Parameters are indicated by an HTML tag of the form

```
<param    name=namestring    value=valuestring>
```

The param tags come after the <applet> tag, and before the </applet> tag. An example of some actual parameters in the applet version of the anagram program might be:

```
<applet  code=anagram.class  width=500, height=500>
    <param  name="target"   value="surfing the net">
    <param  name=wordlist   value="words.txt">
    <param  name=minsize    value="2">
</applet>
```

It does not matter if strings are quoted or not, unless the string contains embedded white space. Inside the program you call getParameter with the name as an argument, and it returns the string representing the value. If there isn't a parameter of that name, it returns null. Here is an example:

```
String s = getParameter("minsize");
// parse to an int.
int minsize = Integer.parseInt(s);
```

Notice that this follows the same conventions as "main(String argv[])"—all arguments are passed as strings, and programmers need to do a little processing to get the values of arguments that are numbers.

To pass a double as a parameter to an applet, the html tag would look like this

```
<param name=peach   value="3.1" >
```

The code to retrieve it would be:

```
String s = getParameter("peach");
double d = Double.valueOf(s).doubleValue();
```

This differs from the int code because the class Double does not have a parseDouble method to create a double from a String. Instead we have to create a double object from the String, then extract the double value from that.

Security Issues of Applets

The term "security" means controlling the resources of your computer system: the files, screen, peripherals and CPU cycles. Even on a single-user system, like Windows 3.11, this is an issue because a computer virus can destroy your valuable work. Some form of security check is especially needed with applets because they are executed automatically on your behalf. Just by browsing a web page embedded applets are sent over and executed on your system. Without a security check an applet could, either through maliciousness or poor programming, corrupt your files or transmit the contents to points unknown.

Viruses are already too prevalent in the PC world. A virus was recently detected that even infected the MS-Word word processor by taking advantage of an "execute macros on start-up" feature. MS-DOS, Windows 3.11, and Windows 95 have little-to-no security. The Microsoft ActiveX frameworkhas security in terms of identification through signing, but no security in terms of resource access permission.

Right from the start, Java improves on this situation by defining and supporting several levels of resource access control. Some of Java's security is user-configurable, and some of it (to avoid a breach of security) is not.

The SecurityManager is a built-in class in package java.lang with about a dozen methods each of which checks access to a particular resource: threads, properties, socket connections, reading a file, and so on.

The java.lang.SecurityManager class contains these public methods:

```
class SecurityManager {
    public void checkCreateClassLoader();
    public void checkAccess(java.lang.Thread);
    public void checkAccess(java.lang.ThreadGroup);
    public void checkExit(int);
    public void checkExec(java.lang.String);
    public void checkLink(java.lang.String);
    public void checkRead(java.io.FileDescriptor);
    public void checkRead(java.lang.String);
    public void checkRead(java.lang.String,java.lang.Object);
    public void checkWrite(java.io.FileDescriptor);
    public void checkWrite(java.lang.String);
    public void checkDelete(java.lang.String);
    public void checkConnect(java.lang.String,int);
    public void checkConnect(java.lang.String,int,java.lang.Object);
    public void checkListen(int);
    public void checkAccept(java.lang.String,int);
    public void checkPropertiesAccess();
    public void checkPropertyAccess(java.lang.String);
    public void checkPropertyAccess(java.lang.String,java.lang.String);
    public boolean checkTopLevelWindow(java.lang.Object);
    public void checkPackageAccess(java.lang.String);
    public void checkPackageDefinition(java.lang.String);
    public void checkSetFactory();
    public boolean getInCheck();
    public java.lang.Object getSecurityContext();
}
```

All but the last 3 methods have names that are self-explanatory; they to scrutinize some specific form of resource access. So checkRead(java.io.FileDescriptor) will return normally if a read may be done using this file descriptor, and throw an exception if it should not. The last three methods carry out this processing:

checkSetFactory()   check whether an applet can set a networking-related object factory. A "factory" is a java term for a class that creates objects of another class. Usually classes are responsible for their own constructors, but sometimes it is convenient to manage this from another class, especially when one of several subtype classes might be needed.

getInCheck()   simply says whether a check is currently taking place.

getSecurityContext()   returns an implementation-dependent Object which holds enough information about the current execution environment to perform some of the security checks later.

You never call these checking methods, they are called at appropriate times by the Java runtime. When a Java system first starts executing, the security manager is set to null and the only access restrictions are those imposed by the underlying OS. In other words, anything goes.

To change that, you can write your own class that extends SecurityManager, and provide new methods to override the checking method for the resources you are interested in. The body of each new method contains your algorithm for deciding whether to grant access or not. It will either return or throw a security exception. Returning without throwing an exception means the access is allowed. If you install a new security manager of your own, then every resource not controlled in your new manager is disallowed. Here is an example that allows access to all System properties and nothing else.

```java
class MySecurityManager extends SecurityManager {

    public void checkPropertyAccess(String key) {
        return;
    }

}


public class foo {
    public static void main(String s[]) {

        SecurityManager msm = new MySecurityManager();

        try {
            System.setSecurityManager(msm);
        } catch(Exception e){}


    }
}
```

A SecurityManager can be set at most once during the lifetime of a Java runtime. There is no way to install a new SecurityManager that includes permission to keep installing new SecurityManagers: it's a one shot deal and cannot later be replaced, changed, or overridden. In an application, you the programmer can define the level of security for your program. In an applet, the browser must do this (and applets must be unable to impose a new security manager).

Different browsers have imposed slightly different SecurityManager policies, and they can take into account whether an applet was loaded from a local file or from browsing over the net. Local files only exist on your system because you put them there, so they are presumed to have more privileges. Table 7-2 is a matrix of broswer characteristics extracted from the JavaSoft site http://www.javasoft.com/sfaq.

Table 7-2: Browser capabilities

Capabilities	Ns/net	Ns/local	Av/net	Av/local	Applic
read/write file in /home/me with acl set	no	no	yes	yes	yes
read the user.name property	no	yes	no	yes	yes
connect to port on client	no	yes	no	yes	yes
connect to port on 3rd host	no	yes	no	yes	yes
load library	no	yes	no	yes	yes
exit(-1)	no	no	no	yes	yes
create a popup window without a warning	no	yes	no	yes	yes

Key:
- Ns/net: Netscape Navigator 3.x, loading applets over the Net
- Ns/local: Netscape Navigator 3.x, loading applets from the Local file system
- Av/net: Appletviewer, JDK 1.x, loading applets over the Net
- Av/local: Appletviewer, JDK 1.x, loading applets from the Local file system
- Applic: Java Standalone applications

The restrictions mean that an applet loaded from over the net:

- Can really read and write files if the ACL has been set, and you run the applet using Appletviewer.

- Cannot make network connections to hosts other than the one it came from

- Cannot start a program on your system by using the equivalent of the system() call in C. An application or local applet can do this with the method "java.lang.Runtime.exec()".

- Cannot load a library

Some browsers may impose other restrictions on top of these. The eventual aim is to provide support for recognizing and executing trusted applets with more capabilities even over the net, without jeopardizing system security.

Default Capability Differences

Note that there is a difference in default capabilities between an applet loaded from over the net, and an applet loaded from the local file system. Where an applet comes from determines what it is allowed to do. An applet brought from over the net is loaded by the applet class loader, and it is subject to the restrictions enforced by the applet security manager.

An applet stored on the client's local disk and accessible from the CLASSPATH is loaded by the file system loader. These applets are permitted to read and write files, load Java libraries and exec processes. Local applets are not passed through the byte code verifier, which is another line of defence against code from the net.

The verifier checks that the byte code conforms to the Java language specification and looks for violations of the type rules and name space restrictions. The verifier ensures that:

- There are no stack overflows or underflows.

- All register accesses and stores are valid.

- The parameters to all bytecode instructions are correct.

- No illegal type conversion are attempted.

Netscape Navigator 3.x disables all privileges for applets browsed over the net. It allows a small number of privileges for applets loaded from a local file system, such as the ability to load a library or read the user.name property. The Sun appletviewer allows applets to read and write files.

You can configure the Sun appletviewer to read and write files on your local disk by editing the file .hotjava/properties. This file is in your home directory on Unix (note its name starts with a dot, so it is not usually visible when you list the directory). Under Windows, the files is in the root directory of the drive you installed java on (the file might be C:\.hotjava\properties).

Then you can set the acl.read and acl.write properties to point to the files or directories that you will allow applets to read or write. For example, if I add these two lines to my ~/.hotjava/properties file, (or my C:\.hotjava\properties file on Windows)

```
acl.read=/home/linden
acl.write=/tmp
```

then applets are allowed to read any files in /home/linden or to write to any files in the /tmp directory. 🐦

Here's an applet that you can run under Sun's appletviewer to confirm this.

```
// <applet code=show.class  height=100 width=200> </applet>
import java.io.*;
import java.awt.*;
import java.applet.Applet;
public class show extends Applet {

    public void Read() throws IOException {

        DataInputStream dis;
        String s, myFile = "show.java";

        dis = new DataInputStream(new FileInputStream(myFile));
        s = dis.readLine();
        System.out.println("line> "+s);
    }

    public void paint(Graphics g) {
        try {
                Read();
                g.drawString("Success in read", 10, 10);
        }
        catch (SecurityException e) {
            g.drawString("Caught security exception in read", 10, 10);
        }
        catch (IOException ioe) {
                g.drawString("Caught i/o exception in read", 10, 10);
        }
    }
}
```

Don't worry about the I/O details—that will be covered in full in the next chapter. For now the purpose is to demonstrate that browsers control the resources accessed by applets, and that file I/O is possible from an applet using the applet-viewer.

Signed Classes

The Java 1.1 release allows classes to be signed, so a user can be confident in identifying who supplied the applet. The goal is to be able to tell if an applet is trusted or untrusted. We want to allow trusted applets access to our computer systems, but we must still ensure that untrusted applets can't steal or damage information on a computer running a Java-enabled browser. Users can configure their browsers with a list of organizations that they trust to have non-destructive code. Applets from these organizations can then be run automatically with more privileges, including file access.

There are several variations on how to sign a class, but the basic algorithm works like this:

The signed class scheme uses a public key encryption scheme, which is based on codes that take two keys. One key is used to encrypt a message and a second is used to decrypt it. The clever part is that knowing one key does not provide any hint on what the other key is. Encrypting things is like translating them into Martian—the encryption key is an English-to-Martian dictionary, and the decryption key is a Martian-to-English dictionary. (The analogy breaks down if you take it too far).

So the key used for decryption can even be made public (hence the name "public key"). You pick up the decryption key from a source you trust to give you the right one, perhaps reading it off the company's Web page. A "signed class" has an identification string added to the class, along with a hash total for the byte code. The values are also stored in the class in encrypted form. Anyone can decrypt them using the public decryption key and check that the encrypted values matches the plaintext values. If they do match, the class has not been tampered with.

When you decrypt something using the Sun decryption key, it will only make sense if it was encrypted with the Sun encryption key. Any other key produces gibberish. Hence, when the class loader of your browser decrypts something and it makes sense, it can be sure that it comes from where it says it comes. An evil hacker cannot make changes to a class and wrap it up with its signature again. No one except Sun has the ability to encrypt a class with Sun's secret encrypting key.

You might adopt the protocol that you trust all classes that come from Netscape and Sun. If determined trustworthy, you may also want the browser to announce other signed classes and let you choose whether to go and get their public key.

Some Light Relief

Did Apple Copy Xerox?

The Apple Macintosh is a marvellous personal computer that featured a windowing interface right from its introduction in 1984. The Mac popularized the use of windows, menus, and mouse pointing devices very effectively. But where did the Mac team get the idea from?

There's a story in wide circulation that the Mac GUI was ripped off wholesale from Xerox! Before starting the Macintosh project, Steve Jobs visited the Xerox Research Center in Palo Alto California (PARC), and was shown a GUI interface running on the Xerox Star computer. Conspiracy theorists then claim that Steve Jobs realized the potential of the Xerox technology and pinched the ideas (and later some of the people) for the Mac.

How shocking. But what are the facts? One indication that things might not have happened quite that way, is the marked lack of innovation at Apple since Steve Jobs was pushed out in 1985. The stagnation at Apple without Jobs suggests that Jobs may well have been an innovator rather than a copier. On the other hand, it might just mean that it is really hard to get anything new done in a huge corporation. Since Jobs and many of his key developers left, the product improvement focus at Apple has largely centered around more memory/bigger screen/newer processor. These are just pedestrian "mid-life kickers" as we call them in Silicon Valley. The one totally new product, the Newton personal digital assistant, was an unmitigated disaster. Ironically, the failure of the Newton led to the firing of John Sculley, the Pepsi executive who had pushed Jobs out. Users don't want small products of increased complexity. They want decreased complexity in existing products.

But to come back to the Macintosh GUI. The man who started the Macintosh project (and named it for his favorite type of eating apple, modified to avoid trademark issues—those fruit farmers are apparently fanatically litigious) was Jef Raskin. The Mac project started early in 1979, long before Jobs ever visited Xerox. In fact, the reason Jobs finally went to PARC was that Raskin asked him to, to help convince Jobs that a WYSIWYG environment was the way to go.

Raskin had been a professor and computer center director at the University of California at San Diego and a visiting scholar at the Stanford Artificial Intelligence Laboratory (SAIL). Raskin was often a visiting academic at the Xerox Research Center in its first few years, but to avoid any possible conflict of interest Raskin stopped visiting PARC after he joined Apple in 1978.

Raskin was an early originator of the idea that user interface and graphics were of primary importance to the future of computing. His 1967 Computer Science thesis argued that computers should be all-graphic, that we should eliminate character generators and create characters graphically and in various fonts, that what you see on the screen should be what you get, and that the human interface was more important than mere considerations of algorithmic efficiency and compactness. The thesis was titled "The Quickdraw System" which is the name of the Mac GUI drawing toolbox.

At Apple, Raskin built on his own earlier work to create click-and-drag for moving objects and making selections. Xerox used a click-move-click paradigm that was prone to error. Raskin hired a former student of his, Bill Atkinson, who extended Raskin's work to pull-down menus.

Larry Tesler was the first PARC ex-employee to join Apple, and some people have claimed that he brought the selection-based editor with him. In reality the concept dates back to an editor Raskin had designed many years before in 1973 while at Bannister & Crun. However, Raskin had discussed his ideas with those of similar interests at Xerox, so perhaps some of the technology transfer was actually from future Apple employee to Xerox!

Summary: Contrary to the widely-accepted version, Steve Jobs didn't totally ripoff the Mac GUI from a visit to Xerox. On the contrary, key elements of the design came from Jef Raskin, a computer science professor who had evangelized WYSIWYG designs for many years, including inside Xerox. Other parts of the Mac interface originated with Bill Atkinson and Bud Tribble who had been students at UCSD when Raskin taught there.

The moral of this story is ... what—you expect every story to end with a moral? Too bad. This one doesn't have one. Raskin did comment on the inaccuracies in the common story, and tried to get his perspective down on paper in the fourth reference below. The only other point to mention is that Raskin gave his three children Palindromic names: Aza, Aviva, and "Sums are" Erasmus (not sure about that last one...)

Exercises

Make the anagram application into an applet.

(Medium) 🍎

1. The scheme for passing parameters to applets from HTML is very flexible, and in fact allows you to pass an arbitrary number of parameters. If you give your HTML parameters names that end with a number in sequence, like this

   ```
   <param   name=myparam1    value="some value" >
   <param   name=myparam2    value="another value" >
   <param   name=myparam3    value="25.2" >
   ```

   it's easy to concatenate a count onto the name, as an argument to get-Parameter like this:

   ```
   next = getParameter( "myparam"+i );
   i++;
   ```

   That way you can keep retrieving parameters until you get a null returned. Write a program with the two statements above in a loop to demonstrate this. Print out the value of the parameters received.

2. Write an applet that reads a file. Run it in the appletviewer and set the properties so it will run successfully.

3. Distinguish between "init()" and "start()" in an applet.

4. Does HTML have to be in a file with the extension .html or .htm? Where else might you put it and why?

Further References

1. "Down With GUIs!" Wired, December 1993, pg. 122. Jef Raskin

2. "Hubris of a heavyweight. A review of Steve Jobs & the NeXT Big Thing" Randall E. Stross, IEEE Spectrum, July 1994 pp. 8-9.

3. "Intuitive Equals Familiar." Communications of the ACM. 37:9 September 1994 pg. 17, Jef Raskin

4. "Holes in the Histories" Interactions 1.3, July 1994 pg. 11, Jef Raskin

CHAPTER
8

- Interative I/O

- File I/O

- Executing a program from Java

- Networking with Java

- Sockets and URLs

I/O and
Networking in Java

A novice of the temple once approached the Chief Priest with a question. "Master, does Emacs have the Buddha nature?" the novice asked.

The Chief Priest had been in the temple for many years and could be relied upon to know these things. He thought for several minutes before replying. "I don't see why not. It's got bloody well everything else."

—Anonymous

This chapter has two major sections: I/O and the network facilities. I/O in Java is highly modular. There are many classes that specialize in one kind of I/O. It is very easy to connect objects of these classes together (like a Unix pipe), so that as the data flows through, they are modified or filtered in the way you need. The key to understanding I/O in Java is getting comfortable with connecting different file processing objects together.

By way of contrast, the biggest obstacle in learning about the Java support for networking *isn't* understanding the Java model—it *is* understanding the network programming terms and capabilities. Accordingly, a summary of TCP/IP networking is presented along with some suggested references for further study.

Interactive I/O

Java has the concept of a standard in, standard out, and standard error that Unix introduced. The class System contains these objects and they are known respectively as

```
System.in     System.out     System.err
```

We have already seen the println method used on standard out. It also has methods to print each of the built-in types. Standard error is very similar. Standard error is separate from standard out in order to provide a separate stream for error messages that might otherwise disappear down a pipe during I/O redirection.

Supporting Non-Blocking I/O

One routine that programmers always want to know about immediately is support for non-blocking I/O. Programmers want to know the method for getting a character from the keyboard without needing to press a carriage return, and returning at once if no character has yet been entered. This facility is much used when writing games software. (It has a much wider applicability for editors and all kinds of interactive software, but games programming is why a lot of programmers first start looking for it).

Java doesn't offer such a feature as part of an input stream (you could program it as a native method). But it is available in the Window Toolkit, and since most games will use the toolkit, games programmers everywhere can breathe a sigh of relief.

Because the in, out, and err streams are used in just about every program, they have been placed in the System class in the lang package, which is imported automatically into each compilation unit. All other I/O is in the package io, which must be imported explicitly.

Interactive Output

The very first thing many programmers want to know is how to print the primitive types. We've already seen that many times, and the approach is different in an applet versus an application. In an application it is just:

```
System.out.print( thing_to_print );
```

The argument can be almost anything. Java usually knows enough to turn an argument into a String and print that.

In an applet, printing to System.out can still be done but it will go to a browser-specified place. For the appletviewer, it is output to the shell from which the appletviewer was started. With Netscape Navigator, it goes to a separate window called the Java Console, which you can choose to show by selecting Show Java Console from the Options menu. For Microsoft Internet Explorer, check "Enable Java Logging," in the advanced options panel. The file goes into <windowsdir>\java\javalog.txt, e.g. c:\windows\java\javalog.txt.

The design paradigm of applets is that inside the paint method

```
public void paint(Graphics g)
```

of the applet, you can draw a String by calling a routine that operates on the Graphics object argument to paint. By convention, the Graphics object is usually given the name "g," so the String will be drawn like this:

```
g.drawString(some_string, x, y)
```

This will place the some_string text in the Applet at position (x,y) in the component you are drawing on. Applets use drawing methods rather than stream I/O because they are by nature graphical windowing objects, not command line text-oriented creatures.

Interactive Input

So much for output. Turning now to input, again the features differ between applet and application. To input some text in an applet, you would use an object called a textField, which is described in a later chapter.

To read values from the keyboard in applications, we use file i/o. The exact combination of features is unfortunately not at all obvious, but it forms a good case study for explaining how Java I/O is modular. First, let's look at the code that executes the interactive input of various primitive types.

Your application must make the declarations given in Table 8-1, then you can read each primitive type as shown.

Table 8-1: **How to read from the keyboard**

Preliminary declarations

```import java.util.*;```
```import java.io.*;```
 	
```static DataInputStream dis = new DataInputStream(System.in);```
```static StringTokenizer st;```

Note: An exception handler declaration is also needed. You can declare the exception as part of the method signature or you can wrap a "try ... catch" around the input statements.

Primitive type	Code to read it from System.in

boolean	```st=new StringTokenizer(dis.readLine());```
	```boolean bo = new```
	``` Boolean(st.nextToken()).booleanValue();```

char	```char ch = dis.readLine().charAt(0);```

int	```st=new StringTokenizer(dis.readLine());```
	``` int myint =```
	```Integer.parseInt(st.nextToken());```

byte	input as int, and cast it to byte.
short	input as int, and cast it to short.

long	```st=new StringTokenizer(dis.readLine());```
	``` long mylong =```
	```Long.parseLong(st.nextToken());```

float	```st=new StringTokenizer(dis.readLine());```
	```float f = new```
	``` Float(st.nextToken()).floatValue();```

double	```st=new StringTokenizer(dis.readLine());```
	```double d = new```
	``` Double(st.nextToken()).doubleValue();```

String	```String s= dis.readLine();```

Notes
 	
Each statement or group of statements must have an exception handler wrapped around it as shown in the opposite column. Or, the method must declare that it throws an IOException.
	```try {```
	```... // put I/O statement in here```
	```}```
	```catch(IOException ioe)```
	```{ioe.printStackTrace();}```

You need to use this until the JDK 1.1 introduces support for scanning character text from an input stream.

Here is an example program showing all of this put together. You should try running it.

```
import java.util.*;
import java.io.*;
public class read {

    static PrintStream p = System.out;
    static DataInputStream dis = new DataInputStream( System.in );

    public static void main(String argv[]) {
    try {
        p.print("Enter int: ");  p.flush();
        st=new StringTokenizer(dis.readLine());
        int myint = Integer.parseInt(st.nextToken());

        p.print("Enter double: ");  p.flush();
        st=new StringTokenizer(dis.readLine());
        double d = new Double( st.nextToken() ).doubleValue();

        p.println("my int = "+myint);
        p.println("my double = "+d);
        } catch(IOException ioe) { p.println(ioe); System.exit(-1); }
    }
}
```

We'll explain in more detail a little later, but for now just note that we are using methods from the class DataInputStream on the System.in FileInputStream object.

A look at the DataInputStream class in $JAVAHOME/src/java/io/ DataInputStream.java will also reveal a method called readInt(). However, you won't get the result you expect if you try to read from the keyboard with:

```
int yourint = dis.readInt();
```

This readInt, like most of the methods in DataInputStream, is intended for files, not interactive I/O. It expects to find its data in binary format, not ASCII. And it expects to read exactly 4 bytes, waiting for further characters until you provide that many. It is quite happy to interpret a carriage return as a character that forms part of the int. 🍎

The worthless "scanf ( ) " of C

Java has slightly better support for interactive I/O than C, but that is hardly saying much. C programmers will probably be nodding in recognition at this point. C features a library call named scanf() that is so riddled with misfeatures and design mistakes that it is more trouble to use than it is worth. The official advice to C programmers who want to do interactive input is: "Do not use scanf. Instead, read an entire line from the keyboard and then use scanf to pick out the pieces you want."

Java is better than this, but not by much. Programmers should not be forced to program their own interactive I/O. They deserve a simple, usable console I/O package as part of the language. This omission is rectified in the JDK 1. 1 release. Similarly, the first major release of Java, JDK 1.0, had no provision for formatting output. It was not possible to say "print this double with 3 places after the decimal point" unless you did all the programming yourself.

A number of talented programmers have stepped up to fill the gap. Jef Poskanzer wrote one package that is available at http://www.acme.com/java/software/ Acme.Fmt.html. This is another area of missing functionality that may eventually be filled in by a standard library.

File I/O: Everything is done by Streams

Java I/O is built on Streams. By itself, a pool of data just lays there inertly: to make it flow into or out of your program, use a stream object. A Stream is just a flow of data. The great beauty of Java Streams is that they are not restricted to files, but can be applied to any source of data, and any destination for data.

In other words, a stream in real life could be supplied by a lake, by another stream, by a pumping station, by a spring, and so on. A Stream in Java could be getting its bytes from (or sending them to) a file, a String, a socket on the net, an array in memory, the terminal and so on. The Stream knows how to pull bytes out of each of these, but you won't necessarily know, nor need to know. The Stream class hides or *encapsulates* all these details. As a result, your program doesn't have to be cluttered with low level detail about how input from a socket differs from keyboard input.

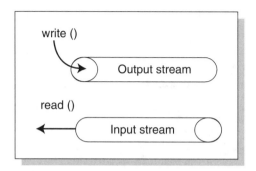

Figure 8-1:   An Input Stream and an Output Stream

An input stream is something that sends us a succession of bytes, and an output stream is something that we can send a series of bytes to.

Another way to understand this is to consider a stream as letting you do much the same things as an open file descriptor, but the focus is on the operations (flow of data) rather than the implementation (file descriptor). A Stream may have a file descriptor as part of its private data.

You also have the ability to "push" streams on top of each other to stack up" several different kinds of processing and accessing data. This is similar to the STREAMS facility in the Unix kernel that connects device drivers to user processes. Java streams are not directly related to Unix kernel STREAMS, but are a similar kind of idea.

The Java source for the I/O classes can (and should) be examined at `$JAVAHOME/src/java/io/*`. You just instantiate a stream object and then can do I/O on it immediately. There is no separate "open()" step. If the instantiation didn't throw an exception, you are ready to go. And there's no concept of "I am opening this file for ASCII writes/binary data writes" as occurs on the PC with other forms of I/O. You write what you write, without making a needless distinction between character and other data.

A given Stream is device-independent, greatly reducing the range of library calls you need to memorize. It makes it easier to change and debug too. Network problems? Temporarily modify your socket stream to receive data from an in-memory array, and change it back when you have everything debugged.

Input Streams

Here are the four fundamental input Streams from the java.io package:

FileInputStream:	Gets bytes from a File
StringBufferInputStream:	Gets bytes from a StringBuffer
ByteArrayInputStream:	Gets bytes from an array
PipedInputStream:	Gets bytes from a pipe (think "hosepipe" it's just a data structure that squirts bytes at you).

All of these classes have some methods in common, especially:

* `public int read();`   get a byte returns -1 on EOF.
* `public int read(byte[] b, int offset, int length);` reads length bytes into your array b starting at offset. Returns -1 if there are no more bytes to read (EOF), otherwise returns the total number of bytes read.

All of these classes operate solely on bytes. If you want to obtain an integer from one of these Streams it's up to you to assemble it from four successive bytes.

The constructors for FileInputStream let you name the file you are interested in. The constructors for ByteArrayInputStream let you indicate the byte array that is the source of your data, and so on.

Here are two examples of how to instantiate a FileInputStream. All of the constructors require that you provide the name of the file either directly, as a literal string or variable, or indirectly by giving a File object that has already been associated with a filename.

Example 1

```
FileInputStream fis;
try  {
     fis = new FileInputStream("animals.txt");
     ...
}
catch (FileNotFoundException fnfe) {
     ...
```

Example 2

```
File f;
FileInputStream fis;
try {
    f = new File("plum");
    fis = new FileInputStream( f );
} catch ...
```

Basic input operates on bytes, and there are three choices for getting data:

- Input a single byte, returning (int) -1 at EOF

- Input filling an array of bytes,

- Input filling a range within an array of bytes.

All reads are blocking reads: if the data is not there, it does not return from the read until it is. These three methods are the "read" methods shown in the class FileInputStream below.

Here is a small program that reads an existing file and echoes its bytes to the screen. Before you run this program, first create the text file "animals.txt" for it to read. Put the names of a few animals in it.

```
// a program to demonstrate reading bytes from a file
import java.io.*;
public class read {

    public static void main(String argv[]) {
        try {

            FileInputStream f = new FileInputStream( "animals.txt" );
            int b;
            while( (b=f.read()) != -1 ) {
                System.out.print( (char) b );
            }

            System.out.flush();
        } catch(IOException ioe) {ioe.printStackTrace() }
    }
}
```

If you compile and run this, you will see the contents of your animals.txt file printed as the file is read, like this

```
% javac read.java
% java read

dog
bandicoot
mouse
```

Some of the input Stream classes have their own quirks. In some classes the methods are synchronized, while in other classes the methods can throw an IOException. There are instances when there are other methods, like `available()`, to say how many bytes the next read can return, `skip()` to advance over some number of bytes, and `reset()` to go back to the beginning of the stream.

Programmers writing applications frequently ask how they can access the RS232 serial port (or modem, etc) on a system. There's a hard way and an easy way. The hard way is to use a native method (a method written in C or some other non-Java language) and link that into your code.

The easy way can only be done if your operating system makes devices appear like files in the file system. For instance, on a Unix system, the serial port typically has a name like "/dev/ttya" and under Windows, the serial port may be called "COM2:".

If you can get at the serial port through the filesystem, then you can open it just as a regular file and have at it. However, note that you can only read *or* write with a stream (not both), so accessing the port with a stream only gives unidirectional access. If you need to read *and* write use two streams. ❦

The basic input streams look like this:

FileInputStream: The basic input operations to read a byte or an array of bytes, skip over some bytes, and close the stream.

Commonly Used Methods:

```
// constructors
 public FileInputStream(String name) throws FileNotFoundException
 public FileInputStream(File file) throws FileNotFoundException

 public native int read() throws IOException
 public int read(byte b[]) throws IOException
 public int read(byte b[], int off, int len) throws IOException

 public native long skip(long n) throws IOException
 public native int available() throws IOException
 public native void close() throws IOException
```

`ByteArrayInputStream:`   Implements a buffer (array of bytes) that can be used as an input stream. Although the byte array is in memory, this stream allows you to access it via read() calls.

Commonly Used Methods:

```
// constructors:
 public ByteArrayInputStream(byte buf[])
 public ByteArrayInputStream(byte buf[], int offset, int length)

 public synchronized int read()
 public synchronized int read(byte b[], int off, int len)

 public synchronized long skip(long n)
 public synchronized int available()
 public synchronized void reset()
```

`StringBufferInputStream:`   Implements a string buffer (modifiable string) that can be used as an input stream. Similar to the ByteArrayInputStream in that it allows you to get data serially from a StringBuffer through read() calls.

Commonly Used Methods:

```
// constructor:
 public StringBufferInputStream(String s)

 public synchronized int read()
 public synchronized int read(byte b[], int off, int len)

 public synchronized long skip(long n)
 public synchronized int available()
 public synchronized void reset()
```

We have already seen in the case study in the previous chapter how to read from a file using a FileInputStream. The following are some examples of typical use of the other classes.

Here is an example using the StringBufferInputStream class to obtain characters from a string with "read()" calls. Bear in mind that this is a small example to show the concept.

```
import java.io.*;
public class test7a {
    static String s = new String( "aardvark butterfly\n" +
        "cat dalmatian\n" +
                "eagle fish\ngopher hippo\ninyala jackal\nkyloe " +
                "lamb\nmoose nanny-goat\nopossum pandora\n" );

    static StringBufferInputStream sbis =
        new StringBufferInputStream( s );

    public static void main (String a[]) {
        int c;
            while ((c=sbis.read())!= -1) {

                System.out.print((char)c);

                }

            }
}
```

The result of running this program is that each call to sbis.read() comes back with one character, which is printed by the call to System.out.print(). The output looks like this:

```
aardvark butterfly
cat dalmatian
eagle fish
gopher hippo
inyala jackal
kyloe lamb
moose nanny-goat
opossum pandora
```

Output Streams

Like regular streams (rivers, creeks, etc.) any given stream only flows in one direction. You can read from a stream, or write to a stream, but if you need to read and write, you will need two different streams. Here are the three fundamental output Streams from the java.io package:

FileOutputStream: Writes bytes to a File

ByteArrayOutputStream: Puts bytes into its own temporary internal storage, for later retrieval

PipedOutputStream: Puts bytes into a pipe (think "drainpipe" it's just a data structure that drinks down bytes that you pour into it).

All of these classes have some methods in common, especially:

- `public int write();` put a byte
- `public int write(byte[] b, int offset, int length);` write length bytes from array b.

All of these classes operate solely on bytes. If you want to write something bigger than a byte (like an int) into one of these Streams, it's up to you to break it down and write a series of successive bytes. There are three ways to write bytes:

- Output a single byte,
- Output an array of bytes,
- Output a range from within an array of bytes.

The output classes are really just the counterparts of the input classes that we have already seen. Instead of providing a couple of "read()" methods they provide some variations on "write()".

All writes are blocking writes: control does not return from the write until the I/O transfer is handed over to the operating system. An I/O operation may or may not block just its own thread. Depending on the underlying implementation it may block the entire process (all threads!) The compiler from Sun Microsystems for Windows 95 has a clever implementation—it turns all I/O into asynchronous I/O, so only the I/O thread is blocked. Watch out for this on other platforms. These three methods are the "write" methods shown in the class FileOutput-Stream below.

The classes look like this:

FileOutputStream: The basic input operations to write a byte or an array of bytes.

Commonly used Methods:

```
// constructors
public FileOutputStream(String name) throws IOException
public FileOutputStream(File file) throws IOException
public FileOutputStream(FileDescriptor fdObj)

public native void write(byte b) throws IOException
public void write(byte b[]) throws IOException
public void write(byte b[], int off, int len)
                        throws IOException

public native void close() throws IOException
public final FileDescriptor getFD()  throws IOException
protected void finalize() throws IOException
```

ByteArrayOutputStream: Implements an in-memory byte array that can be written to as an Output Stream. The array grows as needed. There are two methods to read (retrieve) the data: toByteArray() and toString().

Commonly Used Methods:

```
// constructors
public ByteArrayOutputStream()
public ByteArrayOutputStream(int size)

public synchronized void write(int b)
public synchronized void write(byte b[], int off, int len)
public synchronized void writeTo(OutputStream out)
                        throws IOException

public int size()
public synchronized void reset()

public synchronized byte toByteArray()[]
public String toString()
public String toString(int hibyte)
```

The constructors for FileOutputStream let you name the file you are interested in. The constructors for ByteArrayOutputStream let you indicate the byte array that the data is coming from. It will write the bytes into its own internal storage, from whence they can be retrieved as a string (by calling toString()) or a byte array (by calling toByteArray()). The benefit of ByteArrayOutputStream is that it will automatically grow its own internal storage array as necessary to store everything you send it. So this makes a great temporary buffer without any programming effort on your part.

Here is a small program that writes the names of some beers to a new file. The name you supply as a command line argument. Proper error handling is omitted from this example for clarity.

```
// a program to demonstrate how to write bytes to a file
import java.io.*;
public class write {

    public static void main(String argv[]) {

        byte beers[] = {'a','l','e','\n','l','a','g','e','r','\n'};
        try {

            FileOutputStream f = new FileOutputStream( argv[0] );
            f.write( beers );
            f.close();

        } catch(IOException ioe) {
            System.out.println(ioe);
            System.exit(-1);
        }
    }
}
```

You can compile and run the program like this:

```
%java write.java

%javac write  beer.txt

%cat beer.txt

ale
lager
```

The Unix command "cat" corresponds to the Windows "type." It lists the contents of a file. Notice especially how easy it is to stream output into a file. There is no separate open() operation—instantiating a FileOutputStream with the name of the file is enough to create and open the file. There are several forms of write(). The one we use here writes the entire byte array to the file. Finally, close() the file to ensure that all internal buffers are flushed.

To make the Stream output to a byte array instead of a file, we would use the ByteArrayOutputStream by changing the constructor, like this:

```
try {
  ByteArrayOutputStream f = new ByteArrayOutputStream( 128 );
    f.write( beers );

    byte plum[] = f.toByteArray();  // gets the bytes back

} catch(IOException ioe) { System.out.println(ioe); }
```

You cannot touch the internal buffer of ByteArrayOutputStream, but you have the whole thing cleared (call reset()), or handed back to you as shown in the code above. This is of the most use when you write several different things into the buffer from several different places, and don't want to keep track of indexes or array sizes yourself.

But we still only have the ability to write bytes. For more advanced I/O features and other types we need filtered I/O, described in the next section.

Layering Streams on Top of One Another

Now, here is the really significant conceptual breakthrough of Streams: you can connect one Stream to another, and the result is also a Stream. Each Stream in this chain has the chance to modify the data as it goes by, and it can also offer a selection of more sophisticated methods to operate on the stream. Remember this piece of important information: *Streams can be "pushed" or layered on top of each other to provide filtered processing,* as shown in Figure 8-2.

The constructors of these filtered streams take a Stream as an argument and give back a filtered stream. Let's show how this works in practice by describing the three filtered output streams that java.io provides

PrintStream: Provides methods to output a printable (Unicode) representation of all the primitive types. This will typically be used when the output will eventually be seen by people.

DataOutputStream: Provides methods to output a binary representation of all the primitive types. This will typically be used when the output will be processed by another program.

BufferedOutputStream: Supports output buffering. Instead of many small writes being made, this Stream will only write to the stream underneath it when the buffer is full, or when you call the flush() method. Buffering I/O almost always gives a performance improvement. The constructors allow you to specify the buffer size or take the default.

Figure 8-2: Layering streams on top of each other

As an example, PrintStream supports these methods:

```
public class PrintStream  extends FileterOutputStream {
    public PrintStream(OutputStream out);
    public PrintStream(OutputStream out, boolean autoflush);

    public void print(Object obj);
    synchronized public void print(String s);
    synchronized public void print(char s[]);
    public void print(char c);
    public void print(int i);
    public void print(long l);
    public void print(float f);
    public void print(double d);
    public void print(boolean b);

    public void println()
    // println versions of all the nine print methods above. E.g.:
    synchronized public void println(Object obj);
    synchronized public void println(String s);

    public void write(int b);
    public void write(byte b[], int off, int len);
    public void flush();
    public void close();
    public boolean checkError();
}
```

We always use a filter stream in conjunction with another stream. Here's an example showing how we can use the methods of Printstream on a FileOutputStream.

```
import java.io.*;
public class write2 {

    public static void main(String argv[]) {

        try {

            FileOutputStream f = new FileOutputStream( argv[0] );

            PrintStream p = new PrintStream( f );

            float fl = 3.1415f;
            p.println( "your float value is: " + fl );

        } catch(IOException ioe) {}
    }
}
```

We are now able to print floats, booleans, ints and other types to a file in Unicode, instead of just being able to write bytes. Running this program gives this result:

```
% java write2 myfile.txt
% cat myfile.txt

your float value is: 3.1415
```

If you had written a float value without using the PrintStream you would have got a binary not a printable value. The standard output Stream System.out is a PrintStream object. Similarly, we strive for a performance gain by pushing a buffered output stream into our file, then pushing a print stream onto that:

```
try {

    FileOutputStream f = new FileOutputStream( argv[0] );

    BufferedOutputStream bos = new BufferedOutputStream( f );

    PrintStream p = new PrintStream( bos );

    float fl = 3.1415f;
    p.println( "your float value is: " + fl );

    p.close();

} catch(IOException ioe) {System.out.println(ioe);}
```

You can instantiate and push streams in one line, but that quickly becomes unreadable, like this:

```
PrintStream p = new PrintStream( new BufferedOutputStream(
                new FileOutputStream( argv[0] ) ));
```

The methods of DataOutputStream are similar to the methods of PrintStream, but the data is written in binary form, not Unicode. The methods are:

```
public class DataOutputStream
    extends FilterOutputStream implements DataOutput {

    public DataOutputStream(OutputStream out);

    public synchronized void write(int b) throws IOException;
    public synchronized void write(byte b[], int off, int len)
       throws IOException;

    public void flush() throws IOException;
    public final int size();

    public final void writeBoolean(boolean v) throws IOException;
    public final void writeByte(int v) throws IOException;
    public final void writeShort(int v) throws IOException;
    public final void writeChar(int v) throws IOException;
    public final void writeInt(int v) throws IOException;
    public final void writeLong(long v) throws IOException;
    public final void writeFloat(float v) throws IOException;
    public final void writeDouble(double v) throws IOException;
    public final void writeBytes(String s) throws IOException;
    public final void writeChars(String s) throws IOException;
    public final void writeUTF(String str) throws IOException;
}
```

It's guaranteed that a DataInputStream can read back anything that a DataOutputStream has written.

Filtered Input Streams

Just as there are input streams and output streams, there are filter input streams as well as filter output streams. The four standard filter input streams provide by Java I/O are:

DataInputStream: Provides methods to input the binary representation of all the primitive types. This is the input class that corresponds to DataOutputStream. DataInputStream can read anything that DataOutputStream can write.

BufferedInputStream: Supports input buffering. Instead of many small reads being made, this Stream will only read from the stream underneath it when the buffer is empty. Buffering I/O almost always gives a performance improvement.

LineNumberInputStream: Provides methods to keep track of the number of lines that have been read. This stream is intended for pushing on top of some stream that's doing textual (not binary) input.

PushbackInputStream: Compiler writers everywhere will love this class. It provides single character look ahead in an input stream, allowing a character to be read once, then pushed back into the input stream so the next read will get it again. This is an idiom used in some parsing algorithms.

Why do we have a PushbackInputStream (which is of use mostly to those writing LALR(1) parsers), but no PrintInputStream to get Unicode text for all primitive types (which would be of use to every Java programmer in the world)? That's a very good question, and if you ever find out the answer be sure to let me know.

The methods for DataInputStream are:

```
public class DataInputStream
        extends FilterInputStream implements DataInput {

    public DataInputStream(InputStream in);

    public final int read(byte b[]) throws IOException;
    public final int read(byte b[], int off, int len) throws IOException;

    public final void readFully(byte b[]) throws IOException;
    public final void readFully(byte b[], int off, int len)
                                       throws IOException;
    public final int skipBytes(int n) throws IOException;

    public final boolean readBoolean() throws IOException;
    public final byte readByte() throws IOException;
    public final int readUnsignedByte() throws IOException;
    public final short readShort() throws IOException;
    public final int readUnsignedShort() throws IOException;
    public final char readChar() throws IOException;
    public final int readInt() throws IOException;
    public final long readLong() throws IOException;
    public final float readFloat() throws IOException;
    public final double readDouble() throws IOException;

    /*
     * Reads in a line that has been terminated by a \n, \r,
     * \r\n or EOF.
     */
    public final String readLine() throws IOException;

    public final String readUTF() throws IOException;
    public final static String readUTF(DataInput in) throws IOException;
}
```

Most of the DataInputStream methods have names that suggest the datatype they operate on: readByte(), readChar etc. The method readUTF() may need explaining.

Universal Transformation Format (UTF) is a hack to support multibyte characters on systems that were only designed for ASCII. In UTF, a character can be one, two, or three bytes long. The first byte of any character specifies whether it is a one, two, or three byte character. If the most significant bit is 0, then it is a one byte character, in ASCII. If the most significant bits are 110, then it is a two byte character. If the most significant bits are 1110, then it is a three byte character. Using this ingenious encoding, programs can use 7-bit ASCII with no change at all, but also have the ability to use multibyte characters, albeit in a highly inconvenient form (you need a special version of strlen() for example).

ReadUTF() will pull in a sequence of 1-3 byte UTF characters and pack them into a regular Unicode String. There's a corresponding writeUTF() that turns a String into UTF. UTF is a compatible interim solution while vendors of ASCII-based systems are figuring out how to move to Unicode to support the two-thirds of the world whose native alphabets can't be expressed in ASCII.

Write your own filters

You can also write your own filters that do anything you like to the bytes as they go by: keep a count, sum up control fields, substitute certain values for other values and so on. Make your code extend FilterOutputStream or FilterInputStream as appropriate. 🐛

Here is an example of a user-programmed filter to change (or "censor") all "+" characters to new lines in an input file.

```java
import java.io.*;
public class filt {

    public static void main(String args[]) {
        FileInputStream fis=null;
        try {fis = new FileInputStream("example.txt"); }
        catch(FileNotFoundException fnf){System.out.println(fnf); }

        Censor c = new Censor(System.out, (int)'+', (int)'\n');
        int i=0;
        try {
        while( (i=fis.read() )!= -1 )
                c.write(i);
        } catch(IOException ioe){System.err.println(ioe); }
    }
}


class Censor extends FilterOutputStream {

    int saved_remove=0;
    int saved_replace=0;
    OutputStream saved_out=out;

    Censor(OutputStream out, int remove, int replace) {
        super(out);
        saved_remove=remove;
        saved_replace=replace;
    }

    public void write(int b) throws IOException {
        if (b==saved_remove) b=saved_replace;
        saved_out.write(b);
    }
}
```

Here is an example of how to push one input stream onto another, to gain the filtered processing of both. The program reads from a string, but also keeps track of the lines in the input using the LineNumberInputStream.

```java
// shows the use of various input streams
import java.io.*;
public class test7b {
    static String s = new String(
        "aardvark butterfly\ncat dalmatian\n" +
                "eagle fish\ngopher hippo\ninyala jackal\nkyloe " +
                "lamb\nmoose nanny-goat\n" );

    static StringBufferInputStream sbis =
        new StringBufferInputStream( s );

    static LineNumberInputStream lnis =
        new LineNumberInputStream( sbis );

    public static void main (String a[]) {
        int c;
        try {
            while ((c=lnis.read())!= -1) {

                System.out.print((char)c);
                if (c=='\n') {
                    System.out.print("that finishes input line "
            + lnis.getLineNumber() + "\n\n");
                }

            }
        } catch (IOException ioe) {
                System.out.println("Exception reading stream");
                ioe.printStackTrace();
                System.exit(0);
        }
    }
}
```

Note that (unlike when using StringBufferInputStream) the use of LineNumber-InputStream may involve an I/O exception, and you must make provision for this. The results of running this program are:

```
aardvark butterfly
that finishes input line 1

cat dalmatian
that finishes input line 2

eagle fish
that finishes input line 3

gopher hippo
that finishes input line 4

inyala jackal
that finishes input line 5

kyloe lamb
that finishes input line 6

moose nanny-goat
that finishes input line 7
```

Using the framework of the above example, push another input stream onto the existing two. Use SequenceInputStream to supply a FileInputStream as well as the StringBufferInputStream that we are using above. Create a file called animals.txt that contains a few more creatures. Instantiate the SequenceInputStream and push a LineNumberInputStream onto it, to demonstrate the seamless flow of data from two different sources. (Easy).

On MS-DOS based systems like Windows 95, a newline in an ASCII file is represented by two characters: ASCII carriage return followed by ASCII linefeed. On Unix systems, a newline is represented by just one character: an ASCII linefeed (0x0a). On a Macintosh, carriage return signals a new line. Having two characters to represent newline is a carryover from the days of mechanical teletypes[1], when it was useful to have one action to advance the roll of paper and another to move the print head back to the left margin. This hasn't been useful for twenty years or more now.

1. Teletype is a trademark of an antique corporation. The sound of a teletype machine ("KERchunk-a-chunk-a-chunk") is often used as a radio special effect to indicate the arrival of timely news. No competent news organization has used teletypes in decades.

The different line delimiters can bedevil programs that are written to expect one convention but are run on a system with the other. For example, without taking this into account, the anagram program will run under Unix, but fail on Windows. The reason is this part of the source:

```
while ( (c=fis.read()) != EOF ) {
// how to read past EOLN on a PC?
    if ( c == '\n' ) break;
    buffer[i++] = (char) c;
```

The key statement says "if this is a newline character, break out of the loop and deal with the string we just completed reading." On a Windows system, this will leave a '\r' character jammed on the end of each token in the input stream.

There's a kludgey way to fix this and a proper way. The kludgey way is to explicitly check for the carriage return character following newlines, and throw it away if it's there. In the anagram program, it would be an extra read, like this:

```
while ( (c=fis.read()) != EOF ) {
// kludge up EOLN on a PC
    if ( c == '\r' ) c=fis.read();
    if ( c == '\n' ) break;
    buffer[i++] = (char) c;
```

A better way to accomplish this is to use the standard DataInputStream or LineNumberInputStream. Both of these Classes are capable of coping with an end of line conveyed by \n or \r\n or \r or EOF.

Modify the anagram program in the previous chapter so that it uses a DataInputStream instead of a FileInputStream, and can be run happily on all platforms.

There is also a `StreamTokenizer` class that can be pushed onto an input stream. It will attempt basic lexing of the stream, namely assembling sequences of characters into string tokens. Use javap java.io StreamTokenizer to review its methods.

When Push Comes to Shove

There are a couple of other Stream classes that are not filters, but have a similar effect. The first is SequenceInputStream, which allows you to concatenate two streams, creating one new stream. The first stream will be read until *end of file* (EOF), but EOF will not be returned. Instead the program will then start reading from the second stream. You can stack up an arbitrary number of input streams together using this class.

An example of its use is: if you had several input files with the same format, and you want to treat them exactly as though they were one big file. Another opportunity to use it is when you have a file and an array with some data in the same format. You can effectively concatenate one to the other and feed it all to the consumer without it ever knowing about the two sources.

The class SequenceInputStream is very brief and just contains the methods:

```
public class SequenceInputStream extends InputStream {

    public SequenceInputStream(Enumeration e);
    public SequenceInputStream(InputStream s1, InputStream s2);

    public int read() throws IOException;
    public int read(byte buf[], int pos, int len) throws IOException;
    public void close() throws IOException;
}
```

There are also two stream classes that we always use together, in a matched consumer/producer pair. The classes are PipedInputStream and PipedOutputStream. An object of one of these is connected to an object of the other class, providing a safe way (no data race conditions) for one thread to send a stream of data to another thread.

PipedOutputStream: Used in conjunction with a PipedInputStream to let threads pass data to each other by means of writes and reads on a common pipe.

Commonly Used Methods:

```
// constructors
public PipedOutputStream(PipedInputStream snk)
                    throws IOException
public PipedOutputStream()

public void connect(PipedInputStream snk) throws IOException

public void write(int b)  throws IOException
public void write(byte b[], int off, int len)
        throws IOException

public void close()  throws IOException
```

PipedInputStream: This class is used in pairs with PipedOutputStream. It allows two threads to communicate using I/O calls.

What one thread writes into the PipedOutputStream, will be read by another thread that has instantiated PipedInputStream. These two classes mean that programmers have a ready-made producer/consumer buffer, and do not have to code this from first principles.

Commonly Used Methods:

```
// constructors:
public PipedInputStream (PipedOutputStream src) throws IOException
public PipedInputStream ()

public void connect(PipedOutputStream src) throws IOException
synchronized void receive(int b) throws IOException
synchronized void receive(byte b[], int off, int len)
                                    throws IOException
synchronized void receivedLast()

public synchronized int read()  throws IOException
public synchronized int read(byte b[], int off, int len)
                                    throws IOException
public void close()  throws IOException
```

As an example of the use of Piped streams, the program below re-implements the Producer/Consumer problem, but uses Piped streams instead of wait/notify. The version using wait/notify was shown in Chapter 5, and if you compare the two versions you'll see that this one is considerably simpler.

```java
import java.io.*;
public class pipes {

   public static void main(String args[]) {
      Producer p = new Producer();
      p.start();

      Consumer c = new Consumer(p);
      c.start();
   }
}


class Producer extends Thread {
    protected PipedOutputStream po = new PipedOutputStream();
    private PrintStream po2 = new PrintStream(po);

    public void run() {
       // just keep producing
       for(;;) produce();
    }

    private final long start = System.currentTimeMillis();
    private final String banana() {
        return "" + (int) (System.currentTimeMillis() - start);
    }

    void produce() {
       String s = banana();
       po2.println( s );
       System.out.println("produced " + s);
    }

}
```

In the code above, notice how we push a PrintStream onto the PipedOutput-
Stream, making it easy to write Strings into the pipe, rather than bytes or byte
arrays.

```java
class Consumer extends Thread {
    private PipedInputStream pip;
    private DataInputStream d;

    // java constructor idiom, save argument.
    Consumer(Producer who) {
        try {
            pip = new PipedInputStream(who.po);
            d = new DataInputStream( pip );
        } catch (IOException ie) {
            System.out.println(ie);
        }
    }

     String get(){
        String s=null;
        try {    s= d.readLine();   // read from pipe.
        } catch (IOException ie) {System.out.println(ie);}
        return s;
     }

    public void run() {
        java.util.Random r = new java.util.Random();
        for(;;) {
            String result = get();
            System.out.println("consumed: "+result);
            // next lines are just to make things asynchronous
            int randomtime = r.nextInt() % 1250;
            try{sleep(randomtime);} catch(Exception e){}
        }
    }
}
```

The Java I/O classes have been criticized (with some justification) as being
too numerous, and too extravagant with their use of inheritance. The
PushBackInputStream, for instance, should have been part of a useful existing
stream (say, BufferedInputStream), rather than adding an extra level of method
calls for each character. But the Piped streams allow for real simplification in
inter-thread communication.

A Word About IOExceptions

Let's say a few words on the subject of IOExceptions. If you look at the runtime source, you'll see that there are four basic I/O related exceptions (there are another five that have to do with network I/O). The basic I/O related exceptions are:

- `FileNotFoundException`

- `InterruptedIOException`

- `UTFDataFormatError`

- `EOFException`

These names are self-explanatory, except for the last one. The name EOFException suggests that it is thrown whenever EOF is encountered, and that perhaps therefore this exception can be used as the condition to break out of a loop. That's not what happens, and no, it can't generally be used that way. The EOFException would be better named UnexpectedEOFException, as it is only raised when the programmer has asked for a fixed definite amount of input, and when the end of file is reached before all the requested amount of data has been obtained. EOFException is only raised in two classes, DataInputStream and RandomAccessFile, (and their subclasses of course). It is never raised when the normal end of file is reached.

Other than in the two classes mentioned, the usual way to detect EOF is to check for the -1 return value from a byte read, not by trying to catch EOFexception.

Interactive Input Redux

Finally we're in a position to explain what all that stuff was at the beginning of the chapter. There isn't a "PrintInputStream" in Java 1.0 (but there should be) so we have to fake one up. We introduced the following kind of code to read an int from the keyboard.

```
import java.util.*;
import java.io.*;

static DataInputStream dis = new DataInputStream( System.in );
static StringTokenizer st;

st=new StringTokenizer(dis.readLine());
int myint = Integer.parseInt(st.nextToken());
```

Let's take these statements step by step. The two imports allow us to use the classes without giving their lengthy entire name each time. The line

```
static DataInputStream dis = new DataInputStream( System.in );
```

pushes a DataInputStream onto the regular input stream whose name is "in" and that lives in object System. That now allows us to use the DataInputStream methods on System.in. Most of the DataInputStream methods are for fetching binary data, but it does have a readLine() that will obtain an entire String (everything up to a newline, and the newline is discarded). We then feed that string into a String-Tokenizer, which is a utility class that removes white space

```
st=new StringTokenizer(dis.readLine());
```

and hands you the next sequence of non-white space characters when you call its method nextToken(). Finally, the last step is to feed the result of that into

```
int myint = Integer.parseInt(st.nextToken());
```

which takes the string, and gives you back the corresponding binary int value. A similar algorithm is followed for reading all the other primitive types interactively.

That deals with the most commonly used input and output streams. There are a couple of other facilities to be aware of, too, such as random access I/O.

Random Access

The class RandomAccessFile allows the file pointer to be moved to arbitrary positions in the file prior to reading or writing. This allows you to "jump around" in the file reading and writing data with random (nonsequential) access. You provide a mode string when you open the file, specifying whether you are opening it for read access only "r", or read and update access "rw".

Here is an example of how you would append to a file, using the RandomAccessFile class. We will write a few more animals on the end of the "animals.txt" file created in the previous programming challenge.

```java
import java.io.RandomAccessFile;
class test7e {

    static public void main(String a[]) {
        RandomAccessFile rf;
        try  {
            rf = new RandomAccessFile("animals.txt", "rw");

            rf.seek( rf.length() );

            rf.writeBytes("ant bee\ncat dog\n");

            rf.close();

        } catch (Exception e) {
            System.out.println("file snafu");
            System.exit(0);
        }
    }
}
```

This example will extend the "animals.txt" file by appending the string on the end.

Write an elementary version of the Unix "cat" (concatenate) command. This should take a list of files on the command line, and type out their contents one after the other to the standard output device. (Easy to Medium difficulty)

The class File

A number of methods are available in the class File to provide information about a file or a directory. Here are the methods:

```
public class File {

    constructors:
        public File(String path)
        public File(String path, String name)
        public File(File dir, String name)

    deleting a file:
        public boolean delete()

    to do with file name:
        public String getName()
        public String getPath()
        public String getAbsolutePath()
        public String getParent()
        public boolean renameTo(File dest)

    getting the attributes of a file:
        public boolean exists()
        public boolean canWrite()
        public boolean canRead()
        public boolean isFile()
        public boolean isDirectory()
        public native boolean isAbsolute()
        public long lastModified()
        public long length()
        public boolean equals(Object obj)

    to do with the directory:
        public boolean mkdir()
        public boolean mkdirs()
        public String[] list()
        public String[] list(FilenameFilter filter)

    miscellaneous:
        public static final char pathSeparatorChar
        public int hashCode()
        public String toString()
```

Write a Java program that creates a subdirectory "Fruit" of the current directory if it does not already exist.

It should then create a file called "yam" in that directory, leaving it if it already existed. Make the program print out what it is doing. Finally it should print the attributes of both the file and the directory it is in. 🍎

Platform Specific I/O

Since file I/O results in something that has an existence outside a program, we should (alas) expect some visible differences between the different platforms. There are several such differences, as shown in Table 8-2.

Table 8-2: Platform differences relating to I/O

Property	Usual Unix Value	Usual Windows Value	Usual Macintosh Value
file.separator	/	\	:
line.separator	\n	\r\n	\r
path.separator	:	;	:

The file separator is the character used to separate components in a path name (e.g. in "c:\windows\bin\foo.exe" the character "\" is the file separator). The path separator is an OS concept, used when you want to specify several path names as starting points for searching for a command or library. Path separators are used when you set, for example CLASSPATH.

On Unix, a new line is just a linefeed character. On Windows, a new line is usually represented by two characters, carriage return followed by linefeed. On the Mac, a new line is represented by a carriage return.

Whatever platform you compile and execute your code on, if you output '\n' or do a System.out.println(), you get exactly the ASCII linefeed hex value 0x0A. You do not get the line separator appropriate for that platform. (This is arguably a bug in the case of println(); it should output the line separator for the system it is running on, rather than the system it was compiled on).

Many Windows programs can cope with reading just linefeed instead of carriage return and linefeed, but some cannot. If the difference matters to you, you need to write your code to get and use the line separator property instead of '\n'.

Even if you take this step, that just makes your program portable—not your data-file. Your data will still have been written with a platform-specific end-of-line character(s). A non-Java program that reads back this file on a different platform may choke on the unexpected format. The only ways to avoid this kind of platform dependency is to write everything in Java, or to give up using characters that are used inconsistently on different computers.

On the other hand, you can use "/" to separate the components in a filename in Windows, just as in Unix. The Windows filesystem calls all use it internally anyway, and only COMMAND.COM (the shell) can't handle it. This is an interesting artifact of history, dating from the origins of DOS as an unofficial port (known as QDOS) of CP/M with a few trivial changes to obscure the copying.

Executing a Program from Java

As the title implies, this section explains how to execute a program from Java, and read the output of that program back into your application. Just as a reminder, untrusted applets cannot do this.

The theory of executing a program from your Java program has three steps:

1. Get the object representing the current runtime environment. There is a call in class Lang.Runtime that does this.

2. Call the "exec" method in the runtime object with your command as an argument. This creates a Process object.

3. Connect the output of the Process (confusingly referred to as an input stream) to an input stream in your program, and read from it.

Here is the code.

```
import java.io.*;
public class who {

    public static void main(String args[]) {
      try {
          Runtime rt = Runtime.getRuntime();        // step 1

          Process prcs = rt.exec("/bin/who");        // step 2

          DataInputStream d = new DataInputStream( // step 3.
                                   prcs.getInputStream() );

          String line;
          while  ((line = d.readLine()) != null)
              System.out.println(line);
      } catch(IOException ioe) { System.out.println(ioe); }
    }

}
```

This uses a class inside System called Runtime that does a couple of runtime related things. The main use is to provide a way to execute other programs, but it also has methods to force garbage collection or finalization, and tell you how much total memory and free memory is available. It also uses the class Process that allows you to get in, out, err streams, and to destroy, or to wait for a process.

Several books use the example of listing files in a directory, but there is already a Java method to do that in class File. The code

```
        File f = new File(".");
      String lst[] = f.list();
```

will return an array of Strings, one string for each filename. The program /bin/who is a Unix program that lists the users on a system. Compiling and running the program above gives this output.

```
        % javac who.java
        % java who
        pvdl       console      Aug 17 12:29
        pvdl       pts/1        Aug 17 12:30
        pvdl       pts/2        Aug 17 12:30
        pvdl       pts/3        Aug 17 12:30
```

Here, it shows that I logged onto my workstation in four different windows at the stated times. Watch out for these common errors when executing a program from your Java code:

- You must provide the complete path name for the command. The exec method does not use a shell, so does not have the ability to look for executables in the search path that your shell (or command interpreter) knows about.

- This also means you cannot use commands that are built in to a shell, unless you explicitly call a shell as the program you wish to run. In MS-DOS the DIR and DEL commands are not programs, but are "internal commands" which are processed by the command interpreter (COMMAND.COM).

- Remember to instantiate an input stream to read the output from running the command. You will only be able to communicate with programs that use standard in, out and err. Some programs like xterm open a new tty, so can't be used as you would wish.

- Remember that an untrusted applet does not have permission to run exceutables.

Networking with Java

"If a packet hits a pocket on a socket on a port,

and the bus is interrupted and the interrupt's not caught,

then the socket packet pocket has an error to report.

—Programmer's traditional nursery rhyme

The biggest difficulty most people face in understanding the Java networking features lies in understanding the network part rather than the Java part. If you learn French, it doesn't mean that you can translate an article from a French medical journal. Similarly if you learn Java, you need to have an understanding of the network services and terminology before you can blithely write Internet code. This section provides a a solid review, followed by a description of the Java support.

Everything You Need To Know about TCP/IP But Failed to Learn in Kindergarten

Networking at heart is all about shifting bits from point A to point B. Usually we bundle the data bits into a packet with some more bits that say where they are to go. That, in a nutshell, is the Internet Protocol or IP. If we want to send more bits than will fit into a single packet, we can divide the bits into groups and send them in several successive packets. These are called "User Datagrams."

User Datagrams can be sent across the Internet using the User Datagram Protocol (UDP), which relies on the Internet Protocol for addressing and routing. UDP is like going to the post office, sticking on a stamp, and dropping off the packet. IP is what the mail carrier does to route and deliver the packet. Two common applications that use the UDP are: SNMP, the Simple Network Management Protocol, and TFTP, the Trivial File Transfer Protocol. See Figure 8-3.

Just as when we send several pieces of postal mail to the same address, the packages might arrive in any order. Some of them might even be delayed, or even on occasion lost altogether. This is true for UDP too; you wave good-bye to the bits as they leave your workstation, and you have no idea when they will arrive where you sent them, or even if they did.

System A has a big block of information to send to system B.

info

various internet paths

The IP software chops it into manageable sized packets, sticks an address on the front, and shoots those user datagrams over to system B.

i + ☒

f

o

n

various internet paths

But the datagrams might not arrive, or might arrive out of order.

i

various internet paths

f n o

That's B's problem!

Figure 8-3: IP and UDP (Datagram sockets)

Uncertain delivery is equally undesirable for postal mail and for network bit streams. We deal with the problem in the postal mail world (when the importance warrants the cost) by paying an extra fee to register the mail and have the mail carrier collect and bring back a signature acknowledging delivery. A similar protocol is used in the network work to guarantee reliable delivery in the order in which the packets were sent. This protocol is known as Transmission Control Protocol or "TCP." Two applications that run on top of, or use, TCP are: FTP, the File Transfer Protocol, and Telnet.

TCP uses IP as its underlying protocol (just as UDP does) for routing and delivering the bits to the correct address. However, TCP is more like a phone call than a registered mail delivery, in that a real end-to-end connection is held open for the duration of the transmission session. It takes a while to set up this stream connection, and it costs more to assure reliable sequenced delivery, but often the cost is justified. See Figure 8-4.

The access device at each end-point of a phone conversation is a telephone. The access object at each end-point of a TCP/IP session is a socket. Sockets started life as a way for two processes on the same Unix system to talk to each other, but some smart programmers realized that they could be generalized into connection end-points between processes on different machines connected by a TCP/IP network.

Sockets can deliver fast and dirty using UDP (this is a datagram socket), or slower, fussier, and reliably using TCP (this is termed a stream socket). Socket connections generally have a client end and a server end. Generally the server end just keeps listening for incoming requests ("operators are standing by" kind of thing). The client end initiates a connection, and then passes or requests information from the server.

There! Now you know everything you need to use the Java networking features.

System A has a big block of information to send to system B.
The data must be sent reliably.

Figure 8-4:   TCP/IP (Stream sockets)

What's in the Networking Library?

If you browse the network library source in $JAVAHOME/src/java/net, you'll find these classes:

InetAddress	The class that represents IP addresses and the operations on them.
DatagramPacket	A class that represents a datagram packet containing packet data, packet length, internet addresses and port. Packets can be sent and received.
DatagramSocket	This class allows datagrams to be sent and received using the UDP.
PlainSocketImpl	This is the default socket implementation. It doesn't implement any security checks nor support firewalls.
SocketImpl	This is the Socket implementation class. It is an abstract class that must be subclassed to provide an actual implementation. The Unix Socket API does not distinguish between client and server sockets, but the Java API does.
ServerSocket	The server Socket class. It uses a SocketImpl to implement the actual socket operations. It is done this way so that you are can change socket implementations depending on the kind of firewall that is used.
Socket	The client Socket class. It uses a SocketImpl to implement the actual socket operations. Again, this permits you to change socket implementations depending on the kind of firewall that is used.
URL	The class represents a Uniform Reference Locator—a reference to an object on the Web. You can open a URL and retrieve the contents, or write to it.

There are a few other classes too, but these are the key ones.

TCP/IP Client Server Model

Before we look at actual Java code, a diagram is in order showing how a client and server typically communicate over a TCP/IP network connection. Figure 8-5 shows the way the processes contact each other is by knowing the IP address (which identifies a unique computer on the Internet) and a port number (which is a simple software convention the OS maintains, allowing an incoming network connection to be routed to a specific process).

Figure 8-5: Client and server communication using a TCP/IP connection

An IP address is like a telephone number, and a port number is like an extension at that number. Together they specify a unique destination. As a matter of fact, a socket is defined as an IP address and a port number.

The client and server must agree on the same port number. The port numbers under 1024 are reserved for system software use. For simplicity, network socket connections are made to look like streams. You simply read and write data using the usual stream methods, and it automagically appears at the other end. Unlike a stream, a socket supports two-way communication. There is a method to get the input stream of a socket, and another method to get the output stream. This allows the client and server to talk back and forth.

Many Internet programs work as client/server pairs. The server is on a host system somewhere in cyberspace, and the client is a program running on your local system. When the client wants an Internet service (such as retrieving a Web page from an HTTP server), it issues a request, usually to a symbolic address such as www.sun.com rather than an IP address.

There will be a Domain Name Server locally (usually one per subnet, per campus, or per company) that resolves the symbolic name into an Internet address.

The bits forming the request are assembled into a *datagram*, and routed to the server. The server reads the incoming packets, notes what the request is, where it came from, and then tries to respond to it by providing either the service (web page, shell account, file contents, etc.) or a sensible error message. The response is sent back across the Internet to the client.

Almost all the standard Internet utilities (telnet, rdist, ftp, ping, rcp, and so on) operate in client/server mode connected by a TCP socket or by UDP. Programs that send mail don't really know how to send mail—they just know how to take it to the Post Office. In this case, mail has a socket connection, and talks to a daemon at the other end with a fairly simple protocol. The standard mail *daemon* knows how to accept text and addresses from clients and transmit it for delivery. If you can talk to the mail daemon, you can send mail. There is little else to it.

Many of the Internet services are actually quite simple. But often considerable frustration comes in doing the socket programming in C and in learning the correct protocol. The socket programming API presented to C is quite low-level, and all too easy to screw up. Needless to say, errors are poorly handled and diagnosed. As a result many programmers naturally conclude that sockets are brittle and error-prone.

The C code to establish a socket connection is:

```
int set_up_socket(u_short port) {
    char    myname[MAXHOSTNAME+1];
    int     s;
    struct sockaddr_in sa;
    struct hostent *he;

    bzero(&sa,sizeof(struct sockaddr_in));/* clear the address */
    gethostname(myname,MAXHOSTNAME);      /* establish identity */
    he= gethostbyname(myname);            /* get our address   */
    if (he == NULL)                       /* if addr not found... */
        return(-1);
    sa.sin_family= he->h_addrtype;        /* host address */
    sa.sin_port= htons(port);             /* port number */

    if ((s= socket(AF_INET,SOCK_STREAM,0)) < )/*finally,createsocket*/
        return(-1);
    if (bind(s, &sa, sizeof(sa), 0) < 0) {
        close(s);
        return(-1);                           /* bind address to socket */
    }

    listen(s, 3);                             /* max queued connections */
    return(s);
}
```

By way of contrast, the Java code is:

```
ServerSocket servsock = new ServerSocket(port, 3);
```

The good news is that Java handles that complexity "under the covers" for you. It doesn't expose the full range of socket possibilities, which lets the novice socketeer choose contradictory options. So, some sockety things cannot be done in Java. You cannot create a raw socket in JDK 1.0, and hence cannot write the ping program that relies on raw sockets. The benefit is overwhelming however: you can open sockets and start writing to another system just as easily as you open a file and start writing to hard disk.

Every computer system on the Internet has a unique IP address consisting of four groups of digits separated by periods, like this: 204.156.141.229

They are currently revising and increasing the IP address specification so that there will be enough new IP addresses to give one to every conceivable embedded processor on earth, and a few nearby friendly planets.

One special IP address is: 127.0.0.1

This is the "loopback" address used in testing and debugging. If a computer sends a packet to this address, it is routed out and back in again, without actually leaving the system. Thus this special address can be used to run Internet software even if you are not connected to the Internet. Set your system up so that the Internet services it will be requesting are all at the loopback address. Make sure your system is actually running the daemons corresponding to the services you want to use.

The special hostname associated with the loopback address is "localhost," if you are requesting services by name rather than IP address. On any system, you should be able to enter the command "ping localhost" and have it echo a reply from the loopback IP address. If you can't do this, it indicates that your TCP/IP stack is not set up properly.

Sending E-mail by Java

As our first example, let's write a Java program to send some e-mail. As we hinted above, e-mail is sent by socketed communication with port 25 on a computer system.

All we are going to do is open a socket connected to port 25 on some system, and speak "mail protocol" to the daemon at the other end. In an applet, open a socket back to the server. In an application, you can open a socket on the same system. If we speak the mail protocol correctly, it will listen to what we say, and send the e-mail for us.

The code to send e-mail is:

```
import java.io.*;
import java.net.*;
public class email {

    public static void main(String args[]) throws IOException {
        Socket sock;
        DataInputStream dis;
        PrintStream ps;

        sock = new Socket("localhost", 25);
        dis = new DataInputStream( sock.getInputStream());
        ps = new PrintStream( sock.getOutputStream());

        ps.println("mail from: trelford");
        System.out.println( dis.readLine() );

        String Addressee= "linden";
        ps.println("rcpt to: " + Addressee );
        System.out.println( dis.readLine() );

        ps.println("data");
        System.out.println( dis.readLine() );

        ps.println("This is the message\n that Java sent");
        ps.println(".");
        System.out.println( dis.readLine() );

        ps.flush();
        sock.close();
    }
}
```

Many of the Internet services are like this one. You set up a socket connection, and talk a simple protocol to tell the server at the other end what you want.

Note that the main() routine has been declared as throwing an Exception. This is a shortcut, permissible in development, to save the necessity of handling any exceptions that might be raised. It only works because exceptions are not considered part of the signature of a method. In production code, it is crucial to catch and handle any exceptions.

You can find all the Internet Protocols described in documents *Request For Comments* (RFCs), the format in which they were originally issued, available online at: http://www.internic.net/std. The mail RFC is RFC821.txt.

You can find all the WWW protocols described in documents linked to from this URL: http://www.w3.org/pub/WWW/Protocols/.

A careful study of some of these documents will often answer any protocol questions you have. ❧

HTTP and Web-Browsing: Retrieving HTTP Pages

Here is an example of using the HTTP daemon to retrieve a Web page from a system on the network. The http daemon sits on port 80 by convention. It understands a dozen or so requests, including "GET" followed by a path name. The argument "sparcs" is the name of a Web-server system on my subnet inside Sun Microsystems in Menlo Park, California, so change that to the name of your local Web server.

```java
import java.io.*;
import java.net.*;
public class http {

    public static void main(String args[]) throws IOException {
        String webserver = "sparcs";
        int http_port = 80;
        Socket sock;
        DataInputStream dis;
        PrintStream ps;

        sock = new Socket(webserver, http_port);
        dis = new DataInputStream( sock.getInputStream() );
        ps = new PrintStream( sock.getOutputStream() );

        ps.println("GET /index.html");
        String s=null;
        while ( (s=dis.readLine())!=null)
                System.out.println( s );

        sock.close();
    }
}
```

Note: If you are not on a network, before you run this code, start the http server daemon on your local system and use the local host address. If you are on a local network, your firewall will probably limit the visibility of outside systems, so pick a local server system that is running httpd as your test case.

The program prints out everything the http daemon sends back to it. In this case, running the program yields:

```
<Html>
<Head>
<Title>SPARCS</Title>
<!-- Author: Susan P. Motorcycles -->
</Head>
<Body>

<h1>SPARCS.ENG </h1>
<p>
<h2>Resources</h2>
<p>
<hr>Go to
<a HREF="estar/public_html/index.html"><u>Estar Homepage</u></a></p>
<p>
<hr>Go to
<a HREF="Kernel/index.html"><u>OS Kernel Homepage</u></a></p>

</Body>
</Html>
```

This is indeed the page at http://sparcs.eng/index.html inside Sun. As may be
expected, Java has some awareness of various net protocols. In particular it can
deal with a URL directly, and not require the programmer to descend into the
underlying netherworld of sockets. So in practice, if we wanted to look at the contents of a URL, we would use the URL class, like this:

```
import java.net.*;
import java.io.*;
public class page {

  public static void main(String a[]) {
    DataInputStream dis;
    try {
      URL u  = new URL( "http://sparcs.eng/index.html" );
      dis = new DataInputStream( u.openConnection().getInputStream() );

      String s ;
      while ( (s=dis.readLine())!=null ) {
        System.out.println( s );
      }
    } catch (Exception e) { System.out.println( e ); }
  }

}
```

A URL can pose a security risk, since you can pass along information via a URL.
For instace, you could request "http://www.spies.com/cgi-bin/secretinfo", and
"secretinfo" would be passed along to the CGI script. Since requesting a URL can
send out information just as a Socket can, requesting a URL has the same security
model as access to Sockets.

Coding the program this way is not only shorter, but allows us to interrogate certain other URL properties, such as the protocol that is being used, and the host system (these methods are of use when you don't use literal values as in this example).

Putting the following lines in the above program

```
System.out.println("    file: "+ u.getFile() );
System.out.println("    host: "+ u.getHost() );
System.out.println("     ref: "+ u.getRef() );
System.out.println("protocol:" + u.getProtocol() );
```

gives the result

```
   file: /index.html
   host: sparcs.eng
    ref: null
protocol:http
```

What if there is a GIF at that URL—won't we print out image information as though it were text? Yes, the program would. You need to build just a little more intelligence into it so it recognizes file types, and handles them appropriately. This is what the content handler/protocol handler guff is about. If a browser doesn't recognize a media type, it should be able to download the code to process it from the same place it got the file. If they ever get this working, it will be (as flaxen-coiffured domestic harpie Martha Stewart likes to say) "a good thing."

If you modify the basic program above so that it transmits the other 10 or 11 http commands and give it a GUI front-end to display the formatted http text, you will have written a Web browser! A Web browser is at heart a fairly simple program. The prototype *HotJava* Web browser, at that time called "Webrunner," was written in just one week according to Patrick Naughton (who was there and worked on it).

Both this example, and the mailer program, are client applications. The server end of the http protocol is not much more complicated. A basic http daemon can be implemented in a few hundred lines of code.

"On the Internet, nobody knows you're a dog."

On the Internet, No One Knows You're a Dog . . .

Let's make a brief digression at this point, and recall the phenomenon in which the Internet entered the public consciousness in a big way. One of the early indicators of this was a 1993 cartoon in the New Yorker Magazine, with the punchline "On the Internet nobody knows you're a dog!" This cartoon was cut out and displayed in every network programmer's office from Albuquerque to Zimbabwe. Mainstream recognition! On the Internet, nobody knows you're a dog.

Our code example is a Canine Turing Test—a Java program to distinguish whether the communicating party is a dog or not. People greet each other by shaking hands, while dogs sniff each other. Dogs are loyal companions, and part of their loyalty is absolute truthfulness. To tell if a dog is at the other end of a socket, just ask the question "If you met me, would you shake my hand, or sniff it?" Depending on the answer that the client sends back over the socket to the server, the server will know if the client is a dog or a human.

Obviously this program is only going to work if you are using a computer that has an IP address and a connection to a TCP/IP network. Or if you run it all on one system, and you have socket support working. On a Unix workstation TCP/IP support is a standard basic part of the operation system. On a PC you'll need to have the TCP/IP "protocol stack" installed. Calling this software a "protocol stack" is a bit of a misnomer, as it has nothing to do with LIFO stacks. "TCP/IP software" would be a more accurate name.

Under Windows 95 the TCP/IP protocol stack (wsock32.dll) is present on the system, but needs to be configured to work. You configure it by clicking on "My Computer" -> "Control Panel" -> "Network" -> "Network." Where the window shows a list reading "The following network components are installed," make sure you have at least "Dial-Up adapter" and "TCP/IP" in the list.

Click on "TCP/IP" to highlight it, and activate the "Properties" button underneath the network component list. Press the button to bring up TCP/IP properties. There are six tabbed entries here, and they all need to be set up correctly for your networking code to work correctly. *Your Internet Service Provider* should supply full instructions.

Under Windows 3.1 there is no standard support for TCP/IP. Every vendor supplies their own custom library, creating a morass of truly hideous software complexity. If you have dial-up access to the Internet, your service provider should provide instructions on how to configure the TCP/IP software. ☕

The code comes in two parts: a server that listens for clients and asks them the question, and clients that connect to the server. The server is going to detect whether clients are dogs or not. First the server code, which looks like this:

```java
/**
 *   a network server that detects presence of dogs on the Internet
 *
 *   @version    1.1 Jan 21 1996
 *   @author     Peter van der Linden
 *   @author     From the book "Just Java"
 */
import java.io.*;
import java.net.*;

class server {
    public static void main(String a[]) throws IOException {
        int q_len = 6;
        int port = 4444;
        Socket sock;
        String query = "If you met me would you shake my hand, "
                    + "or sniff it?";

        ServerSocket servsock =
            new ServerSocket(port, q_len);

    while (true) {
        // wait for the next client connection
            sock=servsock.accept();

        // Get I/O streams from the socket
          PrintStream out =
           new PrintStream( sock.getOutputStream() );
          DataInputStream in  =
          new DataInputStream( sock.getInputStream() );

        // Send our query
        out.println(query);
        out.flush();

        // get the reply
        String reply = in.readLine();
        if (reply.indexOf("sniff") > -1)
            System.out.println(
            "On the Internet I know this is a DOG!");
            else System.out.println(
            "Probably a person or an AI experiment");

        // Close this connection, (not overall server socket)
          sock.close();
      }
   }
}
```

Now the client end of the socket, which looks like this:

```java
// On the Internet no one knows you're a dog...
// unless you tell them.

import java.io.*;
import java.net.*;

class dog {

    public static void main(String a[]) throws IOException {
        Socket sock;
        DataInputStream dis;
        PrintStream dat;

        // Open our connection to positive, at port 4444
        sock = new Socket("positive",4444);

        // Get I/O streams from the socket
        dis = new DataInputStream( sock.getInputStream() );
        dat = new PrintStream( sock.getOutputStream() );

        String fromServer = dis.readLine();

        System.out.println("Got this from server:" + fromServer);

        dat.println("I would sniff you");
        dat.flush();

        sock.close();
    }
}
```

When you try running this program, make sure that you change the client socket connect to refer not to "positive" (my workstation) but to a system where you intend to run the server code. You can identify this system by using either the name (as long as the name will uniquely locate it on your net), or the IP address. (If in doubt, just use the IP address).

Here's how to run the example:

1. Put the server program on the system that you want to be the server. Compile the server program, and start it:

```
javac server.java
java server
```

2. Put the client program on the system that you want to be the client. Change the client program so it references your server machine, not machine "positive." Then compile it.

```
javac dog.java
```

3. When you execute the client program, on the client system you will see the output:

```
java dog
```

Got this from server: If you met me would you shake my hand, or sniff it?

4. On the server machine, you will see the output.

```
On the Internet I know this is a DOG!
```

Make sure the server is running before you execute the client, otherwise it will have no one to talk to.

Write a second client program that would reply with the "shake hands" typical of a person. Run this from the same or another client system. (Easy). 🐦

There's one improvement that is customary in servers, and we will make it here. For all but the smallest of severs, it is usual to spawn a new thread to handle each request. This has three big advantages:

- The program source is less cluttered, as the server processing is written in a different class

- By handling each request in a new thread, clients do not have to wait for every request ahead of them to be served

- Finally, it makes the server scalable: It can accept new requests independent of its speed in handling them (of course you better buy a server that has the mippage to keep up with requests).

The following code demonstrates how we would rewrite the Internet dog detector using a new thread for each client request.

```
/**
 *   a network server that detects presence of dogs on the Internet
 *   and which spawns a new thread for each client request.
 *   @version   2.0 Aug 19 1996
 *   @author    Peter van der Linden
 *
 */
import java.io.*;
import java.net.*;

class Worker extends Thread {
   Socket sock;
   Worker(Socket s) { sock =s; }
   public void run(){
      System.out.println("Thread running:"+currentThread() );
      // Get I/O streams from the socket
        PrintStream out = null;
        DataInputStream in  = null;
      try {
        out = new PrintStream( sock.getOutputStream() );
        in  = new DataInputStream( sock.getInputStream() );
      // Send our query
      String query = "If you met me would you shake my hand, or sniff it?";
      out.println(query);
      out.flush();

      // get the reply
      String reply = in.readLine();
      if (reply.indexOf("sniff") > -1)
        System.out.println("On the Internet I know this is a DOG!");
      else System.out.println("Probably a person or an AI experiment");

         // Close this connection, (not the overall server socket)

         sock.close();
      } catch(IOException ioe){System.out.println(ioe); }
   }
}

public class server2 {
   public static void main(String a[]) throws IOException {
      int q_len = 6;
      int port = 4444;
      Socket sock;

      ServerSocket servsock = new ServerSocket(port, q_len);

   while (true) {
      // wait for the next client connection
        sock=servsock.accept();
      new Worker( sock ).start();
    }
   }
}
```

Page Counters in Web Pages

Finally, lets answer a question that many people have, namely: "How do I use Java to implement a counter on my web page?" It seems like this should be trivial to do—there's probably even a class to increment a count every time a web page is accessed and display the new value on the page.

Well it turns out that this can be done in Java, but it's a little more work than just calling a method. The problem is that an applet can't write files on the server. Only the server can write files on the server, although you can set up a daemon on the server to listen to and act on "write this file" requests from applets.

Here are the obvious steps to set up a page counter in Java:

1. Keep the "page access count" in a file on the server, which is referred to by an HTML document.

2. When the page is accessed, an applet in the page executes on the client.

3. Send a message to a daemon running on the server to say "add one to the number in the page access count file."

4. The daemon on the server reads and updates the file.

People always want to be able to do this totally from the applet, but that is not possible. The cooperation of the server is required. This kind of communication was traditionally done with CGI scripts, with the following new steps replacing previous steps 3 and 4, respectively.

- Open a socket and write an http GET or POST request to the server.

- The http request will start up the CGI script. The output of the script (with a MIME header stripped off) will be sent back down the socket to the applet.

However, Java now offers the "Jeeves" framework for servers (geddit? Named after P.G. Wodehouse's genius server, Jeeves). The Jeeves API for "servlets" is intended to replace work formerly done by CGI scripts.

More information on Jeeves, including a white paper is available at http://java.sun.com/products/jeeves/index.html.

Jeeves allows you to program everything in Java, and leave the CGI muddle alone. You get the benefit of doing everything in one language plus Java's security.

How to Find the IP Address Given a Machine Name

This code will be able to find the IP address of all computers that it knows about. That may mean all systems that have an entry in the local hosts table, or (if it is served by a name server) the domain of the name server, which could be as extensive as a large subnet or the entire organization.

```
import java.io.*;
import java.net.*;

class who {

    public static void main(String a[]) throws IOException {

        InetAddress InetAddr =
            InetAddress.getByName (a[0]);
        System.out.println(
            "inet address is " + InetAddr.toString() );


    }
}
```

Some Notes on Protocol and Content Handlers

Some of the Java documentation makes a big production about the extensibility of the HotJava browser. If it is asked to browse some data whose type it doesn't recognize, it can simply download the code for the appropriate handler and use that to grok the data. Or so the theory runs. It hasn't yet been proved in practice.

A prime opportunity to showcase dynamic handlers arose when the Java Development Kit was switching over from the Alpha to Beta versions in late 1995. There were significant applet incompatibilities between the two. It provided a fine opportunity to use dynamic content handling. The browser source (which worked exclusively with Alpha applets) was widely available for the asking. No beta-capable version of the alpha Browser has appeared to date. The general wonderfulness of dynamic handlers in the browser has still to be proven in practice.

The theory of the handlers is this. There are two kinds of handler that you can write: protocol handlers and content handlers.

A **protocol handler** talks to other programs. Both ends follow the same protocol in order to communicate ("After you.", "No, I insist, after you.") If you wrote an Oracle database protocol handler, it would deal with SQL queries to pull data out of an Oracle database.

A **content handler** knows how to decode the contents of a file. It handles data (think of it as the contents of something pointed to by a URL). It gets the bytes and assembles them into an object. If you wrote an MPEG content handler, then it would be able to play MPEG movies in your browser, once you had brought the data over there. Bringing MPEG data to your browser could be done using the FTP protocol, or you might wish to write your own high performance protocol handler.

Content handlers and protocol handlers may be particularly convenient for web browsers, and they may also be useful in stand-alone applications. There is not a lot of practical experience with these handlers yet, so it is hard to offer definitive advice about their use. Some people predict they are going to be very important for decoding file formats of arbitrary wackiness, while other people are ready to be convinced by an existence proof.

Some Light Relief

The Nerd Detection System

Most people are familiar with the little security decals that electronic and other high-value stores use to deter shoplifters. The sticker contains a metallic strip. Unless deactivated by a store cashier, the sticker sets off an alarm when carried past a detector at the store doors.

These security stickers are actually a form of antenna. The sticker detector sends out a weak RF signal between two posts through which shoppers will pass. It looks for a return signal at a specific frequency, which indicates that one of the stickers has entered the field between the posts.

All this theory was obvious to a couple of California Institute of Technology students Dwight Berg and Tom Capellari, who decided to test the system in practice. Naturally, they selected a freshman to (unknowingly) participate in the trials. At preregistration, after the unlucky frosh's picture was taken, but before it was laminated into his I.D. card, Dwight and Tom fixed a couple of active security decals from local stores onto the back of the photo.

The gimmicked card was then laminated together hiding the McGuffin, and the two conspirators awaited further developments. A couple of months later they caught up with their victim as he was entering one of the stores. He was carrying his wallet above his head. In response to a comment that this was an unusual posture, the frosh replied that something in his wallet, probably his bank card, seemed to set off store alarms. He had been conditioned to carry his wallet above his head after several weeks of setting off the alarms while entering and leaving many of the local stores.

The frosh seemed unimpressed with Dwight and Tom's suggestion that perhaps the local merchants had installed some new type of nerd detection system. Apparently the comment got the frosh thinking though, because the next occasion he met Dwight, he put Dwight in a headlock until he confessed to his misdeed. **Moral**: never annoy a nerd larger than yourself.

Exercises

1. Write a stream that censors output. It should delete all occurrences of the word "red" and instead substitute "scarlet." Make sure it doesn't replace "red" in the middle of a word, like "credit." Your stream should be put into use by being pushed onto another stream, so it will need a constructor that does that.

2. Extend the example mail program above so that it prompts for user input and generally provides a friendly front-end to sending mail.

3. Write a socket server program that simply returns the time on the current system. Write a client that calls the server, and sends you mail reporting on how far apart the time on the local system is, versus the time on the current system.

4. In the previous exercise, the server can only state what time it is at the instant the request reaches it, but that answer will take a certain amount of time to travel back to the client. Devise a strategy to minimize or correct for errors due to transmission time. (Hard—just use a heuristic to make a good guess.)

Further Reading

"More Legends of Caltech"

William A. Dodge, Jr.
published by the California Institute of Technology, Pasadena, Calif., 1989.
(This book has no ISBN).

TCP/IP Network Administration

Craig Hunt
O'Reilly & Associates, Sebastopol CA, 1994
ISBN 0-937175-82-X
The modest title hides the fact that this book will be useful to a wider audience than just network administrators. It is a very good practical guide to TCP/IP, written as a tutorial introduction.

Teach Yourself TCP/IP in 14 Days

Timothy Parker
Sams Publishing, Indianapolis, 1994
ISBN 0-672-30549-6
When a book starts off with an apology for the dullness of the subject material, you just know that the author has some unusual ways about him.

Unix Network Programming

W. Richard Stevens
Prentice Hall, NJ 1990
The canonical guide to network programming.

Answer To Programming Challenge

Here is a Java program that creates a subdirectory, and a file in it.

```java
// create a subdirectory Fruit
// then create a file called yam in that directory
import java.io.*;
class files {
    public static final PrintStream o = System.out;

    public static void main(String a[]) throws IOException {
        File d = new File("Fruit");
        checkDirectory(d);
        checkFile("Fruit/yam");
    }

    static void checkFile(String s) {
        File f = new File(s);
        if (!f.exists() ) {
            o.println("File " + f.getName() + " doesn't exist");
            FileOutputStream fos;
            try { fos = new FileOutputStream(f);
                  fos.write(' ');
            } catch (IOException ioe) {
                  o.println("IO Exception!");
            }
        } else {
            o.println("File " + f.getName() + " already exists");
        }
    }

    static void checkDirectory(File d) throws IOException {
        boolean success;
        if (!d.exists() ) {
            o.println("Directory "
              + d.getName() + " doesn't exist");
            if (success=d.mkdir())
                o.println("Have created directory " + d.getName());
            else
                o.println("Failed to create directory "
                + d.getName());
        } else {
            o.println( d.getName() + " exists already");
            if (d.isDirectory()) {
                o.println( "and is a directory.");
            } else {
                o.println( "and is a file.");
                throw new IOException();
            }
        }
    }
}
```

Answer To Programming Challenge

This program uses a SequenceInputStream to jam two different sources of data seamlessly together. It pushes a LineNumberInputStream on top of that, to keep track of line numbers.

```java
// shows the use of various input streams
import java.io.*;
public class test7c {
    static String s=new String("aardvark butterfly\n" +
        "carp dalmatian\n" +
            "eagle fish\ngopher hippo\ninyala jackal\nkyloe " +
            "lamb\nmoose nanny-goat\nopossum pandora\n" );

    static StringBufferInputStream sbis=
        new StringBufferInputStream(s);

    public static void main (String a[])
        throws FileNotFoundException {
          int c;
          FileInputStream fis = new FileInputStream("animals.txt");

          SequenceInputStream sis =
                new SequenceInputStream( sbis, fis );

          LineNumberInputStream lsis =
          new LineNumberInputStream( sis );

          try {
              while ((c=lsis.read())!= -1) {

                  System.out.print((char)c);
                  if (c=='\n') {
                      System.out.print("that finishes input line "
                              + lsis.getLineNumber() + "\n\n");
                  }

              }
          } catch (IOException ioe) {
                System.out.println("Exception reading stream");
                ioe.printStackTrace();
                System.exit(0);
          }
    }
}
```

The file "animals.txt" contains
queenbee raven
swan terrier
urchin vixen
wallaby xoachi
yellowjacket zebra

Running the program results in
aardvark butterfly
that finishes input line 1

carp dalmatian
that finishes input line 2

eagle fish
that finishes input line 3

gopher hippo
that finishes input line 4

inyala jackal
that finishes input line 5

kyloe lamb
that finishes input line 6

moose nanny-goat
that finishes input line 7

opossum pandora
that finishes input line 8

queenbee raven
that finishes input line 9

swan terrier
that finishes input line 10

urchin vixen
that finishes input line 11

wallaby xoachi[2]
that finishes input line 12

yellowjacket zebra
that finishes input line 13

2.   An "xoachi" is a little-known animal whose name I made up.

CHAPTER
9

- What's New in JDK 1.1

- Java APIs: Present and Future

- Delving Into Remote Method Invocation

- All About JDBC

Utilities and Libraries

"There's a tomato in every automaton."

—*Professor Rudolph's Big Book of Finite State Machines and Fruit Fancies*

At first, Java came with only a dozen or so basic classes that implemented common data structures and operations. As Java began to grow in popularity, it grew in size too as JavaSoft and other interested parties hurried to announce and support more libraries. This chapter provides an overview of the utility classes and libraries that accompany Java.

The Java libraries and products can be divided into three broad categories:

- Utilities bundled with the JDK

- Optional additions to the JDK

- Other Java-related products and services

There are so many additional libraries and packages announced for Java at this point, that that aspect alone would make a topic for a pretty thick book. What we'll do here is provide an overview of everything that has been announced at the

time of this writing. We will also provide a complete working example of Remote
Method Invocation, and of Java database access using the JDBC.

New Features of the Java Development Kit 1.1 Release

The following is a summary of everything new that was introduced with the JDK
1.1 release.

Java Archive (JAR) Files. These are intended to solve two problems. First,
address poor http performance due to making a socket connection for every individual file to be downloaded. Second, they support individual files being signed
to authenticate their origin. JAR files combine several files into one Java archive,
and support compression of the individual files. JAR files use a new applet tag,
called the *archive* tag, as in:

```
<applet archive="Nuclear.jar"
  code="NuclearPlant.class"
  width=680 height=473  >
```

The system will bring the entire Nuclear.jar file over, and start executing in the
NuclearPlant class.

Better Support for Internationalization. There is now some support for local-
ized applets, so that the same program can display its messages in German in
Germany, in French in France, and so on. There is also support for obtaining
the date and time in the right format for the locale. This can be different even
when the language is the same. In the United States the date is written as
month.day.year, but in Britain the usage is day/month/year.

Security. The introduction of libraries to support cryptography and digital signatures. Developers will be able to build cryptography into their products. Additionally the features will be used internally to sign files of code, data and images.
The first support comes in with JDK 1.1, and more will be phased in with later
releases.

Abstract Windowing Toolkit (AWT) Improvements. Much work has been done
to raise the quality and performance of the AWT. Several new widgets have
appeared: scroll panes, pop-up menus, cursors per component, and some clipboard support. There is now a way to print the screen from within the AWT.

Network Enhancements. Some BSD-style options for sockets have been added,
along with some new subclasses of SocketException for better error reporting.

The class MulticastSocket has moved from the vendor hierarchy sun.net into the standard Java.net.

Remote Method Invocation. This is, or will be, the basis of the long sought network "killer app!" Remote Method Invocation is best described as "RPC for Java." It allows a client system to make calls into another computer system. To the client it just looks like invoking a method within its own process, but it actually executes code on another system. There is a fuller description of this later in the chapter.

Object Serialization. This means that there are now ObjectOutputStream and ObjectInputstream classes, just as there are DataInputStream and DataOutput-Stream. You can now write objects into files or sockets for persistent storage or transmission across the ether. RMI uses object serialization.

Reflection. Reflection is a way for Java code to find out what methods and fields are in any loaded class. It can then construct new instances of classes and arrays, and call methods on the classes. Reflection is useful to have when you are building object frameworks, such as Java Beans. It is reflection in the sense of "what I see when I look in the mirror."

Byte, Short, and Void Classes. These just round out the standard classes for the primitive types. They are needed now that we have serialization and reflection. The class void is a wrapper class, which Javasoft has yet to describe detail. The name suggests it is used when you want to pass any general object around, but the class Object already does that.

Database Connectivity. Now there is a standard way to access SQL databases from Java. The Java Database Connectivity (JDBC) library provides uniform access to a wide range of relational databases. A complete example is given later in this chapter.

New Native Method Interface. There will be a new interface for calling code written in C or other non-Java language. The main goal is to get binary compatability of all native method libraries on a given VM. This means that Hot Java, Internet Explorer, and Netscape Navigator should not each require a different convention for the same Java-to-C call. To a user, it means that code containing native methods can be executed in any browser (once signed classes make it feasible to execute native methods from a browser).

A Standard Interface for the Just-in-Time Compiler Crowd. This is intended for tool implementors, and essentially documents the interfaces that people were already using, bringing them to an official standardization.

Nested Classes. Nested classes are an experimental technique allowing a simpler syntax for a nested class. This gives Java the lexical scoping used in block structured languages like Pascal.

General Performance Improvements. The JDK 1.1 release includes many bug fixes, and many performance improvements. The AWT peer class was re-implemented for Windows 95. On the Macintosh, fragmented heaps were allowed (the heap does not have to be all in one place). On Windows 95 and Solaris/SPARC, a critical portion of the inner loop of the interpreter was recoded in assembler. A compile time option now allows the use of native threads on Solaris.

Never in the past has a language evolved as rapidly as Java. The FCS release is not even past its first birthday, and it has already gained a road map that will make it the most richly-featured portable language in computer history. The JDK 1.1 release is a big first step in that direction.

Overview of All APIs

This section provides a list of everything that will eventually be in Java, and in some cases is already here. In an amazingly short space of time, a rich variety of Java tools, APIs, and services has already sprung up. Sun has taken the unusual step of providing a complete road map showing how future libraries will be added to enable Java to evolve from a programming language to a full operating environment. The initiative is clearly aimed at moving Java to become a complete software solution, scalable from the smallest applet to the biggest corporate data center.

We're going to be using the term API a lot in this section, so let's review the meaning. An API is an *Application Programmer Interface*. It is a specification of a software library, detailing all the function calls, arguments, and results you get back from them. An API exists on paper and is just a design. To actually use an API, you need a real library that implements the API.

Chapter 7 of the ANSI C specification is an API describing many functions like printf() in the C runtime library. On Unix, the file libc.so is the library that implements the API. An API promises some services on paper, a library delivers them in code.

When Jorge Luis Borges commented that "I have always imagined that paradise will be a kind of library," he surely had the JDK road map in mind.

Some of these libraries are being shipped with JDK 1.1, while others are planned to come in future releases. The new libraries shipped with JDK 1.1 will be described at length in this chapter. It's helpful to start by providing a thumbnail description of all of them. When your boss thunders into your office and demands to know if you can integrate Java programs with the Solaris CORBA implementation, you'll be able to give the right answer: "Certainly. Java fits into Neo using the Joe software. How about moving me to a corner office with a window?"

There are eight families, each containing several new APIs. The APIs are classified as either a *core* API or a *standard extension* (in most cases all the APIs in a family are classified the same way). A core API is one that comes with the JDK, is part of Sun's standard implementation, and must be supported by every Java system. A standard extension is a library that does not have to be supported, but if the feature is supported, it must be done in exactly that standard way. Some of these software components, like the JDBC, moved into the core Java Development Kit with the 1.1 release. More will migrate in over time. The API families are shown in Table 9-1:

Table 9-1: The API family tree

Core	Standard Extension
Java Security	Java Management
Java Beans	Java Embedded
Java Media	
2D, graphics, audio	3D, video, telephony

Several of the APIs are complete now, one or two are available in early form, and the rest are currently under development. Sun is developing these APIs using an open process that is unprecedented in the industry.

The API proposals are being drafted in partnership with industry leaders in each area. Lucent Technologies (the new name for Bell Labs) is working on the telephony API. The 2D graphics API in the Media family is based on Adobe's Bravo document imaging system. Intel and Silicon Graphics assisted in the development of a media framework API covering audio, video, and MIDI.

The results of these collaborative efforts will be available for public comment and review before the specifications are finalized. Most of these specifications will be published by the end of 1996. The extensions to the Java Media API are more complicated, and will be published in 1997. Everything will be completed by the end of 1997.

Now let's look at these eight API families in greater detail.

Java Enterprise

These APIs allow Java applications to be integrated with corporate database and legacy applications. Within Java Enterprise, four APIs have been designed:

- JDBC. A standard SQL database access interface, providing access to many different relational databases.

- Java IDL. Implements the OMG Interface Definition Language specification, as a language-neutral way to specify an interface between an object and a client on a different platform. It allows Java to call out to other object frameworks.

- Java RMI. A remote method invocation between peers, or between client and server, when both ends are written in Java. RMI is an object-oriented protocol that does the same kind of thing as RPC. RMI is built on Object Serialization.

- Object Serialization. A new I/O library to turn an object into a byte stream, and later reconstitute it back into an object.

All four of these APIs are available now. People who wondered whether Java would ever be used for anything more than scrolling text in Web pages have their answer. The Java Enterprise APIs make it easy to create large-scale commercial and database applications that can share multimedia data with other applications inside an organization or across the Internet.

Java Commerce (Java Wallet)

The Java Commerce APIs will (finally!) bring secure purchasing and financial management to the Web. These APIs, also called *Java Wallet*, are the first step towards the goal. It defines and implements a client-side framework for credit card, debit card, and electronic cash transactions. Java Wallet will provide a purchasing framework for consumers to buy goods, and pay for them using a payment-service API. The merchant APIs will provide shopping-cart and billing capabilities to vendors.

The term Java Wallet is carefully chosen. You don't pay for things with your wallet itself. Your wallet is the place you safely keep the objects that really pay for things: credit cards, money, check book. And so it is with the Java Wallet: a secure receptacle for holding electronic financial instruments known as "cassettes" (because they plug in like tape cassettes). Java Wallet builds on the *Java Security* family described in the next paragraph.

There is a tremendous profit waiting for the first organization to bring simple and secure financial transactions to the Net. So the competition is heating up. Netscape already has a proposal in place, and Microsoft is not far behind.

Java Security

Java Security APIs are a framework to let developers put security-related features in their applets and applications. The features include cryptography with digital signatures, encryption, and authentication. Respectively, these allow you to say who you are, secretly, and have other people believe it.

Instead of every programmer having to implement an authentication class, the class will be part of a library. The design provides a clean interface between applications and the cryptography, so that developers (or users) can plug in one of several alternative cryptographic algorithms. This simplifies matters for US vendors, as the US Government currently insists on putting cryptographic software in the same category as machine guns, bazookas, and artillery pieces, and forbids export under Arms Trade regulations.

US computer companies usually bear the expense of preparing two versions of their products: one with cryptography for the domestic market, and one with no or weaker cryptography for export. Now systems developers will use the Java Security APIs, and provide the receptacle into which alternative encryption modules can easily be placed.

If you agree with the current position of the US Government that software (like Netscape Navigator and the Unix operating system) are munitions, that cryptography should be restricted so the US Government can break it, and that the US Government should have a "back door" key to read anyone's encoded messages (including yours), then here are some things to consider:

- *Do not* visit the URL http://www37.netscape.com/eng/US-Current/itar.hmtl and read the Internation Traffic in Arms Regulations.

- *Do not* look at the Usenet newsgroups alt.security.pgp, talk.politics.crypto, or sci.crypt.

- *Do not* download and use PGP (Pretty Good Privacy), a package of strong encryption available for all popular systems, written by Phil Zimmermann. Do *not* visit http://web.mit.edu/pgp, and follow the directions to download. Overseas readers should avoid visiting the alternative site http://www.ifi.uio.no/~staalesc/PGP/language.html. in Norway.

- *Do not* buy Phil Zimmermann's books available in many bookstores. Do not specify "The Official PGP User's Guide," by Philip Zimmermann, from MIT Press, 128 pages, ISBN 0-262-74017-6, $14.95. Nor should you read "PGP Source Code and Internals" by Philip Zimmerman, published by MIT Press 1995, ISBN 0-262-24039-4. This book contains the entire source code for PGP, and almost put the US Government in the medieval position of banning the sale and distribution of a book.

Note that everybody in the world already has access to the Data Encryption Standard (DES), the strong encryption technique standardized by the US Government in 1977. Prohibiting its export doesn't keep it out of any nation's hands. So why do it? Some people speculate that the real agenda driving the NSA is their fear that bundling DES in popular American software products will encourage routine use of good cryptography both inside and outside the US; this makes traffic analysis much harder for them.

Therefore (the theory runs), the US Government wants cryptography to be awkward to deploy, not because they can't break it, but because they want to discourage people inside the US from using better products by default. If you spend a long time in the counter intelligence world, I guess that's how you end up thinking.

There is genuinely a certain amount of nonsense or misinformation fed to the media, who are all too ready to report it unquestioningly. *Parade Magazine* of Sept. 29, 1996 printed a reader's letter than asked "If we know so much, how come we can't catch terrorists?" *Parade* printed an answer from "an expert" claiming "they started using codes on the Internet." This is such a blatant falsehood, one can only presume they are trying to soften up public opinion to accept restrictions on privacy on the Internet.

For three years, Zimmermann was the target of a US Customs criminal investigation to determine if he violated federal export laws after he programmed, and gave away free, the PGP software. Finally in 1996, after years of expense and strain for Zimmermann, the Feds dropped the case against the computer programmer. If you want to read some press stories about the case, see the following references:

> Steven Levy, "The Encryption Wars: Is Privacy Good or Bad?" Newsweek, 24 April 1995, page 55.
>
> Vic Sussman, "Lost in Kafka Territory," US News and World Report, 3 April 1995, page 32.
>
> Ken Hoover, "Indictment Possible in Cyberspace Privacy Case," San Francisco Chronicle, 29 May 1995, page A15.
>
> William Bulkeley, "Cipher Probe," Wall Street Journal, Thursday 28 April 1994, front page.
>
> John Markoff, "Federal Inquiry on Software Examines Privacy Programs," New York Times, Tuesday 21 Sep 1993, page C1.
>
> Steven Levy, "Battle of the Clipper Chip," New York Times Magazine, Sunday 12 Jun 1994, page 44.
>
> John Markoff, "Cyberspace Under Lock and Key," New York Times, Sunday 13 Feb 1994.
>
> Philip Elmer-DeWitt, "Who Should Keep the Keys," Time, 14 Mar 1994, page 90.
>
> An excellent source of general information on cryptography and algorithms is the book "Applied Cryptography, 2nd Edition," by Bruce Schneier, published by John Wiley and Sons, 1995. 🍒

Java Beans

After the Enterprise API family, Java Beans is probably the most significant API. It is also the least well-defined at this point. It is a component object model that ties all the other APIs together.

It's a little hard to describe something this abstract, but the Java Beans family defines a portable, platform-neutral set of APIs for software components to talk to each other. The avowed intention is for Java Bean components to be able to plug into existing component architectures such as Microsoft's COM/Active-X architecture. Unlike Active-X, Beans will be supported on all systems that support Java, not just on Windows 95 and NT. JavaSoft also plans Beans to "play well" with Apple's OpenDoc, and Netscape's LiveConnect component object models. However, another (conflicting) goal is to be simple and lightweight.

Java Beans will make it easier for developers to write applications that use a common framework to blend programs seamlessly. The usual example people give is embedding a spreadsheet in a word processor document, and a chart program in the spreadsheet. The application is much wider and more significant than that. If the promise of Beans is fulfilled it could provide a complete desktop environment largely independent of the underlying operating system (OS). See Figure 9-1. It could even replace the underlying OS on a single-user system, just as Netscape ultimately desires its browser to be the universal GUI.

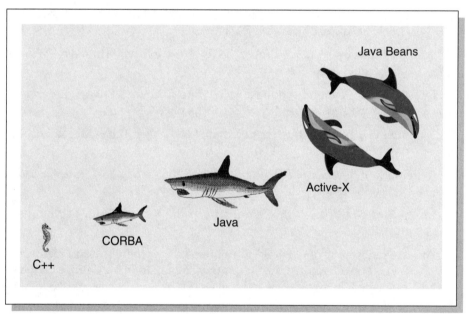

Figure 9-1: A strange food chain can be found in the ocean

Java Beans implies some change or refinement to the AWT used by Java. Outwardly, it will need to support Drag and Drop, and integration with the clipboard (a place to paste and temporarily save information). Internally, it will use object persistence and a finer-grained model for event handling.

When Sun Microsystems licensed Java back in December 1995, many industry commentators wondered if Microsoft would try to subvert the language in some way. The answer wasn't long in coming. Microsoft's plan was to retain their desktop monopoly by taking every possible opportunity to undermine, or weaken the portable, platform-independent nature of the language and protocols. One opportunity involves using the proprietary Active-X C library so that Java programs wouldn't be portable to non-Microsoft desktops. The Java beans initiative was born to counter Microsoft's plan, and retain platform independence. It will allow users to do everything that ActiveX can do, but in a portable way. In this way, users have already benefited from competition on the desktop: they now have an open alternative to Microsoft's object model.

Microsoft has already launched the next phase of their plan: a strident marketing campaign to try to win people over to the Active-X lock-in. Part of this campaign involves handing the Active-X specification to an outside standardization body (if one can be found that is stooge enough to take it). Unless Active-X becomes ubiquitous on all desktops, programmers need to be clear about this: using Active-X means you are restricting your code (and hence your market) to only work on Microsoft-blessed desktops. Staying with just Java means "write once, run anywhere."

Java Media

Java Media APIs are designed to deliver multimedia over the Internet. The simpler media support is part of the core system, and the more advanced features are initially intended as standard extensions. Table 9-2 lists the six API clans within the Media family.

Table 9-2: Six clans of the Media family

Core	Standard Extension
Java 2D	Java Telephony
Java Share	Java 3D
Java Animation	
Java Media Framework	
Clocks, Audio	Video, MIDI

In greater detail, the APIs cover these areas:

- Java 2D provides an abstract imaging model that extends the 1.0.2 AWT package, including scalable fonts, line art, images, color, transforms and compositing.

- Java Share provides for sharing of applications among multiple users, such as a shared white board.

- Java Animation provides for motion and transformations of 2D objects. It makes use of the Java Media Framework for synchronization, composition and timing.

- Java Media Framework has clocks for synchronizing sound, vision and external events. It also has media players for playing audio, video and MIDI. You will be able to play MPEG video by virtue of having Java on your system, and will not need to download additional plug-ins. The framework will allow users to do full audio and video streaming. Programmers will be able to create applications with moving backgrounds, foregrounds, and sprites. Intel is working on implementing the API, and the first implementation will be for the Windows platform.

- Java Telephony integrates telephones with computers. It provides basic functionality for a full range of telephone services including simple phone calls, teleconferencing, call transfer, caller ID and *dual tone multi-frequency* (DTMF) decode/encode. Java applications will be able to interact with the phone system to place calls, automatically identify incoming calls, and interface with voice mail systems—all in a standard way. ISVs and companies that build communications cards have expressed great interest in JavaTel. It ties in well with recent interest in TCP/IP as a network control interface. People are also experimenting with using Internet to carry voice traffic. JavaTel will handle call control both for the desktop and for enterprise-wide telephony. It is a layer over other computer-telephony integration middleware such as Microsoft's TAPI, Novell and Lucent's TSAPI, and the Sun's own SunXTL.

- Java 3D provides an abstract, interactive imaging model for behavior and control of 3D objects. Objects can be viewed in light or shade, rotated to view from different angles, and seen as solid or wire frames.

Java Server

JavaSoft marketing literature says that the Java Server API is "an extensible framework that enables and eases the development of a whole spectrum of Java-powered Internet and Intranet servers. The APIs provide uniform and consistent access to the server and administrative system resources required for developers to quickly develop their own Java *servelets*—executable programs that users upload to run on networks or servers."

In English, that means "this is going to replace CGI." You'll be able to write your server code and client code in the same language. The APIs will let developers create servelets that run on servers, much like applets run on clients. Servelets are directly invokable via URL, and are activated by the Jeeves server on demand. A servelet may be automatically uploaded from the net, so there must be support for an "untrusted servelet" to run without compromising the server.

The server API doesn't have a GUI (since it's on the server), but file access, controlled by ACLs is important. There may be additional access to network administration and server system data.

When an applet accesses a servelet, a dynamically created document will be returned. If the servelet was browsing financial data in a company, it could provide different levels of access, depending on the applet making the query. If the applet was associated with a clerk, it would give access to individual invoices. If it was associated with the company accountant, it would provide overall totals as well.

Java Management

The short insight into this API family is that there will be some libraries to allow network adminstrators to use Java tools to manage their networks. The marketing talk is the usual guff about "a rich set of feature-full extensible object-oriented libraries to ease and enable" etc., etc., etc. What that means is that you'll have the libraries to talk *Simple Network Management Protocol* (SNMP), and thence to build applets that manage an enterprise network over Internet. The API includes support for events, topology discovery and access to SNMP through use of a Java SNMP proxy.

The Management API should really be called the Network Management API. It has been developed jointly with a broad range of industry leaders including AutoTrol, Bay Networks, BGS, BMC, Central Design Systems, Cisco Systems, Computer Associates, CompuWare, LandMark Technologies, Legato Systems, Novell, OpenVision, Platinum Technologies, SunSoft, Tivoli Systems, and 3Com.

Java Embedded

The Java Embedded APIs specify how the Java API may be reduced or divided into a subset for embedded devices that can't support the full Java Core API. For example, a Java chip in a cell phone usually won't be able to do file I/O. It may have a small LCD display on which some windowing can be done however. The Embedded API is based on java.lang, java.util and parts of java.io. It also defines a series of extensions for networking and GUIs.

At least two telephone companies are building Java chips into phones. If you think about it, a cell phone has a CPU, a network interface (to the telephone exchange), a keyboard (strictly a keypad), and a screen (LED display). The embedded API will allow everyone to program to the same feature subset. The embedded API is useful for much more than phones. It can be expected in almost every device that has, or could have, a CPU, such as cars, video cameras, printers,or copiers.

It doesn't take much imagination to see that if every intelligent appliance had a $5 serial port in it, and the Java Embedded API in ROM, you could program them and get them all working the way you want. If your VCR had this, you could hook it up to your computer and write a program to record shows, change channels, play tapes, or adjust the color balance automatically when needed. If your stereo had this, you could get it to talk to your TV, or even call you at work to play you soothing music. People who don't want to program would buy the applets from people like you and I.

Related Non-Java Object Products

This section contains a description of some Java-related products. It provides useful background information on non-Java object software.

CORBA

If you read the object-oriented trade press, one term you may have seen more and more is CORBA. CORBA is the *Common Object Request Broker Architecture*. In a single sentence, it is a framework to let objects on one computer to talk to objects on another computer. Note that I wrote "objects talk to one another" not "programs talk to one another." CORBA is a true object-oriented distributed processing framework. The "common" part means that it is not tied to any one language, or any one hardware vendor, but can inter-operate among all. CORBA was designed over the course of several years in an open industry-wide process, with the main participants being the Unix hardware vendors: DEC, H-P, Sun, and IBM.

Why do you want objects on different computers to talk to each other? Trust me on this, you really do. It allows you to build much more complicated and capable systems that support true distributed processing. It's not intended for a single programmer working on a lone PC. It is highly useful in a large enterprise with Terabytes of data distributed in databases on dozens of mainframe class systems.

CORBA implementations have just started to be deployed. Sun has an implementation known as NEO. Like all CORBA implementations, NEO is language-neutral, and it achieves this by having an interface language (it looks close to C) that other languages must map into. Making CORBA language independent was a very far-sighted decision on the part of the original designers, and it means there is a place for CORBA in the Java world.

CORBA implementations were often deployed with C++, but with the right "glue" or interface definitions, they can talk to Java programs and supply object services across a Net. In the case of Sun's NEO implementation of CORBA, the right glue is a Java package called *Joe*. Joe provides the interface definitions (known as IDL) to allow Java to make requests of NEO.

When you want objects to communicate across different systems, there are two main reasons for using CORBA instead of just using Java's RMI:

- CORBA provides an object framework that is language independent. If you're using multiple languages, or you wish to leave that option open for the future, or you want to access C++ legacy systems, CORBA makes it easy.

- The CORBA initiative started before Java, and the CORBA code is a little more tried and tested. The Java RMI code is currently in Beta form and doesn't have an extensive user base. Nor does CORBA, but it is further along.

If neither of these is a "must have" feature for you, then don't use CORBA—it's simpler and easier to use the Remote Method Invocation of Java.

IDL

IDL or *Interface Definition Language* is the way CORBA achieves language-neutrality. You describe in IDL the signature of the methods and data that CORBA will pass back and forth for you. IDL looks somewhat like C, but it is purely for describing interfaces, not writing actual programs. IDL is only for people using CORBA. Most Java systems won't use the CORBA framework, so most Java programmers will never use IDL.

NEO and Joe

Sun has a CORBA implementation named NEO. Joe is the productization of the IDL technology, specialized for the NEO product. In other words, the Joe libraries let Java run in the NEO Object Request Broker. Joe integrates Java applications with Solaris NEO object servers. A Java ORBlet is automatically downloaded to a client browser to support Java client requests.

Remote Method Invocation

Remote Method Invocation content.

responsible for getting the incoming arguments and transmitting them over to its buddy on the server machine. It does this by opening a socket, serializing the objects, and passing the data across.

The buddy routine on the server machine is called a *skeleton* because it's just the bare bones of a routine. It doesn't do anything except unmarshal the data passed to it, and call the real server routine. The algorithm is then reversed to communicate the result back to the method on the client machine. And so a remote method has been invoked on one system by another, as shown in Figure 9-3.

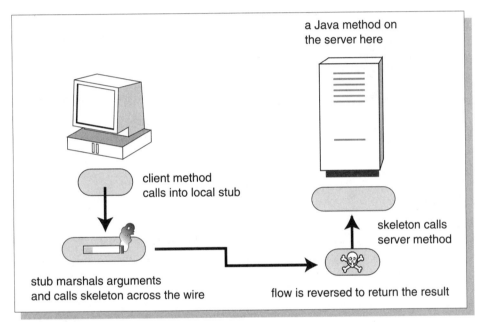

a Java method on the server here

client method calls into local stub

skeleton calls server method

stub marshals arguments and calls skeleton across the wire

flow is reversed to return the result

Figure 9-3: How RMI does it

Various extra cleverness takes place to support sending Objects across the network, including sending the exact type of the object arguments with the data. If that class doesn't exist on the receiving side, the corresponding class object itself is also loaded over the network.

How the RMI Code Looks

Let's look at a code example to make this abstract description a little more concrete. Suppose we have a computer system that is physically connected to all sorts of weather-monitoring equipment: rain gauges, thermometer, anemometer, barometer, and so on. This will be our server system. The remote method we want to invoke is getWeatherReadings(). We need to provide an implementation of this on the server, and we need to provide an interface for it on the client, so it can compile against it.

We should note at this point that the example is based on the alpha 2 version of RMI, released in July 1996. Some changes can be expected as the design proceeds to final form. Be sure to look at the JavaSoft site http://java.sun.com to get the latest update, which will be released with JDK 1.1 in any event.

The class that encapsulates our weather readings looks like this:

```
public class GaugeReadings {
    public String forecast;
    public float  rain;
    public float  temp;
    public float  windspeed;
    public String barometer;

    public GaugeReadings(String s, float r, float t, float w, String b) {
        forecast =s;
        rain=r;
        temp=t;
        windspeed=w;
        barometer=b;
    }

}
```

The class GaugeReadings has 5 public variables that hold the current value of various gauges. There is a constructor that loads these values. There aren't any other methods in this example. Somebody else will construct the object on the server. We'll simply obtain an object of GaugeReadings and read the current values of the public variables on the client.

We will pass an object of this class back from the server when the client requests the current readings. The interface for requesting the readings will simply look like this:

```
import java.rmi.*;

public interface WeatherIntf extends java.rmi.Remote {

    public GaugeReadings getWeatherReadings()
                    throws java.rmi.RemoteException;
}
```

The first line says we use the RMI packages. The interface declaration says that we extend the type Remote. Remote is the counterpart of Object. It's the most general type of thing you can hold. All you know about it is that it represents some Java object outside this virtual machine. The next line declares that when we call the getWeatherReadings() method of something that implements the WeatherIntf, we will get back an object of our GaugeReadings class. That call may throw a remote exception, which we can catch just like any exception. Figure 9-4 illustrates how everything fits together.

If we compile these two files, we now have enough to develop code on both the server and the client. We need both these classes to be present on the server and the client, so that further compilation and program development can take place.

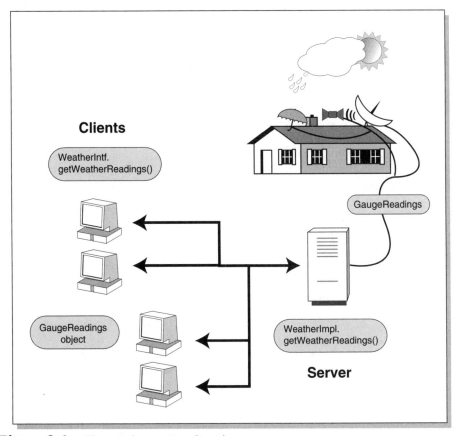

Figure 9-4: The weather station client/server

RMI Client Code

The client code is slightly simpler, and it looks like this:

```
import java.rmi.*;
import java.net.*;

public class Client {

  static public void main(String a[]) {

    GaugeReadings g = null;

    System.setSecurityManager(newjava.rmi.server.StubSecurityManager());

    String where ="rmi://localhost/Weather";
    try { Remote robj = Naming.lookup(where);
      WeatherIntf wi = (WeatherIntf) robj;
      g = wi.getWeatherReadings();
    } catch(Exception e) {System.out.println(e);}

    System.out.println("On the server, the weather is "+g.forecast);
    System.out.println(g.rain+" in. of rain fell recently");
    System.out.println("the temp. is "+g.temp+", wind is "+g.windspeed+"mph");
    System.out.println("the barometer is "+g.barometer);

  }

}
```

You should find nothing new or remarkable about this code. Compile it as usual. It sets a new security manager to an example from the java.rmi package. Then it creates something that looks a lot like a URL that says:

- The protocol to use—rmi

- Where to search—localhost (use a different system once you have this working locally)

- What to look for—the service called "Weather"

There needs to be some way for the client to express what service it wants, and this URL is the way it captures that information. It then does a naming lookup (the call is even called "Naming.lookup") to see who on the local net can offer the weather service.

There is a central table called the Registry that has a list of service names paired with (essentially) socket connections. This exists on as many or as few systems as we like. The client must know where to look for its registry. This may well be kept on the same system as the server, or it could be on a third system that is dedicated to providing naming services. From our lookup, we get a Remote object that implements the WeatherIntf interface. We cast it to the correct type, and then use it to call for the weather readings. We catch any exceptions, and finally print out what we received. Apart from the references to Remote, there is nothing at all in this code that is different from a wholly local system. What a marvelous advantage to have code that works the same in the local case and across the network.

RMI Server Code

Finally we come to the server code that has a little bit of RMI magic dust sprinkled over it to make everything work. The code looks like:

```
import java.net.*;
import java.rmi.*;
import java.rmi.server.UnicastRemoteServer;

public class WeatherImpl extends UnicastRemoteServer implements WeatherIntf {
    public WeatherImpl() throws java.rmi.RemoteException {super();}

    public static void main(String arg[]) {
        System.setSecurityManager(
            new java.rmi.server.StubSecurityManager() );

        try { WeatherImpl wi = new WeatherImpl();
            Naming.rebind("Weather", wi);
        } catch(Exception e) {System.out.println(e);}

    }

    GaugeReadings g = new GaugeReadings("sunny", 0.0F, 75.0F, 5.0F, "steady");
    public GaugeReadings getWeatherReadings() throws java.rmi.RemoteException {
        return g;
    }

}
```

Here we extend the UnicastRemoteServer class. This tips off the system that we are expecting to hear from remote clients. We extend the WeatherIntf. This promises that we will provide an implementation of the getWeatherReadings() method. Sure enough, we do. We simply return an object that we just constructed; a real weather station would actually take readings from the instruments on its roof.

Again, we set the security manager. Then we create a new instance of this WeatherImpl class, and register it in the Registry. We have to use the same registry and service name that the client will be using, of course. The service name we have chosen is "Weather." The last part of this class is the method that can be remotely invoked.

Compiling and Running the System

We compile the server class `javac WeatherImpl.java`.

Then we have to run the RMI compiler on its class file to produce the stub and the skeleton files:

```
rmic WeatherImpl
```

At this point you should have the client/server files listed in Table 9-3.

Table 9-3: The files from these two systems should appear

Client	Server
Client.java Client.class	
GaugeReadings.class	GaugeReadings.java GaugeReadings.class
WeatherIntf.class	WeatherIntf.java WeatherIntf.class
	WeatherImpl.java WeatherImpl.class
	WeatherImpl_Stub.class WeatherImpl_Skel.class

Now we can start to run it. The stub class is supposed to be downloaded to the client automatically when needed. First, start the standard registry naming service on the machine where the client will look for it (probably the machine the server is on):

```
java  java.rmi.registry.RegistryImpl
```

Then, on the server, start the server program

```
java  WeatherImpl
```

Use two different windows, as both these programs need to be running at once. Finally, on the client, start your client program:

```
java Client
```

The client system will click and ìwhirrî for a few seconds as objects "whizz" back and forth over the ether. Then you should see your weather report:

```
On the server, the weather is sunny
0 in. of rain fell recently
the temp. is 75, wind is 5mph
the barometer is steady
```

Although we have been referring to client/server all along, this works just the same with two peers. Or with two systems that mutually invoke methods on the other, sometimes acting as client, sometimes as server.

RMI is a very powerful technique for building large systems. The fact that the technique can be described, along with a working example, in just a few pages, speaks volumes in favor of Java. RMI is tremendously exciting and it's simple to use. You can call to any server you can bind to, and you can build networks of distributed objects. RMI opens the door to software systems that were formerly too complex to build.

Object Serialization

Serializing an object just means writing the values of all its data fields into a stream of bytes. You already know how to serialize an array or a String. The two new classes let you serialize/serialize other objects too.

Once you can turn an object into a stream, you can write it to a file (which gives you a persistent object that lives on after the program in which it was created), print it, pipe it to a thread, or even send it down a socket to another system on the other side of the world. All of these are useful things.

Object serialization is in the java.io class, along with all the other classes that process streams shown here. The new classes are:

```
public class java.io.ObjectOutputStream
    extends java.io.DataOutputStream implements java.io.ObjectOutput {
  public java.io.ObjectOutputStream(java.io.OutputStream);

  public final void writeObject(java.lang.Object);
}


public class java.io.ObjectInputStream
    extends java.io.DataInputStream implements java.io.ObjectInput {
  public java.io.ObjectInputStream(java.io.InputStream);
  public final java.lang.Object readObject();
  public synchronized void registerValidation(java.io.ObjectInputValidation,int);
}
```

A whole slew of exceptions can be thrown by the readObject routine, namely ClassNotFound Exception, MethodMissingException, ClassMismatchException, StreamCorruptedException, and of course IOException. The method writeObject can throwMethodMissingException, ClassMismatchException, and IOException. Primitive data types can be written directly, and object data types can be written by applying the routine recursively. If an object points to other objects, those objects are saved too, and so on.

The registerValidation() method lets you register an object to be validated before the entire graph is handed back to you. Validating an object means checking that it still points to all the things it pointed to before.

The new keyword *transient* marks data as not having a value that is saved when the class is serialized. One example would be anything whose value is only valid at a given moment in time, like:

```
transient int current_speed
```

The serializer knows it has to reserve space for the value, but it doesn't save the soon-to-be outdated value there. For this reason, transient fields should usually be marked private too, as you don't want other objects using the values they find there. Static (class-level) data is not serialized either.

Do you want to serialize something from the class? You already have. That's what a class file is. You don't have to write out methods, because you already have those in the .class file, and can get them by loading it at any time. Different data values are what distinguish two objects of the same class. No special code is needed to allow a class to be serialized. In fact, you have to take steps to stop a class being serializable, usually by overloading writeObject for it, to make it throw an IOException.

If you just use write out the data values, you've got no guarantee that someone hasn't since modified its class and recompiled it, so the serializer calculates a hash value on the class and saves that too. If the saved hash value from the object you bring in matches the hash value for the class in memory, we figure it's the same class. Note that when you read an object back in, after you have written it out, you do not get back the same object. You get back a different object with identical values in the data fields.

There are some commonly used terms for serializing an object. Writing it to disk is called *pickling* or *preserving* the object. People also talk about marshalling and unmarshalling an object when it is being sent somewhere. I prefer the term lyophilize (pronounced "laff-alize") as it is a better description. When you pickle something you add brine to it.

Lyophilize is a term from chemistry meaning "freeze-dry." When you freeze dry something you take the water out and just leave the dry stuff. When you lyophilize an object you remove the code and just save the data.

Serialization Code Example

We should note at this point that the example is based on the alpha 2 version of RMI, released in July 1996. Some changes can be expected as the design proceeds to final form. Be sure to look at the Javasoft site http://java.sun.com to get the latest update, which will be released with JDK 1.1 in any event.

```
import java.io.*;

public class writeobj {

    public static void main(String arg[]) {
        Integer I = new Integer(65);
        try {
          FileOutputStream fos = new FileOutputStream("plum.dat");
          ObjectOutputStream oos = new ObjectOutputStream(fos);
          oos.writeObject(I);
        } catch(Exception e) {System.out.println(e);}

        try {
          FileInputStream fis = new FileInputStream("plum.dat");
          ObjectInputStream ois = new ObjectInputStream(fis);
          Object o = ois.readObject();
          I = (Integer) o;
          int i = I.intValue();
          System.out.println("i="+i);
        } catch(Exception e) {System.out.println(e);}

    }

}
```

This little program creates a FileOutputStream then pushes an ObjectOutputStream on it, to write an Integer object to the file "plum.dat." It then reads it in again. Notice that you just read in a raw object, and need to cast it back to its original type. You need to have some way of remembering what that type is, such as only writing one kind of object in a given file.

Java and Databases: JDBC

Right at the beginning it was realized that getting information into and out of databases would be a really useful ability to give Java. Large enterprises stand or fall by the quality of their corporate databases, and Java has a bright future in enterprise computing. So the very first library that Sun provided after the Java Development Kit was the Java DataBase Connectivity (JDBC). Sun designed the JDBC to allow access to any ANSI SQL-2 standard database.

We'll describe the JDBC in full here, and show a working example that you can copy and try. To get the most out of this section, you really need to understand database terms and techniques (like "SQL"). We'll sketch out some of these, but the topic really requires a complete book of its own. A good one is recommended at the end of this chapter.

The JDBC API defines Java classes to represent database connections, SQL statements, result sets, database metadata (data about data), etc. It allows a Java programmer to issue SQL statements to read/write a database.

The JDBC itself is written entirely in Java, will run anywhere and (from JDK 1.1 on) can be downloaded as part of an applet. However, more software than just the JDBC is needed to talk to a database, so the security model needs careful consideration if you want to use applets.

The JDBC consists of an API (the specification of a library or application programmer's interface), and a package containing about 20 Java classes to implement the application program side of the API. Some of the classes are interfaces, and the code that implements them must be provided by an additional database-specific piece of software called a driver.

Java programs call methods in the JDBC package to connect with databases through their drivers, then retrieve, process, and write information. See Figure 9-5. The package that holds the Java code for the JDBC is called java.sql. We'll be saying more about SQL later. For now, just note that it is a specialized programming language used to access just about all databases. We don't want to make Java replace SQL, we just want Java to be able to bundle up SQL queries, direct them to the right database, and listen for the answers.

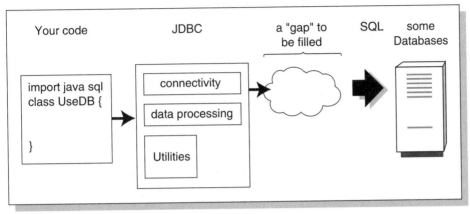

Figure 9-5: Where the JDBC fits

Note that we are not saying what kind of database is upstream from the JDBC. Your Java code knows very little about this. What your program does know is that by talking to the JDBC it can indirectly talk to a database, just as by talking to a broker you can accomplish a transaction (sell a house, buy a diamond) through a third party you might never meet directly.

Vendor independence is one of the reasons that the large commercial database users are excited by the Java-DBMS integration. These companies see great value in front-end software that doesn't lock them in to one particular database supplier. The network distributed feature of Java is an additional boost, making it almost trivial to build true distributed data processing systems.

The Classes in the JDBC

The JDBC Application Programmer Interface is implemented by about 20 Java classes, in the java.sql package. In Table 9-4, the 20-odd classes are divided into three groups concerned with connectivity, data processing, and utility functions.

Table 9-4: JDBC classes can be divided into three groups

Class	Purpose
Connectivity java.sql.DriverManager java.sql.Driver java.sql.DriverPropertyInfo java.sql.Connection	Manages the drivers that are registered with it Handles one specific type of database Gets and sets Connection properties Represents a session with a specific database. SQL statements are executed and results are returned for an individual connection
Data Processing java.sql.DatabaseMetaData java.sql.Statement java.sql.CallableStatement java.sql.PreparedStatement java.sql.ResultSet java.sql.ResultSetMetaData	Provide information on the database as a whole. Sends over an SQL statement. A variant on Statement (used to execute an SQL stored procedure). Another variant on Statement (holds a static pre-compiled SQL statement). These are often more efficient to execute. Holds the result of executing an SQL statement. Provides information on the types and properties of a ResultSet
Support java.sql.Types java.sql.Numeric java.sql.Date.java java.sql.Time.java java.sql.Timestamp.java java.sql.SQLException.java java.sql.SQLWarning.java java.sql.DataTruncation.java	Constants used by SQL Supports arbitrary precision numbers Supports dates Supports times Supports a combined date/time A database access exception class with more information added about the error A subclass of SQLException A subclass of SQLWarning relating to a data value being unexpectedly cut short.

The source for these classes and interfaces is provided, too.

Using the JDBC

There are four steps that all Java programs follow to talk to a database using the JDBC.

1. Load any drivers you are going to need.
2. Tell the JDBC what database you want to use.
3. Connect to that database.
4. SQL statements across the connection, and get results back.

Step 1: Load any drivers you are going to need

This is a system-specific step that depends on how exactly you will connect to the database. The drivers are the software component that "fill the gap" in Figure 9-5. There are several possibilities for how the gap may be filled. In Java, you will simply invoke the static method Class.forName("drivername"); using the actual name of the driver. The forName() method gets the runtime class descriptor, and has the side effect of loading the associated library or class into your Java runtime.

All databases have a driver at their end to accept queries, feed them into the database's internal form and deliver results. As Figure 9-6 shows, the driver for Oracle is specific to Oracle, the driver for Sybase is specific to Sybase and so on. Although just about all databases speak SQL in theory, they all actually have slightly incompatible local dialects of SQL.

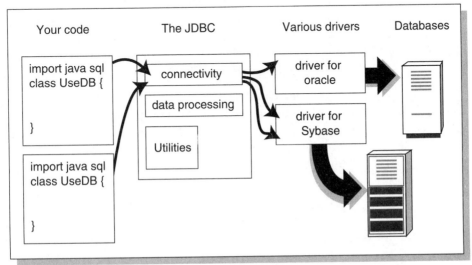

Figure 9-6: Where the drivers fit in

What's needed is a driver or a pipeline of drivers that speak to the JDBC at one end, and can speak the database dialect at the other end. Right here is where you can start to get into trouble, because there are no drivers supplied with the JDBC. You have to obtain them from the database vendors or from the third party tools companies. These companies are flourishing filling this need and will usually let you download an evaluation copy of a driver for a limited use period.

Although these driver components are essential to use the JDBC, this is a "batteries not included" kind of deal. If you want to run a Java program that accesses a database, you need to additionally procure both the database and its drivers. The drivers could be in the form of a Java program, or (more likely at this point) a dynamically linked library of native code, which must be loaded into your running Java system.

The slickest kind of driver implements the JDBC interfaces and talks directly to the database server with no other intervening code. It's a big programming job to get the proprietary and usually unpublished database protocols working, and it must be rewritten for each kind of database. It offers the best performance however.

Another implementation possibility is a bit simpler: provide some code that talks to the JDBC at one end, and can speak the language expected by an existing database driver at the other. This code in the middle is, of course, termed *middleware*. Such a driver would be a bridge between JDBC and the database driver at the back end. We'll say more about this later.

Step 2: Specify what database you want to use

There can be several programs active on one system and talking to different databases at one time. You need to tell the JDBC which one will be used by this program. Rather than giving a filename (which doesn't scale across different machines very well), you tell the JDBC what database you want to use in the form of a URL. An example URL might be like the one shown in Figure 9-7.

As you might guess, the form and content of the URL is very specific to individual databases and the drivers you will use for access. Whether or not the port number is necessary, or even required, is a driver-dependent feature, as are the parameters in the URL after the subprotocol (odbc, here). You just have to read the documentation that comes with the driver.

This is the protocol
to follow. The main
protocol is jdbc. The
subprotocol is odbc

The port number
to use for the
socket connection

The system on
which the database
resides

The pathname to
the database

Figure 9-7: A URL tells the JDBC what database to use

Step 3: Connect to that database

This is the point where your code registers with the JDBC. You will use the connectivity classes to connect to the database of interest. Your program can be talking to several different databases at once. For this reason, the JDBC package is
sometimes called a *driver manager*, which can be anything that controls multiple
drivers. However, the JDBC does a lot more than just manage a few drivers.

Your application program needs to tell the driver manager to open a connection to
the URL you put together in Step 2. Making the connection is an iterative process:
the JDBC driver manager will load all the drivers it can find and ask each in turn
to try to process the URL. The driver manager looks up a property called
"jdbc.drivers" in the system properties table. This should contain a list of class
names for driver classes, separated by colons. You can set these in a ~/.hotjava/
properties file, which might contain a property key/value pair like:

```
jdbc.drivers=foo.bah.Driver:wombat.sql.Driver:some.other.ourDriver
```

The DriverManager class will attempt to load each of these driver classes. If
you have all the right software "glue" in place, then one of them will be able to
connect to that URL successfully. The rest will fail silently, without throwing an
exception. Typically there will only be a handful of drivers on any given system,
so the connection is established very quickly.

Step 4: Send SQL statements across the connection and get results back

Once you have a connection open to your database, you will start sending SQL statements across and getting back result sets. Some database APIs have special mechanisms to support asynchronous querying, but this is not needed by Java. You simply create a new thread for any SQL statement that might take a long time. Be careful to ensure that you only use the java.sql classes in a "thread-safe" manner. That is, you are responsible for providing synchronization and avoiding data races where necessary.

Queries and updates are sent across to the database in the form of SQL statements, which are just Strings containing the SQL text. The results usually come back as something called a "Result Set." Some SQL statements just return an integer, while one SQL statement (DDL) returns nothing. If you refer back to the list of classes in the JDBC, you'll notice there is one called ResultSet that has many methods for retrieving the result of executing an SQL statement.

The result will usually be in the form of a table (several rows each of several columns of data). There are methods to access individual rows by index and to get the data back as a String or some other type. There is also a class ResultSetMetaData. *Meta* is a Greek word meaning "I will try to impress you by using Greek words." In computer science it means "information about," so the meta-data of a result set is merely the information about the data in a result set (the number of columns and rows, their names and sizes, and so on). The ResultSet lets you look at the values you got back. The ResultSetMetaData lets you look at the types.

When you have finished all the processing, close everything down in an orderly manner.

About SQL and Relational Databases

As we mentioned above, actually extracting information from a database and writing it back is done in Structured Query Language. SQL has been refined over more than two decades, and is the language used to access essentially all modern databases.

Years ago, there used to be several fundamentally different architectures for databases: there were hierarchical databases, network databases, and relational databases. It is now almost universally accepted that the relational design is superior to the other alternatives. We're also starting to see early use of object-oriented databases, some of which are accessed in a relational fashion. The collision between *object-oriented* and *relational-databases* is an area of emerging technology.

The database gurus have their own terminology of relations, tuples and N'th normal form, but (in plain words) the central idea to a relational database is that data is kept in tables. In a way, a table in a relational database is like an enormous spreadsheet. It might have millions of rows and hundreds of columns. Each column contains only one kind of data. A row in a table corresponds to a record. The database can contain several tables. A programmer will use SQL statements to merge tables and extract data from them.

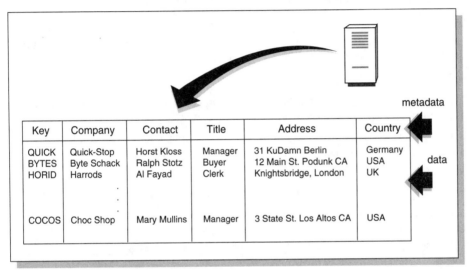

Figure 9-8:   A relational database

At first every database vendor had its own special database query language. Users eventually got fed up enough to create an industry standard around IBM's SQL. There was the SQL'89 standard, followed by the SQL'92 standard, both created under the ANSI umbrella. But SQL is still fragmented into many subtly-different slightly incompatible dialects.

The JDBC classes do their work in terms of SQL, so it takes an understanding of SQL to describe what these are. SQL is a pretty elaborate programming language in its own right, customized to handle tables, rows and columns. Describing SQL would take more room than is available here. Suffice it to say that SQL has statements like SELECT, INSERT, DELETE, and UPDATE. Interested readers are referred to the further reading. SQL operates on tables; merging, matching and extracting from them and provides its result sets in the form of tables.

The JDBC-ODBC Bridge

In the early 1990s there was a further development in the SQL world. Microsoft got involved in the process and used its monopoly leverage, just the way IBM used to, to impose the *Open DataBase Connectivity* (ODBC) standard on the industry. ODBC is an Application Programmer Interface that allows C programs to make calls into an SQL server and get back results. ODBC provided a unified way for Microsoft applications such as Access, Excel, FoxPro, and Btrieve to talk to IBM, Oracle, Paradox and other back end database systems.

Every database vendor was then pretty much obliged to provide not just a driver for their own dialect of SQL, but also a driver that would allow ODBC to communicate with their protocols. If they didn't support ODBC they would be locked out of the high volume PC desktop market.

Most of the ANSI SQL-2 databases out there now have ODBC drivers. So in order to provide instant Java connectivity to lots of products, Sun joined with Intersolv to create the jdbc.odbc package that implements the java.sql package for ODBC databases. This was a brilliant move as it leveraged (some would say "finessed") Microsoft's earlier work.

By creating an open standard for its desktop applications to connect to anybody's database, Microsoft also inadvertently provided a way for Java to connect to their standard, and thence to anybody's database. The JDBC-ODBC bridge implements the JDBC by making the appropriate calls to the ODBC Standard C API.

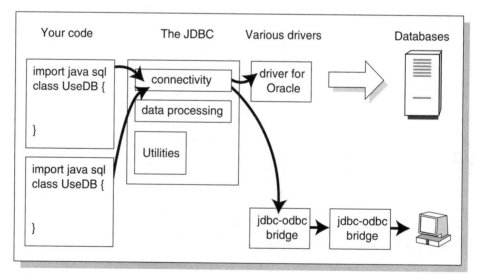

Figure 9-9: The JDBC-ODBC bridge

The JDBC-ODBC bridge is a little inefficient perhaps, using a driver to talk to a driver, but it provides instant connectivity to all popular databases. ODBC is a C language interface so the bridge needs to take Java types, and unhand them into C types on the way over to ODBC, and re-hand them on the way back. The JDBC-ODBC bridge is a separate C library that needs to be accessible to your code. There's a Java part that is a driver manager for the bridge, and a native code part that's the driver. Since it's native code, there are separate versions of the bridge driver for Windows and for Solaris.

People also talk about *tiers* of database access. This has nothing to do with how many drivers and driver managers are in the chain between the application and the database. It has to do with how the application code is partitioned. Before client/server, you had to connect directly to the system with the database and run your program on it. Such a mainframe might have hundreds or even thousands of terminals like the IBM 3270 attached to it. This was a one-tier solution.

In the early days of client/server, there was a simple split between code on the client and data on the server. That was the so-called "fat client" or two-tiered approach with no middleware. Now the model has become more refined: often the client only has code for the GUI, and there is separate application logic on a server, which the client accesses (often by browsing an applet on a Web page). The application logic in turn may talk to a database server on another system. The client never talks directly to the database. This is the three-tiered approach.

If you want browser access to a database, the three-tiered approach is the fastest way to avoid security issues and get everything working. Write your program as an application, and when it's all working, make the application serve client applets through a socket.

Code Example of Database Access

This section presents a step-by-step example of the actual set-up and code for an access to a database using Java. This is a one tiered access because everything is on one system: the application, the JDBC, the bridge, and the database. On the other hand we are stringing all these components together in just the way you need to for a multi-tiered approach. There is a large number of different databases, access methods, and host platforms, so the example I have chosen to present is the one that can be tried at least cost for most people. It uses a small scale database MS-Access on Windows 95, rather than an industrial-strength database like Oracle, Sybase or Informix on an enterprise server system. The principle remains the same however.

The example has a Java application that talks to the JDBC, and then a bridge from JDBC to ODBC, ending up at an ODBC database. This example shows how to configure everything if you are going in across the bridge. But, bear in mind that the JDBC-ODBC bridge is really just an interim solution while we wait for vendors to provide direct access drivers. You don't have to use the bridge and if you have a more direct driver, you wouldn't. Before a direct driver is available, developers can use the ODBC drivers to begin development, and later switch to a JDBC driver and avoid two layers of driver software.

The JDBC-ODBC bridge (which also contains a driver to interface to the ODBC driver) translates JDBC calls into ODBC calls. Thus, it allows the JDBC to talk to an ODBC driver front ending a database. It's a bridge in the sense that it allows you to pass over a rocky chasm separating two different protocols.

This example describes how your Java application can use the JDBC to process a Microsoft Access database running under Windows 95. Frankly, the process depends on a long chain of actions, each of which must be done exactly right, to avoid mysterious failures. You should read through all these steps before trying it for yourself. And with that warning in mind, here goes.

Step 1. Make sure you have MS-Access for Windows 95, version 7.00 or later running on your Windows 95 system.

Typical error: Trying to use MS Access version 2.0. The 16-bit Windows 3.1 version of MS Access cannot be used as JDBC uses the 32-bit ODBC which Microsoft only supplies in Access for Windows 95/NT. The downrev version of Access will result in the following error in Step 7:

```
Unable to load dll "JdbcOdbc.dll" (errcode = 45a)
*** SQLException caught ***

SQLState: 08001
Message:  No suitable driver
Vendow:   0
```

The message indicates that you do not have the 32-bit ODBC driver for the database you are trying to access.

Step 2. The "typical installation" option of MS Access for Windows 95 does not include the ODBC drivers you require. If necessary, go back and reinstall everything in MS Access to get the ODBC drivers on your system. This will make a "32-bit ODBC" icon appear on your control panel.

The 32-bit MS-Access driver for ODBC comes with Access 95 / Office Pro. It is not a standard part of Windows 95.

Typical error: Mistaking the "ODBC" icon on your Windows 95 control panel for the required "32bit ODBC" icon.

Step 3. Set up a Data Source Name for the sample database. Open ODBC32 to bring up the "Data Sources" panel then press "add" to bring up "Add Data Source" and highlight "Microsoft Access Driver (*.mdb)" and press "OK."

This brings up a panel labeled "ODBC Microsoft Access 7.0 Setup" in which you enter a Data Source Name. Use "myDSN." Also enter the description "bananas." Then press Database: "Select," which brings up a file chooser panel.

Choose the pathname C:\Access\Samples\Northwind.mdb, which is one of the sample databases that comes with Access, assuming you installed in C:\Access. If you installed in a different place, use that path to the Northwind.mdb file instead.

Press "OK" and get back to the "Data Sources" panel, where you should now see the entry "myDSN." You have successfully associated the Data Source Name and 32bit ODBC with the Access database.

Step 4. Set up the Java side to match this DSN. Make certain that the Java program names the right database. The program is on the CD and is called simple.java. It contains:

```java
import java.sql.*;
class simple {

   public static void main (String args[]) {

               String url   = "jdbc:odbc:myDSN";
               String query = "SELECT * FROM Customers "
                            + "WHERE CustomerID = 'QUICK'";
       try {
         // Load the jdbc-odbc bridge driver
         Class.forName ("jdbc.odbc.JdbcOdbcDriver");

         // Attempt to connect to a driver.
         Connection con = DriverManager.getConnection (
                                       url, "", "" );

         // Create a Statement object so we can submit
         // SQL statements to the driver
         Statement stmt = con.createStatement ();

         // Submit a query, creating a ResultSet object
                    ResultSet rs = stmt.executeQuery (query);

         // Display all columns and rows from the result set
                    printResultSet (rs);

         rs.close();
         stmt.close();
         con.close();
       }
       catch (SQLException ex) {
          while (ex != null) {
         System.out.println ("SQL Exception:   " +
                 ex.getMessage ());
             ex = ex.getNextException ();
           }
         }
         catch (java.lang.Exception ex) {
           ex.printStackTrace ();
         }
       }

   private static void printResultSet (ResultSet rs)
         throws SQLException
    {
      int numCols = rs.getMetaData().getColumnCount ();

      while ( rs.next() ) {
         for (int i=1; i<=numCols; i++) {
           System.out.print(rs.getString(i) + " | " );
             }
         System.out.println();
      }
   }
 }
}
```

The SQL statement in this program retrieves the record for the customer key "QUICK." There are two declarations right at the beginning of the main routine, URL and query. When you have this working, you can try changing

```
String url = "jdbc:odbc:myDSN";
```

to point to another database. You could also change query to:

```
String query = "SELECT * FROM Customers";
```

This would make it retrieve every customer record. Half a dozen lines down, the connection line is:

```
Connection con = DriverManager.getConnection(
                           url, "", "" );
```

The two null strings are for user-id and password. The program source is set up correctly as it is, but these are some things to try experimenting with.

Step 5. Ensure your classpath is set correctly. Make sure your Java classpath contains the directory with the jdbc code, namely

```
C:\java\jdbc\jdbc\classes
```
(or wherever you put it)

and the directory with the jdbc-odbc code, namely

```
C:\java\jdbc\jdbc-odbc\classes
```
(or wherever you put it)

Typical error: If you leave one of these out Java will give you a pretty reasonable error message. Some people copy these classes to the JDK library, so they don't have to add more to their classpath. In the JDK 1.1 release, the JDBC class is part of the standard class library.

Step 6. Ensure your path is set correctly. Make sure your Windows path contains the directory with the jdbc-odbc dll code, namely

```
C:\java\jdbc\jdbc-odbc\classes\jdbc\odbc
```
(or wherever you put it)

Typical error: If you leave a .dll directory out of your path, the code won't work, but you might not get a message that helps pinpoint the problem.

Step 7. Compile the Java program

```
javac Simple.java
```

Fix any compilation errors that show up (typically problems caused by not setting classpath correctly).

Step 8. Run the Java program

```
java Simple
```

You should see one entry in the Customers table print out.

```
QUICK | QUICK-Stop | Horst Kloss | Accounting Manager | ....
```

You can look at this table using Access, and confirm that the record is correct.

Review of Classes

This section takes a closer look at some of the important classes used in the preceding program and in the JDBC generally. It highlights some of the important methods of each.

Connectivity classes

`java.sql.DriverManager` manages the drivers that are registered with it.

```
public static synchronized Connection getConnection(String url)
        throws SQLException;
// try to establish a connection to the given database URL

public static Driver getDriver(String url)
        throws SQLException;

// try to find a driver that understands this URL.

public static synchronized void registerDriver(java.sql.Driver driver)
        throws SQLException;
// how a newly loaded driver tells the driver manager about itself

public static void setLoginTimeout(int seconds) {
// maximum time a database login can take before failing.

public static void setLogStream(java.io.PrintStream out) {
// Set the logging/tracing PrintStream
```

`java.sql.Driver` handles one specific type of database. This class is an interface.

```
Connection connect(String url, java.util.Properties info)
        throws SQLException;
// try to connect to the database at the given URL

boolean acceptsURL(String url) throws SQLException;
// return true if the driver thinks it can process this url.
```

java.sql.Connection represents a session with a specific database. SQL state-ments are executed and results are returned for an individual connection. This class is an interface.

```
Statement createStatement() throws SQLException;
// a statement is an SQL string to send to the database.

void setAutoCommit(boolean autoCommit) throws SQLException;
// By default the Connection automatically commits
// changes after executing each statement. If auto commit has been
// disabled an explicit commit must be done or database changes will
// not be saved.

DatabaseMetaData getMetaData() throws SQLException;;
// get the metadata.

void commit() throws SQLException;
// makes all changes since the previous commit/rollback

void rollback() throws SQLException;
// drops all changes made since previous commit/rollback
```

There are other, more advanced methods in this interface, too.

Data processing classes

java.sql.Statement sends over an SQL statement. This class is an interface.

```
ResultSet executeQuery(String sql) throws SQLException;
// Execute a SQL statement that returns a single ResultSet

int executeUpdate(String sql) throws SQLException;
// Execute a SQL DDL, INSERT, UPDATE or DELETE statement

void close() throws SQLException;
// close the database

void cancel() throws SQLException;
// can be used by one thread to cancel a statement being executed
// by another thread.

SQLWarning getWarnings() throws SQLException;
// executing a statement clears the old value of Warnings
// and possibly creates a list of new warnings.
```

java.sql.ResultSet holds the result of executing an SQL statement. This class is an interface. A ResultSet provides access to a table of data generated by executing a Statement. The table rows are retrieved in sequence. Within a row its column values can be accessed in any order.

```
String getString(int columnIndex) throws SQLException;
// Get the value of a column in the current row as a String

boolean getBoolean(int columnIndex) throws SQLException;
// ... as a boolean
// there are also corresponding methods to get the value of the
// entry in that column as any kind of Java primitive type,
// and as an SQL.Numeric, a byte array, a Time, Date, or Timestamp,
// an ASCII stream, a Unicode Stream, a binaryStream, or an Object!
// if you can put it into a database, Java can pull it out.

SQLWarning getWarnings() throws SQLException;
// get warning messages

void clearWarnings() throws SQLException;
// clear warning messages

ResultSetMetaData getMetaData() throws SQLException;
// get metadata describing the number, types and properties of
// a ResultSet's columns. The first column number is 1, not zero.

boolean next() throws SQLException;
// return true if the current row is valid. False when no more rows.
```

java.sql.ResultSetMetaData provides information on the types and properties of a ResultSet.

```
int getColumnCount() throws SQLException;
// the number of columns in this result set

boolean isCaseSensitive(int column) throws SQLException;
// does upper/lower case matter in this column?

boolean isSearchable(int column) throws SQLException;
// can this column be used in a 'WHERE' clause?

boolean isCurrency(int column) throws SQLException;
// is this column a cash value?

int isNullable(int column) throws SQLException;
// can you store null in this column

String getColumnLabel(int column) throws SQLException;
// what is the full name of the column?

String getColumnName(int column) throws SQLException;
// what is the column known as internally?

String getSchemaName(int column) throws SQLException;
// get the schema (loosely "plan") name for the table that
// this column came from.

boolean isReadOnly(int column) throws SQLException;
// is this column definitely not writeable?
```

Useful URLs

You will find more information about Java database connectivity at the following URLs:

http://www.xdb.com/home.htm

http://www.weblogic.com

http://www.microsoft.com/vfoxpro/vfinfo/vfpodbc.htm

http://dataramp.com/

http://splash.javasoft.com/jdbc/

http://www.vincent.se/

These URLs are for companies that are producing commercial JDBC (or jdbc-odbc) drivers and tools.

If you are on a tight budget, then consider the Postgres95 software. It can be downloaded for free, and it has a Java class library available. Further details are at URL: http://www.ki.net/postgres95/

Some Light Relief

Those Messy Messages

How many times have you encountered some kind of software failure, and ended up with an error message that told you precisely nothing? If you've been programming for any length of time at all, you'll recognize this as an all-too-familiar source of frustration.

The all time classic used to be the Unix "bus error-core dumped" but that has been replaced in recent years by the infamous Microsoft Windows "GPF." What are systems programmers thinking of when they design error messages like that? Are they deliberately trying to confuse and annoy applications programmers?

Well, no. We hardly ever try to do that deliberately. The problem arises because at the point where the problem is detected in the operating system kernel, there is no application-specific knowledge to report the problem in terms meaningful to the user. Let me give you an example of what I mean.

Inside Sun's operating system development group, there is a special interest committee known as the Ease-of-Use group. I was a co-founder and ardent supporter of this free-ranging think tank some years ago, and was for a long period the representative from kernel software development.

One day the Ease-of-Use committee decided to study kernel messages and see if there were any candidates for improvement. The person who did the study was an experienced technical writer, skilled in the art of communication, and she found many kernel error messages to complain of, including these ones:

Bad terminal owner

bread error, fatstart

Error walking tree %s.

FAT size error

Flushing job

Hit BOTTOM

lpExec confused.

object exists in wastebasket

Out of register space (ugh) allocator

POSSIBLE ATTACK from %s: newline in string "%s"

That must be tomorrow

real error

repeated leap second moment

runt packet

Bogus wildcard from %s

I read through this list, and the first thing that jumped out at me was that these were all reasonable error messages, so what was the problem? Then I read the list again, and thought about it a bit longer and the reason became clear: Every one of these messages was ambiguous. If you didn't have programming experience, you would only see the English meaning. If you did have programming experience, in this context you would only see the programming meaning. The Table 9-5 explains this more clearly.

Table 9-5: Interpreting error messages

Error	English Meaning	Programming Meaning
Bad terminal owner device.	The person who bought the system has been naughty.	The system has lost track of the process that controls this.
bread error, fatstart.	Something to do with putting on weight if you eat too much bread.	There was an error when we tried to read one of the blocks near the beginning of the File Allocation Table.
Error walking tree.	Something went wrong when we were trying to take a tree for a walk.	An invalid pointer was found as we were traversing the data structure known as a "tree."
Hit BOTTOM	User needs spanking.	Unexpectedly encountered the end of a table
Flushing job.	More toilet humor.	This process is being completely removed from the queue of the shell.
real error	As opposed to a fake one?	An error in a real (floating-point) number calculation.
repeated leap second moment	What? We have leap years and leap days, but surely we don't have leap seconds?	Actually we do, perhaps James Gosling was right after all to comment on it at length in the Date.java class.
object exists in wastebasket	How can the computer possibly know how untidy my office is?	The wastebasket icon on the window desktop has a discarded object in it.
Out of register space (ugh) allocator.	What is "ugh" supposed to add to this?	I'm tempted to pretend that "ugh" is the Universal Graphic Hash code, but actually it conveys that a distasteful and irrecoverable error situation has occurred in the code generator. It has encountered an expression so complex that it has bedeviled the register.
That must be tomorrow	Too whimsical?	This message is the response from shutdown when you give an invalid time.

. . . and so on. The point is that both parties have merit here. The programmer has chosen brief messages that describe the situation well—to other programmers. The Ease-of-Use fan has demonstrated that the messages are surprisingly easy to misinterpret. Neither party has understood the perspective of the other. It's clearly a mistake to demand that users have a programming background. On the other hand we can't expect every diagnostic message from the kernel to be meaningful to the lay person, but neither should it be ambiguous.

The moral is clear: As systems programmers we must avoid ambiguous messages. We must spell out the full name of data structures where possible. We don't necessarily have to make a message meaningful to the end user, but at least it must be incapable of misinterpretation. Don't tell users "hit bottom" when "item not found in table" will do just as well. Whenever you write an error message that will be seen by the user, take an extra minute to phrase it with care.

I'll finish by presenting one final example. I like this because it reveals a programmer who's trying hard, but can't quite let go of the techno-babble:

```
Printer out of media (paper).
```

That error used to be in PrintTool, but we have since sent the programmer to a re-education camp, and it has now been changed to

```
Printer out of paper (media).
```

Hey, even small improvements count.

Further Reading

Java Database Programming with JDBC

by Pratik Patel
published by Coriolis, 1996.

CHAPTER 10

The Abstract Window Toolkit

"Mach is the biggest intellectual fraud of the last decade."
"Really, not X-Windows?"
"I said 'intellectual'."

—Overheard in Silicon Valley

The Java Abstract Window Toolkit (AWT) continues the portability goals of the language. It provides a single-windowing user interface on systems with wildly different native window systems. It does this in a clever way: it supports only the functions that are common to all the window systems. The Java window system then uses the underlying native window system to actually render the screen images, and manipulate GUI objects.

One word of caution: as with any significant piece of software, there are some bugs in the 1.0.2 release of the AWT. If something doesn't work quite the way this text suggests it should, then collect some further information and see if you can categorize the conditions under which it fails.

You may have found a bug (report it by following the procedure at http://www.javasoft.com/intouch.html), you may have found a bug in this text (in which case claim your bounty as described at the front), or you may just fill a gap in your understanding of what is supposed to happen.

For example, FileDialogs work under Windows 95, but do not always work under Solaris 2. 🍎

385

The Role Of Objects

Object-oriented programming fits well with window systems. The concept of making new widgets by subclassing existing ones, and overriding part of their behavior is a time-saver. Another philosophical similarity is the way that widgets have to handle events just as objects handle messages.

Method inheritance is a key part of the window interface in Java. Programmers are expected to override routines and extend classes to gain the exact behavior that they want. The basic components of a GUI (buttons, textfields, scroll bars, lists, and so on) are all created by subclassing the superclass called "Component."

How the Java Abstract Window Toolkit Works

The AWT requires the native window system to be running on the platform, as it uses the native window system to implement windows within Java. Figure 10-1 (opposite page) shows this. Be warned that this means the behavior of the AWT widgets is that provided by the native window toolkit. This can be subtlely different on different platforms. For example, the TextField widget behaves differently between Motif and Windows.

Mnemonic: Peer objects let your Java runtime "peer" at the underlying window implementation. They are only of interest to people porting the Java Development Kit. To a Java applications programmer all window system code is written in Java.

The policy of supporting the "highest common factor"[1] of all the supported native window toolkits works well. The windowing operations that are common to all toolkits tend to be the most useful ones. Highest common factor GUI toolkits are not a new idea. It is a new idea to support a highest common factor toolkit as a class library that is highly integrated with its own general purpose programming language.

---

1.   Some people call it the "lowest common denominator" instead.

native window system

1 Java program issues call to add a button to a window on the screen

2 AWT runtime makes the request of the native window system..

3 . . .which puts the button on the screen

4 button is pressed by mouse

5 native window system passes event to Java event handler system

6 and from there into Java app's code

Figure 10-1:   How the Java abstract window toolkit works

The Different Faces of the AWT

Where there are big differences in the AWT, Java adopts conventions that smooth over the differences. For example, Macs have one button on the mouse, PCs have 2 buttons on the mouse, Unix has 3 buttons on the mouse (left, right, and center)

Java deals with this hardware difference by adopting the convention that mice have three buttons. If the GUI invites a user to "click on the right button," mice with fewer than three buttons can simulate it by holding down the meta and alt keys while mouse clicking. This shows up in the "modifiers" field of the event. However this isn't a perfect solution, as it doesn't detect when multiple mouse buttons are pressed simultaneously. But that is a very unusual event.

It would be possible to approach the GUI with a different philosophy and have the Java AWT support on every platform every operation that is supported by one native toolkit. This would require a huge amount of extra implementation and maintenance effort for a small increase in functionality.

Window systems have become too complicated and overblown in recent years. When there are 1,000 page manuals explaining the Microsoft Windows API, and when it takes hundreds of lines of code to put a window on the screen (using X-windows) you know that it's time for something simpler and better. Supporting only the window operations that are common to all toolkits means that programmers have an easier job learning the window toolkit. Software gets written faster and it is less buggy. Sure, it may not feature "balloon help," but you can have it now, and it works.

You can write Java windowing programs with one specific platform in mind, but you get code that runs on all the other platforms for free.

Application software companies no longer have to produce different versions of their software for each supported platform. As soon as these companies transition their products to Java, we will no longer need to see "123 for Windows 3.x, 123 for Windows 95, 123 for Solaris." There will just be "123 for Java." It's a huge and compelling reason to program in Java. 🍃

General Remarks on Window Systems

A few words of explanation about the programming model for window systems are in order. Unlike procedural programs in which things happen sequentially from beginning to end, windowing programs are asynchronous. You cannot predict at any given instance which of the on-screen buttons, menus, frames etc., the user will touch. Accordingly a model known as "event-driven programming" is used.

In event-driven programming, the logic of your code is inverted. Instead of one flow of control from beginning to end, the program mostly waits for user input. When the user touches something on screen with the mouse pointer, the window system catches that event and passes it on to a handler that you earlier supplied. This is known as a callback, and your handler is a "callback routine" because the window system calls back to it when the event happens. Your handler will deal with the graphics event, and the action that is associated with it. If a button says "press here to read the file," then your button handler must handle the button event, and also read the file in. Handling a button event just means noticing that it occurred, but other events like dragging something with the mouse take a bit more work to make it appear correctly on the screen.

Almost the whole of window programming is learning about the different objects that you can put on the screen (windows, scrollbars, buttons, etc.). Your event handling code for each widget (as these windowing objects are termed) will be invoked as needed. Let's take a look at the very simplest example just to get started.

We have already seen the code to pop-up a window for an applet (since all applets run in a window, having an applet at all means that we have already implicitly created a window). The most frequently-used kind of window is a subclass of Window, known as a Frame. Here is the code to put up a Frame from an application.

```java
import java.awt.*;
public class cherry {
    static Frame f = new Frame("cherry");

    public static void main(String[] a) {
        f.resize(300,100);
        f.show();
    }
}
```

Compiling and executing this program will cause a Frame like that shown in Figure 10-2 to appear on the screen.

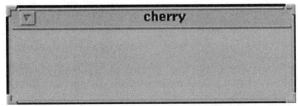

Figure 10-2:   Executing the program above will create this screen

As is usual in a programming language, there is more than one way to accomplish this. As an alternative, we could have made class cherry extend class Frame, and instantiate itself inside cherry. A "Frame" is a window with a title bar on which title strings and pull-down menus can be placed. Here, we just gave it the title on the title bar of "cherry".

Almost everything that you can see on the screen from Java is ultimately taking place in a Frame or a Panel. These are the "corkboards" or backdrops to which we attach scrollbars, textfields, menu items, etc.

Details of the AWT

The AWT provides five services to the programmer:

- A set of the usual GUI widgets:[2] buttons, pull-down menus, choices, checkboxes, text input fields, and so on.

- An event handling system that notices when the user adjusts one of these widgets, and conveys that information to the program.

- The concept of "containers"—objects that you attach a widget to. A container can hold a number of related widgets, and deal with them as a group. Typically you do not display an individual widget, you add it to a container. It is the container that is displayed.

- Some "layout managers" that provide help in automatically positioning where a widget goes when you add it to a container. This frees up the programmer from the responsibility of prescribing where every last widget in the GUI should go. (Although you can do it that way too, if you want). Each container will have a layout manager associated with it.

- Simple support for graphics operations: draw an arc, fill a polygon, etc.

AWT Containers

We have already seen how to get a basic backdrop on the screen both with an applet, and with an application. Here is a little more information about these backdrops, or containers. Containers are a subclass of something called a Component. Almost everything in the AWT is a subclass of Component. Having an ultimate common parent makes it easy to build up GUIs recursively: all these components fit in this container, which fits in this component. . . It is easy to render everything onto the screen, by simply painting the backdrop, and then having all the nested Components paint themselves too.

Components are the most general kind of GUI object. They do two principal things:

1. Display themselves and all contents on the screen.

2. Catch and handle events relating to the widgets, keyboard and mouse when the focus is on the Component.

2. "widget" is a term popularized by the X-Window system. It conveys the idea of "window gadget"—a gadget or thingummy that has some handy interaction with the user in a window. For example, scrollbars, cursor icons, and buttons are all widgets.

Containers are the specific backdrops to which you will add your GUI widgets. The two important things you do with a Container:

1.   Add/remove widgets from it, according to some layout policy.

2.   Override a method in a Component, for event handling.

There is a difference between Component and Container. Component is really general. It can be any GUI piece, even a Container. (Examples: Scrollbar, Button, Panel) Containers are the specialized GUI pieces that hold widgets. It has the method add() for adding a widget. (Examples: Panel, Window)

The class hierarchy looks like that in Figure 10-3.

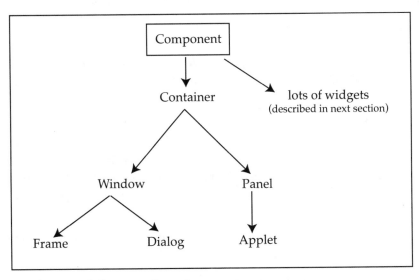

Figure 10-3:   Class hierachy

As Figure 10-3 above shows, "Containers" are of two kinds:

•   Subclasses of Window, which are separate pop-up windows in their own right, and

•   Subclasses of Panel, which are containers that generally represent a smaller part/area of a larger Window (that is to say, they will have been added to a Window). Applets appear on the screen as a Panel.

A description of Component and its container subclasses follows.

Component Everything on the screen is built out of Components. A Component has a size and position, and can be rendered onto the screen. This is a very general class that has methods to check whether the instance is on screen, is visible, what its size and location are, and whether to show it or not. It also has methods to capture events and deal with them (described below).

Component also has a method

```
public boolean handleEvent(Event evt)
```

to process user input events when the user presses a button, drags the mouse, and so on.

```
handleEvent()
```

is the most basic handler. It does some analysis of the input event, and will call one of about a dozen other methods like these:

```
public boolean action(Event evt,Object what)
public boolean keyDown(Event evt, int key)
public boolean mouseMove(Event evt, int x,int y)
```

The programmer overrides these to provide the callback routines that window systems use for event handling. There are also methods in Component to set colors, fonts, and new sizes and places on the screen.

Finally, Component gets painted on the screen when the runtime system calls its method:

```
public void paint(Graphics g)
```

We have seen this method several times before, and now we know the class to which it belongs.

```
"paint" should really be called:
do_This_To_Draw_Me
as that is what it really does.
```

Any object that belongs to a subclass of Component can override paint to provide specialized instruction on how to paint itself. ☕

Container A data structure class that is used to hold several widgets, and treat them as a related group. Typically, all the widgets in one window, or one part of a window will be in the same container, and the container will be displayed. It has the method

```
public Component add(Component comp)
```

to add a widget to the container. Most of its other methods are to do with layout managers, or choosing a size for the container.

A container in itself is not displayable. It is only when you get down to the subclasses of Container that you have something that can be shown on the screen. Container has 2 subclasses: Window and Panel.

Window This is a totally blank window. It doesn't even have a border or a menu bar. It could be used to implement a pop-up window. Typically you don't use Window directly, but use its more useful subclasses (**Frame** and **Dialog**).

Window has a few methods to do with showing and hiding the window, bringing it to the front and back, and packing together the components in the window.

Frame This is a specialization of Window, on which Menu bars (which can be multilevel) are created and processed.
It has a border and possibly a menu bar attached to it. When you create a **Frame**, it is not physically displayed inside the applet or other Container, but is a separate free floating window on the display monitor.

An example of the code to create a Frame, and how it looks on the screen appeared in Figure 10-2 earlier.

Dialog   The Dialog class can be used to pop-up a window that has an area where the user can type a line of text. Dialogs can be modal (no further user input can occur until it is dismissed) or non-modal (the dialog can be ignored or dealt with when desired). This is controlled by a boolean flag in the constructor.

There is also a subclass called **FileDialog** that brings up the native "file chooser" window, allowing a filename to be selected. Because of the file access restrictions on applets FileDialog is most useful in applications.

The code to put up a FileDialog is:

```
import java.awt.*;
public class fd {
    static Frame f = new Frame("cherry");

    public static void main(String[] a) {
        FileDialog fd = new FileDialog(f, "grapes");
        fd.show();
        f.add(fd);
        f.show();
    }
}
```

It will display a window like the one in Figure 10-4.

Figure 10-4: A typical display window of Dialog

The filter box and button is supposed to say "only show me filenames of this form." Some aspects of FileDialogs were buggy in JDK 1.0.2.

The code to retrieve the filename string that the user chose looks like this.

```
String s = fd.getFile();
```

FileDialogs look quite different on different operating systems. The example (opposite) is the appearance under OpenWindows on Solaris.

Panel A container with a built-in way to layout on the screen everything it contains. A Panel is a smaller region that is usually contained within a Frame.

Figure 10-5 is a picture of a panel that has been nested within an applet. The panel has been colored so you can see it. By default it has the same color as the applet, so is invisible. Many smaller panels can be added to one applet container. Each panel can then be treated as a container in its own right: have things added to it, catch events, and have a layout policy.

Figure 10-5: Panel nested within an applet

Panel has almost no methods of its own, and none of general interest. The major purpose of the Panel class is to provide a default "FlowLayout" manager for its Applet subclass. The code to display this panel is:

```java
import java.awt.*;
import java.applet.*;
class MyPanel extends Panel {
    public void paint(Graphics g) {
        resize(200,25);
        setBackground(Color.green);
        g.drawString("I am in the Panel",10,10);
    }
}
public class cucumber extends Applet {
    MyPanel p = new MyPanel();
    public void init() {
        add(p);
    }

}
```

Applet Applet is a subclass of **Panel**. The major thing this says is that Applets come readymade with some GUI stuff in place. We've seen applets many times now. Figure 10-6 is another example screendump of one.

Figure 10-6: Just another applet

Here is the code that created that applet:

```
import java.awt.*;
import java.applet.*;

public class plum extends Applet {

    public void init() {
        setBackground(Color.green);
        resize(250,100);
    }

    public void paint(Graphics g) {
        g.drawString("I am in the Applet", 35,15);
    }

}
```

One advantage of an applet over an application for a GUI program is that you can start adding components and displaying them without needing to create an underlying backdrop, as one already exists.

Here are some popular methods of Applet:

```
public URL getDocumentBase()
public URL getCodeBase()

public String getParameter(String name)
public void resize(int width, int height)

public void showStatus(String msg)
public Image getImage(URL url) //bring in an image
public Image getImage(URL url, String name)

public AudioClip getAudioClip(URL url) //bring in a sound file
public void play(URL url)
```

These four methods are for the stages in the applet lifecycle:

```
public void init()
public void start()
public void stop()
public void destroy()
```

As you can see, Applet has several methods that deal with sounds and pictures. For both of these, it uses a URL (the "Universal Resource Locator" that we met in Chapter 1) to pinpoint the file containing the goodies. You do not have to do anything special to make an Applet retrieve an image from its server over the Internet—it is a built-in method for you. A URL can locate something that is local to your system, or anywhere remote on Internet. Some people like to imagine that is why it is a "Universal" resource locator. It will look anywhere in the Universe.

The DocumentBase referred to in the first method, is simply the directory containing the HTML page that you are currently visiting. Similarly, the CodeBase is the directory that contains the applet you are currently executing. Often these two directories will be the same. Since the codebase is a URL, it can be anywhere on the Internet though.

Applet has other methods too. The source can be seen in

```
$JAVAHOME/src/java/applet/Applet.java
```

AWT Widgets

This section describes how to add widgets to Frame or Panel, and how to process the input that you get back from widgets. The widgets that we will cover here are shown in Figure 10-7. The class hierarchy is quite flat. The widgets are subclasses of the general class Component that we have already seen.

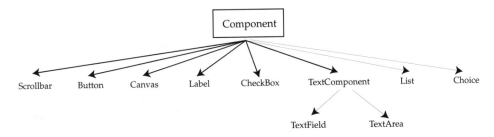

Figure 10-7: The class hierarchy of a widget

These classes are the widgets or building blocks from which you will create your GUI. What you do with all these components is:

1.   Add them to a Frame or Applet, then display it.

2.   Get back input when the user presses buttons, makes selections, etc., and process it. 💝

Fortunately both of these activities are quite straightforward, and we'll cover them here in source code, words, and pictures. The add method can be applied to a Frame in an application, like this:

```
Frame f = new Frame();
        ...
f.add( something );
```

Or it can be applied to the Applet's panel in an applet, like so:

```
public static void init () {
    this.add( something );
```

or, more simply:

```
public static void init () {

    add( something );
```

Recall the Applet lifecycle described in Chapter 6. That made clear that there is an "init()" method which each Applet can override. It will be called when the Applet is loaded, and it is a good place to place the code that creates these GUI objects. We will use "init()" for that.

A Few Words on Getting a GUI Event

Just as adding widgets to a panel or frame is easy, so getting back user input is also straightforward. Everything hinges on the method with this signature:

```
public boolean action( Event e, Object o)
```

The method is part of every Component, so all of the buttons, choices lists, etc., inherit it and can override it.

Whenever a user operates a Component (presses a button, clicks on a choice), the action event is called. The "Event e" argument contains much information about the coordinates of the event, the time it occurred, and the kind of event that it was. If the event was a keypress, it has the value of the key. The other argument is a generalized object that contains extra information in some cases.

The event contains a field called "id" that indicates the type of event it is (e.g. KEY_PRESS, MOUSE_DOWN, LIST_SELECT, etc), and hence which other Event variables are relevant for the event. For keyboard events, the field called "key" will contain a value indicating the key that was pressed/released and the modifiers field will contain the modifiers (whether the shift key was down, etc).

For KEY_PRESS and KEY_RELEASE event ids, the value of key will be the unicode character code for the key; for KEY_ACTION and KEY_ACTION_RELEASE, the value of key will be one of the defined action-key identifiers in the Event class (PGUP, PGDN, F1, F2, etc).

The class Event can be seen in full in directory $JAVAHOME/src/java/awt/Event.java.

A summary of the event class is:

```
public class Event {
    public static final int SHIFT_MASK;
    public static final int CTRL_MASK;
    public static final int META_MASK;
    public static final int ALT_MASK;

    public static final int F1; // the F1 function key
    public static final int F2;
      // ...
    public static final int F12; // the F12 function key

    public static final int KEY_PRESS;
    public static final int KEY_RELEASE;
    public static final int KEY_ACTION;
    public static final int KEY_ACTION_RELEASE;

    public static final int MOUSE_DOWN;
    public static final int MOUSE_UP;
    public static final int MOUSE_MOVE;
    public static final int MOUSE_ENTER;
    public static final int MOUSE_EXIT;
    public static final int MOUSE_DRAG;

    public static final int ACTION_EVENT;
    public static final int GOT_FOCUS;
    public static final int LOST_FOCUS;

    public int id; // what the event was (uses the constants above)

    public Object target;  // the component generating the event.
    public long when;     // the timestamp

    public int x;
    public int y;     // x and y are where the event happened.

    public int key;  // the key that was pressed

    public int modifiers;   // the state of the modifiers

    public int clickCount; // number of clicks from the mouse

    public Object arg;    // an arbitrary argument, not always used

    public boolean shiftDown();   // true if shift key down
    public boolean controlDown(); // true if ctrl key down
    public boolean metaDown();    // true if meta key down

}
```

You get an object of this class sent to the action routine for each GUI event.

So for example, if the "Q" key is pressed, these fields (others will be set too) will have the values shown in the event object sent to the container of the key:

```
id=KEY_PRESS, key=81, modifiers=SHIFT_MASK
```

For some events (like key presses, and mouse movements), the target is the container. For others (like buttons, scrollbars, and text fields), the target is the widget itself. Don't be fooled by the implication that the "target" is where the Event is going to. Sometimes it is where it has come from.

If the mouse is dragged, this event object will be sent to the container of the key:

```
id=MOUSE_DRAG, x=x_coord, y=y_coord,  modifiers=0
```

When you drag a mouse or a scrollbar, many, many events are sent. It doesn't wait until you have stopped moving the object, it generates an event for each slight movement (not necessarily each pixel of movement).

If the center button of a 3-button mouse is pressed, these are some of the fields of the Event object:

```
id=MOUSE_DOWN, modifiers=ALT_MASK
```

If the right button of a 3-button mouse is pressed, these are some of the fields of the Event object:

```
id=MOUSE_DOWN, modifiers=META_MASK
```

The modifiers field in the event is how Java portably handles the different number of mouse buttons Mac: one, Windows: two, and Unix: three). You should be able to hold down the ALT or META (shift or control) key and click the left mouse button to make it appear as a center or right mouse button event. This is totally broken in JDK 1.0.2.

The object o in the action routine is not always used. When the event is a button, it holds a string that is the label of the button. When the event is a menu item being selected, it holds a string that is the menu item's name.

For each container that a widget is added to, the programmer has the opportunity to provide an overriding version of:

```
public boolean action(Event e, Object o)
```

and to use that to determine exactly what the event was, and from that take action to deal with it. The action method must return true to indicate it has consumed (dealt with) the event.

Having explained the theory of widgets and widget input, lets take a look at how they appear on the screen, and typical code to handle them. You'll notice that the format in the following pages deviates a bit from the rest of the chapter. The recurring subheadings are designed to illustrate the commonality between all the widgets. So, let's go.

Scrollbar

What it is

In fancy words, a Scrollbar is a draggable analog component. The user slides a bar along, and the program gets back a numeric value from that. A Scrollbar can be freestanding, or attached to a canvas or other component.

What it looks like on screen

You will typically override the init() method to add these objects to the Applet's panel as shown in Figure 10-8. In an application, you can set them up where you like. (Note: in future examples in this section, we won't bother repeating the context that this is part of the init() method in an applet).

Figure 10-8:   Freestanding Scrollbar

The code to create it

```
public void init() {
    Scrollbar s  =
          new Scrollbar(Scrollbar.VERTICAL,20,10,5,35);
    add(s);
```

The arguments are

- Whether the bar should go up, or along (`Scrollbar.HORIZONTAL`)
- The initial position for the slider (bar)
- The size of the visible portion of the scrollable area
- The value at the low end of the scale
- The value at the high end of the scale

The code to retrieve user input from a Scrollbar

Scrollbars are the only widget that does not have an action() method. Scrollbar events use the underlying method "handleEvent()." All widget events start out in handleEvent(), but the Event class does some preprocessing, and splits out most of them into a call to action() or one of the mouse action methods. This isn't done for Scrollbars. The method handleEvent() is used to get the position of the slider when it is moved.

```
public boolean handleEvent(Event e) {
    if (e.target instanceof Scrollbar) {
        value = ((Scrollbar)e.target).getValue();
        return true;
    }   else return super.handleEvent(e);
    ...
```

Scrollbars are often teamed up with another widget, for example, a text entry field. This allows a limited screen area to be assigned to it, while allowing the whole thing to be viewed in pieces. Scrollbars cause a whole series of events the whole time you are moving the slider. The runtime system doesn't wait until you have stopped and call handleEvent once; it may call it dozens of times as you scroll.

There are four methods to get and set the line and page increments of a scrollbar (the amount it moves on a line or page up or down event). These are:

```
setPageIncrement(int i).
setLineIncrement (int i)
getPageIncrement ()
getLineIncrement()
```

Button

What it is

This is a GUI button. You can program the action that takes place when the button is pressed.

What it looks like on screen

In Figure 10-9, the button "peach" can be pressed.

Figure 10-9:   Here's your peach button

The code to create it

```
Button b = new Button("peach");
add(b);
```

The code to retrieve user input from it

```
public boolean action(Event e, Object o) {
    if (e.target instanceof Button)
        if( "peach".equals( (String) o ) ) {
          System.out.println("peach button pressed");
          return true;
    ...
```

Note: there is an alternative, perhaps uglier way to obtain the label of the button that was pressed, using the Event e:

```
if( "peach".equals( ((Button)e.target).getLabel()) )
```

You can only cast the target to a button if it actually is a button or button subclass.

Program an "Alice in Wonderland" applet: a panel with two buttons, one of which makes the panel grow larger, the other smaller.

```
resize(int width, int height)
```

will resize a Container. (Easy—about 20 lines of code).

Canvas

What it is

A Canvas is a screen area that you can use for drawing graphics or receiving user input. A Canvas contains almost no methods. All its functionality is inherited from Component (setting font, color, size, and receiving events) or from you giving it functionality when you extend the class. When you extend the class, you can override the "paint()" method for this Canvas, and *that* gives you a Graphics context in which to use the Graphics methods. There's more about Graphics in a later section.

What it looks like on screen

Figure 10-10 shows a canvas.

Figure 10-10:   A typical canvas

The screen dump is not very exciting, merely showing a rectangular area that has been highlighted with a different color to make it visible (see code below). Canvases are pretty inert until you extend them and use them to display images, or do other graphics programming.

The code to create it

The following code gives the Canvas a red color, so you can distinguish it from the Panel (as long as your Applet panel isn't red to begin with of course). It then gives the Canvas a size of 80 pixels wide by 40 high, and adds it to the Applet.

```
Canvas n = new Canvas();
n.setBackground(Color.red);
n.resize(80,40);
add(n);
```

Here is how you would extend Canvas to provide a surface that you can draw on. Remember that you don't really draw on anything; you place the statements to say how it should be drawn in its paint() method to override the paint method of the parent class.

```
//<applet code=can.class width=300 height=150> </applet>
import java.awt.*;
import java.applet.*;
public class can extends Applet {
    myCanvas c = new myCanvas();

    public void init() {
        c.resize(190,65);
        add(c);
    }
}

class myCanvas extends Canvas{
    public void paint(Graphics g) {
        g.drawString("don't go in the basement", 10,25);
        g.drawLine(10,35, 165,35);
    }
}
```

As usual, compile with:

```
    javac  can.java
```

Execute with

```
    appletviewer can.java
```

It will put a window like that shown in Figure 10-11 on the screen:

Figure 10-11:   Pay attention to this message

A common idiom with Canvas is the old "pass something to the constructor for later use." It's often convenient to pass the constructor an Image that will be drawn on the Canvas. If you make it an argument to the constructor, you can use the same class for many different images as in this example:

```
class myCanvas extends Canvas {
    Image saved_i;
    public myCanvas(Image i) {
        saved_i = i;
    }

    public void paint(Graphics g){
        g.drawImage(saved_i,0,0,this)
    }
}
```

We'll get to what an image is, and the drawImage() method later. The thing to note here is how a class can extend Canvas, and how different objects of that class can display different backgrounds.

The code for that would be used like the following:

```
Image dog_picture = getImage( ...
Image cat_picture = getImage( ...
myCanvas c1 = new myCanvas(dog_picture);
myCanvas c2 = new myCanvas(cat_picture);
```

A canvas is similar to a Panel, in that you can make it paint itself, render images, and accept events. A Canvas is not a container however, so cannot hold other components.

Label

What it is

This is a very simple component. It is just a string of text that appears on screen, like that shown in Figure 10-12.

What it looks like on screen

Figure 10-12:   A simple string of text

The code to create it

```
Label la = new Label("Grapes");
add(la);
```

Labels are write only, so there is no code to retrieve user input from it. Labels are typically used as a cheap, fast way to get some text on the screen, and to label other widgets with descriptions or instructions.

CheckBox

What it is

A screen object that represents a boolean choice "pressed" or "not pressed" or "on" or "off." Usually has some text (often a label) explaining the choice. For instance, "Press for fries" would have a Checkbox "button" allowing yes or no, as shown in Figure 10-13.

What it looks like on screen

Figure 10-13: What, no burger?

The code to create it

```
Checkbox cb  = new Checkbox("Fries?");
add(cb);
```

The code to retrieve user input from a CheckBox

```
public boolean action(Event e, Object o) {
    if (e.target instanceof Checkbox) {
        System.out.println("Fries status flipped");
        return true;
    }
    ...
```

Note that you can keep track of the state of a Checkbox, by invoking its method "get State()" which returns true if the Checkbox is selected, false otherwise.

Also note that there is a way to group a series of Checkboxes together to create a CheckboxGroup of "radio buttons." The term "radio buttons" arises from the old manual station selection buttons in car radios. When you pressed in one of the buttons, all the others would pop out and be deselected. CheckboxGroups work the same way.

CheckboxGroups work in a funny way. To create a group of checkboxes, first you instantiate a CheckboxGroup. Then when you instantiate each checkbox, you pass the checkboxgroup object to the checkbox constructor, and that tells it which group it is in. Only one box in a checkboxGroup can be selected at a time. Pressing one de-selects the previous selection.

TextField

What it is

A single line of text that the user can type in. The number of characters shown is configurable, as shown in Figure 10-14.

What it looks like on screen

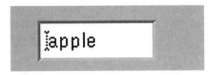

Figure 10-14:   Type in any line of text

The code to create it

This creates a TextField with eight characters showing, and initialized to the characters "apple." You type different characters in there and more than eight, but only eight will show at a time.

```
TextField tf = new TextField("apple",8);
add(tf);
```

If you want people to enter a password in the TextField, you can hide the keys they press by

```
tf.setEchoCharacter('*')
```

The code to retrieve user input from it

A TextField causes an event when a return is entered in the field. At that point you can retrieve the text.

```
public boolean action(Event e, Object o) {
    if (e.target instanceof TextField) {
        String readthis = (String) o;
        return true;
    }
    . . .
```

Note that this widget doesn't offer an event for each character entered, only when the carriage return is pressed at the end of the String. So you can't validate each character as it is entered.

List

What it is

A scrolling list of text strings, from which the user can select one or several (single or multiple selection is configurable). See Figure 10-15.

What it looks like on screen

Figure 10-15:   A scrolling list of text strings

The code to create it

This creates a scrolling list with three items visible initially, and does not allow multiple selections at the same time (multiple selections is false).

```
List li = new List(3,false);
li.addItem("carrot");
li.addItem("parsnip");
li.addItem("sprout");
li.addItem("cabbage");
li.addItem("turnip");
add(li);
```

The code to retrieve user input from it

```
public boolean action(Event e, Object o) {
if (e.target instanceof List) {
    String readthis = (String) o;
```

The action handler is called when the selection is made by clicking on the list entry.

If you have allowed multiple selections to be active in the list at one time (the list represents say pizza toppings, where you might want pepperoni and black olives and mushrooms), then you should use a different widget to signal that the input is ready. A button or a checkbox can be used for this. The list has a method called "getSelectedItems()" that will return each of several one by one.

Choice

What it is

A selection from several text strings. This is a pop-up list, akin to a pull-down menu. See Figure 10-16. When you hold the mouse button down on the choice, a list of all the other choices appears, and you can move the mouse over the one you want as shown in Figure 10-17.

What it looks like on screen

Figure 10-16:   You can have lemon . . .

When you select the list, it pops up the full range of choices, looking like this

Figure 10-17:   . . . or orange or lime

The code to create it

```
Choice c = new Choice();
c.addItem("lemon");
c.addItem("orange");
c.addItem("lime");
add(c);
```

The code to retrieve user input from it

```
public boolean action(Event e, Object o) {
if (e.target instanceof Choice) {
    String result = (String) o;
```

Menu

What it is

A Frame can hold a MenuBar, which can have several pulldown Menus, as shown in Figure 10-18. The MenuBar runs along the top of the Frame and lists the names of each Menu that has been added to it. Each pulldown Menu has selectable MenuItems on it, each identified by a String. You can populate a Menu with MenuItems and also with other menus. In the second case it forms a multi-level menu.

What it looks like on screen

Figure 10-18: Typical pull down Menus

The code to create it

```
Frame f = new Frame("my frame");
MenuBar mb = new MenuBar();

f.setMenuBar(mb);
    Menu nuts = new Menu("nut", true); //tear-off is true
        nuts.add(new MenuItem("almond"));
      nuts.add(new MenuItem("-") );    // a separator in the menu
        nuts.add(new MenuItem("filbert"));
        nuts.add(new MenuItem("pecan"));

    mb.add(nuts);
```

The code to retrieve user input from it

```
public boolean action(Event e, Object o) {
    if (e.target instanceof MenuItem) {
        if ( "almond".equals((String) o) )
        ... // take some action
    return true;
    ...
```

An alternative to adding a MenuItem is to instantiate and add a CheckboxMenuItem:

```
nuts.add(new CheckboxMenuItem("shelled"));
```

As the name suggests, this is a menu item that can be "checked off" or unselected (like a Checkbox). It has a method `getState()` to say whether it is currently selected or not. Other than that it works like a MenuItem, because it is a subclass of MenuItem. With all these widgets, there are more methods than are shown here. Use `javap java.awt.Menu` to see all the methods

A Menu has a constructor to make it a "tear-off" Menu meaning that the Menu stays up even when you take your finger off the mouse button. A menu item can be disabled so it can't be selected, then enabled again.

As well as pull down menus, most modern systems have pop-up menus, which are menus that are not attached to a menu bar on a Frame.

JDK 1.1 introduced support for pop-up menus, making menus much more useful in applets. Until then, people tended to avoid using menus in applets because the top level container is a Panel (not a Frame) and can't have a MenuBar added to it. You can create Frames in applets, but they are independent windows, floating free on the desktop.

To create a pop-up menu, JDK 1.1 has a method saying where it is to appear, and the container that is to own it. The pop-up menu will have the same look-and-feel of the native pop-up window. To see an example of a pop-up menu, on most window systems you can click on the background screen to produce a pop-up menu introducing a myriad of useful options.

`TextArea`

What it is

A TextField that is several lines long.

What it looks like on screen

Figure 10-19: This TextArea accepts many lines of text.

The code to create it

```
TextArea t = new TextArea("boysenberry", 4, 9);
add(t);
```

This creates a text area of four lines, each showing nine characters. The first line shows the first nine characters of the string "boysenberry." You can place text on the next line in the initializer by embedding a '\n' character in the string. TextAreas come with scrollbars, so you can type an unbounded amount of text.

The code to retrieve user input from it

Unlike a TextField, a TextArea might have embedded newlines, so a newline can't be used to cause the event that says "I am ready to present my value."

The same solution is used as with a multiple-selection list. Use another widget, say a button, or checkbox, to signal that the text is ready to be picked up.

```
public boolean action(Event e, Object o) {
if (e.target instanceof Button)
   if( "text ready".equals( (String) o ) ) {
     String my_text = t.getText();
     return true;
     . . .
```

The capacity of a TextArea is large but is not infinite. Some users have reported that it seems to hold around 32 Kbytes of characters, less some overhead, on Windows 95.

ScrollPane

What it is

A ScrollPane is a Component that acts exactly like a regular Component—but with scrollbars attached. TextAreas and scrolling lists already come this way, however Panels and Canvases don't.

You can just add a component to a ScrollPane Container and you get the scrolling behavior automatically. This widget was introduced with JDK 1.1. Prior to that, many people implemented their own versions, which usually had horrible results because the underlying peer window system was not used.

What it looks like on screen

A ScrollPane will have the general appearance of a TextArea, but instead of being restricted to something that can accept text, it can hold any kind of widget. It will commonly be used for Canvas and Panel.

Figure 10-20: A ScrollPane comes with two ScrollBars built in

The code to create it

At the time this book went to press, ScrollPanes had been publicly announced, but the details of how to use them had not been finalized.

As with a scrollbar there will be methods to retrieve, and set the page and line increments. There will also need to be a way to distinguish between the horizontal and the vertical scrollbars on the pane.

The code to retrieve user input from it

At the time this book went to press, ScrollPanes had been publicly announced, but the details of how to use them had not been finalized. It is likely they will be similar in use to a Scrollbar.

Widget Wrap-up

Finally, Figure 10-21 is the applet that consists of the widgets described above, placed in the Applet panel.

Figure 10-21:   One big happy family of widgets

The code for this is on the CD in the directory containing all the other AWT programming material.

Rewrite the above program so that it is an application not an applet. Create a Frame, add all the components to it, and then "show()" the Frame. (Easy)

Note that there is a significant GUI difference between applications and applets. Applets display their components as soon as they are added to the panel, but in an Application you must call "show()" to display the Frame and widgets you created. E.g. one way to do it would be:

```
Frame f = new Frame("Even more Fruit");
   ... lots of widget adding ...

f.show()
```

Obtaining Mouse and Keyboard Input

The previous section described how various widgets interact with the user. This section describes how mouse and keyboard events are passed to your program. It is done in a very similar way to what we have already seen for widgets.

Events go to the Component that is the immediate Container of the place where the event happened. The class Component has a method `handleEvent()` with this signature:

```
public boolean handleEvent(Event evt)
```

If you look at handleEvent in file $JAVAHOME/src/java/awt/Component.java, you'll see that it contains a switch statement based on what the event was, and it really factors out all the keyboard and mouse events calling individual methods to handle all the possibilities for those.

A list of some of the specific Event handlers that `handleEvent()` factors out is:

```
public boolean mouseDown(Event evt, int x, int y)
public boolean mouseDrag(Event evt, int x, int y)
public boolean mouseUp(Event evt, int x, int y)
public boolean mouseMove(Event evt, int x, int y)
public boolean mouseEnter(Event evt, int x, int y)
public boolean mouseExit(Event evt, int x, int y)

public boolean keyDown(Event evt, int key)
public boolean keyUp(Event evt, int key)

public boolean action(Event evt, Object what) //when a widget is touched
```

The programmer can override these to provide the callback routines that window systems use for event handling.

To see what's really going on with events, insert this line at the start of your version of handleEvent.

```
System.err.println("Event: " + e.toString() );
```

You'll be amazed at the number of events that are generated by the simplest mouse motions. This method converts each to a string and prints it. 🍃

Use inheritance to create your own version of the Button and Choice classes in an example Applet. Override "action()" within each of these two classes. Now it is much easier to decode which event has come in. If the "myButton.action()" has been invoked, it must have been an instance of myButton that was operated. (Easy). 🍃

Capturing Individual KeyPresses

Write an action() method that will handle all of the widgets in the previous section, and for each print out what the event is. (Medium).

Here is an example of how a game program might capture individual key presses as they are made. Note that only certain events are available from certain widgets. In particular, non-blocking key presses are available in Panels, but not in TextFields. This can be even more annoying than those smirking kids in the Mentos commercials.

```java
import java.awt.*;
import java.applet.*;
public class game  extends Applet {

    public void init() {
        resize(450,200);
    }

    public boolean keyDown(Event evt, int key) {
        System.out.println("Got: " + (char)key );
        return true;
    }

}
```

What could be simpler?

Handling the Quit Event

You will usually want to put the three or four lines of code that deal with a window being quit or destroyed (when the user has finished with it—this is usually a standard choice on the frame menu bar). The code looks like:

```java
public boolean handleEvent(Event e) {
    if (e.id == Event.WINDOW_DESTROY) {
        System.exit(0);
    }
    return false;
}
```

You don't have to exit the program. That would be appropriate when the user quits from the top-level window. For a lower-level window, the right thing to do may be to hide the window, and release the resource for garbage collection by removing any pointers to it.

All the Event handling methods have a boolean return type. This is used to answer the question "Did this method fully handle the event?" If it did, return true. If it did not, (Whoa! Trick answer coming!) return the result of calling the superclass's event handler to propagate the event up the containment hierarchy. To understand why, let's look at a partial solution to the previous Programming Challenge.

```
import java.awt.*;
import java.applet.Applet;

public class mb extends Applet {
    myButton mb;

    public void init() {
        add(new myButton("press me") );
    }
}

class myButton extends Button {

    public myButton(String s) {
        super(s);
    }

    public boolean action(Event e, Object arg) {
        System.out.println("myButton pressed!");
        return true;
    }
}
```

Here we see a very common form of inheritance: subclassing an AWT widget to provide some slight refinement of behavior. Normally, our "action()" method is a common method that might handle a dozen kinds of event. In this case, when the button is pressed, control is transferred to the myButton.action() method and no decoding of "what Event was this?" is needed. We know it must have been a myButton that was pressed. 🦋

Now, we may have created several levels of subclass of Button, myOtherButton extends... extends myButton extends Button. Each adds some slight twist, and each has its own overriding action() routine. Our intent will be to first try handling the special button event in the lowest subclass. If that doesn't want it, then we almost certainly want to pass the event up the inheritance hierarchy. (If that isn't what we want then why did we bother creating the inheritance hierarchy?) However, what will actually happen is that the runtime system will propagate the unconsumed event up the containment hierarchy.

For Advanced Students Only

The fact that you return "true" from the Event handler leads the normal programmer to assume that one should return "false" if more processing is required by the containing class.

Bzzzt! The idiom is that you "return super.handleEvent(e)" to pass the event up the inheritance chain if your method doesn't consume the event.

This is because there are two possible chains to follow to look for the event handler:

1. Up the chain of containers: (Event is in a Panel which is in a Frame which is in a Window...)

2. Up the chain of subclasses: (Event is from myOtherButton which is a subclass of myButton, which is...)

What you usually want to happen is for the runtime to try both hierarchies. The runtime system should make the event go up the chain of superclasses for a given widget, and then go to the enclosing container, exhaust all its superclasses, and so on.

This will occur if your Event handler, instead of returning false, does:

```
return super.handleEvent(e);
```

None of this is necessary if you do not have a chain of subclassed widgets. On the other hand, it doesn't hurt to write the statement this way regardless. If you don't have a big inheritance hierarchy myButton.action() will call Button.action() which simply returns false anyway.

Layout in a Container

You may be wondering how the Applet knows where to put the individual elements that have been added to it. The answer is Layouts. Layout Managers are classes that specify how components should be placed in a Container. You choose a layout manager for a Container with a call like this:

```
setLayout( new FlowLayout() );
```

Flow Layout

Figure 10-22 is an Applet full of buttons laid out with FlowLayout (the default for all Panels).

Figure 10-22:   In this applet, buttons are laid out left to right and centered

A flow layout means that Components are added left to right keeping them centered in the Container, and starting a new line whenever necessary. When you resize the applet components might move to a new line. There are possible "left" and "right" arguments to the constructor to make the components be left or right justified instead of centered, as shown here:

```
setLayout (new FlowLayout (FlowLayout.RIGHT));
```

Most of the layouts allow you to specify the gap in pixels between adjacent components, by specifing the values to the constructor. One FlowLayout constructor looks like this:

```
public FlowLayout(int align, int hgap, int vgap);
```

Grid Layout

Figure 10-23 is the same applet with a one-line change to give it a grid layout.

Figure 10-23: A grid layout puts things in equal sized boxes starting from top, left

In the constructor you specify the number of rows and columns, like this:

```
setLayout( new GridLayout(2,3) );
```

That creates a two-row grid, with three boxes in each row. Grid layouts are simple and somewhat rigid. One thing that always surprises and annoys programmers is the way the widgets change in size to match the grid size. To avoid this, add a button to a panel, and add the panel to the container with the grid layout.

BorderLayout

The third popular type of layout is BorderLayout. As the name suggests you can put four components around the four edges of the Frame, with a fifth component taking any remaining space in the middle. The default layout for a Frame or Window is BorderLayout. You can set it in another kind of Container with a line like:

```
setLayout( new BorderLayout() );
```

Then you add up to five widgets, specifying whether they go at the North (top), East (right) and so on. Actually, for consistency, you can specify this for the other layout managers, too. The same applet with a one-line change to use BorderLayout looks like that shown in Figure 10-24.

Figure 10-24: Grid set-up using BorderLayout

Here is the code used to generate the three preceding examples.

```java
// <applet code=lay.class     height=100 width=200>  </applet>

import java.awt.*;
import java.applet.*;

public class lay  extends Applet {
    public void init(){
    Button b1     = new Button("fold");
    Button b2     = new Button("spindle");
    Button b3     = new Button("pound");
    Button b4     = new Button("twist");
    Button b5     = new Button("mutilate");

    // setLayout( new FlowLayout() );
    // setLayout( new GridLayout(2, 5) );
    setLayout( new BorderLayout() );

    add("North",b1);
    add("South",b2);
    add("East",b3);
    add("West",b4);
    add("Center",b5);
    show();

    }

}
```

Two important points to watch with BorderLayout: First, you have to set BorderLayout before adding components otherwise you mysteriously see nothing (however, this isn't true for the other two layout managers). Second, letter case is significant when setting the position (you can't use "north" instead of "North").

CardLayout

A fourth kind of Layout Manager is CardLayout, named with a deck of playing cards in mind. You can only see one card at a time, but you can shuffle through the deck and pull another card to the top to display at any time. You use this when you have several alternative screens to present in succession. Perhaps a button on each screen leads you to the next. Each "card" in the CardLayout will typically be a Panel with its own layout manager, as shown in Figure 10-25.

Figure 10-25: A screen shot using CardLayout

The code to generate this card layout is:

```
// <applet code=card2.class    height=200 width=200>  </applet>

import java.awt.*;
import java.applet.*;

public class card2  extends Applet {
    Button b1      = new Button("next");
    Panel p = new Panel();
    CardLayout c = new CardLayout();

    public void init(){
       p.resize(100,100);
       p.setLayout( c );

       myCanvas mc1 = new myCanvas( Color.green );
       myCanvas mc2 = new myCanvas( Color.red );
       myCanvas mc3 = new myCanvas( Color.blue );

       add(b1);
       add(p);
       p.add("starter", mc1);
       p.add("middle", mc2);
       p.add("finish",  mc3);
    }

    public boolean handleEvent(Event e) {
        if (e.target instanceof Button){
                c.next(p);
                System.out.println("button press");
                return true;
        }
    return false;
    }

}


class myCanvas extends Canvas {
  // this simply sets up a colored canvas, so you
  // can see when a new one is brought to the front.
    public myCanvas(Color c) {
       setBackground(c);
       resize(75,150);
    }

}
```

The card layout code above creates three canvases of different colors and adds them to a panel P using a card layout. We've used canvases in the example so that the container that had the card layout (here a Panel) was a different type to the individual cards (here, canvases) to minimize confusion.

The example code also creates a button. When the button is pressed, the next card is brought to the front, and you will see the color change as a different canvas comes up to the front. Unlike the other layout managers, you need to keep a reference to this one. That is, you cannot write:

```
setLayout( new CardLayout() );
```

you must write

```
CardLayout c = new CardLayout();
something.setLayout( c );
```

This is because you need to reference the first(), last(), next(), and previous() or show() methods of the card layout manager to flip through the cards. You also need to pass the container that is card-laid-out as an argument. Here are two examples:

```
c.next( p );
```

or

```
c.show(p, "middle");
```

The second example will bring up the card with the name "middle."

GridBagLayout

The final kind of Layout Manager is GridBagLayout, which is a variation of GridLayout. It doesn't force you to fit components one per grid position, but allows you to let a component take up the space of several adjacent grid positions. It uses a series of constraints and weights to work out what goes where.

Frankly, GridBagLayout is excessively complicated, and I'm not recommending it to anyone. Its value lies in demonstrating that ordinary programmers can write new implementations of the public interface LayoutManager. GridBagLayout was written by a public-spirited programmer outside Sun and donated out of a desire to advance the Java effort. If you really want to spend time on GridBagLayout there is a tutorial about it online at:

```
http://java.sun.com/doc/tutorial.html
```

The hope is that much of this will go away and programmers will expect to use a GUIbuilder for exotic layouts. In the meantime, nest components on panels and then layout the panels using the first four layout managers.

Layouts are funky. You probably won't find any one layout that does exactly what you want. The solution is to divide your Panels and Frames into sub-panels, and use a different layout manager (as appropriate) for each panel. Then display the different panels together in a single frame. ✌

Even More About Components

At this point we have seen all the building blocks that make up a GUI and how they fit together and operate. It's time to wrap up with some final remarks on Components and highlight some useful methods. Component is the very general class that means "any widget." It's actually an abstract class, that gets more specific within each widget (as you'd expect).

Cursors

One piece of functionality that is expected to move into Component is the ability to set the cursor type. In JDK 1.0, the cursor could be set only for a Frame, but all containers should be able to say what their cursor is. There are 13 different kinds of cursor icon, including the default (usually an arrow), 8 different directions for resizing, a crosshair, text, hand, wait and move cursor icons. Some of these cursors are shown in Figure 10-26.

Arrow	Busy	Resize	SizeEast	Text	CrossHair
⬉	⧗	✛	↔	I	+

Figure 10-26:   Just some of the many cursor icons

Cursors have the look of the native platform, and the examples here are from Microsoft Windows. You set the cursor on a Frame with:

```
Frame f2 = new Frame("My Frame");
f2.setCursor(Frame.CROSSHAIR_CURSOR);
```

This will continue to be supported for backward compatability.

Useful Methods of Component

There is a long list of useful methods in Component, many of which occur in pairs. The ones explained here are the most popular ones. Remember, almost every GUI element is a Component, so these methods can be invoked pretty universally.

`public synchronized void enable()` Allow this component to interact with the user.

`public synchronized void disable()` Prevent this component from interacting with the user.

`public synchronized void hide()` Makes the component invisible.

`public synchronized void show()` Makes the component visible.

`public void validate()` Lays out the component and all its subcomponents. This will usually be done after changing its size.

`public void invalidate()` Marks the component as invalid (i.e.: it requires attention from its layout manager to regain its proper appearance on the screen.

`public synchronized void setBackground(Color c)` Gives the component the specified background color. If you make the background and foreground colors too similar, you won't see anything!

`public synchronized void setForeground(Color c)` Gives the component the specified forground color. Anything drawn on the component (lines, shapes, text etc, will have this color).

`public void resize(int width, int height)` Changes the component to have the specified size.

`public void move(int x, int y)` Moves the component to the specified coordinates. You normally let the layout manager do all this work.

`public void reshape (int x, int y, int width, int height)` This is the combination of a move and a resize together.

`public void addNotify()` You'll never call this, unless you're creating your own peer objects in the native window system. It's another really badly named method. It creates the peer object for this component.

`public Container getParent()` Returns the object that contains this component. There are also methods called getParent in the classes MenuComponent, File (gets the directory the File is in), and ThreadGroup. They do the same thing, so they have the same name.

`public Toolkit getToolkit()` Returns the "toolkit" of this component. The toolkit has some useful methods of its own: you can get information about the fonts and screen resolution, you can call getDefaultToolkit which in turn lets you get an Image (examples coming up later).

`public synchronized void setFont(Font f)` Lets you set the font (typeface) which will be used when you drawStrings on this component. Font information is in the next chapter.

There is an example on the CD in file ch10/q.java of using Component.move().

We have already seen how the add(something) method is used to add a component to a container. There is a corresponding remove(something) method that takes it away.

Currently, Java doesn't have a way to layout overlapping unrelated windows so that the one you want is on top. One (platform dependent) trick that programmers sometimes use to get this effect is to remove() the components, then add them again. If you try a couple of alternatives, you can usually find the right order to do the add()s leaving your desired window on top. ❦

Printing the Screen

From the start, programmers have asked for a way to print the screen. JDK 1.1 introduced the facility. Since the underlying support for printing is so different on each platform (there's no POSIX PrintScreen() function!) this is something that will have to be implemented in native code. Since the support will be a standard part of the run time library, that won't affect applet portablity.

The exact way in which a print job is started hasn't been announced yet, but it looks like a natural function to put into the window toolkit (mentioned above). The most obvious approach is to have it bring up the system specific dialog for choosing the right printer and spawning the job.

Programmers have also frequently requested a way to save screen images. By printing to a file, rather than a printer, this can easily be done. There's also a slightly more complicated way to do it by grabbing the pixels. This will be explained in Chapter 11.

Some Light Relief

The Domestic Obfuscated Java Code Non-Competition

Readers of my book "Expert C Programming" will be aware of the International Obfuscated C Code Competition (IOCCC). It's an annual contest run over Usenet since 1984 to find the most horrible and unreadable C programs of the year. Not horrible in the sense of badly written, but the much subtler concept of horrible to figure out what they do and how they work.

The IOCCC accepts entries in the winter, they are judged over spring, and the winners are announced at the summer Usenix conference. It is a great honor to be one of the dozen or so category winners at the IOCCC, as many very good programmers turn their talents to the dark side of the force for this event. If you know C pretty well you might be interested in figuring out what this IOCCC past winner does:

```
main(){printf(&unix["\021%six\012\0"],(unix)["have"]+"fun"-0x60);}
```

Hint: it doesn't print "have fun."

Here, in the spirit of the IOCCC are two Java programs that I wrote for April Fool's Day. You should be pretty good at reading Java code at this point so I won't spoil your fun. This program is on the CD in directory justjava/ch10/h.java. It looks like one big comment, so it should compile without problems. When you run it, it greets you! But how?

```
/*    Just Java
      Peter van der Linden
      April 1, 1996.

\u0050\u0076\u0064\u004c\u0020\u0031\u0020\u0041\u0070\u0072\u0039\u0036
 \u002a\u002f\u0020\u0063\u006c\u0061\u0073\u0073\u0020\u0068\u0020\u007b
  \u0020\u0020\u0070\u0075\u0062\u006c\u0069\u0063\u0020\u0020\u0020\u0020
   \u0073\u0074\u0061\u0074\u0069\u0063\u0020\u0020\u0076\u006f\u0069\u0064
    \u006d\u0061\u0069\u006e\u0028\u0020\u0053\u0074\u0072\u0069\u006e\u0067
     \u005b\u005d\u0061\u0029\u0020\u007b\u0053\u0079\u0073\u0074\u0065\u006d
      \u002e\u006f\u0075\u0074\u002e\u0070\u0072\u0069\u006e\u0074\u006c\u006e
       \u0028\u0022\u0048\u0069\u0021\u0022\u0029\u003b\u007d\u007d\u002f\u002a

*/
```

The second program is my attempt to greatly improve program portability. This one source file can be compiled by an ANSI C compiler, and executed. The same code can also be compiled by a Java compiler, and executed. True source portability! Every program should do as well. This program is on the CD in directory justjava/ch10/b.java .

```
/*  Peter van der Linden,    "Just Java"
    April 1, 1996
    Real portability: this is both a Java program and a C program.

    Compile and run this Java program with:  javac b.java    java b
    Compile and run this C program with:     cc   b.c        a.out
    \u002a\u002f\u002f*/

#define String char*
#define t struct
#include <stdio.h>
t{t{int(*print)(const char*,...);}out;}System={{printf}};/*\u002a\u002f

public class b {
                              public static void
/* The main routine                            */    main (
/* The number of arguments \u002a\u002f\u002f*/          int    argc,
/* The array of argument strings         */          String argv[] )
                     {
                              System.out.print("Hi!\n");
                     }

/*\u002a\u002f}/**/
```

How does this bi-lingual program work?

Please don't suggest an International Obfuscated Java Code Competition! It works for C because there are so many opportunities to abuse the preprocessor, the expression semantics, the library calls, and so on. Java doesn't offer half so many opportunities to unscrew the unscrutable, so let's keep things that way, OK?

CHAPTER 11

- Color and Fonts

- Drawing Lines and Shapes

- Drawing Images

- Advanced Image Processing

- Audio

Graphics
Programming

"A disciple of the temple once asked a Zen master "What is Risk?" The master patiently explained, "It is that which has caused men to venture everything in its pursuit. It is associated with intense speed, and it is prominent in the overlapping flow of events. It embraces the simplest and most consistent of designs in life."

"I see," said the disciple, "so that is peril, hazard, chance, or risk." "Risk?" said the master, "I thought you said RISC."

-Anonymous

This chapter covers the more advanced features of window programming, namely those associated with graphics rather than window widgets. In this chapter we will cover color, fonts, and how to draw shapes on a Canvas or Panel. We will then look at Images and some Image Processing. We'll finish up with an explanation and some sample programs showing Java's support for audio output. Table 11-1 lists the methods that cause the screen to be displayed.

Table 11-1:   Common Graphic methods

Method	Description
void repaint()	You or the window system may call this to request that the window be refreshed. Typically, you would call it if you have changed the appearance of something, and you want to see it on the screen. It calls update()
void update(Graphics g)	This is a step in repainting the window. It defaults to clearing the area then painting it, but you can conceivably override it to do something additional. However, most of your programs will not override this, and will not call this.
void paint(Graphics g)	Will be called by the window system when the component needs to be redisplayed. You will not call this. You will override this if you dynamically change the appearance of the screen, and want to see it appear.

Colors

Naturally, Java allows you to put colors on the screen and there is a class called Color in the java.awt package. The basic color model used by Java is a common one in the computer industry. Colors are made up of a red, a green, and a blue component, each of which is described by a byte value saying how vivid that color is, ranging from 0 (darkest shade) to 255 (lightest shade). This is known as the RGB model. The actual color used in rendering will be the best match in the color space available for a given output device. Images (like JPEG files) also have an "alpha" component that describes how transparent a pixel[1] is.

Again this is stored in a byte, so it takes 32 bits just to store a single pixel on the screen. This is why some graphics programs can swamp your system. For large images, megabytes of data need to be moved around. The "alpha" comes in later with images, it isn't part of the Color class.

You need to experiment with this a little to get a feel for it. Figure 11-1 shows an applet that allows you to set the R, G, and B values and see the resulting color mix.

---

1.   A Pixel is a "Picture Element." It is a dot on a computer screen. When people say screens are 1024 by 786 (or whatever) they are referring to the number of pixels it can display. A pixel is like a grain of sand. By itself it is almowt unnoticeable, nothing happens until you have thousands of them.

Figure 11-1: The RGB can be set like this

To get these results, type in the following 30-line program (or copy it off the CD in file ch10/col.java):

```
// <applet code=col.class    height=100 width=300>   </applet>
import java.awt.*;
import java.applet.*;
public class col extends Applet {

    Scrollbar s1 = new Scrollbar(Scrollbar.VERTICAL,0,400,0,255);
    Scrollbar s2 = new Scrollbar(Scrollbar.VERTICAL,0,400,0,255);
    Scrollbar s3 = new Scrollbar(Scrollbar.VERTICAL,0,400,0,255);
    Canvas c = new Canvas();

    int r=0,g=0,b=0;
    public void init () {
        add(s1); add(s2); add(s3); add(c);
        c.resize(75,75);
    }

    public void paint(Graphics gr) {
        c.setBackground(new Color(r,g,b) );
        gr.drawString("r="+r+ ",g="+g+ ",b="+b, 20,100);
    }

    public boolean handleEvent(Event e) {
        if (e.target instanceof Scrollbar) {
            r=s1.getValue();
            g=s2.getValue();
            b=s3.getValue();
            repaint();
            return true;
        }
        return false;
    }
}
```

We've already seen how you can use a Color object to set the color of a component. Here's an example of how that might be done in practice.

```java
Frame f = new Frame("my frame");
f.setForeground( Color.white );

f.setBackground( new Color(255,175,175) ); //pink
```

The class Color has the following methods and constants, among others:

```java
public final class Color {

    public final static Color white = new Color(255, 255, 255);
    public final static Color gray = new Color(128, 128, 128);
    public final static Color black = new Color(0, 0, 0);
    public final static Color red = new Color(255, 0, 0);
    public final static Color pink = new Color(255, 175, 175);
    public final static Color orange = new Color(255, 200, 0);
    public final static Color yellow = new Color(255, 255, 0);
    public final static Color green = new Color(0, 255, 0);
    public final static Color magenta= new Color(255, 0, 255);
    public final static Color cyan = new Color(0, 255, 255);
    public final static Color blue = new Color(0, 0, 255);

    public Color(int r, int g, int b);
    public Color(int rgb);
    public Color(float r, float g, float b);

    public int getRed();
    public int getGreen();
    public int getBlue();
    public int getRGB();

    public Color brighter();
    public Color darker();

    public static int HSBtoRGB(float hue, float saturation, float brightness);
    public static float[] RGBtoHSB(int r, int g, int b, float[] hsbvals);
    public static Color getHSBColor(float h, float s, float b);
}
```

There's an alternative color model, known as HSB, meaning *Hue Saturation and Brightness*. Java doesn't use this, but it allows easy translations using the methods just described.

So when will I use the `paint()`, `repaint()`, **or** `update()` **methods?**

If you just use the static display typical of a GUI, you might never need to override any of the three above methods. You can often just hide() and show() Components as needed. Let's explain when you use paint().

Normally the window system keeps track of what you have put on the screen. If you obscure it with other windows and then bring it to the front, the window system is responsible for restoring the state.

If, however, you wish to *change* what you have put on the screen (say you have displayed a GIF that you now want to replace with something else), this would be accomplished by overriding paint(). Code in init() can get something on the screen to begin with. Code in paint() can change the screen and get something different up there. You call repaint() to signal to the window system that it needs to update the screen. The window system will then call your paint() method to put the new image on the screen. It's done this way because paint takes an argument (a Graphics context) that you don't normally have (or need to have) access to. Repaint() doesn't need any arguments.

Repaint() calls update() which calls clear() and then paint(). You might override update() if you are doing some advanced graphics work, and you know that you only need a small portion of the screen to be changed (e.g. in an animation). Update gives you the opportunity to achieve this, by providing a point where you can insert your own code between repaint() and paint(). In addition,

```
repaint(x,y,w,h);
```

will repaint just the stated size rectangle at the given coordinates. Paint may be called by the runtime independent of update.

Summary: You never call paint() yourself. You may override it, but the understanding is always that it will be called for you at the times the window system thinks it needs to update the screen. If you want to force the window system to think that, then call "repaint()."

Repaint() simply lodges a request to update the screen, and returns immediately. Its effect is asynchronous, and if there are several paint requests outstanding it is possible that only the last `paint()` will be done.

Fonts and Font Metrics

Fonts and information about font size are encapsulated into two classes: Font and FontMetrics. Just as with Colors, whatever font is current will be used in all text drawing operations in the AWT. However, it will not be used in operations like System.out.println. Think about it: Those are Stream operations that merely push data in and out. Only the window system cares about the physical appearance of that data.

Notice in the following example that the "foo" text will appear in the current font.

```
    paint(Graphics g) {
        g.drawString("foo",10,10);
}
```

You're given a default font to start you off, then you can change any of the characteristics, or construct a new font and set it as the font to use.

> Try modifying the "mobile button" program q.java mentioned a couple of sections back, so that the button has a background color of red, a foreground color of white, and is labeled in italic courier size 18 point. The source is on the CD. Setting colors on buttons is buggy in JDK 1.0.2.

You can construct a new font with:

```
    Font loud = new Font  ("TimesRoman", Font.BOLD, 18);
```

You can make that the current font for any Component (any Button, Label, MenuItem, Canvas) or Graphics object, with:

```
        this.setFont(loud);
```

The constructor for a Font is simply:

```
        public Font( String name, int style, int size);
```

You can set the font (`courier`, **helvetica**, etc.), the style (PLAIN, **BOLD**, *ITALIC*, or combinations of the three), and the size (8 point, 10 point, 12 point etc.) any way you like.

Different computer systems will have different fonts installed on them. For example, the closest thing available to the Windows WingDings font on Unix is called Zapf Dingbats (really). It's a screwy font, so everyone gives it a screwy name. Java copes with this by mapping your font request to the closest font, size and style that is on the underlying system. These five font names can be taken for granted:

- Times Roman

- Courier

- Helvetica

- Symbol

- Dialog

Fonts are very straightforward. The FontMetric class allows you to compute the exact position of Strings, namely how wide and high they are in terms of pixels. This will allow you to lay out strings exactly centered or to mix Strings of different styles and get the spacing right. You might do this if you were writing a word processor in Java, but it's a bit fussy for everyday use.

FontMetrics has these methods, which return values in units of a pixel (a dot on the screen).

```
public abstract class FontMetrics {
    public Font getFont() {

    public int getLeading(); // print term for line spacing
    public int getAscent();
    public int getDescent();
    public int getHeight() // leading + ascent + descent

    public int getMaxAscent() {
    public int getMaxDescent() {

    // For backward compatibility only.
    public int getMaxDescent() // some programmers can't spell...

    public int charWidth(char ch);
    public int stringWidth(String str);
}
```

The font metrics give you the real measurements of the font that is actually in use on your system, not the theoretical measurements of the font you asked for. The two may well be different.

The Graphics Context

A Graphics object is what you ultimately draw lines, shapes and text on. It is also called a "graphics context" in some window systems because it bundles together information about a drawable area, plus font, color, clipping region, and other situational factors. If you look at the code in $JAVAHOME/src/java/awt/Graphics.java, you will see that it is an abstract class:

```
public abstract class Graphics { ...
```

Therefore it cannot be instantiated directly, and you will never see code like:

```
Graphics gr = new Graphics(); // NO!
```

The most common way to obtain a Graphics object is as the argument to a paint() routine in a Canvas or Panel. (You'll actually get some concrete subclass of graphics, the details of which you never need worry about). Less commonly, you can explicitly ask for the Graphics object belonging to any Component or any Image with the call:

```
myComponent mc ...

Graphics mg = mc.getGraphics();
```

When you call getGraphics() it is usually for an Image, Panel or Canvas. It's unlikely you'll get the Graphics object for anything else, such as a button. There is too much peer behavior associated with it for you to be able to add to it sensibly. If you do explicitly call:

```
Graphics g = myPanel.getGraphics();
```

make sure you also call this when you are done with it:

```
g.dispose();
```

Graphics objects take up operating system resources (more than just memory), and a window system may have a limited number of them. When you clean them up explicitly without waiting for garbage collection to kick in, your system will usually tick along more smoothly.

Drawing Text, Lines, and Shapes

These are the methods of Graphics that draw text, lines, and shapes. Most of these come in two varieties: a drawXXX and a fillXXX. The first puts an empty outline on the screen, the second puts the outline and fills the interior with a solid color. In both cases the foreground color is used. A graphics object has the method set-Color(Color c) to change the foreground color, but it doesn't have any direct way to change the background color. The underlying panel (or whatever) must do that, as shown in the following cases.

```
public void drawString(String str, int x, int y);
```

Here, the string is placed at location x,y on this component. For example:

```
    public void paint(Graphics g) {
        g.drawString("The Princess whined incessently", 10, 15);
    }
```

A common pitfall with this method and the next two is drawing with y coordinate zero. That makes the characters disappear as they will be almost completely off the top of the canvas.

```
public void drawChars(char data[], int offset, int length, int x, int y)
public void drawBytes(byte data[], int offset, int length, int x, int y)
```

These two methods place characters or bytes from the array data[offset] to data[offset+length-1] on the component starting at location (x,y).

```
public void drawLine(int x1, int y1, int x2, int y2);
```

A line one pixel wide is drawn from (x1,y1) to (x2,y2). There is no support for drawing lines thicker than one pixel. The workaround is to use the fillPolygon described later. Like all of these methods, the rendering is done in whatever you have set the color to. The default foreground color is black.

```
public void drawRect(int x, int y, int width, int height);
public void fillRect(int x, int y, int width, int height);
```

A rectangle of the stated width and height is drawn with its top left corner at (x,y). There is also a void clearRect(x,y,w,h) that gets rid of a rectangle.

```
public void draw3DRect(int x, int y, int width, int height, boolean raised);
public void fill3DRect(int x, int y, int width, int height, boolean raised);
```

A rectangle of the stated width and height is drawn with its top left corner at (x,y). The rectangle is artfully shaded on two sides to make it appear to be standing out (raised=true) or to be impressed (raised=false). A raised rectangle is shaded with brighter color, and a non-raised one with a darker color. Figure 11-2 shows some 3D rectangles.

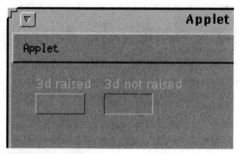

Figure 11-2: 3D raised and unraised

Here is the code that generated the screen shot:

```
// <applet  code=graf.class  height=300 width=500> </applet>
 import java.awt.*;
 import java.applet.*;
 public class graf  extends Applet {

     public void paint(Graphics g) {
         g.setColor(Color.cyan);
         g.drawString("3d raised", 25,25);
         g.draw3DRect(25,30,50,20,true);
         g.drawString("3d not raised", 95,25);
         g.draw3DRect(95,30,50,20,false);
     }
 }
```

Here are two more ways to draw a rectangle

```
public void drawRoundRect(int x, int y, int width, int height, int
    arcWidth, int arcHeight);
public void fillRoundRect(int x, int y, int width, int height, int
    arcWidth, int arcHeight);
```

There are Like drawRect and fillRect, only these rectangles have rounded corners.

You control the diameter of the rounded corners by setting the width and height of the curved portion in pixels. If you use values that are comparable to the width and height of the rectangle, you end up with an oval not a rectangle, as shown in Figure 11-3. Rule of thumb: use arc width and height that are 15-25% of the rectangle width and height

Figure 11-3: A rounded rectangle

Here is the code that generated the diagram:

```
// <applet   code=graf.class   height=300 width=500> </applet>
import java.awt.*;
import java.applet.*;
public class graf  extends Applet {

    public void paint(Graphics g) {
        g.setColor(Color.cyan);
        g.drawString("round", 25,25);
        g.fillRoundRect(25,30, 50,100,15,25);
    }
}
```

```
public void drawOval(int x, int y, int width, int height);
public void fillOval(int x, int y, int width, int height);
```

These two methods draw ovals. The arguments are easy to understand if you compare the methods to drawRect(). The oval that is drawn is one that fits exactly in the rectangle of that width and height. The imaginary rectangle's top left corner is at the (x,y) location.

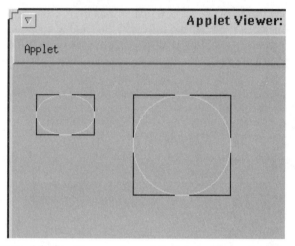

Figure 11-4: Two ovals, and their bounding rectangles

Here is the code that generated the diagram:

```
// <applet   code=graf.class   height=300 width=500> </applet>
 import java.awt.*;
 import java.applet.*;
 public class graf  extends Applet {

     public void paint(Graphics g) {
         g.drawRect(25,30, 60,40);
         g.drawRect(125,30, 100,100);

         g.setColor(Color.cyan);
         g.drawOval(25,30, 60,40);
         g.drawOval(125,30, 100,100);
     }
 }
```

As can be seen, an oval with the width=height is a circle.

```
public void drawArc(int x, int y, int width, int height,
            int startAngle, int arcAngle);
public void fillArc(int x, int y, int width, int height,
            int startAngle, int arcAngle);
```

Again, the starting point for understanding these two methods is the rectangle located at (x,y). Then imagine dividing the rectangle into four quadrants. This x axis from the origin of the quadrants represents 0 degrees. The starting point for the arc is the offset from this line: 90 is straight up (along the y axis), 270 is straight down.

Finally, the arcAngle is how many degrees to sweep from that starting point. See Figure 11-5. Note that it is *not* the end angle as many people assume. A negative arcAngle sweeps clockwise, and a positive one counter clockwise. You never need use a negative angle because an arc sweeping 40 degrees forward from 90 degrees is the same as an arc sweeping 40 degrees back from 50 degrees.

Figure 11-5:   An arc has the same concept of bounding box as an oval

Here is the code that generated the diagram:

```
import java.awt.*;
import java.applet.*;
public class graf  extends Applet {

    public void paint(Graphics g) {
        g.drawRect(25,30, 60,40);
        g.drawRect(125,30, 80,100);

        g.setColor(Color.cyan);
        g.fillArc(25,30, 60,40, 135,45);
        g.fillArc(125,30, 80,100, 135,45);
    }
}
```

```
public void drawPolygon(int xPoints[], int yPoints[], int nPoints);
public void fillPolygon(int xPoints[], int yPoints[], int nPoints);
```

Polygons are shapes with an arbitrary number of straight sides. To draw or fill one using these methods, you provide an array of x coordinates, and an array of corresponding y coordinates, along with the total number of points.

If you want the polygon to be drawn closed you have to duplicate the starting point at the end of the arrays. Figure 11-6 is an example of polygons:

Figure 11-6:   A filled polygon connects arrays automatically as it fills

Here is the code that generated the diagram:

```
// <applet   code=graf.class    height=300 width=500> </applet>
import java.awt.*;
import java.applet.*;
public class graf  extends Applet {

    public void paint(Graphics g) {
        g.setColor(Color.cyan);
        int x_vals[] = {75,45,15,45,45 };
        int y_vals[] = {40,70,40,10,40 };

        g.drawPolygon(x_vals, y_vals, x_vals.length);

        for (int i=0;i<5;i++) x_vals[i]+=80;
        g.fillPolygon(x_vals, y_vals, x_vals.length);
    }
}
```

```
public void drawPolygon(Polygon p);
public void fillPolygon(Polygon p);
```

These two overloaded methods draw or fill a Polygon object. A Polygon object is constructed from the same arrays of (x,y) pairs as used previously:

```
Polygon(int xPoints[], int yPoints[], int nPoints);
```

However, you can also add new points to a polygon, simply by calling this method with an (x,y) pair:

```
pol.addPoint(10,20);
```

A Polygon also knows what its bounding box is.

That concludes most of the important routines for drawing text, lines and shapes. The next section covers the topic of loading images into memory and rendering (drawing) them onto a graphics context.

Loading and Drawing Images

An Image, as the name suggests holds a picture in memory. Originally, a picture will have been scanned in and stored in a file in GIF, JPEG, raster, postscript or other format. Java can currently only process the GIF and JPEG format.

A GIF is a file format for storing pictures. GIF stands for Graphic Interchange Format, and it was originally developed by CompuServe to be a system-independent way to store images. GIFs only store 8 bits of color information per pixel. Just adequate for run-of-the-mill PCs that only allow 256 different colors on screen at once, it is rapidly heading for technical obsolescence. Only use GIFs for cartoons and line drawings. GIF includes compression based on the Lempel-Ziv-Welch (LZW) algorithm, so the files are smaller than they would otherwise be. LZW compression is protected by a software patent filed by Unisys a few years ago. A copy of the public record for this patent is on the CD in just-java/ch1. If you've never seen a software patent before, take a look at this example.

A JPEG is a newer and superior file format for compressing images. It's an acronym for Joint Photographic Experts Group (the committee that wrote the standard). An image in JPEG format can take much less storage space than the same picture in GIF format. However, the JPEG format also allows you to tradeoff image quality against storage needs—more requires more. When you save an image in JPEG format, you can specify a percentage for the image quality. JPEG stores full color information: 24 bits per pixel.

Before you can draw an Image onto a Graphics object, you must have an Image to draw. The most common way of getting one is to load it from a file. Another way of getting an Image is to call createImage() for a particular Component. We'll start by dealing with an image in GIF or JPEG format in a file. An image can be displayed in either an applet or an application. The two alternatives vary slightly.

Loading an Image File in an Application

Here is some code to display a file in an application. We create a Frame, read in the image file from our URL, instantiate a canvas, and off we go.

The only novelty about this is the way we get the image. We have to use something called the "default toolkit" which is available in the AWT. It provides a getImage() method for applications. Note that you can get an Image from a URL (i.e. anywhere on the Internet) as well as from a file pathname.

```java
import java.awt.*;
import java.net.*;
public class display {

    static public void main(String a[]) {
        Image i = Toolkit.getDefaultToolkit().getImage("dickens.jpg");
        Frame f = new Frame("my frame");

        myCanvas mc = new myCanvas(i);
        f.resize(350,200);
        f.add(mc);
        f.show();
    }
}

class myCanvas extends Canvas {
    Image saved_i;
    public myCanvas(Image i) {
        this.resize(300,200);
        saved_i = i;
    }

    public void paint(Graphics g){
        g.drawImage(saved_i, 10, 10, this);
    }
}
```

There are plenty of pitfalls to avoid when you type in this code. If you get one of these wrong, your image will not appear and you will not get any kind of helpful error message either. Here are some potential problems:

*   You must resize the frame in order to see it!

*   If you provide a file name which doesn't exist or can't be accessed, it will fail silently. The same if you use the URL alternative for getImage.

*   If you don't resize the canvas, it won't show up.

If you get all this correct, Figure 11-7 will appear.

Figure 11-7:   See Dickens lay down

Loading an Image File in an Applet

To load an image file in an Applet, we simply reference its URL. File access is usually restructured in an Applet, so there is no getImage that takes a pathname as an argument. However, Recall that a URL can point to a resource anywhere on the Internet, so if the file is local to your system it can find it (if your security manager allows your applet to read local files). The Applet method is:

```
public Image getImage(URL url);
```

It allows you to specify a complete absolute URL to the image file. Some examples would be:

```
URL u1 = new URL("http://sparcs/images/ball.jpg");    //remote
URL u2 = new URL("file:///home/linden/puppy.jpg");    // local
```

The other alternative lets you specify a URL and an image filename that is relative to where the URL points.

```
public Image getImage(URL url, String name);
```

This is more common in an applet because the images files are usually stored in the same directory as the HTML document or the class files. For these cases you can use

```
getDocumentBase() // the URL of the document containing the applet
getCodeBase() // the URL of the applet class file
```

So an example would be:

```
Image i;
    . . .
i=getImage( getDocumentBase(), "puppy.jpg");
```

Note there is a pitfall here! A very common mistake is to try to call getImage() to initialize the image as you declare it, like this:

```
Image i1 = getImage(getDocumentBase(), "spot.jpg");
```

That compiles without a problem, but (if the Image is declared outside any method, as normal) it fails at runtime like this:

```
java.lang.NullPointerException
    at java.applet.Applet.getDocumentBase(Applet.java:59)
    at jpg.<init>(jpg.java:7)
    at sun.applet.AppletPanel.runLoader(AppletPanel.java:386)
```

The reason is that before the init() method of an Applet is called there isn't enough structure in place for calls to other methods of Applet to succeed. You can't do much with an Applet until its init() method has been called, which is the right place to put this getImage() call.

If you can't remember which methods belong to Applet, just use the following rule of thumb: In an applet don't call any methods to initialize data fields in their declaration. Instead declare them, then initialize them separately in the init() method.

A related pitfall concerns the createImage() method. Many people want to create an Image in the constructor of, for example, a Canvas.

```
public class MyCanvas extends Canvas{
    Image myImage;
    Graphics myGraphics;

    public MyCanvas(){
        myImage=this.createImage(100,50); //  this returns Null.
        myGraphics=myImage.getGraphics(); // so this throws NullPtrExcptn.
    }
```

The createImage() method does not work until *after* the Canvas has been added to a Container. So in general you can't create the Image in the constructor. One workaround is to also add the Canvas to its Container in the constructor. This is because a peer for the Canvas component must have been created before we can get its image. But we are still in the class constructor, so unless we force peer creation by doing an add(), createImage here will always fail and return a null pointer.

That brings the image into memory, and holds it in the Image object. The next step is to render it on the screen.

How do you get a Java applet to load an HTML page into the browser?

The method `this.getAppletContext().showDocument(URL)` will make the browser load the page from the specified URL. There is also a version that takes a String argument:

```
public abstract void showDocument(URL url, String target)
```

The string says where to show it:

- "_self" (bring the URL up in the current frame)

- "_parent" (bring it up in the parent frame)

- "_top" (show it in the top-most frame)

- "_blank" (show it in a new unnamed frame)

Similarly, this.getAppletContext().showStatus("Get out in the fresh air more."); will put the message on the browser status line. 🍀

Drawing an Image Onto a Graphics Object

The Graphics object has four variations of the drawImage() method:

- ```
  public boolean drawImage(Image img, int x, int y,
      ImageObserver observer);
  ```

  This draws the specified image at the specified coordinates (x, y). The image is cut off as necessary if it is larger than the area it is being drawn onto.

- ```
  public boolean drawImage(Image img, int x, int y,
      int width, int height,
      ImageObserver observer);
  ```

  This scales the image as needed to fit within the width and height specified as it draws it. Depending on the values you supply, that might change the proportions of the picture stretching or shrinking it in one direction.

- ```
  public boolean drawImage(Image img, int x, int y,
      Color bgcolor,
      ImageObserver observer);
  ```
  ```

- ```
  public boolean drawImage(Image img, int x, int y,
          int width, int height,
      Color bgcolor,
      ImageObserver observer);.
  ```

These last two methods are just variations on the first, with the addition of providing a solid background color behind the image being drawn.

At this point, you are probably asking yourself what is that final parameter called "ImageObserver." If you have a good memory, you might recall that we described it in Chapter 6. We will review it again shortly, but for now let's note that an Applet is an example of an ImageObserver, so wherever one is required, we can just provide the "this" of an Applet. The entire code to load and display a file in an Applet is thus just this:

```
// <applet code=jpg.class height=250  width=300> </applet>
import java.awt.*;
import java.applet.*;

public class jpg extends Applet {

    Image i;

    public void init() {
        i=getImage( getDocumentBase(), "puppy.jpg");
    }

    public void paint(Graphics g) {
        boolean b = g.drawImage(i,25,25, this);
    }
}
```

Running this code results in Figure 11-8 appearing on the screen.
```

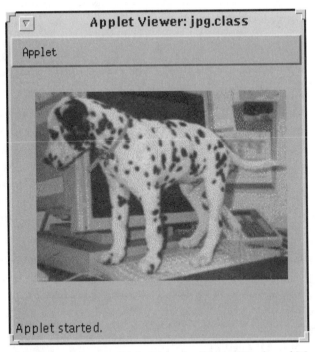

Figure 11-8: See Young Dickens do the "Type-5 Keyboard Macarena"

The ImageObserver Argument

Let's get back to the ImageObserver argument used in drawImage. When you call getImage() to bring an image file into memory, the method returns at once, and in the background at some point a separate thread starts reading the file off disk somewhere on the Internet. That incoming image data is said to be an observable event. And you can specify who or what is going to observe it.

As a matter of fact, Component implements the ImageObserver interface. Every button, frame, canvas, panel, label etc is an ImageObserver and able to register its interest in observing incoming images. An applet being a subclass of Panel is also therefore an ImageObserver. We normally just put "this" down as the argument and the right thing happens by default. As the image comes in gradually, more and more of it is painted onto the screen.

The reason it's done this way, instead of the obvious implementation of making getImage() stall until the bytes are loaded, is twofold:

1. The human factors of waiting for an image file to load are truly horrible. In other words, few things make users angrier than being forced to sit idle while some hideous GIF loads scanline by scanline, so

2. Everyone would end up writing every getImage() as a separate thread. This way, your applet is decoupled from the slow net for free.

Better yet, as pieces of the image are gradually loaded into memory, there will be a number of times when there is enough information to call ImageObserver.imageupdate(). It may be called when the image file header has been read, when we have decoded enough to know the height of the image, when we know the width, and when the entire transfer has been completed.

The Component class contains an imageUpdate() method. When it is called, it schedules a repaint, allowing a little more of the image to be drawn without interfering at all with your thread of control. There are a couple of properties in Table 11-2 that affect this.

Table 11-2: System Properties

Property	Effect
"awt.image.incrementaldraw"	True: (default) draw parts of an image as it arrives. False: don't draw until all the image is loaded.
"awt.image.redrawrate"	The default value is 100. It is the minimum period in milliseconds between calls to repaint for images. This property only applies if the first one is true.

JDK1.0 doesn't support setting an individual property. You change a property by instantiating a new property table based on the system one, then appending your modifications.

The code below updates the entire system properties table. If you just want to add one or two properties, you can't do it directly, but you can do it indirectly as shown in Chapter 6. You create a new properties table, supplying the system properties table to the constructor. You add properties one by one to your new table. When you search, if a property isn't found in your new table, the program will proceed to look in the system properties table. Clumsy but it works.

```java
import java.io.*;
import java.util.*;

public class y {

  public static void main(String args[]) {
    try {
      //String p = System.getProperty("os.version"); // get one property
      //System.out.println("ver="+p);

      ByteArrayOutputStream bos = new ByteArrayOutputStream();
      Properties P = new Properties(System.getProperties());
      System.getProperties().save(bos,"basic props");
      DataOutputStream ds = new DataOutputStream(bos);
      ds.writeBytes("awt.image.incrementaldraw=true\n");
      ds.writeBytes("awt.image.redrawrate=50\n");
      ds.close();

      byte[] tmp = bos.toByteArray();
      ByteArrayInputStream bis = new ByteArrayInputStream(tmp);
      P.load(bis);
      System.setProperties(P);
      System.getProperties().list(System.out); // list all properties

      } catch (Exception e) {e.printStackTrace();}

    }
}
```

Here we use a ByteArrayOutputStream to buffer the properties read in. When you change a property, the change only lasts for as long as your program runs. If you want to permanently change a property you need to write the property file out to disk (with your change) and read it back in at the start of each program.

Image Update

If you want to retain really tight control over an incoming image you can overload imageUpdate() in your applet that will override the regular version in the Component parent class. Whenever there is more information available, your imageUpdate() will be called repeatedly until you return a value of false to indicate that you've got enough information. The following code example will clarify how this works:

```
import java.applet.*;
import java.awt.*;

public class iu extends Applet {
    Image    i;
       int times=0, flags=0,x=0,y=0,w=0,h=0;

    public void init() {
       i = getImage(getDocumentBase(), "spots.jpeg" );
       w = i.getWidth(this);   System.err.println("INIT:w="+w);
       h = i.getHeight(this);   System.err.println("INIT:h="+h);
    }

    public boolean imageUpdate(Image i, int flags,
                            int x, int y, int w, int h) {
                if (times++<5)
                    System.err.println("my IMAGEUPDATE: flags="
                                    +flags+ " w="+w+ " h="+h);
                return true;
    }

    public void paint (Graphics g) {
       g.drawImage(i,50,50, this);

    }

}
```

This clearly shows how imageUpdate is a callback routine. Experiment with this example (invoke with the usual html file), including removing the limitation of 5 prints in the middle of imageUpdate (done so that the information doesn't scroll off the screen the first time you try it).

The Media Tracker

The ImageObserver interface is good for really low-level control of loading media files. But for some purposes it's a bit too low-level. If you just want to wait till a file is loaded completely, and you don't care to hear about the 57 intermediate stages of loading it, then the MediaTracker class is for you.

MediaTracker is actually built using ImageObserver, and it allows you to track the status of a number of media objects. Media objects could include audio clips, though currently only images are supported.

To use MediaTracker, simply create an instance and then call addImage() for each image to be tracked. Each image can be assigned a unique ID for indentification purposes. The IDs control the priority order in which the images are fetched as well as identifying unique subsets of the images that can be waited on independently. You then waitForID(n), which will suspend the thread until the image is completely loaded. The methods isErrorAny() and isErrorID(i) let you know if everything went OK for all the images or for a particular ID group.

Here is an example of the MediaTracker in use:

```
public void init() {
    MediaTracker t = new MediaTracker (this);
    Image i = getImage (getDocumentBase "spots.gif");
    t.addImage (i,1);
    try    {t.waitForID(1);}
    catch  (InterruptedException ie) {return;}
    //Image is now in memory, ready to draw
}
```

Image Processing

By putting together the basic classes that have already been described, and sprinkling a couple of new ones in, some pretty sophisticated image processing can be achieved. This section will describe the standard techniques for getting smoother animation by overriding update and double buffering. Start with this brief applet. The code and JPEG image files are on the CD in directory justjava/ch11.

```
//<applet  code=pin.class   width=600 height=350>   </applet>
import java.awt.*;
import java.awt.image.*;

public class pin extends java.applet.Applet {
    Image spirit, rolls;
    int new_x=550;
    int new_y=100;

    public void init () {
        spirit = getImage(getDocumentBase(), "spirit.jpg");
        rolls = getImage(getDocumentBase(), "rolls.jpg");
    }

    public void paint (Graphics g) {
        g.setColor(Color.gray);
        g.fillRect(0,0,size().width, size().height );
        g.drawImage (rolls,5, 5, this);
        g.drawImage (spirit, new_x-25, new_y-25, this);
    }

    public boolean mouseDrag(Event e, int x, int y) {
        new_x=x;
        new_y=y;
        repaint();
        return true;
    }

}
```

The code implements a simple "Pin the tail on the donkey" game. In other words, you can use the mouse to drag the image of the Spirit of Ecstasy over to its place on the Rolls Royce radiator. Incidentally, the Spirit of Ecstasy was modeled on a real person: Eleanor Thornton. She was the paramour of early motoring pioneer, the second Lord Montagu. He artfully suggested to his pals on the Rolls-Royce board in 1911 that their cars would be enhanced by a graceful radiator mascot, and he "just happened to know a good one." Sadly, Eleanor Thornton perished in a tragic torpedo mishap in 1915, (Lord Montagu on the same boat was wearing an inflatable cork waistcoat and he made it back to England in time to read his obituary in *The Times*). Thornton's spirit lives on, immortalized on the bonnet of every Rolls-Royce motor car for the last 85 years. But I digress. The applet screen looks like that in Figure 11-9.

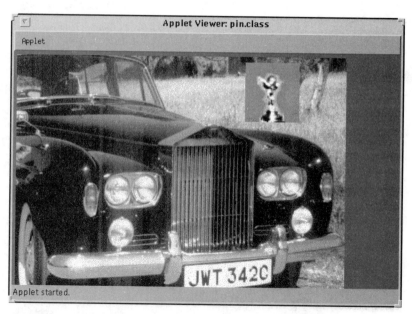

Figure 11-9: A moment of silence for Eleanor Thornton

When you run the code you will notice that the applet flickers annoyingly as you drag the mouse. The flickering problem is a well known artifact of imaging programs in all languages. To fix this, there are some Java-specific things to try and some algorithmic things to try. The first and easiest improvement is to look at the default implementation of one of the utility routines, update().

As we drag the mouse, each event causes the new_x and new_y coordinates to be noted, then a request to repaint() is made. Repaint will call Component.update, which looks like this:

```
public void update(Graphics g) {
    g.setColor(getBackground());
    g.fillRect(0, 0, width, height);
    g.setColor(getForeground());
    paint(g);
}
```

It sets the color to the background color, then fills the whole Graphics context with it (in other words erases whatever image is currently there). It then sets the foreground color, and calls paint.

However, we are already painting the whole background in our paint routine. So, repaint calls update which paints the whole panel, then calls paint, which again paints the whole panel. Voila: a flicker or flash is seen as an unnecessary paint is done. We could remove the fillRect() in paint, for it was put there precisely to demonstrate this flicker as a teaching example (and it represents some more general background painting that you may do). A better solution is to override update(), and provide your own version that doesn't clear the applet panel.

```
public void update(Graphics g) {
    paint(g);
}
```

You can (and should) do this whenever your paint routine updates the entire component. If your paint didn't update the entire component, then you couldn't override update in this manner. You'd get pieces of the old image left in place as you dragged it to a new location. Overriding update with a more sensible version reduces flashing considerably, but doesn't eliminate it. For that we'll use a technique called double buffering or offscreen imaging (they mean the same thing).

Double Buffering

Double buffering, or *offscreen imaging* (a more accurate description), is the process of doing all your (slow) drawing to a graphics area in memory. When the entire image is complete, it zaps it up onto the screen in one (fast) operation. The overall time is slightly longer because of the overhead, but the overall effect is stunning because the new graphics context appears instantly.

Here is the code to make the image rendering be double buffered.

```
//<applet   code=pin2.class    width=600 height=350>  </applet>
// double buffered
// PvdL Sept 1996.
import java.awt.*;
import java.awt.image.*;

public class pin2 extends java.applet.Applet {
    Image spirit, rolls;
    Image myOffScreenImage;
    Graphics myOffScreenGraphics;
    int new_x=400;
    int new_y=100;

    public void init () {
        spirit = getImage(getDocumentBase(), "spirit.jpg");
        rolls = getImage(getDocumentBase(), "rolls.jpg");
        myOffScreenImage= createImage(size().width, size().height );
        myOffScreenGraphics = myOffScreenImage.getGraphics();
    }

    public void paint (Graphics g) {
        g.setColor(Color.gray);
        g.fillRect(0,0,size().width, size().height );
        g.drawImage (rolls,5, 5, this);
        g.drawImage (spirit, new_x-25, new_y-25, this);
    }

    public boolean mouseDrag(Event e, int x, int y) {
        new_x=x;
        new_y=y;
        repaint();
        return true;
    }

    public void update(Graphics g) {
        paint(myOffScreenGraphics);      // draws on the db
        g.drawImage(myOffScreenImage,0,0, this); // draws the db onto applet
    }

}
```

We don't change paint() at all. Paint will still do its rendering thing onto whatever Graphics context you give it. Here's where the magic comes in. We have added two off-screen objects:

```
Image myOffScreenImage;
Graphics myOffScreenGraphics;
```

In init() these two are initialized. We create an Image the same size of the applet. Then we get a graphics context for it. Now the clever part. We modify update so *first* it paints the offscreen image myOffScreenGraphics. It simply uses the regular call to paint, with myOffScreenGraphics as the argument. That painting won't appear on the screen, as it would if the AWT had called paint with the Graphics object for the applet. Instead it goes to myOffScreenGraphics object. (Sorry to belabor the point, but it is important to understand this thoroughly).

Finally, instead of update() calling paint() as it did in the previous version, we now do a very quick g.drawImage() to get the just-painted myOffScreenImage onto the Applet's graphics context! Drawing a single pre-constructed image onto the screen is a lot faster than building up a screenful of images one at a time. And that is double buffering.

Clipping Rectangles

The final possible optimization is to use a clipping rectangle to only draw where the image has changed. Clipping is a standard graphics technique to optimize the amount of (slow) drawing that takes place. When you clip, you are telling the paint routine "I know that the only changes in this image are inside this rectangle, so you only need paint inside the rectangle. Everything else remains unchanged."

The clipRect method of Graphics, namely

```
public void clipRect(int x, int y, int width, int height);
```

cuts down the size of the area that is painted to just the _intersection_ of what it was, and the new rectangle specified by the arguments. This is an optimization used in animations and other graphics programming to speed up output and make it smoother. Many people have complained about the way the clipping rectangle can only be reduced in size. It is expected that some more methods or different semantics will be added to allow it to grow as well as shrink.

When the clipping region only shrinks, it presents a problem when you want to clip several areas on the same graphics context. The workaround shown here is to make a copy of the Graphics context, but that is a little self-defeating, as the purpose of clipping is to speed things up by reducing overhead.

```
public void paint (Graphics g) {
    Graphics gCopyClip = g.create();
    gCopyClip.clipRect(clipX, clipY, clipWidth, clipHeight);
      . . .
}
```

Then, you draw with gCopyClip instead of g.

Depending on how much can be clipped and how long it takes to calculate the overall image, clipping can save a lot of time and effort. Clipping works best on big images where only a little changes at a time. It's tailor-made for animations.

Taking Images Apart: java.awt.image

Java features some pretty substantial support for pulling Images apart to get at individual pixels. It also has a class that takes bytes from memory and assembles them into an Image. One problem with mastering this area of Java is that there is a lot of classes, generality, and infrastructure. As with the stream I/O classes, the profusion of abstractions creates a learning barrier for programmers.

We'll look at two concrete classes in java.awt.image that allow you to have absolute control over your screen images, namely:

- PixelGrabber (implements the abstract class ImageConsumer)

- MemoryImageSource (implements the abstract class ImageProducer).

As the names suggest, ImageConsumer takes an Image away from you (giving you something else you'd rather have, like an array of pixels), while ImageProducer takes something and gives you back the Image that it created from it.

Here's how PixelGrabber works:

1. You construct a new instance of the class supplying the image (or ImageProducer) and lots of sizes and an int array as arguments:

    ```
    PixelGrabber pg = new PixelGrabber ( .... );
    ```

2. You call grabPixels(), which fills the int array with the pixels from the image:

    ```
    pg.grabPixels();
    ```

3. You check the status to see if all bits were grabbed without problems:

    ```
    if (pg.status() & ImageObserver.ALLBITS) != 0)
            // we grabbed all the bits OK
    ```

The two constructors of PixelGrabber are:

```
public PixelGrabber(Image img, int x, int y, int w, int h, int[] pix,
int off, int scansize);

public PixelGrabber(ImageProducer ip, int x, int y, int w, int h,
int[] pix, int off, int scansize);
```

As you can see, the second constructor has an ImageProducer as its first parameter, but the other arguments (defined here) are the same.

- img   is the image to retrieve pixels from

- x   is the x coordinate of the upper left corner of the rectangle of pixels to retrieve from the image, relative to the default (unscaled) size of the image

- y   is the y coordinate of the upper left corner of the rectangle of pixels to retrieve from the image

- w   is the width of the rectangle of pixels to retrieve

- h   is the height of the rectangle of pixels to retrieve

- pix   is the array of integers which are to be used to hold the RGB pixels retrieved from the image

- off   is the offset into the array of where to store the first pixel

- scansize   is the distance from one row of pixels to the next in the array

Here's how MemoryImageSource works. It is essentially the complement of Pixel-Grabber. It reads an int array of pixels and gives you back the corresponding image. First, you construct a new instance of the class MemoryImageSource supplying arguments of the int array, and lots of sizes (height, width, scanline size, etc). That will get you a MemoryImageSource object, which implements ImageProducer, and hence can be fed into the Component.createImage() method to obtain a real renderable Image.

There are six constructors for MemoryImageSource. The simplest one is:

```
public MemoryImageSource(int w, int h, int pix[], int off, int scan)
```

This instantiates a w-by-h MemoryImageSource starting from the pix[off] element in the array of pixels, and with scan pixels in each line. The other five constructors allow various combinations of with and without HashTables and ColorModels.

Transparent Backgrounds

We are going to use these two classes on our image of the Spirit of Ecstasy. We are going to grab the pixels, and turn all the pink ones transparent, by setting the alpha byte to zero. If the alpha value of a pixel is 0 it is totally invisible. If the alpha value is 255 it is totally solid color. Values in between allow for varying degrees of translucence or opacity. Since the background is mostly pink, this will turn it transparent, and allow Eleanor Thornton to be seamlessly reunited with her pedestal.

FAQ

How do I turn the background of my image transparent?

In general, there is no way to say "filter this image, and give it a transparent background." You need a way to identify what is a background pixel and what is a foreground pixel. Here we are using color to identify the background. If the foreground is a regular shape you could use (x,y) position. For more on this, read on. 🍂

I touched up these images in Adobe Photoshop beforehand to give them a uniform background and sharper edges. If your company won't spring for Adobe Photoshop so you can play around with stuff like this, use the public domain "xv" software that can do many of the same things.

To minimize the learning curve here, let's highlight the new code by making this class extend the class pin2 above. (Isn't Object-Oriented Programming wonderful?)

```
//<applet  code=transp.class   width=600 height=350>  </applet>
// double buffered
// transparent image
// Peter van der Linden, Sept 1996, Silicon Valley, Calif.
import java.awt.*;
import java.awt.image.*;

public class transp extends pin2 {

  public void init () {
   spirit = getImage(getDocumentBase(), "spirit.jpg");
   rolls = getImage(getDocumentBase(), "rolls.jpg");
   myOffScreenImage= createImage(size().width, size().height );
   myOffScreenGraphics = myOffScreenImage.getGraphics();

   spirit = getRidOfPink(spirit);    // filter the image

  }


  int  width=475, height=265;
  public Image getRidOfPink(Image im) {
   try {
// grab the pixels from the image
   int[] pgPixels = new int [width*height];
   PixelGrabber pg = new PixelGrabber (im, 0, 0,
     width, height, pgPixels, 0, width);

  if (pg.grabPixels() && ((pg.status() & ImageObserver.ALLBITS) != 0)) {
   // Now change some of the bits
    for (int y=0;y<height;y++) {
     for (int x=0;x<width;x++) {
      int i = y*width+x;
      int a = (pgPixels[i] & 0xff000000)>>24;
      int r = (pgPixels[i] & 0x00ff0000)>>16;
      int g = (pgPixels[i] & 0x0000ff00)>>8;
      int b = pgPixels[i] & 0x000000ff;
      // turn the pink-ish pixels transparent.
      if (r>200 && g>100&&g<200&&b>100&&b<200) {
       a=0;
       pgPixels[i] =  a  | (r<<16) | (g<<8) | b;
      }
    }
   }
   im = createImage (new MemoryImageSource (width, height, pgPixels, 0, width));
   }
   } catch (InterruptedException e) { e.printStackTrace (); }
       return im;
  }

}
```

We have overriden init() to add the filtering statement:

```
spirit = getRidOfPink(spirit);    // filter the image
```

And we have added the routine getRidOfPink(). That routine looks fearsome at first, but it quickly breaks down into four simple stages:

1. Grab the pixels

2. Look at each individual pixel. You may be wondering why the pixel array isn't two dimensional, just as an image is. The reason is to keep it closer to the model the hardware uses. Frame buffer and CPU memory is one dimensional.

3. If the RGB values are within the range of "generally pink" then make the pixel transparent by setting its alpha value to 0.

4. Reassemble the pixel array into an image with MemoryImageSource.

It's as simple as that. When you run this, you'll see a picture like that in Figure 11-10.

Figure 11-10:   Eleanor transparently on her pedestal

Comparing this image with Figure 11-9, you'll see that the ugly pink background has disappeared.

There's a couple more points to note before we move onto our next image processing topic of animation. First, note that it is a very expensive operation to grab pixels and look at them. To help your program performance you should do this as sparingly as possible, and look at as few pixels as you can. Don't grab pixels from the whole image if you don't need to. On a SPARCStation 5 desktop computer, this applet took about five seconds to intialize. On an Intel Pentium 66Mhz system, it took about twice as long.

How do I save to a file an Image I have created on the screen?

FAQ

The beauty of pixel grabbing is that it turns a picture into an array of ints. You can do anything you like with that array of ints including process it, send it down a socket, or write it out to a file. If you write it out to a file, you have saved your image to disk. It will not be in a recognized standard format like GIF or JPEG, and you will not get the benefit of compression. But it does let you save an image to a file.

The final point is that the java.awt.image package has a couple of other specialized classes for filtering RGB values and for chaining ImageProducers together so you can do multiple filtering.

> **Exercise:** Try filtering an image by adapting the code above. Turn the black Rolls-Royce into a pink one.

Animation

Animation is the last major Image Processing topic we are going to cover, and it is thankfully simple. In fact if you already know how to get an image on the screen, you already know how to animate. Just as in cartoon movies, Java animation consists of showing several images (known as "frames") in quick succession. The human eye has a quality called *persistence* that means a series of successive slightly different frames fools us into thinking we see movement. When we change the entire image it is called "frame animation." When we just change a small area of the image, that area is called a "sprite" and we do "sprite animation."

So all we do for animation is bring all our frames in memory and display them one after the other. If we need to we will also use double buffering and clipping to make things appear smoother. There is a cheesy example of Animation that comes with the JDK in directory $JAVAHOME/demo/Animator. If you go to that directory, you can run the following to see some jumping beans.

```
appletviewer  example4.html
```

You can also review the Animator.java source code. As an example here, let's make Dickens the Dalmatian wag his tail in Figure 11-11.

Figure 11-11: See Dickens wag his tail

Before we show the code, let's look at the Java idiom for starting a thread in an Applet. You don't need a user thread in an applet if all you do is respond to GUI events. You *do* need one if you are animating, though.

A regular applet has the framework shown in Figure 11-12

```
public class foo extends java.applet.Applet {

    public void init() { ... }

    public void start() { ... }

    public void stop() { ... }

    public void paint (Graphics g) { ... }

}
```

Figure 11-12:   Framework of a normal applet

To give yourself a thread, the idiom is that you do these five things:

- Make your applet class implement runnable.
- Add the run() method of the thread. Inside here will be the statements to do all the work that your thread must do.
- Declare a Thread object: Thread t;
- Inside start(), instantiate the thread with the Applet:

      t = new Thread(this);

  the thread running:

      t.start();

- Inside stop(), stop the thread running by

      t.stop();
      t=null; // so it can be garbage collected.

So the applet framework with a thread looks like Figure 11-13.

```
public class foo extends java.applet.Applet
implements runnable{

    Thread t;

    public void run()  { ...}

    public void init() { ... }

    public void start() {
        t = new Thread(this);
        t.start();    }

    public void stop() {
        t.stop();
        t=null;        }

    public void paint (Graphics g) { ... }

}
```

Figure 11-13: Threaded applet

Here is the code to animate the tail. It closely follows the preceeding framework. Again, by making this extend the "transp" class of the previous example, we can present the minimum new code. It's not too surprising that we can use the framework of the "pin the silver lady on the Rolls" code as the basis of the "animate the dog's tail" program. They both involve putting images on the screen and moving them about. All animation programs will have the same general form.

```
//<applet  code=wag.class    width=280 height=200>   </applet>
// double buffered
// transparent image
// animated tail
// Peter van der Linden,   Sept 10 1996.

import java.awt.*;
import java.awt.image.*;

public class wag extends transp implements Runnable {
    Image dal, appendage, tail1, tail2;
    Font f;

    public void init () {
        tail1 = getImage(getDocumentBase(), "tail.jpg");
        tail2 = getImage(getDocumentBase(), "tail2.jpg");
        dal = getImage(getDocumentBase(), "dickens.jpg");
        dal = getRidOfPink(dal);
        tail1 = getRidOfPink(tail1);
        tail2 = getRidOfPink(tail2);
        appendage=tail2;

        f = new Font("Helvetica", Font.BOLD, 18);

        myOffScreenImage = createImage(size().width, size().height );
        myOffScreenGraphics = myOffScreenImage.getGraphics();
    }
    public void paint (Graphics g) {
        g.setColor(Color.lightGray);
        g.fillRect(0,0,size().width, size().height );
        g.setColor(Color.yellow);
        g.setFont(f);
        g.drawString("Dickens is a happy dog",10,20);
        g.drawImage (appendage, 10, 50, this);
        appendage= (appendage==tail2?tail1:tail2); // swap frames
        g.drawImage (dal, 35, 65, this);
    }
        public void run() {
        while (true) {
            try{Thread.sleep( 100 ); }
            catch(InterruptedException ie){}
            repaint();
            }
        }

        Thread t;

        public void start() {
            t = new Thread(this);
            t.start();
        }

        public void stop() {
            t.stop();
            t = null;
        }
}
```

The init() method brings in an extra image, tail2.jpg, which looks similar to tail, but is slightly displaced. All the images are filtered to give them a transparent background.

The two tails look like those shown in Figures 11-14 and 11-15.

Figure 11-14: Dickens tail can look like this . . .

Figure 11-15: . . . or this

I created Figure 11-15 from Figure 11-14 by rotating it 10 degrees in Adobe Photoshop (image rotation is one of the features that xv doesn't offer). If you don't have Photoshop, it doesn't matter—you now know enough Java to whip up a special purpose program to do any image processing you want!

In the paint method, I added some text at the top just for fun. The only other change is we now draw an "appendage" instead of a tail. The appendage just holds a reference to either tail1 or tail2. Immediately after we have drawn the appendage, this line:

```
appendage= (appendage==tail2?tail1:tail2); // swap frames
```

swaps it over to point to the other one. In this way, when paint is called, it alternates between Figure 11-14 and Figure 11-15. Another way to accomplish this is to change what appendage refers to in the run() routine. It doesn't have to alternate between two images; you may have dozens in your animation.

The run routine just spins in an infinite loop, sleeping for a tenth of a second, then issuing a repaint request. About 24 frames per second is all you need to fool the eye into seeing continuous motion. Here we're running at 10 frames per second.

The start() instantiates and kicks the thread off. The stop() is equally important. It's very poor programming to leave a thread running after the user leaves a page, so you kill the thread in the stop routine. And that is image animation. Finally, putting the whole thing together, so you can see all the code in one place, here is the program written without inheritance:

```
//<applet  code=fullwag.class    width=280 height=200>  </applet>
// double buffered
// transparent image
// animated tail
// Peter van der Linden,   Sept 10 1996.

import java.awt.*;
import java.applet.*;
import java.awt.image.*;
public class fullwag implements Runnable {
   Image da1, appendage, tail1, tail2;
   Image myOffScreenImage;
   Font f;
   Graphics myOffScreenGraphics;

   public void update(Graphics g) {
      paint(myOffScreenGraphics);      // draws on the db
      g.drawImage(myOffScreenImage,0,0, this); // draws the db onto applet
   }

   int  width=475, height=265;

   public Image getRidOfPink(Image im) {
      try {
// grab the pixels from the image
         int[] pgPixels = new int [width*height];
         PixelGrabber pg = new PixelGrabber (im, 0, 0,
            width, height, pgPixels, 0, width);

   if (pg.grabPixels() && ((pg.status() & ImageObserver.ALLBITS) != 0)) {
// Now change some of the bits
      for (int y=0;y<height;y++) {
        for (int x=0;x<width;x++) {
           int i = y*width+x;
           int a = (pgPixels[i] & 0xff000000)>>24;
           int r = (pgPixels[i] & 0x00ff0000)>>16;
           int g = (pgPixels[i] & 0x0000ff00)>>8;
           int b = pgPixels[i] & 0x000000ff;
           // turn the pink-ish pixels transparent.
           if (r>200 && g>100&&g<200&&b>100&&b<200) {
             a=0;
             pgPixels[i] =  a  | (r<<16) | (g<<8) | b;
           }
        }
      }
    }
    im = createImage (new MemoryImageSource (width, height, pgPixels, 0, width));
    }
   } catch (InterruptedException e) { e.printStackTrace (); }
   return im;
   }
```

```
public void init () {
   tail1 = getImage(getDocumentBase(), "tail.jpg");
 · tail2 = getImage(getDocumentBase(), "tail2.jpg");
   dal = getImage(getDocumentBase(), "dickens.jpg");
   dal = getRidOfPink(dal);
   tail1 = getRidOfPink(tail1);
   tail2 = getRidOfPink(tail2);
   appendage=tail2;

   f = new Font("Helvetica", Font.BOLD, 18);

   myOffScreenImage = createImage(size().width, size().height );
   myOffScreenGraphics = myOffScreenImage.getGraphics();

}

public void paint (Graphics g) {
   g.setColor(Color.lightGray);
   g.fillRect(0,0,size().width, size().height );
   g.setColor(Color.yellow);
   g.setFont(f);
   g.drawString("Dickens is a happy dog",10,20);
   g.drawImage (appendage, 10, 50, this);
   appendage= (appendage==tail2?tail1:tail2); // swap frames
   g.drawImage (dal, 35, 65, this);
}

   public void run() {
   while (true) {
      try{Thread.sleep( 100 ); }
      catch(InterruptedException ie){}
      repaint();
      }
   }

   Thread t;

   public void start() {
      t = new Thread(this);
      t.start();
   }

   public void stop() {
      t.stop();
      t = null;
   }
}
```

Table 11-3: Image Utilities

Here are some Image Processing utilities:	
Windows	The windows equiv to xv is Lview pro, downloadable from http://world.std.com/~mmedia/lviewp.html
	Other people like Paint Shop Pro from Jasc, downloadable from http://www.zdnet.com
Solaris	xv is an interactive image manipulation program for X windows (i.e. Unix). It understands all popular formats and can be downloaded for free from ftp.cis.upenn.edu in directory pub/xv.
Mac	Mac image processing software can be downloaded from: ftp://rever.nmsu.edu/pub/macfaq/JPEGView.* ftp://rever.nmsu.edu/pub/macfaq/GIF_Converter.sit.bin

Now try these exercises:

1. Add to the filtering, to turn Dickens into a black lab, by turning all his white fur black.

2. Change the animation so the "tail wags the dog."

Sounds

Applets have some simple methods to play sound files. The 1.0 release can deal with sounds in the .au format, but support for more formats is surely on the way. There are a number of sound files on the CD that comes with this book, in the top level "noises" directory. You can use these as datafiles to experiment with. You can search at http://www.yahoo.com on ".au" to find dozens and dozens more sites and soundfiles.

You can also browse the site http://cuiwww.unige.ch/OSG/AudioFormats

which describes the implementation of all the popular sound file formats including:

.WAV   **Windows**

.au   **Sun and NeXT.**

.AIF   **Mac and SGI**

There are 4 kinds of information making up a Digital Audio stream. The man page explains that digital audio data represents a quantized approximation of an analog audio signal waveform. In the simplest case, these quantized numbers represent the amplitude of the input waveform at particular sampling intervals.

Sample Rate

> This says how many times per second we sample (take a reading from) our noise source. Java currently supports only 8000 Hz.

Encoding

> The encoding says how the audio data is represented. Java uses u-law encoding (pronounced mew-law) which is the standard CCITT G.711 for voice data used by telephone companies in the United States, Canada, and Japan.

> There is an alternative A-law encoding (also part of G.711) which is the standard encoding for telephony elsewhere in the world. A-law and u-law audio data are sampled at a rate of 8000 samples per second with 12-bit precision, with the data compressed to 8-bit samples. The resulting audio data quality is equivalent to that of standard analog telephone service, i.e. in technical terms, pretty crappy.

Precision

> Precision indicates the number of bits used to store each audio sample. For instance, u-law and A-law data are stored with 8-bit precision. 16 bit precision is common elsewhere but not used in Java.

Channels

> This basically says whether the audio is stereo or mono. Since it is basically telephone audio, Java is mono (single channel).

For a standard audio CD the audio is sampled at 44.1KHz which means that for every second of music (or silence, or the conductor coughing) the CD has to take 44,100 16bit samples for each of the two stereo channels.

Java sounds are encoded at 8,000 Hz, 8-bit mono, using u-law compression

> mono (1 channel)
> 8 bit (as opposed to 16)
> u-law (not A-law or CD quality)

The whole is stored in .au files (not .wav or .aif).

One minute of monaural audio recorded in u-law format at 8 KHz requires about 0.5 megabytes of storage, while the standard Compact Disc audio format (stereo 16-bit linear PCM data sampled at 44.1 KHz) requires approximately 10 megabytes per minute.

Table 11-4: Sound Utilities

Here are some sound utilities:	
Windows	One sound utility that works is is SOund eXchange or SOX, available at http://www.spies.com/Sox. There are many others that work, and also a few that don't. Q: How do I use it? A: sox file.wav -r 8012 -U -b file.au
Solaris	One Solaris Unix sound utility that works is /usr/demo/SOUND/bin/soundtool. Another is audiotool. All modern desktop SPARCs with the exception of the SS4 come with the audio hardware and software needed to record input from line-in or headphone jack. I recorded my message on the CD in the goodies directory using the little microphone that came with my SS5. It plugs into a port on the back. You can also use audiorecord to record the incoming audio data in any format supported by the audio device. For example, use /bin/audiorecord -p line -c 2 -s 44.1k -e linear -t 15 foo.au to record 15 seconds of cd quality sound to file foo.au. Use /bin/audiorecord -p line -t 15 foo.au to record 15 seconds of 8 Khz ulaw data (default) to file foo.au. You can use audiotool to edit the resulting file if needed.
Mac	One Mac sound utility that works is ConvertMachine at http://www.anutech.com.au/tprogram/SoundMachine_WWW

Here is a minimal applet to play a sound effect:

```
import java.applet.*;
public class noise extends Applet {
    public void init() {
        play( getCodeBase(), "danger.au");
    }
}
```

The file "danger.au" is on the CD. It makes a noise like a drumstick rattling on the side of a tin cup. The program would be invoked from the usual html file:

```
<applet code=noise.class  width = 150 height =100> </applet>
```

The applet directory $JAVAHOME/src/java/applet contains several other useful methods:

```
public AudioClip getAudioClip(URL url)
```

Once you have retrieved an AudioClip from a URL, you can play it once, play it in a loop continuously, or cease playing it with these methods:

```
    play()
    loop()
    stop()
```

If you play it continuously, make sure that you stop playing it in the stop() method, called when the applet's Panel is no longer on the screen. Otherwise the noise will continue longer than you probably want.

Write an applet that plays a sound file, and evaluates it for hidden Satanic messages. There is an easy way to do this and a hard way. The easy way is to play the sound file, and then conclude:

```
    println("That contained 0 Satanic messages \n");
```

The hard way would actually involve some analysis of the sound waveforms, but it would probably produce exactly the same result. ❦

In the first edition of this book I threw down the challenge to readers inviting them to submit code to play a sound file backwards. It would be a non-trivial task to figure out the .au format and do that, but alert programmer Manfred Thole from Germany realized that the task would be considerably simplified by using one of the vendor-specific classes that turns a FileInputStream into an AudioStream. This was a clever piece of programming to get the job done more simply.

```java
import java.io.*;
import sun.audio.*;


/**
 *
 * This application plays audio files backwards!
 * Only applicable for "8-bit u-law 8kHz mono" encoded audio files.
 * Usage: BackwardAudio audio-file-to-play-backwards
 */



public class BackwardAudio {

    static void swap(byte [] b) {
        int l = b.length;
        int i;
        byte tmp;

        for (i = 0; i < l/2; i++) {
            tmp = b[i];
            b[i] = b[l-i-1];
            b[l-i-1] = tmp;
        }
    }
```

```
public static void main(String[] args) {

    AudioPlayer ap = AudioPlayer.player;
    AudioStream as = null;
    byte [] ad = null;

    if ( args.length != 1 ) {
      System.err.println("Usage: BackwardAudio audio-file-to-play-backwards");
      return;
    }
    try {
      as = new AudioStream(new FileInputStream(args[0]));
      // Some files give strange results...
      // Maybe they have an incorrect file header.
      if ( as.getLength() < 1 ) {
        System.err.println("Length: "+as.getLength()+"!");
        return;
      }
      ad = new byte[as.getLength()];
      as.read(ad, 0, as.getLength()-1);
      swap(ad);
      //ap.start(new ByteArrayInputStream(ad));
      ap.start(new AudioDataStream(new AudioData(ad)));
      // We have to wait for the ap daemon thread to play the sound!
      Thread.sleep(as.getLength()/8+100);
    }
    catch (FileNotFoundException fne) {
      System.err.println(fne);

    }
    catch (IOException ioe) {
      System.err.println(ioe);
    }
    catch (InterruptedException ie) {
      System.err.println(ie);
    }
  }
}
```

As well as the java.*.* hierarchy of packages, Java vendors can supply vendor-specific packages under <vendor>.* Sun has a large number of sun.* packages that it does not tell you about explicitly. . . . Good programmers will find them because good programmers tend to investigate on their own.

The classes are in the $JAVAHOME/lib/classes.zip file. Copy this file somewhere safe, and unzip it. By the way, this is the file that the JDK README warns you not to unzip. I think they are trying to use reverse psychology on you.

You'll see all the standard java.*.* classes in there, and several dozen interesting looking Sun ones, too, including these:

```
Extracting: sun/misc/Ref.class
Extracting: sun/misc/MessageUtils.class
Extracting: sun/misc/CEStreamExhausted.class
Extracting: sun/misc/UUEncoder.class
Extracting: sun/misc/CharacterEncoder.class
Extracting: sun/misc/HexDumpEncoder.class
Extracting: sun/misc/UUDecoder.class
Extracting: sun/misc/BASE64Encoder.class
Extracting: sun/misc/UCDecoder.class
Extracting: sun/misc/CacheEnumerator.class
Extracting: sun/misc/Timeable.class
Extracting: sun/misc/TimerThread.class
Extracting: sun/misc/UCEncoder.class
Extracting: sun/misc/CRC16.class
Extracting: sun/misc/ConditionLock.class
Extracting: sun/misc/BASE64Decoder.class
Extracting: sun/misc/CacheEntry.class
Extracting: sun/misc/CEFormatException.class
Extracting: sun/misc/Timer.class
Extracting: sun/misc/TimerTickThread.class
Extracting: sun/misc/Lock.class
Extracting: sun/misc/CharacterDecoder.class
Extracting: sun/misc/Cache.class
  Creating: sun/audio/
Extracting: sun/audio/AudioStream.class
Extracting: sun/audio/InvalidAudioFormatException.class
Extracting: sun/audio/AudioStreamSequence.class
Extracting: sun/audio/ContinuousAudioDataStream.class
Extracting: sun/audio/AudioDevice.class
Extracting: sun/audio/AudioPlayer.class
Extracting: sun/audio/AudioData.class
Extracting: sun/audio/AudioTranslatorStream.class
Extracting: sun/audio/NativeAudioStream.class
Extracting: sun/audio/AudioDataStream.class
```

That gives you the package name. Of course, you remember that you can use javap to look at any of the methods of these!

```
    % javap sun.audio.AudioStream
Compiled from AudioStream.java
public class sun.audio.AudioStream extends java.io.FilterInputStream {
    sun.audio.NativeAudioStream audioIn;
    public sun.audio.AudioStream(java.io.InputStream);
    public int read(byte [],int,int);
    public sun.audio.AudioData getData();
    public int getLength();
}
```

Fuller documentation on these Sun classes has been put together by some Swedish programmers and is available at: http://www.cdt.luth.se/java/doc/sun

Some Light Relief

Satan: oscillate my metallic sonatas

Some people claim that "backwards masking" conceals satanic messages in popular music. They believe that if you play the music backwards (like reading the phrase above backwards) a hidden message will be revealed.

You can easily play a piece of music backwards by recording it onto a cassette tape. Then take the cassette apart by unscrewing the little screws, and swap the reels left to right (don't flip them upside down). You will have to thread the tape a little differently onto one spool.

You've done it correctly if the feed and take-up spools revolve in opposite directions to each other when you hit "play." Rewind once to remove this anomaly, and away you go with your backwards masking. This experiment is so much fun, you should drop whatever you're doing (you're probably reading a book) and go and try this *right now*.

For advanced students: overdub a tape to produce a gimmicked version on which you have added some suitable wording ("Sacrifice homework. Cthulu is our thesis advisor. Wear leather and stay out late on Fridays. Stack dirty dishes in the sink, and cut in line at supermarkets"). Leave the tape out for a suitable colleague to "discover" your backwards masked work.

Finally, I urge you to try running the Backward audio class on the file yenrab.au on the CD: `java  BackwardAudio  yenrab.au`

If that sound file isn't evidence of demonic possession, I don't know what is.

CHAPTER
12

- Getting Internet access
- Downloading software
- Future Java developments
- Further Java resources

Future Developments

> *"Lord Hippo suffered fearful loss.*
> *By putting money on a horse*
> *Which he believed, if it were pressed,*
> *Would run far faster than the rest."*
>
> —*Hilaire Belloc, Selected Cautionary Verses.*

This chapter gives you the information you need to move forward from here. It is in two sections. First, how to get Internet access and updates to the software. Second, what lies ahead in terms of Java products and services.

As everyone knows, the only real way to learn a programming language is to write some programs in it. For that you need the Java system, and a Java-capable Web browser. This book comes with a CD that contains the Java compiler system for Windows NT, Windows 95, Macintosh, and Solaris 2.x. However, you may want to download a Web browser, or later releases of Java. This chapter explains how to get these pieces of software. It assumes elementary familiarity with utilities like anonymous FTP for retrieving files from Internet hosts.[1]

---

1. If you do not have this knowledge, the Krol book referenced at the end of the chapter will provide it.

In theory, you could forego the Web browser and Internet access, and just learn Java application programming on your local system. In practice, however, this would be a mistake. You would be missing a key part—seamless client-server programming on the network—which is responsible for the vast interest in Java.

Getting Internet Access

As a preliminary to obtaining the software, you should get an Internet connection. Many readers of this book will already have Internet access through their employer or educational institution. If neither of these sources is available to you, perhaps your town has a library service that offers an online connection, or perhaps you can sign up for a computer class that comes with a student account at a local college. Or you may just prefer the convenience of Internet access in your own home, just as most people have a phone connection and some people have a cable TV connection. An Internet connection at home is readily obtained in most parts of the developed world with a commercial Internet Service Provider (ISP). You connect to the ISP via a phone call, and the ISP is directly connected to the Internet.

Choosing your ISP

In many cases, you will have a choice of Internet Service Provider (ISP), so these two checklists indicate the ways to evaluate them. The first checklist is mostly about the way you connect to the ISP. The second checklist covers the services the ISP offers.

You will need some kind of personal computer at home: a Macintosh, a "Wintel" (MS Windows/Intel) box, a workstation running Unix or one of its variants like Linux. Your system must support a graphical user interface. A VT100 compatible ASCII terminal is no longer good enough.

ISP connections are invariably provided by dialling in from your home, so a large part of the first check list has to do with the telephone service. You may well find that the other members of your household make you get a second phone line instead of tying up your family's main number.

Checklist—ISP connectivity

[   ] **Local calling area** (not a toll call)

So that you don't bankrupt yourself with long distance phone charges you need an ISP to have a Point of Presence (POP) local to your home. An acceptable alternative is a dial-back system where you call in, and they immediately call you back so that the call is billed to them (their size gives them bulk discount with the Telco). A toll-free call-in number is also acceptable.

[   ] Free communications software

You will likely need some communications software for your system. This software is needed to make the connection and keep it going. The ISP should know what is needed for the different Operating Systems, and supply it without charge.

[   ] 28.8kbps lines (V34) or better

The phone line between your home and the ISP is going to be the slowest link in the system. The ISP needs to use the fastest commercially-available modems. At the time of writing (10:17pm, Saturday December 2 1995) these are 28.8kbps modems. These will adapt to slower speeds automatically, so even if your modem is not rated that high, it can still communicate. You will get frustrated with a slow modem before very long, and when you finally upgrade no change is needed at the ISP end. If you need to buy a modem, don't fall for the false economy of a slow one.

[   ] An adequate modem pool

It's frustrating to get a busy signal when you dial in to your ISP. They need to keep adding modems as their business grows, and preferably have a policy such as "at least one SS20 class machine per 100 users" or "no new clients if the modem pool is maxed out more than 3 hours/day."

[   ] SLIP/PPP

To run a Web browser on the Internet, your computer system will need an IP connection. This can be provided over a phone line by one of two alternatives:

- SLIP   Serial Line Internet Protocol
- PPP   Point-to-Point Protocol

Either is adequate, but PPP provides more features (none of which you will be using if you only ever connect to your ISP from home).

[   ] No or low hourly connect fee

The Internet can be an interesting place, and you might spend more than a few hours there. Ideally, there will not be a "per-hour" connection time fee. Some ISPs offer no fee access outside normal business hours. It's also OK if there is a large monthly allowance of free connect time, with a low hourly charge when that is used up.

[   ] Base monthly charge

You'd like the monthly charge to be as low as possible. Expect to pay about the same as basic cable tv service costs. In my area (Silicon Valley, California) that's about $25–30 per month.

[   ] System support

This is where most ISPs fall down. Support is expensive to provide, but usually generates no revenue. As a result, you may find almost no help is available if you have an unusual connection or set up problem. Ask questions to gauge how much system support is offered. What happens if you delete a file by accident? Will they recover it from backup for you?

Sometimes a lively user community can partly compensate for lack of support, by answering common questions.

[   ] Amount of disk space provided

You are going to be downloading files, and perhaps saving them temporarily in your ISP account. How much disk space is bundled in with your account, and how much do they charge for extra use? Some ISPs will provide bulk storage for short periods of time so that large file transfers will complete, but you must dispose of the file shortly thereafter.

There are certain items that the ISP may boast, which you don't actually care about. These include:

- **56K, T-3, or T-1 service**
  You don't care about the bandwidth of the ISP's pipe to the Internet. As long as it's big enough, that's all that matters.

- **Internic registration**
  Most people don't need their own domain name.

- **Static vs. dynamic IP addressing**
  Either is fine for you.

- **Co-location (where you have your machine at their site)**
  This is really for business and commercial users. For you, half the fun is frobbing the hardware personally.

That covers the connection between your home and the ISP. Now you need to consider the range of Internet services that you will get.

Internet Connectivity

There are different levels of Internet connectivity, each providing different services and applications. Although the terminology is not yet in general use, Internet document RFC1775 describes the hierarchy of services. You can retrieve the description via anonymous FTP from "ftp.internic.net" in file /pub/rfc1775.txt

The levels of service available through most ISPs are:

Client Access

The user runs applications that employ Internet application protocols directly on their own computer platform, but might not be running underlying Internet protocols (TCP/IP), might not have full-time access, such as through dial-up, or might have constrained access, such as through a firewall. When active, Client users might be visible to the general Internet, but such visibility cannot be predicted. "Visibility" means "able to chat on-line."

Mediated Access

The user runs no Internet applications on their own platform. An Internet service provider runs applications that use Internet protocols on the provider's platform, for the user. User has simplified access to the provider, such as dial-up terminal connectivity. For Mediated access, the user is on the Internet, but their computer platform is not. Instead, it is the computer of the mediating service (provider) which is on the Internet.

Messaging Access

The user has no Internet access, except through electronic mail and through netnews, such as Usenet or a bulletin board service. Since messaging services can be used as a high-latency (i.e., slow) transport service, the use of this level of access for mail-enabled services can be quite powerful, though not interactive.

Your ISP needs to offer "client access" in the above sense. Mediated access or messaging access are not good enough for the WWW.

Checklist—ISP Services

[   ] **Web access and a Java-capable Web browser**

You absolutely need access to the World Wide Web, through a browser with a graphical user interface (not text-only). This is why you need a computer system at home, rather than just an ASCII terminal. The browser must be Java capable.

You will want to put up a Web home page announcing your existence to Cybernauts. The ISP should provide you the disk space and connectivity to create your own home page.

[   ] FTP access

The File Transfer Protocol allows you to retrieve files from remotes sites. Eventually this will all be done with WWW access, but until the entire world has converted, you still need the lower-level functionality that FTP provides.

[   ] WAIS, gopher, and archie

These are all ways to search the Internet, to locate sites and files of interest. The ISP must provide easy access to these utility programs.

[   ] No censorship

Some ISP's (notably AOL) impose censorship on their customers. This behavior is often a misguided response to pressure from political or watchdog groups flexing their muscle. Censorship occasionally makes ISP's look ridiculous, as in 1993 when Prodigy was using an automated screening program. One contributor to a musical discussion had a posting returned on the grounds that he was using language "inappropriate to the Prodigy service." He was discussing Bach's B Minor Mass—the movement titled "Cum Sancto Spiritu." America Online committed the same faux pas in November 1995, when they declared the word "breast" taboo—thereby making it impossible for breast cancer patients to contact one another for information and support. The major use of the keyword was allowing these patients to find each other. Check the censorship policies of your ISP, and give your business to companies that provide unrestricted access.

[   ] Usenet news and other services

If the ISP provides Web access (which is essential), they are almost certain to provide Usenet news access, telnet, and e-mail services too. These are not essential, but they are very nice to have and there is no reason to exclude them. Usenet news should include the alt or alternative newsgroups, not just the mainstream collection. Check whether these services are bundled in with your Internet access.

It is no exaggeration to say that Java is being ported to more platforms, with more urgency than any other piece of software in the history of the computer industry. People want this software and they want it now.

The market share among high-volume desktop platforms looks roughly like this:

IBM PC and PC compatibles	90%
Macintosh	9%
Unix (all versions)	1%

ISDN: Integrated Services Digital Network

For now, the most common dial-up connection is via a modem. Even the fastest modems are several orders of magnitude slower than dedicated network connections. People use modems because there has been nothing better.

The better alternative will not be long in coming. In fact it has been waiting in the wings for at least a decade. ISDN or "Integrated Services Digital Network" is a digital service (in contrast to the existing analog phone wiring) providing an effective 128Kbit/sec channel across a phone line. Compare that to the best modems that are only one quarter the rate. Faster throughput speeds can be achieved by installing higher rated lines with multiple ISDN channels. The key fact about ISDN is that it brings the speed and reliability of digital transmission to the desktop, rather than relying on analog technology for the last leg.

Your ISP should have an ISDN plan. ISDN is currently only available in urban areas.

Engineers used to joke that ISDN meant "It Still Does Nothing" because the service is taking so long to catch on. In truth, it was a solution in search of a problem. That will change when ISDN finally solves the "vicious circle" that has bedeviled it:

ISDN is not popular because it is costly.

ISDN is costly because it is not popular.

The Web is the problem that ISDN has been waiting to solve.

However a different picture emerges if you tabulate only desktop platforms that are connected to the Internet. The breakdown is roughly:

Unix (all versions)	90%
IBM PC and PC compatibles	9%
Macintosh	1%

For this reason, the first 3 ports were done in this order. Coming from Sun, Java was naturally developed on Sun workstations under the Solaris 2.x (Unix) Operating System. A port to Windows 95 and Windows NT rapidly followed, and was released at the same time as the Solaris version. Sun staff are also completing the Mac port and have announced availability beginning in March 1996.

Ports are also underway or nearing completion to most other platforms of significance. Details can be obtained from these sites:

Other Platforms

IBM: Windows 3.1, AIX and OS/2 ports are underway by IBM, they have announced products under the code name of "Cyberparts." See the IBM Web page at   http://ncc.hursley.ibm.com/javainfo/

DEC: a port to Alpha OSF/1 is being done by the Open Software Foundation. For information, see   http://www.gr.osf.org:8001/projects/web/java/

SGI: See http://www.sgi.com/fun/free/web-tools.html

Hewlett-Packard: The Open Software Foundation (OSF) is working on a port to HP/UX on the Precision Architecture. For information, see
http://www.gr.osf.org/java/

linux: Several independent ports to linux have been made.
See   http://www.blackdown.org

NeXT: A port to the NeXTstep environment is underway.
See   http://www.next.com

AT&T: The Open Software Foundation (OSF) is working on a port to AT&T Unix. For information, see   http://www.gr.osf.org:8001/projects/web/java/

Amiga: http://www.yahoo.com/Computers/PCs/Amiga
http://www.lls.se/~matjo/PJAmi/PJAmi.html

Hardware Needs

Java itself doesn't lay down many specific demands on the hardware. The Web browser probably will. For example, Netscape Navigator 2.0 specifies that users need:

Unix

+ 16Mb memory
+ Solaris 2.3 or later

Windows

+ Windows 95 or Windows NT
+ i386 processor or later
+ 8Mb memory
+ sound blaster card

Macintosh

> + Macintosh System 7.5 or later
> + 8Mb memory
> + PowerPC

Java itself is not a resource hog. If the system is sufficiently configured to run a fully-featured Web browser, it meets the minimum needs for Java too.

The system is referred to as the JDK—Java Development Kit. It includes a java compiler (javac), a java bytecode interpreter (java), a debugger (jdb), and an applet viewer ("appletviewer") that lets you run an applet in the absence of a Web browser.

Getting a Browser

The next piece of software you need is a Java-capable Web browser. At the start of 1996, that means Netscape Navigator version 2.0 or later, or Sun's own HotJava browser or Microsoft's Internet Explorer. These are the first two Java-capable browsers available, but all other browser suppliers are racing fast to catch up. Simply put, if a Web browser is not Java-capable from this point on, it will not be used by anyone knowledgeable. You need a Java-capable browser so you can:

- Experiment with www browsing

- Run applets (little Java applications) that are embedded in Web pages.

In these early days of the Web and Java, companies are eager to meet the pent-up demand for products. They are releasing early so-called Beta versions of their software. They are even making the Beta versions available without charge. The Beta versions are not supported products, and often are very buggy. It can be a frustrating experience trying to work with Beta software.

Software is often available on a choice of media, commonly CD and diskettes. If your system has a CD ROM reader, look for the software on CD ROM, because it avoids swapping 11 diskettes in and out (e.g. to install Win-95). 🍌

The Birth of a Software Product

The classic model for software product releases follows three phases:

Alpha release. The alpha software is the first version that has the major functionality in place. The software will still be very buggy, but enough of it works well enough to release to other departments in the company for test and use. As the inevitable defect reports come back, the problems will be tracked and fixed, so it can move to the next phase of the cycle.

Beta release. You enter the Beta cycle immediately after the alpha cycle is complete. As many as possible of the bugs have been found and fixed, and a new release is generated. This Beta software is made available to outside testers. It may be made widely available to anyone who asks for it (like Windows NT Beta) or it may be given only to a small group of highly qualified partner companies.

The point of Beta test is to locate bugs that can only be found with use and misuse in typical customer environments. The big problem with Beta testing is that you are now so far advanced in the development cycle that it may not be possible to fix any but the most heinous bugs that are uncovered, and perhaps not all of them.

FCS release. FCS stands for "First Customer Shipment." As the Beta period (typically some multiple of months) winds up, the bug-fixing criteria get stricter and stricter. This is because unrestricted bug fixing will destablize the product, at a time when you are aiming for maximum reliability. Typically no new functionality is allowed in the Beta period, and towards the end, only really serious bugs can be fixed: bugs that eat data (data corruption) or bugs that cause core dumps. Finally 6-8 weeks before the end of Beta the software is built for the final time, and put through in-house regression testing. Any last minute problems are noted and either reported in the release notes, or fixed on a case-by-case basis. The CDs are duplicated, sent out to the distribution channels and become available for purchase on the FCS date.

Getting the Netscape Software

Here's how to get the latest Netscape release. Netscape has released several updates to the original Beta release, so there has been more than one Beta.

1.   Use anonymous FTP to the Netscape site ftp.netscape.com. The netscape site is very heavily used. You might consider access outside prime hour. There are no mirror sites (except inside certain educational institutions).

2. The directories are named to reflect their contents. If you wanted the original Beta release (you don't) you could retrieve it from the pathname that matches your system:

Unix
> /2.0beta/unix/netscape-v20b2-export.alpha-dec-osf2.0.tar.Z
> netscape-v20b2-export.hppa1.1-hp-hpux.tar.Z
> netscape-v20b2-export.i486-unknown-linux.tar.Z
> netscape-v20b2-export.sparc-sun-solaris2.4.tar.Z

Windows
> /2.0beta/windows/n16e20b2.exe
> n32e20b2.exe

Mac
> /2.0beta/mac/netscape-2.0b2.hqx

The point is that you have to use some intelligence to choose which file to download.

Use the most recent release that is on the site. The name of the directory should be obvious when you get to the netscape site.

3. Do a binary transfer on the file whose name matches your platform.

If you are running windows on your system, there are two choices for the executable file:
n16e20b3.exe -- for Windows 3.x
n32e20b3.exe -- for Windows 95 and NT.

If running windows you must choose the 32-bit version for windows 95 and NT. Netscape announced in October 1996 that they will support Java on Windows 3.1, so this may change in the future.

4. The Netscape binary is several Mb in size, and will take about 25 minutes to download using a 28.8Kbps line.

When you finally have the Netscape binary on your system, unpack it. On Windows it is a self extracting archive: just execute it, and it will create several programs in the directory. On Unix, it is a compressed tar file, so run uncompress, followed by tar -xvf.

At this point you will have several files in the directory, one of which is called setup. Run the setup program, choose where you want to install it, look at the readme file (it says you promise not to give Netscape to any Syrians, Libyans, North Koreans, Yugoslavs etc.)[2] choose the default security level, configure in the TCP/IP support according to the instructions in the Netscape support/client support/release notes or handbook at http://www.netscape.com and you are ready to go.

The Beta versions of Netscape have a limited shelf life. They expire after a predetermined date, to encourage you to either retrieve a newer beta, or buy the FCS product.

Microsoft Trojan Horse?

In a news report headlined "Microsoft Trojan Horse stymies net use" Interactive Week reported in September 1995, that the use of Microsoft Network removed a file that was essential for network software (like Netscape Navigator) from competitors.

The news story went on to explain if you upgrade from Windows 3.x to Windows 95, it automatically replaces the windows socket library Winsock.dll with a new version that only works with Microsoft's Internet access software. Not only is Microsoft Network given the most prominent place of display on the window interface, it also disables all its competitors.

Only the most knowledgeable of users will be able to track down the problem, and reconfigure the compatible version of the library. Suppliers of competing software only had two options: rewrite their software to use the new Microsoft library—except that Microsoft was very reluctant to release information on the Application Program Interface (API) of the new Winsock environment. The only other choice, which Netcom and many others took, was to immediately abandon use of the new winsock.dll, move the old compatible winsock code elsewhere and hide it from the Microsoft upgrade program that overwrites it.

In December 1995, the United States Department of Justice (the arm of the Federal Government that enforces anti-monopoly laws) announced it was investigating the incident.

Getting Java Updates

Finally, you want to acquire updates to the Java software. As with Netscape there have been several preliminary releases, leading up to an FCS on January 23, 1996. If the Java FCS version is available for your platform, use it in preference to Beta.

---

2. This is because the encryption software in Netscape is deemed a "munition" by the U.S. Government.

The FCS version contains fewer bugs, is better documented, and is better supported. Beta software is for the adventurous.

How to Download Java

Assuming you need to download Java, the process is very similar to downloading Netscape.

1. Use anonymous FTP to your closest mirror to the Java site. The mirrors are:

    USA: Wayne State University
     ftp://ftp.science.wayne.edu/pub/java

    USA: SunSITE at University of North Carolina
     ftp://sunsite.unc.edu/pub/languages/java

    USA: The Blackdown Organization
     ftp://www.blackdown.org/pub/Java

    USA: Dimension X
     ftp://java.dnx.com or
     ftp://www.dnx.com

    UK: SunSITE Northern Europe, Imperial College, London
     ftp://sunsite.doc.ic.ac.uk/packages/java

    Sweden: Luleå University
     ftp://ftp.luth.se/pub/infosystems/www/hotjava

    Germany: SunSITE Central Europe, Aachen
     ftp://sunsite.informatik.rwth-aachen.de/pub/mirror/
     java.sun.com

    Japan: Center for Global Communication (GLOCOM), Tokyo
     ftp://ftp.glocom.ac.jp/mirror/java.sun.com

    Singapore: SunSITE Singapore, National University of Singapore
     ftp://ftp.iss.nus.sg/pub/java

    Korea: Korea Advanced Institute of Science and Technology CAIR, Taejon
     ftp://ftp.kaist.ac.kr/pub/java

    If none of these work for you, the Sun Java site is at ftp.javasoft.com. The Java site and its mirrors are very heavily used. You might consider access outside prime hours. Log on for anonymous ftp.

2. At the Java site, the files are in the pub directory, and are named to reflect their contents.

   Beta release
   /pub/JDK12-beta-solaris2-sparc.tar.Z
   /pub/JDK12-beta-win32-x86.exe

   Although the Java system is architecture neutral to programmers and users, the software that implements the system is different for each platform [1 second puzzler for readers: explain why.]

3. Switch to binary mode, and get the file whose name matches your platform. You only need get the most recent version of the JDK, as indicated by its name.

What's in the JDK

When you unpack the Java Development Kit and install it, you'll find that you have these components:

filename	what it is
javac	compiler, java source to byte code
java	interpreter, runs byte code
jdb	debugger
appletviewer	Allows java programs in Web pages to be run without using a Web browser.

These are the tools you will use most frequently. There are also a few special purpose utilities.

javadoc	Creates html documentation files from clues embedded in Java source.
javah	Creates C header files that correspond to Java objects. This is useful when creating programs that mix languages.
javap	A tool to print out byte codes and class information
javaprof	A profiling tool to tell you which statements in your program were executed the most often.

Let's quickly review what you've learned before exploring the latest Java Developments. We've just described the steps you need to do to assemble a computer system that allows you to run Java. The steps are:

1. Obtain Internet access.

2. Get a Web browser, such as Netscape version 2.0 or later, install it on your system.

3. Get the Java Development Kit (either from the CD that came with this book, or by downloading it) install, and test it on your system. The installation and testing is described in the Introduction at the front of this book.

Java is still at an early stage in its lifecycle. The version 1.0 software only became available to the public on January 23, 1996. However many related products have already been announced, or are being frantically worked on in great secrecy.

Java Developments

The development of Java-related products can be classified under six primary headings: performance, development tools, library enhancements, networking, security, and hardware. Here are the high points of those we have not covered earlier in the book.

Performance

This is the number one request from users, and probably the single highest priority item. Java, being an interpreted system, is currently an order of magnitude slower than C. But C was designed to be close to the hardware and only has built-in datatypes that are directly supported in hardware.

You have to pay something for the abstractions that Java provides and for the built-in structured types like String. On the positive side, modern workstations have MIPS to burn compared with earlier hardware, and are only going to improve. But there are a number of improvements that can be made in the software too.

Performance-oriented implementations of the Java virtual machine are on the way. We can expect optimizing runtimes that detect the frequently traveled paths in a program, and compile down to native code as the program is being executed. More performance improvements can come from a "Just-In-Time" compiler that does an additional step of compiling the byte code to native code on the client, as well as interpreting it. Thus the first pass through a block is interpreted, then you pay the cost of compilation, then passes are done at compiled code speed.

Some people have suggested compressing the byte code of an applet (or anything that is downloaded), and uncompressing it at the client end. This is likely to yield useful results for distributed applications, as the network download time is often the bottleneck.

Development Tools

Just as C is ubiquitous on hardware now, there will be Java ports to many more platforms—everything from a Cray to your TV remote control. At that point the consumer electronics goal of the original project will have been met, proving that if you wait long enough the world will eventually pass by your front door. But for some of the world it's only because they're lost.

We've already mentioned the just-in-time compilers, and we can expect the full range of conventional development tools too. I, for one, would like "indent" to properly format programs, and "java lint" to warn about questionable code constructs. Tip: the Unix C version of indent works fine on Java source and does 95 percent of what you want.

Java is a perfect match for the kind of integrated development environment which is commonplace in the PC space, but which has yet to become established among Unix professionals. If such an environment is written in Java (and it's hard to believe that anyone would be dumb enough to use a different language), then of course it is instantly portable to Unix, Windows, Macs, etc.

Some of the first IDEs on the market are quick adaptions of C++ IDEs, with time-to-market as a major goal. Hence these are not written in Java, and not available for all platforms yet.

The Abstract Window Toolkit is still in need of some help: a GUI-builder that lets a programmer draw images on the screen showing how the interface should look, and which then generates the Java to implement it.

The Javascript language will get some practical use. Javascript is completely unrelated to Java. It is a simple scripting language which can be embedded in an HTML file. It offers loops, and conditional tests. The idea is to put some of the power of a programming language in the hands of non-programmers who want to create Web pages with applets, without needing to become Java-heads. Javascript was briefly named "Livescript" before Netscape saw which way the wind was blowing. The intersection of Java and Javascript is the empty set. Microsoft have a knock off of Javascript, known as JScript.

Networking and Distributed Processing

In its brief life, Java has already become the de facto WWW programming API, and may soon become the Internet programming API. There are more innovations possible, including client/server windowing. At present, the Java AWT and its native peer window component have to be on the same system. There is no technical reason why they cannot be separated, so that users can run a window sys-

Here's an amazing fact about Java portability. One large company developed a Java IDE completely written in Java. It was targeted to Windows and Solaris platforms, and never tested on anything else. Customers lliked it so much they started to run it on their Macs, SGIs, and other systems, *and it just worked!* Some very low level stuff to do with debugging wasn't functional but 95% of the system developed for Windows and Solaris just worked on other platforms right out of the box. A tremendous testament to the portability of Java and the skills of the programming team.

tem down a PPP connection.[3] In practical terms this would allow you (well, alright, me) to dial into the office and run Java applets on a powerful office workstation, displaying the results on a PC at home. One of the design achievements of NeWS (Sun's Network-extensible Window System) was the decoupling of displays. A NeWS program could send its results to any workstation on the same net. This can soon become true for Java.

Java will consolidate its distributed processing and windowing capabilities, and move to provide a common windowing front end to databases, in particular. Several companies announced that they are developing tools in this area.

- Oracle is making its corporate "PowerBrowser" Java capable. Oracle recently stunned the computer industry by demonstrating a prototype $500 "Internet terminal."

- Sybase announced it is licensing the Java system for use with its database products.

- WebLogic offers a portfolio of DBMS tools and services based on Java connectivity and portability. These are further described at: http://weblogic.com/

Tools like these ae placing Java squarely in the enterprise computing sector. We are starting to see strong indications that Java is completely displacing C++ for application development. Tools and compiler companies are making more money from Java, so are switching their investment to it. Some people predict that by the end of 1998, essentially all new application development will be done in Java.

---

3. Think of PPP ("Point to Point Protocol") as carrying TCP/IP services to a system without a dedicated IP address. PPP is often run down a telephone line, e.g. between your workstation and your home PC, so you can work from home.

Adobe has licensed Java and announced that it will integrate Java into both its PageMill authoring tools, and Adobe Acrobat. Adobe Acrobat is a software product aimed at interactive browsing. Just as Postscript is a language that describes how a document should look, allowing different output devices to do the best they can to render it, Acrobat is a language that describes in a device-independent manner how a screen should look. If it's written in Java, it can also be platform independent. Acrobat is really just a sophisticated version of HTML. A publisher can put text on a CD in Acrobat format, and anyone with an Acrobat browser can view the text in a nice formatted and font-rich form, regardless of whether they are on a Unix system, a Mac or a PC.

Security

The restrictions imposed on applets for security reasons are a little onerous with good reason. Everyone wants Java to be free from the kinds of viruses that pervade the MS Windows environment. No one wants to see the return of the 1988 Internet worm[4]. More work remains to be done to ease the restrictions without compromising system integrity.

Hardware and Firmware

A recurring idea in computer science is designing an architecture that is particularly convenient or efficient at executing a specific language. Past attempts include:

Algol-60:	early Burroughs processors
Lisp:	the Symbolics Lisp Machine
COBOL:	many processors optimized for BCD arithmetic.
Ada:	Rational Computers

None of the examples to date have been conspicuously successful. The Lisp Machine was driven out of business by general purpose Unix workstations. The end of the Cold War spelled the end of massive budgets for defense contractors to blow on "cost-plus" contracts, taking the Ada machine down with it. Burroughs was swallowed by Unisys which in turn isn't exactly breaking any new ground in computing these days. Will the Java machine fare any better?

4. See "With Microscope and Tweezers: An Analysis of the Internet Virus of November 1988" by Mark W. Eichin and Jon A. Rochlis, Mass. Institute of Technology, February 1989. This paper starts off describing the Internet as "a collection of networks linking 60,000 host computers" which seems hilariously insignificant in contrast to today's Internet. We've come a long way.

A lot of companies think so, and are betting on it. It costs upwards of $1 billion to design and build a completely new computer architecture these days. If you can leverage existing facilities and technology, you can possibly do it on a shoestring of just $100 million, so anyone betting on a Java-specific chip is making a pretty significant investment.

Oracle has already demonstrated their Internet terminal, and you don't exactly have to be Nostradamus to predict that the lights are burning late in their handsome Redwood Shores, CA offices as they try to figure out exactly how best to bundle Java with it. Silicon Valley is a pretty small community when you get right down to it, and one hears all kinds of talk about Java chips, Java workstations, Java PCs, Java terminals, Java supercomputers and Java microcomputers. Who knows, some of it may even be true.

What is The Future For This Hardware?

The Oracle Corporation's $500 Network Computer.

model name:	NC (Network Computer)
CPU:	Acorn ARM7500 RISC
OS name:	NC-OS (no prizes for creativity in naming)
	based on Acorn Computer Group Plc's RISC OS

NC-OS will be ported to x86 platforms, and is also intended to be portable to any WWW, Internet, or communications device.

enclosure design: Frog Design Inc. (The same creative consultants who worked on the Mac packaging with great success).

Acorn is an enormously capable British computer engineering company. They have been held back by their small size and limited installed base, but have a long track record of innovative and well-thought-out designs.

These are about the only features of the NC system that are known at this point. Oracle's plan for marketing, supporting, or even manufacturing the NC has yet to be announced.

Sun Microsystems has announced a family of Java chips, Pico Java, Micro Java, and Ultra Java, covering a range of price performance points.

Companies can license picoJAVA today, and chips based on the picoJAVA design will generally available in 1997.

picoJAVA is not a chip, but rather a core design around which a variety of chips for different target markets can be implemented. Some information was released at Hot Chips in August about the picoJAVA architecture and more information was disclosed at the Microprocessor Forum in October.

From this, it is public knowledge that several large semiconductor companies intend to license picoJAVA, including LG Semicon, Mitubishi, NEC, and Samsung). In addition, Sun will produce a chip based on picoJAVA known as microJAVA.

Some points that came out at Hot Chips were:

- The picoJava core directly executes the Java bytecodes

- It maintains an on-chip stack

- Can "fold" many common, simple stack/local variable movement byte-codes into the following instruction and execute both in a single cycle.

- It has a modern, pipelined, RISC-style of design. "This isn't your father's Burroughs B5000." It has one cycle execution of simple ALU operations and the like.

- Provides hardware support to facilitate GC, thread management, and object creation (what exactly that support may be is still under wraps. It speeds up all phases of Java program execution, not only the instruction execution time.

LSI Logic at least has gone public with some of its plans for what they call the "Internet on a Chip." This chip is targeted at Java/Internet terminals and other embedded systems. The chip uses one of the MIPS RISC microprocessor designs. More information is at http://www.lsilogic.com/mediakit/unit3_1x.html.

Two big characteristics working in favor of Java-on-a-chip are: (1) the performance speed-up; and (2) the well-defined virtual machine which makes the task easier than trying to "siliconify" other high-level languages. Java is built on a well-defined stack-based virtual machine with the byte code instruction set, supported by a runtime library. It's also possible that tighter integration into the operating system could provide some of the benefits of a Java chip at a fraction of the cost.

The virtual machine was defined with the Java language in mind, but people were quick to realize that other compilers could be targeted to it. This would provide them with instant ports to any platform that supported Java. Not all languages are good candidates for meeting the requirements of the Java VM. C++ is a little too lax in its use of pointer arithmetic to be a good fit. However, the language experts at compiler company Intermetrics have already targeted their Ada 95 compiler to the Java VM, and created quite a stir by demonstrating it working at a 1995 Ada convention. Their Web site is at http://www.inmet.com

---

What Will Microsoft Do?

One of the big wildcard questions was "what does Microsoft intend to do?"

People questioned whether Microsoft sincerely plans to embrace the technology, or will somehow try to act as a spoiler. Certainly it is very hard to find examples of companies that have succeeded in a collaborative venture with Microsoft. The mighty IBM was humbled, burned even, by its abortive attempt at joint development on OS/2 with the Redmond giant.

Stac Electronics tried to make a deal with Microsoft for Stac's data compression software. According to court documents, the deal fell apart on Microsoft's unwillingness to pay per copy royalties. But Microsoft just went ahead and put Stac's software technology into MS-DOS 6 anyway[a]. Stac won a court judgement for $120 million against Microsoft in February 1994, later settling for $90M to avoid a lengthy appeal. In the book "Start-Up", Jerry Kaplan claims that Microsoft pinched his idea for pen computing when he showed them the concept to ask for applications porting. Instead Microsoft started a project to produce their own pen computing OS.

The whole concept of platform independence strikes at Microsoft's lock on desktop software. Microsoft must be furious about this, to say the least. It was faced with choosing between embracing the technology or ignoring it. If Microsoft embraced Java, Microsoft risked appearing to endorse a competing technology. If Microsoft ignored Java, Microsoft risked being left behind.

Before Java, Microsoft owned the desktop absolutely. Now they have already lost the browser desktop to Netscape, and are fast losing control on interesting desktop APIs to Java and Sun. Microsoft's answer is to try to embed Java in a honey pot of proprietary ActiveX code. Developers who want to push the limits of Windows will use these ActiveX controls, and their code will only ever run on Microsoft platforms. Developers who are interested in portability will carefully avoid these lock-ins and their code will run everywhere.

---

[a]One journalist asked "Just what kind of game does Microsoft think it's playing here?" and immediately provided his own answer: "Monopoly." Monopoly is a trademark of Parker Brothers.

We can also expect to see a lot more demand for graphics designers, illustrators, and artists. Java can animate your Web page, true, but you still need something to say, and an interesting way in which to say it. Consider the "Neon sign" applet that used to be at

http://java.sun.com/JDK-prebeta1/applets/contest/NeonSign/index.html.

This is an impressive looking applet that shows a flickering neon sign, spelling out the name of the applet author. The more you look at this, the less there is to it.

The applet just consists of two images, one with the neon sign dark, and one with it lit up. The applet randomly switches back and forth between them, so it appears that the sign is flashing. But all the cleverness of this applet is in the glossy artwork—and *that* is precisely the part that most programmers cannot supply for you.

Other Java Resources

Half the point of Java is accessing the resources of the WWW. Here is a collection of favorite sites. If you check in with the Java ones periodically, you will always be well-informed about new developments.

http://www.javasoft.com (also reachable as http://java.sun.com)   The Sun Java site. Download software, look at applets, read the most up-to-date documentation and user guides.

http://www.gamelan.com   The Gamelan site. Named after an Indonesian musical ensemble, the Gamelan (pronounced to rhyme (approximately) with "come along") site is a rich resource for Java code, Java applets, hints, libraries and all kinds of information.

Gamelan is sponsored by the EarthWeb organization, an Internet consulting and services company. The Gamelan site is a treasure house that should be your second port of call after the Sun site.

http://www-net.com/java/faq   The mother of all FAQ lists. This site contains pointers to the various and several Java FAQ lists that public-spirited programmers are maintaining to help spread the information.

You can also access some of these individual FAQ sites directly at:

http://sunsite.unc.edu/javafaq/javafaq.html
http://www-net.com/java/faq/faq-java.txt
http://www.city-net.com/~krom/java-faq.html
http://java.sun.com/faqIndex.html
http://www.digitalfocus.com/digitalfocus/faq/index.html

http://www.io.org/~mentor1/jnIndex.html   This is the URL for Digital Espresso—a weekly summary of traffic on the comp.lang.java newsgroup. The volume of traffic there is enormous (several thousand messages per week), so a weekly summary really helps those who want to keep up without getting mired in the detail.

http://www.javaworld.com   The best online Java magazine. Has back issues at http://www.javaworld.com/common/jw=backissues.html

http://java.sun.com/doc/language_specification   The Java language specification. Also available as a 700 page book.

http://www.yahoo.com   Yahoo started life as a part-time project by a couple of Stanford students. It has rapidly blossomed into one of the premier Web searching and indexing sites. You are not a Web aficionado until you have a "connection timed out" while trying to reach yahoo.

http://www.dimensionx.com or http://www.dnx.com   Another early adopter of Java. This site is rich with applets, ideas and general Java know-how. Well worth a visit.

http://www.fbi.gov/topten.htm   The FBI "Top Ten most wanted" list. Check this every month to see if any of your co-workers have made it onto the list. If so, make history and be the first to turn them in by e-mail.

http://www.ccil.org/jargon/jargon.html   The Jargon File. Everything you don't need to know about programmer slang, and less. Also available as a book, lord help us. Version 3.0 came out in August 1993 as The New Hacker's Dictionary second edition (ISBN 0-262-68079-3), published by MIT Press. They finally re-edited that bizarre and confusing saga of Guy Steele's about the Palo Alto ice cream store. It's still not a very funny story, but at least now you can understand what the point would be, if it had one. Guy Steele is currently responsible for writing the Java Language Specification.

ftp://ftp.ora.com/pub/examples/windows/win95.update/regwiz.html   Find out the truth about the Microsoft Registration Wizard snooping your hard disk for competitors' products! Learn how expert programmers use debugging and file monitoring tools to see what is really happening in a system. A detective story with a moral at the end.

Don't forget to read the Java newsgroups, starting at comp.lang.java.programmer. There are about half-a-dozen Java newsgroups, and they are very high volume. Maybe I'll see you there.

Conclusion

Programmers get interested in Java for many different reasons. Perhaps you started out by hearing that Java made possible executable content in Web pages. Perhaps your initial reaction, like mine, was "So what?" Maybe your boss asked you to investigate Java after reading something in "The Economist" magazine, or the Wall Street Journal, or Time, or Newsweek, or the New York Times. It's highly unusual for a programming language to receive so much attention from the mainstream media, especially before the product has even reached the First Customer Shipment milestone.

The amount of media coverage of Java naturally raises some questions in the minds of programmers. It begins to look like the kind of exaggeration more usually associated with the entertainment industry. But that is not what is happening here at all. Sun was completely taken by surprise by the Java phenomenon, just as much as everyone else. As the significance of the language grew and grew, a series of increasingly senior managers were brought in to lead the program. Investment in the language—inside Sun and outside—grew too.

Scott McNealy, the CEO of Sun, has occasionally remarked that Sun made a mistake by not whole-heartedly backing the NeWS window system when it was first developed in 1987. As a result, it has taken nearly a decade for the Unix world to resolve the conflicting windowing system alternatives. Scott has commented in the past that he will personally ensure that superior Sun software technology is never again stifled through wavering commitment, and he is certainly delivering on his promise. The chief architect of NeWS was James Gosling—the chief architect of Java.

Sometimes tremendous interest in a product is not the result of overselling or collective trend-following. Sometimes it really does happen because the world recognizes the right product, in the right place, at the right time. Java is a better mousetrap, and the world is beating a path to Sun's door. There has been a convergence of mighty trends that Java is well placed to address.

© 1996 Matthew Burtch

> **Convergence of Mighty Trends**
>
> As the computer industry closes out the last five years of the Millennium, the times are characterized by the following mighty trends:
>
> • Popularization of the Internet
>
> • Computer industry blending into telecom industry
>
> • Consumer electronics merging with PC technologies
>
> • Computer industry drive to multimedia everything
>
> • Rejection of the complexity of C++
>
> • Desire for independence from Intel and Microsoft desktop monopolies
>
> • Resurgence of threads and object-oriented programming.
>
> and, as always,
>
> • More and more computing power for less and less investment.
>
> Partly by accident, partly by design, Java is located at the point where all these paths come together.

Not much in Java is completely new. What is new is the combination of all the things, put together in a simple package, and made available on highly-generous terms from computer industry technology leader, Sun Microsystems. While executable content in Web pages is novel, it isn't such a big deal in itself. Java is an enabling technology for what will follow.

Java is producing a "paradigm shift"—a fundamental rethinking of the established ways of software development. Paradigm shifts lead to tremendous upsets, but also tremendous opportunities. The development of the internal combustion engine was a paradigm shift, and there were undoubtedly people in 1876 who were asking "But Herr Otto, so what if you can spin that big flywheel with a petrol motor?" What implications does it have for software distribution channels if you can pull applets to your system with a Web browser?

Past computer industry paradigm shifts have included the trend to minicomputers, which DEC rode to great prosperity throughout the 1970s. That was followed by the "migration to the desktop" spearheaded by the Apple II PC and reinforced (tardily) by the IBM PC. The "migration to the desktop" paradigm shift almost bankrupted DEC as they failed to anticipate it and then came up with a succession of failing strategies to cope with it. It did bankrupt other, even less well-prepared companies like Wang.

First, take an ordinary sheet of 8.5" by 11" paper, and make it narrower by cutting off 1.5" or so, to make 7" by 11". Then follow these instructions:

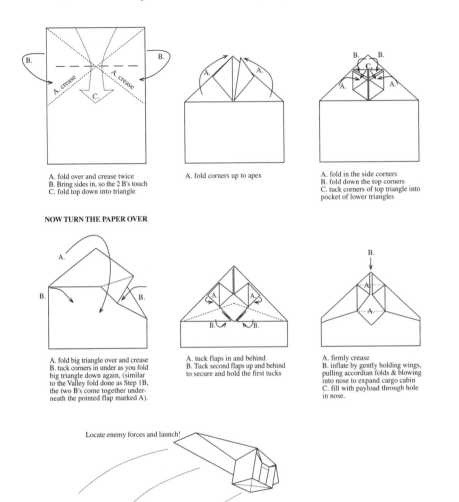

A. fold over and crease twice
B. Bring sides in, so the 2 B's touch
C. fold top down into triangle

A. fold corners up to apex

A. fold in the side corners
B. fold down the top corners
C. tuck corners of top triangle into pocket of lower triangles

NOW TURN THE PAPER OVER

A. fold big triangle over and crease
B. tuck corners in under as you fold big triangle down again, (similar to the Valley fold done as Step 1B, the two B's come together underneath the pointed flap marked A).

A. tuck flaps in and behind
B. Tuck second flaps up and behind to secure and hold the first tucks

A. firmly crease
B. inflate by gently holding wings, pulling accordian folds & blowing into nose to expand cargo cabin
C. fill with payload through hole in nose.

Locate enemy forces and launch!

Figure 12-1: The Kamikaze water bomber

Fold up wings, and fill with payload through hole in nose. Umm, the hole in the *plane's* nose, that is. Launch and enjoy.

Origami is relaxing and fun. Just the thing for unwinding after a busy day chasing electrons. If you've really got a lot of spare time, check the origami models at http://www.cs.ubc.ca/spider/jwu/origami.html

There's a praying mantis there that takes 100 steps to complete!

P.S. My Origami Java chip will be released soon.

By The Way. . .

Some companies are so desperate for Java programmers, that they are stating their requirements in terms of "hours of experience" in the same way that flying experience is measured.

Seen recently on comp.lang.java

```
From: (name removed to protect the guilty)
Newsgroups: comp.lang.java
Subject: Freelance job for C++/Java Programmer
Date: 27 Jan 1996 23:26:28 -0800
Distribution: world
We are now looking for: an experienced C/C++, Java programmer.
Around 4 years experience on Windows & Mac preferred,
minimum of 100 hours with Java required.
```

Personally, I never hire programmers based on how long they have been in the workforce. It's much more relevant to find out what programs they have written and what they're interested in. But this posting is an interesting insight into market economics.

Further Reading

LAN Times Encyclopedia of Networking

by Tom Sheldon
publ by Osborne McGraw-Hill, 1994
ISBN 0-07-881965-2

The back cover describes this as "covering A (Appletalk) through X (X Windows)" and it is absolutely right: the sections on Y and Z were completely missing from my copy. Har har. Just funning you. This is an excellent and easily-understood encyclopedia of anything and everything to do with networks. If you can only afford one book on data communications, this is absolutely the one to buy.

The Whole Internet

by Ed Krol,
publ. O'Reilly & Associates, Sebastapol CA, 1994, (second edition).
ISBN 1-56592-063-5

An excellent and exceptionally able description of all key aspects of the Internet for the intelligent lay-reader. Also contains detailed descriptions of the applications that you can run on Internet.

APPENDIX A

Powers of 2 and ISO 8859

Refer to Table A-1 for Powers of 2

With n bits in integer two's complement format, you can count:

unsigned from 0 to (one less than 2^n)
signed from -2^{n-1} to (one less than 2^{n-1})

Refer to Table A-2 for ISO 8859

Characters 0x0 to 0x1F are the C0 (control) characters, defined in ISO/IEC 6429:1992

Characters 0x20 to 0x7E are the G0 graphics characters of the 7-bit code set defined in
ISO/IEC 646-1991(E) — essentially the 7-bit ASCII characters.

Characters 0x80 to 0x9F are the C1 (control) characters, defined in ISO/IEC 6429:1992

The unshaded characters comprise the Latin-1 code set defined in ISO/IEC 8859-1:1987 though the symbols "Φ" and "Φ" (0xDE and 0xFE) are approximations to the capital and small Icelandic letter "thorn." The actual letters are too weird to be in character sets anywhere outside a 12-mile radius of Reykjavík.

Table A-1: Powers-of-two from 2^1 to 2^{64}

2^1	2	2^{17}	131,072	2^{33}	8,589,934,592	2^{49}	562,949,953,421,312
2^2	4	2^{18}	262,144	2^{34}	17,179,869,184	2^{50}	1,125,899,906,842,624
2^3	8	2^{19} **megabyte**	524,288	2^{35}	34,359,738,368	2^{51}	2,251,799,813,685,248
2^4	16	2^{20}	1,048,576	2^{36}	68,719,476,736	2^{52}	4,503,599,627,370,496
2^5	32	2^{21}	2,097,152	2^{37}	137,438,953,472	2^{53}	9,007,199,254,740,992
2^6	64	2^{22}	4,194,304	2^{38}	274,877,906,944	2^{54}	18,014,398,509,481,984
2^7	128	2^{23}	8,388,608	2^{39} **terabyte**	549,755,813,888	2^{55}	36,028,797,018,963,968
2^8	256	2^{24}	16,777,216	2^{40}	1,099,511,627,776	2^{56}	72,057,594,037,927,936
2^9 **kilobyte**	512	2^{25}	33,554,432	2^{41}	2,199,023,255,552	2^{57}	144,115,188,075,855,872
2^{10}	1,024	2^{26}	67,108,864	2^{42}	4,398,046,511,104	2^{58}	288,230,376,151,711,744
2^{11}	2,048	2^{27}	134,217,728	2^{43}	8,796,093,022,208	2^{59}	576,460,752,303,423,488
2^{12}	4,096	2^{28}	268,435,456	2^{44}	17,592,186,044,416	2^{60}	1,152,921,504,606,846,976
2^{13}	8,192	2^{29} **gigabyte**	536,870,912	2^{45}	35,184,372,088,832	2^{61}	2,305,843,009,213,693,952
2^{14}	16,384	2^{30}	1,073,741,824	2^{46}	70,368,744,177,664	2^{62}	4,611,686,018,427,387,904
2^{15}	32,768	2^{31}	2,147,483,648	2^{47}	140,737,488,355,328	2^{63} **bubbabyte**	9,223,372,036,854,775,808
2^{16}	65,536	2^{32}	4,294,967,296	2^{48}	281,474,976,710,656	2^{64}	18,446,744,073,709,551,616

Table A-2: ISO 8859 8-bit Latin-1 character set and control characters

Least significant 4 bits of the byte

	0	1	2	3	4	5	6	7	8	9	A	B	C	D	E	F
0	nul	soh	stx	etx	eot	enq	ack	bel	bs	ht	lf\n	vt	ff	cr\r	so	si
1	dle	dc1	dc2	dc3	dc4	nak	syn	etb	can	em	sub	esc	is_4	is_3	is_2	is_1
2	space	!	"	#	$	%	&	'	(	)	*	+	,	-	.	/
3	0	1	2	3	4	5	6	7	8	9	:	;	<	=	>	?
4	@	A	B	C	D	E	F	G	H	I	J	K	L	M	N	O
5	P	Q	R	S	T	U	V	W	X	Y	Z	[	\	]	^	_
6	'	a	b	c	d	e	f	g	h	i	j	k	l	m	n	o
7	p	q	r	s	t	u	v	w	x	y	z	{	|	}	~	del
8	*n/a*	*n/a*	bph	nbh	*n/a*	nel	ssa	esa	hts	htj	vts	pld	plu	ri	ss2	ss3
9	dcs	pu1	pu2	sts	cch	mw	spa	epa	sos	*n/a*	sci	csi	st	osc	pm	apc
A	nbsp	¡	¢	£	¤	¥	¦	§	¨	©	^{a}	«	¬	shy	®	‾
B	°	±	^{2}	^{3}	´	µ	¶	•	¸	^{1}	^{o}	»	$^1/_4$	$^1/_2$	$^3/_4$	¿
C	À	Á	Â	Ã	Ä	Å	Æ	Ç	È	É	Ê	Ë	Ì	Í	Î	Ï
D	Ð	Ñ	Ò	Ó	Ô	Õ	Ö	×	Ø	Ù	Ú	Û	Ü	Y	Φ	β
E	à	á	â	ã	ä	å	æ	ç	è	é	ê	ë	ì	í	î	ï
F	∂	ñ	ò	ó	ô	õ	ö	÷	ø	ù	ú	û	ü	y	Φ	ÿ

Index

SUNSOFT PRESS

Prentice Hall PTR is pleased to publish SunSoft Press books. This year's SunSoft catalog has unprecedented breadth and depth, covering not only the inner workings of Sun operating systems, but also guides to multiprocessing, internationalization of software, networking, and other topics important to anyone working with these technologies.

These and other Prentice Hall PTR books are available at your local Magnet Store. To locate the store nearest you fax (201) 236-7123 or visit our web site at:

http://www.prenhall.com

THE PROFESSIONAL'S CHOICE

ALL ABOUT ADMINISTERING NIS+, Second Edition

Rick Ramsey

Updated and revised for Solaris™ 2.3, this book is ideal for network administrators who want to know more about NIS+: its capabilities, requirements, how it works, and how to get the most out of it. Includes planning guidelines for both new installations and for transitions from NIS; detailed descriptions of the structure of NIS+ objects and security; and setup instructions for both standard NIS+ comands and NIS+ shell scripts. Presents modular, fully-tested, step-by-step instructions and many illustrations, examples, and tips.

1995, 480 pp., Paper, 0-13-309576-2 (30957-5)

AUTOMATING SOLARIS INSTALLATIONS

Paul Anthony Kasper and Alan L. McClellan

If you want to minimize the time you spend installing the Solaris environment on SPARC™ or x86 systems, this book is for you! It describes how to set up "hands-off" Solaris installations for hundreds of SPARC or x86 systems. It explains in detail how to configure your site so that when you install Solaris, you simply boot a system and walk away—the software installs automatically! Topics covered include setting up network booting, enabling automatic system configuration, setting up custom JumpStart files, booting and installing, debugging and trouble-shooting. A diskette containing working shell scripts that automate pre- and post-installation tasks is provided.

1995, 320 pp., Paper, 0-13-312505-X (31250-4) Book/Disk

CONFIGURATION AND CAPACITY PLANNING FOR SOLARIS SERVERS

Brian L. Wong

Written for MIS staff, this book provides information on planning and configuring Solaris servers for use in NFS™, DBMS, and timesharing environments. The material concentrates on applied computer architecture, case studies and experimentally-based, real-world results rather than on queueing models.

1996, 300 pp., Paper. 0-13-349952-9 (34995-1)

NEW!

THE UNIX BOOK OF GAMES

Janice Winsor

A collection of classic games with complete rules and illustrated tips and hints. Includes commentary by the programmers who created each game. Includes complete source code and binaries for SCO and Linux.

1997, 256 pp., Paper, 0-13-490079-0 (49007-8) Book/CD-ROM

DESIGNING VISUAL INTERFACES:
Communication Oriented Techniques

Kevin Mullet and Darrell K. Sano

Useful to anyone responsible for designing, specifying, implementing, documenting, or managing the visual appearance of computer-based information displays, this book applies the fundamentals of graphic design, industrial design, interior design, and architecture to solve the human computer interface problems experienced in commercial software development. It describes basic design principles (the what and why), common errors, and practical techniques (the how). Readers will gain a new perspective on product development as well as an appreciation for the contribution visual design can offer to their products and users. Six major areas: Elegance and Simplicity; Scale, Contrast, and Proportion; Organization and Visual Structure; Module and Programme; Image and Representation; and Style.

1995, 304 pp., Paper,
0-13-303389-9 (30338-8)
(includes 4-color plates)

DEVELOPING VISUAL APPLICATIONS XIL:
An Imaging Foundation Library

William K. Pratt

A practical introduction to imaging into new, innovative applications for desktop computing. For applications in the technical, commercial, and consumer environments, imaging should be considered as basic as putting text or user interface elements into an application. This book breaks down the barriers that developers may have in integrating imaging into their applications. It acquaints developers with the basics of image processing, compression, and algorithm implementation by providing clear, real-world examples of how they can be applied using XIL, a cross-platform imaging foundation library. This book acquaints knowledgeable imaging developers with the architectural features and capabilities of XIL. It can also serve as a primer for new XIL programmers.

1996, 400 pp., Paper,
0-13-461948-X (46194-7)

HTML FOR FUN AND PROFIT, Gold Signature Ed.

Mary E. S. Morris

This book is about writing HTML pages for the World Wide Web. Written in a step-by-step, hands on, tutorial style, it presents all the information needed by an aspiring web page author. Platforms are also discussed. Includes:

- Setting up your server
- Learning HTML formatting basics, including lists and special characters
- Integrating multimedia into web pages
- Formatting tables in HTML
- Creating interactive HTML documents with CGI scripting
- Customizing HTML pages with Server Includes
- Designing effective web page layouts
- Appendices on installing and using Xmosaic, WinMosaic, and Mac-Mosaic browsers are included.
- A CD-ROM containing shareware and extensive examples of sample HTML pages and sample perl scripts is also provided.

This book also includes a chapter on Netscape with HTML examples on the CD-ROM. The CD-ROM includes a web server for Microsoft Windows 3.1, NT, Macintosh and UNIX.

1996, 330 pp., Paper,
0-13-242488-6 (24248-7)
Book/CD-ROM

EXPERT C PROGRAMMING:
Deep C Secrets

Peter van der Linden

Known as "the butt-ugly fish book" because of the coelacanth on the cover, this is a very different book on the C language! In an easy, conversational style, *it* reveals coding techniques used by the best C programmers. It relates C to other languages and includes an introduction to C++ that can be understood by any programmer without weeks of mind-bending study. Covering both the IBM PC and UNIX systems, this book is a *must read* for anyone who wants to learn more about the implementation, practical use, and folk lore of C!

1994, 384 pp., Paper, 0-13-177429-8 (17742-8)

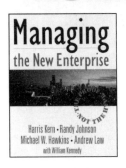

MANAGING THE NEW ENTERPRISE:
The Proof, Not The Hype

Harris Kern, Randy Johnson, Andrew Law, and Michael Hawkins with William Kennedy

In this follow-up to the best selling *Rightsizing the New Enterprise*, the authors discuss how to build and manage a heterogeneous client/ server environment. *Managing the New Enterprise* describes in detail the key technology support infrastructures, including networking, data centers, and system administration, as well as how Information Technology must change in order to manage the New Enterprise. This is an indispensable reference for anyone within Information Technology who is facing the challenges of building and managing client/server computing.

1996, 240 pp., Cloth, 0-13-231184-4 (23118-3)

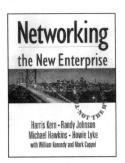

NETWORKING THE NEW ENTERPRISE:
The Proof, Not The Hype

Harris Kern and Randy Johnson

The final volume in the New Enterprise Trilogy, this book focuses on planning network projects, developing architectures, and implementations of expanding distributed computing and client server technologies. A must for any business in today's growing marketplace.

Networking the New Enterprise includes in-depth ideas for developing network architectures; including, key methods, and strategies for network management, security and design; details on implementing Network Management Systems; Methods for enhancing, securing and optimizing Networks.

1997, 350 pages, paper, 0-13-263427-9 (26342-6)

INTERACTIVE UNIX OPERATING SYSTEM:
A Guide for System Administrators

Marty C. Stewart

Written for first-time system administrators and end users, this practical guide describes the common system administration menus and commands of the INTERACTIVE UNIX System V/386 Release 3.2, Version 4.0 and SVR 3.2 UNIX in general. Loaded with step-by-step instructions and examples, it discusses how to install and configure the INTERACTIVE UNIX system, including the hardware requirements. It describes the unique CUI menu interface, basic OS commands, administration of new user accounts, configuration of customized kernels, and working with the INTERACTIVE UNIX system as an end user.

1996, 320 pp., Paper, 0-13-161613-7 (16161-2)

PC HARDWARE CONFIGURATION GUIDE:
For DOS and Solaris

Ron Ledesma

This book eliminates trial-and-error methodology by presenting a simple, structured approach to PC hardware configuration. The author's time-tested approach is to configure your system in stages, verify and test at each stage, and troubleshoot and fix problems before going on to the next stage. Covers both standalone and networked machines. Discusses how to determine x86 hardware configuration requirements, how to configure hardware components (MCA, ISA, and EISA), partitioning hard disks for DOS and UNIX, and installing DOS and/or UNIX (Solaris x86). Includes configuration instructions, checklists, worksheets, diagrams of popular SCSI host bus, network, and video adapters, and basic installation troubleshooting.

1995, 352 pp., Paper, 0-13-124678-X (12467-7)

MULTIPROCESSOR SYSTEM ARCHITECTURES:
A Technical Survey of Multiprocessor / Multithreaded Systems Using SPARC, Multi-level Bus Architectures and Solaris (SunOS)
Ben Catanzaro

Written for engineers seeking to understand the problems and solutions of multi-processor system design, this hands-on guide is the first comprehensive description of the elements involved in the design and development of Sun's multiprocessor systems. Topics covered include SPARC processor design and its implementations, an introduction to multilevel bus architectures including MBus and XBus/XDBus, an overview of the Solaris/SunOS™ multithreaded architecture and programming, and an MBus Interface Specification and Design Guide. This book can serve as a reference text for design engineers as well as a hands-on design guide to MP systems for hardware/software engineers.

1994, 528 pp., Paper, 0-13-089137-1 (08913-6)

PANIC! UNIX System Crash Dump Analysis
Chris Drake and Kimberley Brown

PANIC! is the first book to discuss in detail UNIX system panics, crashes and hangs, their causes, what to do when they occur, how to collect information about them, how to analyze that information, and how to get the problem resolved. *PANIC!* presents this highly technical and intricate subject in a friendly, easy style which even the novice UNIX system administrator will find readable, educational and enjoyable. It is written for systems and network administrators and technical support engineers who are responsible for maintaining and supporting UNIX computer systems and networks. Includes a CD-ROM containing several useful analysis tools, such as adb macros and C tags output from the source trees of two different UNIX systems.

1995, 496 pp., Paper, 0-13-149386-8 (14938-5) Book/CD-ROM

PROGRAMMING WITH THREADS
Steve Kleiman, Devang Shah, and Bart Smaalders

Written by senior threads engineers at Sun Microsystems, Inc., this book is the definitive guide to programming with threads. It is intended for both novice and more sophisticated threads programmers, and for developers multithreading existing programs as well as for those writing new multithreaded programs. The book provides structured techniques for mastering the complexity of threads programming with an emphasis on performance issues. Included are detailed examples using the new POSIX threads (Pthreads) standard interfaces. The book also covers the other UNIX threads interface defined by UNIX International.

1996, 250 pp., Paper, 0-13-172389-8 (17238-9)

RIGHTSIZING THE NEW ENTERPRISE:
The Proof, Not The Hype
Harris Kern and Randy Johnson

A detailed account of how Sun Microsystems implemented its rightsizing strategy going from a mainframe data center to a heterogeneous client/server distributed environment. This book covers the key infrastructures of an IT organization (the network, data center, and system administration), the rightsizing/management tools, and the training/resource issues involved in transitioning from mainframe to UNIX support. The facts contained in this book provide you with the PROOF that 'right-sizing' can be done.and has been done.

1995, 352 pp., Cloth, 0-13-490384-6 (49038-3)

RIGHTSIZING FOR CORPORATE SURVIVAL:
An IS Manager's Guide
Robert Massoudi, Astrid Julienne, Bob Millradt, and Reed Hornberger

This book provides IS managers with "hands-on" guidance for developing a rightsizing strategy and plan. Based upon research conducted through customer visits with multinational corporations, it details the experiences and insights gained by IS professionals that have implemented systems in distributed, client-server environments. Topics covered include:

- Why rightsize?
- What business results can rightsizing produce?
- Key technologies critical to rightsizing
- Good starting points for rightsizing
- What is the process to rightsize an information system?
- Cost considerations and return on investment (ROI) analysis

• How to manage the transition

Throughout the book, case studies and "lessons learned" reinforce the discussion and document best practices associated with rightsizing.

1995, 272 pp., Paper,
0-13-123126-X (12312-5)

READ ME FIRST!
A Style Guide for the Computer Industry
Sun Technical Publications

A comprehensive look at documenting computer products, from style pointers to legal guidelines, from working with an editor to building a publications department—in both hard copy and electronic copy with an on line viewer, FrameMaker templates for instant page design, and a detailed guide to establishing a documentation department and its processes. Based on an internationally award-winning Sun Microsystems style guide (Award of Excellence in the STC International Technical Publications Competition, 1994)

1996, 300 pp., Paper,
0-13-455347-0 (45534-6)
Book/CD-ROM

SOLARIS IMPLEMENTATION:
A Guide for System Administrators
George Becker, Mary E. S. Morris and Kathy Slattery

Written by three expert Sun system administrators, this book discusses real world, day-to-day Solaris 2 system administration for both new installations and for those migrating an installed Solaris 1 base. It presents tested procedures to help system administrators to improve and customize their networks by eliminating trial-and-error methodologies. Also includes advice for managing heterogeneous Solaris environments and provides autoinstall sample scripts and disk partitioning schemes (with recommended sizes) used at Sun.

1995, 368 pp., Paper,
0-13-353350-6 (35335-9)

CREATING WORLD WIDE WEB SOFTWARE:
SOLARIS, Second Edtion
Bill Tuthill and David Smallberg

Written for software developers and business managers interested in creating global applications for the Solaris environment (SPARC and x86), this second edition expands on the first edition and has updated information on international markets, standards organizations, and writing international documents. New topics in the second edition include CDE/Motif, NEO (formerly project DOE)/ OpenStep, Universal codesets, global internet applications, code examples, and success stories.

1996, 250 pp., Paper,
0-13-494493-3 (49449-2)

SOLARIS PORTING GUIDE,
Second Edition
SunSoft Developer Engineering

Ideal for application programmers and software developers, the *Solaris Porting Guide, Second Edition*, provides a comprehensive technical overview of the Solaris 2.x operating environment and its related migration strategy. The second edition is current through Solaris 2.4 (both the SPARC and x86 platforms) and provides all the information necessary to migrate from Solaris 1 (SunOS 4.x) to Solaris 2 (SunOS 5.x). Other additions include a discussion of emerging technologies such as the Common Desktop Environment (CDE), hints for application performance tuning, and extensive pointers to further information, including Internet sources.

1995, 752 pp., Paper,
0-13-443672-5 (44367-1)

SUN PERFORMANCE AND TUNING:
SPARC and Solaris
Adrian Cockcroft

An indispensable reference for anyone working with Sun workstations running the Solaris environment, this book provides detailed performance and configuration information on all SPARC machines and peripherals, as well as on all operating system releases from SunOS 4.1 through Solaris 2.4. It includes hard-to-find tuning information and offers insights that cannot be found elsewhere. This book is written for developers who want to design for performance and for system administrators who have a system running applications on which they want to improve performance.

1995, 288 pp., Paper,
0-13-149642-5 (14964-1)

State Sales/Use Tax

In the following states, add sales/use tax: CO-3%; GA, LA, NY-4%; VA-4.5%; KS-4.9%; AZ, IA, IN, MA, MD, OH, SC, WI-5%; CT, FL, ME, MI, NC, NJ, PA, TN-6%; CA, IL, TX-6.25%; MN, WA-6.5%;DC-5.75%.

Please add local tax for AZ, CA, FL, GA, MO, NY, OH, SC, TN, TX, WA, WI.

Order Information:

- Please allow 2-4 weeks for processing your order.
- Please attach the order form with your payment.
- No P.O. boxes and no C.O.D.s accepted.
- Order form good in the U.S. only.
- If you are tax exempt, please include exemption certificate or letter with tax-exempt number.
- Resellers not eligible.
- Offer not valid with any other promotion.
- One copy per product, per order.

THE ARCHIVE UTILITY FOR WINDOWS

WINZIP®

Nico Mak Computing, Inc.

KEY FEATURES

- Brings the convenience of Windows to Zipping
- Built-in PKZIP-compatible ZIP & UNZIP (PKZIP & PKUNZIP are not required)
- Built-in support for popular Internet file compression formats TAR, gzip, and Unix compress
- Full drag and drop support
- Works with ARJ, ARC, and LZH files
- Optional virus scanning support

Have you ever used the Internet, a BBS, or CompuServe? If so, you've probably encountered .ZIP, .TAR, .GZ, and .Z files. Are you a Windows user? If so, WinZip is the way to handle these archived files.

WinZip brings the convenience of Windows to the use of ZIP files without requiring PKZIP and PKUNZIP. It features an intuitive point-and-click drag-and-drop interface for viewing, running, extracting, adding, deleting, and testing files in ZIP, LZH, ARJ, and ARC files. Optional virus scanning support is included. Windows and Windows 95 versions are included in the same package.

Shareware evaluation versions of WinZip are available on better bulletin boards and online services everywhere. Be sure to get version 6.0 or later.

"These days everyone needs a good unzipping utility. This is the best."
PC Computing, 12/95

"Recommended download"
Windows Magazine, 9/95

"Cadillac of unzippers"
PC Magazine, 3/95

Voted "Best Utility"
1994 Annual Shareware Industry Awards

SPECIAL OFFER!

SAVE $5 OFF THE $29 PRICE (includes shipping) with this coupon.

- -

Offer good only when paying by check to Nico Mak Computing, Inc., P.O. Box 919, Bristol, CT 06011-0919. Connecticut residents please add 6% sales tax.

NAME: _____

COMPANY: _____

ADDRESS:_____

CITY _____ STATE _____ ZIP: _____

COUNTRY: _____

Payment must be in US funds. Offer expires April 1997. Original coupons only. Price subject to change without notice. This coupon in not valid in France or French speaking territories.

IMPORTANT—READ CAREFULLY BEFORE OPENING SEALED CD-ROM

This CD-ROM contains the Java Development Kit and sample code from Just Java, as well as other copyrighted software.

SUN MICROSYSTEMS LICENSE AGREEMENT

This is a legal agreement between the purchaser of this book/CD-ROM package ("You") and Sun Microsystems, Inc. By opening the sealed CD-ROM you are agreeing to be bound by the terms of this agreement. If you do not agree to the terms of this agreement, promptly return the unopened book/CD-ROM package to the place you obtained it for a full refund.

SOFTWARE LICENSE FOR SAMPLE CODE

1. Grant of License. Sun Microsystems grants to you ("Licensee") a non-exclusive, non-transferable license to use the software programs (sample code) included on the CD-ROM without fee. The software is in "use" on a computer when it is loaded into the temporary memory (i.e. RAM) or installed into the permanent memory (e.g. hard disk, CD-ROM, or other storage device). You may network the software or otherwise use it on more than one computer or computer terminal at the same time.

2. Copyright. The CD-ROM is copyrighted by Sun Microsystems, Inc. and is protected by United States copyright laws and international treaty provisions. Therefore, you must treat the CD-ROM like any other copyrighted material. Individual software programs on the CD-ROM are copyrighted by their respective owners and may require separate licensing. The Java Development Kit is copyrighted by Sun Microsystems, Inc. and is covered by a separate license agreement provided on the CD-ROM and reprinted below.

3. Just Java Sample Code. Sun Microsystems, Inc. grants you a royalty-free right to reproduce and distribute the sample code or applets provided that you: (a) distribute the sample code or applets only in conjunction with and as a part of your software application; (b) do not use Sun Microsystems, Inc. or its authors' names, logos, or trademarks to market your software product; and (c) agree to indemnify, hold harmless and defend Sun Microsystems, Inc. and its authors and suppliers from and against any claims or lawsuits, including attorneys fees, that arise or result from the use or distribution of your software product.

DISCLAIMER OF WARRANTY

The SOFTWARE (including instructions for its use) is provided "AS IS" WITHOUT WARRANTY OF ANY KIND. SUN MICROSYSTEMS and any distributor of the SOFTWARE FURTHER DISCLAIM ALL IMPLIED WARRANTIES INCLUDING WITHOUT LIMITATION ANY IMPLIED WARRANTIES OF MERCHANTABILITY OR OF FITNESS FOR A PARTICULAR PURPOSE. THE ENTIRE RISK ARISING OUT OF THE USE OR PERFORMANCE OF THE SOFTWARE OR DOCUMENTATION REMAINS WITH YOU.

IN NO EVENT SHALL SUN MICROSYSTEMS, ITS AUTHORS, OR ANY ONE ELSE INVOLVED IN THE CREATION, PRODUCTION, OR DELIVERY OF THE SOFTWARE BE LIABLE FOR ANY DAMAGES WHATSOEVER (INCLUDING, WITHOUT LIMITATION, DAMAGES FOR LOSS OF BUSINESS PROFITS, BUSINESS INTERRUPTION, LOSS OF BUSINESS INFORMATION, OR OTHER PECUNIARY LOSS) ARISING OUT OF THE USE OF OR INABILITY TO USE THE SOFTWARE OR DOCUMENTATION, EVEN IF SUN MICROSYSTEMS HAS BEEN ADVISED OF THE POSSIBILITY OF SUCH DAMAGES, BECAUSE SOME STATES/COUNTRIES DO NOT ALLOW THE EXCLUSION OF LIMITATION OF LIABILITY FOR CONSEQUENTIAL OR INCIDENTAL DAMAGES, THE ABOVE LIMITATION MAY NOT APPLY TO YOU.

U.S. GOVERNMENT RESTRICTED RIGHTS

The SOFTWARE and documentation are provided with RESTRICTED RIGHTS. Use, duplication, or disclosure is subject to restrictions as set forth in subparagraph (c)(1)(ii) of The Rights in Technical Data and Computer Software clause at DFARS 252.227-7013 or subparagraphs (c)(1) and (2) of the Commercial Computer Software—Restricted Rights 48 CFR 52.227-19.

Java Development Kit, Version 1.0.2, Binary Code License

This binary code license ("License") contains rights and restrictions associated with use of the accompanying software and documentation ("Software"). Read the License carefully before installing Software. By installing Software, you agree to the terms and conditions of this License.

1. Limited License Grant. Sun grants to you ("Licensee") a non-exclusive, non-transferable limited license to use Software without fee. Licensee may re-distribute complete and unmodified Software to third parties provided that this License conspicuously appear with all copies of the Software and that Licensee does not charge a fee for such re-distribution of Software.

2. Java Platform Interface. In the event that Licensee creates any Java-related API and distributes such API to others for applet or application development. Licensee must promptly publish an accurate specification for such API for free use by all developers of Java-based software. Licensee may not modify the Java Platform Interface ("JPI," identified as classes contained within the "java" package or any subpackages of the "java" package), by creating additional classes within the JPI or otherwise causing the addition to or modification of the classes in the JPI.

3. Restrictions. Software is confidential copyrighted information of Sun and title to all copies is retained by Sun and/or its licensors. Licensee shall not modify, decompile, disassemble, decrypt, extract, or otherwise reverse engineer Software. Software may not be leased, assigned, or sublicensed, in whole or in part. Software is not designed or intended for use in on-line control of aircraft, air traffic, aircraft navigation or aircraft communications; or in the design, construction, operation or maintenance of any nuclear facility. Licensee warrants that it will not use or redistribute the Software for such purposes.

4. Trademarks and Logos. Licensee acknowledges that Sun owns the Java trademark and all Java-related trademarks, logos, and icons including the Coffee Cup and Duke ("Java Marks") and agrees to: (i) comply with the Java Trademark Guidelines at http://java.com/trademarks.html; (ii) not do anything harmful to or inconsistent with Sun's rights in the Java Marks; and (iii) assist Sun in protecting those rights, including assigning to Sun any rights acquired by Licensee in any Java Mark.

5. Disclaimer of Warranty. Software is provided "AS IS," without a warranty of any kind. ALL EXPRESS OR IMPLIED REPRESENTATIONS AND WARRANTIES, INCLUDING ANY IMPLIED WARRANTY OF MERCHANT-ABILITY, FITNESS FOR A PARTICULAR PURPOSE OR NON-INFRINGEMENT, ARE HEREBY EXCLUDED.

6. Limitation of Liability. SUN AND ITS LICENSORS SHALL NOT BE LIABLE FOR ANY DAMAGES SUF-FERED BY LICENSEE OR ANY THIRD PARTY AS A RESULT OF USING OR DISTRIBUTING SOFTWARE. IN NO EVENT WILL SUN OR ITS LICENSORS BE LIABLE FOR ANY LOST REVENUE, PROFIT OR DATA, OR FOR DIRECT, INDIRECT, SPECIAL, CONSEQUENTIAL, INCIDENTAL OR PUNITIVE DAMAGES, HOWEVER CAUSED AND REGARDLESS OF THE THEORY OF LIABILITY, ARISING OUT OF THE USE OF OR INABILITY TO USE SOFTWARE, EVEN IF SUN HAS BEEN ADVISED OF THE POSSIBILITY OF SUCH DAMAGES.

7. Termination. Licensee may terminate this License at any time by destroying all copies of Software. This License will terminate immediately without notice from Sun if Licensee fails to comply with any provisions of this License. Upon such termination, Licensee must destroy all copies of Software.

8. Export Regulations. Software, including technical data, is subject to U.S. export control laws, including the U.S. Export Administration Act and its associated regulations, and may be subject to export or import regulations in other countries. Licensee agrees to comply strictly with all such regulations and acknowledges that it has the responsibility to obtain licenses to export, re-export, or import Software. Software may not be downloaded, or otherwise exported or re-exported (i) into, or to a national or resident of, Cuba, Iraq, Iran, North Korea, Libya, Sudan, Syria or any country to which the U.S. has embargoed goods; or (ii) to anyone on the U.S. Treasury Department's list of Specially Designated Nations or the U.S. Commerce Department's Table of Denial Orders.

9. Restricted Rights. Use, duplication or disclosure by the United States government is subject to the restrictions as set forth in the Rights in Technical Data and Computer Software Clauses in DFARS 252.227-7013(c) (1) (ii) and FAR 52.227-19(c) (2) as applicable.

10. Governing Law. Any action related to this License will be governed by California law and controlling U.S. federal law. No choice of law rules of any jurisdiction will apply.

11. Severability. If any of the above provisions are held to be in violation of applicable law, void, or unenforceable in any jurisdiction, then such provisions are herewith waived to the extent necessary for the License to be otherwise enforceable in such jurisdiction. However, if in Sun's opinion deletion of any provisions of the License by operation of this paragraph unreasonably compromises the rights or increase the liabilities of Sun or its licensors, Sun reserves the right to terminate the License and refund the fee paid by License, if any, as Licensee's sole and exclusive remedy.

Sysdate 7/28/96
JUS100 -tNB050-067993669
↑
0 = zero Not O

Read before
opening
CD package!

LICENSE AGREEMENT
AND LIMITED WARRANTY

BY OPENING THIS SEALED SOFTWARE CD PACKAGE, YOU ACCEPT AND AGREE TO THE TERMS AND CONDITIONS PRINTED BELOW AND IN THE FULL AGREEMENT PRINTED ON THE PAGES FOLLOWING THE INDEX. IF YOU DO NOT AGREE, DO NOT OPEN THE PACKAGE.

The software is distributed on an "AS IS" basis, without warranty. Neither the authors, the software developers, Sun Microsystems, nor Prentice Hall make any representation, or warranty, either express or implied, with respect to the software programs, their quality, accuracy, or fitness for a specific purpose. Therefore, neither the authors, the software developers, nor Prentice Hall shall have any liability to you or any other person or entity with respect to any liability, loss, or damage caused or alleged to have been caused directly or indirectly by the programs contained on the CD. This includes, but is not limited to, interruption of service, loss of data, loss of classroom time, loss of consulting or anticipatory profits, or consequential damages from the use of these programs. If the CD medium is defective, you may return it for a replacement CD.

This CD-ROM is a standard ISO-9660 disc. Software on this CD-ROM requires Windows 95, Windows NT, Solaris 2.x or Macintosh (System 7.5).

Windows 3.1 IS NOT SUPPORTED